Psycholinguistics

An Introduction
to the
Psychology of Language

DONALD J. FOSS
DAVID T. HAKES

University of Texas at Austin

PRENTICE-HALL, INC., Englewood Cliffs, New Jersey 07632

Library of Congress Cataloging in Publication Data

Foss, Donald J.,
    Psycholinguistics: an introduction to the
psychology of language.

    Bibliography: p.
    Includes index.
    1. Psycholinguistics. I. Hakes, David T.,
    joint author. II. Title.
P37.F66   401'.9   77-27826
ISBN 0-13-732446-4

Printed in the United States of America

10 9 8 7 6 5 4 3 2 1

PRENTICE-HALL INTERNATIONAL, INC., *LONDON*
PRENTICE-HALL OF AUSTRALIA PTY. LIMITED, *SYDNEY*
PRENTICE-HALL OF CANADA, LTD., *TORONTO*
PRENTICE-HALL OF INDIA PRIVATE LIMITED, *NEW DELHI*
PRENTICE-HALL OF JAPAN, INC., *TOKYO*
PRENTICE-HALL OF SOUTHEAST ASIA PTE. LTD., *SINGAPORE*
WHITEHALL BOOKS LIMITED, *WELLINGTON, NEW ZEALAND*

For
Pat
Melissa & Lara

And For
Judy & Linzee

Contents

V Applications and Relations

11 Reading, *322*

12 Language and the Brain, *350*

Preface

The present century could be called the age of communication. The telephone was patented a little over 100 years ago and came into common use in this century. Also during this time radio and television have revolutionized communication, permitting vast numbers of people to experience the same event simultaneously. More recently, computers have added a new dimension to the communication age. A substantial fraction of the gross national product is generated by individuals who are primarily communicators: journalists, teachers, advertising and public relations agents, and many others.

Because of its immense importance, communication has become an area of study in its own right—and it is a large and diverse one. Among those interested in studying the various phenomena of communication are speech scientists, mass media researchers, and communications engineers, to name a few. Since most communication occurs via language, it too is a topic that is studied extensively. There is also another engine that propels the study of language. Throughout history, many philosophers and scientists have believed that language is a unique human possession and that by studying it we can gain insight into the workings of the human mind. So the study of language promises to illuminate both our public, outer activities and our private, inner ones.

Among the scientists studying language are the psycholinguists. Like most areas of study, psycholinguistics is defined by the questions that it asks, and by the mysteries that it is trying to solve. Psycholinguists are typically concerned with three broad questions. The first is: What does one know when one knows a language? In other words, how can we describe the knowledge that is possessed by someone who can speak a language? The second question is: How does an individual use his or her knowledge when producing or comprehending speech? This is a question about how we function when we are talking, listening, reading, writing, and perhaps thinking. The third question is: How did we get this way? That is, how does one acquire the knowledge about language and the ability to use it?

As these questions indicate, psycholinguists are concerned primarily with the mental structures and operations that make communication possible, although many psycholinguists are also interested in the act of communication itself. Those who study mental structure and processes are called cognitive psychologists; psycholinguistics is, therefore, one branch of cognitive psychology. Other branches involve the study of such topics as memory, problem solving, attention, and perception. Cognitive psychologists want to describe and explain these various processes, and the past twenty years have seen a remarkable surge of interest in doing so. The branches of cognitive psychology are intertwined. The findings of psycholinguistics affect theories of memory, for example, and the findings in memory studies can bear upon the answers that are given to the above questions.

The aim of this book is to explain more thoroughly the nature of the questions themselves and to describe and discuss the proposed answers that have been given to them. The book is divided into five sections. In the first we introduce the study of language and discuss some aspects of language structure. This is the linguistics part of the psycholinguistics enterprise. It occurs first because we believe that it is necessary to know something about the structure and organization of the activities that one is trying to explain. In the second section we discuss the comprehension of spoken language. We take an "outside-in" approach, following a message from the time its sound arrives at the ear to the time that it has affected the memory system of the listener. In the third section we discuss the production of spoken language. Here we turn the direction of information flow around, from "inside to out." We begin with the processes involved in planning to speak, and end with the muscle activities that carry out these plans. In the fourth section we describe the process of language development, starting with the pre-linguistic child and following the child to the point where complex utterances are being comprehended, spoken, and judged. In this section we also describe and evaluate some theories of language acquisition. In the fifth section we discuss some important topics related to comprehension, production, and acquisition. These include the process of reading, language and the brain, aphasia, language in non-humans, linguistic diversity (including Black English), and the relationship between language and thinking.

The reader will quickly become aware that we cannot answer the questions that we have posed, at least not completely. But he or she will get a good grasp of the problems and will understand something about the kinds of answers that are being given today. We have tried to present an accurate picture of the field without being afraid of saying where we are ignorant. We are convinced that it is better to admit such ignorance than to pretend that there are answers where, in fact, such answers have not yet been found. Of necessity we have often had to simplify issues; when we did, we tried to tell the truth even though we couldn't tell the whole truth.

The reader of this book needs no background training in linguistics or in advanced psychology. Terms are defined when needed, and we have tried to state the issues in such a way that they can be understood without prior knowledge of them.

Although the present book is a collaborative effort, primary responsibility for the various chapters was divided between us. D. J. F. drafted Chapters 1, 2, 4, 5, 6, 11, and 13; D. T. H. drafted Chapters 3, 7, 8, 9, 10, and 12.

It is a pleasure to acknowledge the assistance of those individuals who aided us in writing this book. A number of colleagues and students commented upon one or more chapters, and the book is better because of their efforts. From among our associates at the University of Texas we particularly benefitted from the comments and criticisms provided by Professors Randy Diehl and Peter MacNeilage, and those provided by Randy Bias and Michelle Blank. We also received very useful and constructive criticism from William Baker, University of Alberta; Arthur L. Blumenthal, Harvard University; Richard Meltzer, Information Systems Program, General Electric Corp.; Elissa Newport, University of California, San Diego; Rose Olver, Amherst College; and N. J. Spencer, Virginia Commonwealth University. Since we did not always take the advice that was offered, we are responsible for all of the errors.

We owe a particular debt of thanks to two individuals: Judy Evans, who did much of the proofreading of our manuscript and who helped in numerous other ways as well; and Pat Childers, who typed and retyped, somehow managing both to stay cheerful and to keep things straight even as we reorganized the book from week to week while she was typing. Finally, we want to thank our families and our friends. They know why.

DONALD J. FOSS AND DAVID T. HAKES
Austin, Texas

I

Introduction: Language and Its Structure

1

The Study of Language

People communicate in many ways—a look can kill, a tone of voice can indicate that a speaker means the opposite of what he or she is saying, and a touch sometimes says more than a book can. Two people will sometimes speak to each other quite differently when they are alone than when a third person is present. A very large part of modern psychology, from physiological studies of muscle control to the social psychology of persuasion, could be considered relevant to the topic of human communication. This book focuses on one mode of communication; it is about language.

Language is surely the most important tool of communication that individuals have at their disposal. Many people have claimed that the possession of language is the single most important distinction between humans and lower forms of life. All humans, with a few pathological exceptions to be discussed later, acquire language; it is a universal human accomplishment. Up to this point, no non-human has acquired a language. (This last claim has recently been disputed. We will also consider that issue later.)

Language permits people to communicate a tremendous range of attitudes and information, biases and truths. It permits the building of a tradition through which a person's actions and thoughts can be influenced by the thoughts of someone who lived hundreds of years earlier. It permits a degree of self-expression impossible to any other species. When used to describe events, it has an evocative power rivaling that of the events themselves. Further, language can be used to request information or action, to challenge, to command, and to perform many other functions.

While it is obvious that language is our central tool of communication and that it has great expressive and informative power, its actual nature is not so obvious. Usually we do not think much about language itself; we simply use it. But in fact there are many different ways to think about language. The point of view we will take is that of *psycholinguistics.*

Psycholinguistics, as we will use the term here, is the study of language as a human activity. It is the study of *what* people acquire when they acquire a language, of *how* they acquire it, and of *how they use* it when producing and understanding messages. As such, it is a sub-field of the general area of cognitive psychology, the psychology of knowing or of thinking. Thus, psycholinguistics is an important part of the study of how the mind is organized and how it works. It is clearly relevant to the study of human communication, and it may have applications in many practical areas, such as teaching reading skills, language acquisition by the deaf, learning foreign languages, and others. But the present focus of the field is not directly on the topic of communication. Rather, it is on the language abilities that make communication possible. In addition, psycholinguistics does not yet have very much to offer in the way of concrete proposals about practical problems. Some people, the present authors included, believe that a study of the basic processes involved in acquiring, understanding, and producing language will be a useful and necessary antecedent to significant advances in these important fields. But for the present this is only a belief and not an established fact.

Linguistic Diversity

On those occasions when language itself has come to your attention it has probably been in conjunction with some aspect of language diversity. If you are a New Yorker and have had occasion to speak with a Texan, or if you are from a white middle-class background and have spoken with a ghetto black, then you have probably become aware of some differences in speech patterns, or dialects. If you have spent a week in Paris without knowing French, the "language barrier" has probably been brought home to you with particular force. Most people have at one time or another mused about the diversity of languages. Still, it sometimes surprises people to learn that there are more than three thousand languages being spoken today. This figure is not a precise one, in part because it is not exactly clear what constitutes a language difference rather than a dialect difference. How different do two dialects have to be before we say that they are different languages?

The rule of thumb is that two people speak the same language if they are mutually intelligible, while those who learn to speak a language in the same community are said to speak the same dialect. But these are only rough and inadequate distinctions. For example, it is sometimes said that speakers of Mandarin and Cantonese speak two dialects of Chinese, even though they are not mutually intelligible. And speakers of Norwegian can make themselves understood by Swedes, even though they are usually said to speak different languages. The distinction between a language difference and a dialect difference is not a sharp one. A whimsical linguist once suggested that a dialect becomes a language when its speakers get an army and a navy! For the present, that is good enough for our purposes.

There are two points about linguistic diversity that should be mentioned at the outset, since a misunderstanding of the issues involved can badly distort one's understanding of the nature of language. We call these the *myth of "pure language"* and the *problem of linguistic chauvinism.* They are related problems.

The Myth of Pure Language

In our experience, almost everyone who is new to the study of language believes in the myth of pure language. According to this myth each language exists in some pure or absolutely correct form. Any deviation from this form is looked upon as an impurity, as sub-standard. This view is represented schematically in Figure 1.1A. At the top of the figure is an L, representing the "pure" form of some language. This is the ideal form in which, say, American English exists. Perhaps it is the English spoken by an educated and articulate network news broadcaster. Related to L are various dialects, D_1, D_2, etc. Some of the dialects are quite close to L, for example D_1. This is the dialect of someone who speaks very much like the newsman, but has some trace of impurity or difference, perhaps a broad Boston *a*. Further away are other dialects, until we reach D_7. This might be the dialect spoken by a poor sharecropper who, when asked what his son does, would reply, "He be workin at farmin."

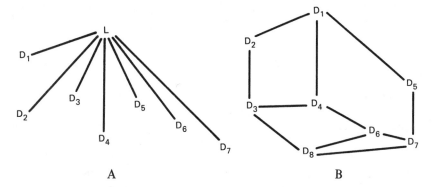

Figure 1.1. (A) The relationships among a language and its dialects, according to the myth of pure language. (B) A more accurate picture of the relationships among dialects.

An alternative picture is presented in Figure 1.1B. In this picture, no one dialect is really at the top. There is, technically speaking, no "top" to Figure 1.1B. Rather, there is a set of dialects that are related to one another. The lengths of the lines connecting the various dialects indicate the degrees of relationship—some are close (e.g., D_2 and D_3), others are more distantly related (e.g., D_2 and D_7). But no particular dialect is any more central or primary than any other. An implication of Figure 1.1B is that each child acquires a dialect that is, for that child, the basic form of the language and not a derived or impure form. Thus, each dialect is worthy of study in its own right. From the point of view of modern linguistics, Figure 1.1B presents the more correct picture. It may certainly be true that the members of the dominant (that is to say, the most powerful) sub-culture in a society speak one of these dialects and that they may punish those who do not. But this is a fact about the society and not a fact about dialects themselves. The myth of pure language leads people to view Figure 1.1A as correctly picturing the relationship among dialects. But those scientists who aim to describe and explain language agree that Figure 1.1A presents an incorrect view; Figure 1.1B is better (see, e.g., Labov, 1970).

Linguistic Chauvinism

A second, related attitude toward linguistic diversity is linguistic chauvinism—the belief that one's own language is the best of all possible languages. This romantic notion has been far from harmless, since a great deal of human strife has been caused, at least in part, by one group of people trying to impose their language on another, generally in the belief that their language was superior to the other, "heathen" tongue. A rather harmless example was provided by the 1923 Illinois legislature which passed a bill stating in part, "Whereas the name of the language of a country has a powerful psychological influence in stimulating and preserving the national ideal, be it enacted: 'The official language of the State of Illinois shall be known hereafter as the "American" language and not as the "English" language,'" (Mencken, 1963, pp. 92-93). We wonder if those who voted "aye" knew that that very word has its roots in Middle English!

Linguistic chauvinism often shows up in the claim that one language is more "complex" than another. Depending upon the mood of the chauvinist at the moment, this alleged fact may be used to condemn or to praise the language under discussion. (For example, the language is complex and therefore overly complicated, confused, and hard to learn. Or, the language is complex and therefore rich in expressive power and useful for communication.) Such claims presuppose a yardstick for measuring complexity, for without one the chauvinist's claims are simply empty. No such yardstick exists.

In fact, if there were such a yardstick, it seems likely that all human languages would register the same on it. Every language so far studied by linguists appears to permit a range of expression as wide as any other. True, one language may have terms for concepts not named in another language (e.g., *electoral college, frisbee*). But this is a fact about the concepts that are of interest to the speakers of that language, it is not a fact about the complexity of the language itself (see Chapter 13).

Linguists do not generally see their task as prescribing what constitutes a correct or "pure" language. Rather, they see it as one of *describing* and *explaining* the facts of language as they find them. It is true that some linguists are involved in constructing grammars and dictionaries for languages, and that such grammars and dictionaries are used to *prescribe* usage. Language teachers use grammars that way, and dictionaries provide their users with information about what one particular group of people considers to be correct. There is a certain usefulness to knowing the grammar and rules of word usage that are common among speakers of a language, for this provides a means of maximizing one's effectiveness when speaking and writing. But it is the convenience of effective communication among speakers, rather than a standard of absolute correctness, that provides the justification for learning a common grammar and common rules of word usage. It is not that other dialects and usages are inherently inferior.

Linguists take a tolerant and anti-chauvinistic attitude toward languages and dialects that differ from their own. In the same way, when anthropologists go to study another culture, they do not do so with the intent of converting members of that culture to their own cultural values. Their intent is rather to describe and explain the culture as they find it. There is no room in their work for a view that one culture is inherently superior to another. So, too, with linguists and psycholinguists. They are trying to explain what they find, not to change it. There is no place for the myth of a "pure" language or for linguistic chauvinism.

Linguistic Universals

Up to this point we have focused on the diversities among languages, since these are noticed most readily. But we can also consider the ways in which languages are similar. In fact, the most influential work in linguistics in recent years has been concerned with the similarities among languages rather than with the differences (see, e.g., N. Chomsky, 1965, 1975). The question here is, what are the things that are common to all human languages? What are the *universal*, as opposed to the language-particular, characteristics?

A linguist might approach the question by asking how the rules of a grammar of English are like those of a grammar of, say, Finnish, and whether these similarities are also reflected in the grammars of other languages. Taking a more psychological approach, we can ask about the similarities between what speakers of English and Finnish know about their languages.

It seems intuitively clear that speakers of both would agree that they speak in "sentences," that the sentences are built up from "words," and that the words are built up out of certain elementary speech sounds (like the sound signified by the letter *s*). Both would probably also agree that the sentences and words have "meaning," while the elementary speech sounds themselves do not. And it seems plausible that speakers of both languages use very similar physiological mechanisms in producing their languages. (No human language user produces sentences from words that are, in turn, built from sounds made by rubbing the legs together! This is one of the characteristics that distinguish us from crickets.) Such observations may seem obvious and quite trivial at first. Yet they describe a part of what is common to human language users and, at the same time, what distinguishes human language from other behavior, both human and non-human.

At a somewhat deeper level, there are a number of properties of human languages that have been claimed to be universal. It is worth describing some of these, for they will shape our thinking about the problems of acquiring, understanding, and producing language. Each linguist or psycholinguist who has considered the problem of linguistic universals produces a list of the important properties. One approach to the question is to consider the characteristics which seem to distinguish human language from the communication systems that occur naturally in other species, e.g., the dance of the honeybee that tells others in the hive the direction and distance of nectar. Hockett (1960, 1966) produced such a list in the course of studying human and animal communication systems. He suggested a number of "design features" that appeared to distinguish the two kinds of systems, features that he claimed are universal among human languages. We will discuss four of Hockett's universal design features.

Discreteness

"*Discreteness.* The possible messages in any language constitute a discrete repertory rather than a continuous one" (Hockett, 1966, p. 10). That is, the messages in a human language are built up from units (i.e., speech sounds), of which there is a limited number. For example, you can say the word *camel* in a number of ways that differ slightly from each other, but a hearer would probably regard all the pronunciations as being variations of *camel.* The variations might indicate something about how important the word was in what you were saying, about whether you were speaking rapidly or slowly, or about your dialect; but they would all be taken as being the *same word.*

There is no logical necessity that it be this way. One could conceive of a language in which different words resulted as the speaker varied, say, the length of time involved in producing the first vowel of *camel.* Perhaps these different words could be used to signal how docile the beast was. A very short *a* might be a word indicating a mean animal, while a very long *a* might yield a word signifying a very tame one. Intermediate durations would indicate intermediate degrees of docility. In this imaginary language utterances could be almost indistinguishably similar. We could make the vowel durations of two utterances of *camel* as close to each other as we pleased to indicate that one camel was just a little bit tamer than another. But although this is a logical possibility, no human language works this way. As Hockett put it, "Utterances cannot be indefinitely similar to one another" (1966, p. 10). No natural language permits fine gradations of meaning to be signalled by such fine gradations of sound. The principle of discreteness is honored by all languages.[1]

Arbitrariness

"*Arbitrariness.* The relation between a meaningful element in language and its denotation is independent of any physical resemblance between the two" (Hockett, 1966, p. 10). That is, words do not have to sound or look like the things they stand for. There are, in every language, a few words (e.g., names for animal noises) where there is a relationship between the word's sound and what the word stands for (onomatopoeia). There also may be a few words in which some aspect of the word's sound appears to be related to the kind of thing the word means. For example, words with vowels like *ee* (*teeny*) seem to refer to small things, while words with vowels like *oo* (*huge*) appear to refer to large things (phonetic symbolism). What is striking about these phenomena is that they are quite rare and perhaps due only to chance (see Taylor & Taylor, 1965).

In general, we could interchange the meanings of any two words if we all agreed to do so. There is nothing about dogs that requires that they be called *dogs* (or *chiens*) rather than *cats* (or *chats*). While there might be some initial confusion if we all decided to use the word *cats* to refer to dogs, there is nothing about either the words or the things to which they refer that prevents us from doing so. Such arbitrariness is not characteristic of all forms of representation. Maps, for example, bear a point-by-point correspondence to the terrain they portray. The same is true of a representational painting or photograph. Not so with language: there is no point-by-point correspondence between words and the world.

We will consider "meaning" and "reference" later, and we will find then that the relationship between them is quite complex. For the moment it is enough to note that the semantic relationship is, in at least one important way, an arbitrary one. We cannot tell what a thing's "name" is by looking at it; learning the meanings of words requires far more than looking, making it a formidable task.

Openness

"*Openness.* New linguistic messages are coined freely and easily" (Hockett, 1966, p. 11). This is one of the most important universal characteris-

---

[1]Some languages (e.g., Swedish) do use vowel duration to signal differences in meaning. But only two or three durations are used, not an indefinitely large number. So, even for these languages, discreteness holds.

tics of human language. Consider for a moment a simple question: How many sentences are there in English? Although it may not be immediately obvious, the correct answer is that there is no limit.

Up to this time an enormous number of English sentences have been spoken or written. But the number so far is finite—a very large number to be sure, but a number that could be counted, at least in principle. But the possibilities for more new English sentences are unlimited, as can be shown by a simple trick. The statement *John's favorite number is one* is a sentence. So is *John's favorite number is two.* Now, since there is no limit to the number of numbers that can be used in sentences of that form, there is no limit to the number of sentences of that form. To demonstrate the same point with a slightly different trick, the statement *Pat buttered the parsnips* is a sentence. So is *I said that Pat buttered the parsnips,* and so too is *I said that I said that Pat buttered the parsnips.* We could extend the example in this way forever. Admittedly, the resulting sentences would become boring and difficult to follow, but we are talking about the possibilities of the English language and not about whether the sentences would be graceful or easily understood. English, like every other language, offers unlimited possibilities for saying new things and for saying old things in new ways.

One consequence of this openness of language is that no one has ever heard more than a very small proportion of the sentences that could occur. Similarly, no one has ever produced more than a very small proportion of the sentences he or she could produce. And this means that whenever someone hears or produces a sentence, it is highly likely that the sentence is *novel,* one that that person has never heard or produced before.

One implication of openness and novelty is that we cannot learn a language by memorizing its sentences. There are far too many of them (i.e., an unlimited number) for this to work. Furthermore, memorizing sentences would not provide us with a way of understanding or producing novel sentences. Clearly, then, a person's knowledge of language cannot be a list of sentences. The list would have to be of unlimited length. Equally clearly, we are finite creatures who can learn and store only a limited, finite amount. So, the limited amount we know must be knowledge that allows us to *construct* or *create* the sentences we produce and to *construct interpretations for* the sentences we hear. One of the central concerns of linguists and psycholinguists is to find a way to characterize and account for this creativity—to specify how, with our limited capabilities, we are able to produce and understand an unlimited number of sentences, most of which are novel.

Openness, arbitrariness, and discreteness are, then, among the most important universal aspects of human languages. As we have suggested, the existence of these characteristics has important implications for how we describe what people know when they know a language and how they go about understanding, producing, and acquiring it. Much of the rest of this book is devoted to exploring these implications. But before we turn to such explorations, there is one additional design feature that Hockett suggested which is important for us to note.

Duality of Patterning

"Duality of patterning." Language is, essentially, a means of relating two different kinds of patterns or forms of representation—sound and meaning.[2] The representation of language sounds, the *phonological system,* is an external representation; the representation of meanings, the *semantic* system, is an internal representation. The means of relating the two is a language's *syntactic system.*

We can think of the external and internal representations as involving different *codes.* The external, phonological code is the one in which language is transmitted from one person to another, from speaker to hearer. It consists of a small number of elements that do not themselves have meanings and which, for the moment, we can consider to be roughly equivalent to the sounds of the letters of the alphabet. Of course, these elements cannot be combined randomly; not all of the sequences of speech sounds that a speaker could produce can be used to convey meanings. Each language involves a phonological system, a set of rules that specify the possible sequences and combinations of elements which the phonological code of that language allows.

The internal, semantic code is the one in which speakers and hearers represent the meanings, or messages, of the sentences they produce and understand. The elements and rules of this system are quite different from those of the phonological system, for the semantic code is used to represent a very different kind of information. It is, in fact, extremely difficult to specify what the elements and rules of the semantic system are because the semantic code is a mental representation and as such cannot be observed directly.

A language's syntactic system is essentially a means of relating a representation in one of these codes to a representation in the other. That is, the syntactic system provides a translation from the phonological representation of a sentence into its semantic form and vice versa. As we saw in discussing arbitrariness, there is rarely a direct relation between a representation in the phonological code and one in the semantic code, and those rare cases where there is involve units no larger than words. For this reason, we might expect the syntactic system itself to be complex. It is, but it is also highly structured and systematic.

We can perhaps make this notion of duality clearer by considering how it applies to understanding a sentence we have heard. Take, for example, the sentence we used earlier, *Pat buttered the parsnips.* The process of understanding the sentence begins with registering the sound pattern the speaker produced,

---

[2] Our characterization of duality differs somewhat from Hockett's, but we make the same distinction as he did—namely, that between sound and meaning.

that is, with forming a representation of the sentence's external form. But understanding the sentence involves a great deal more than this. Understanding the sentence involves getting out its meaning—forming a representation of the message the speaker was trying to communicate. For *Pat buttered the parsnips,* this will roughly be a representation of the information that there exists some person (Pat, whom we may or may not know) who performed a particular kind of action, and that the action was performed on a particular kind of thing. The representation would specify the kind of action performed, which is given by the meaning of the verb, *butter,* and also the kind of thing upon which that action was performed.

As we saw earlier, there is nothing about the sound pattern of *parsnips* itself that indicates what kind of things parsnips are. We know what they are because we know the meaning that is associated with that sound pattern. Furthermore, there is nothing about the sound pattern of *Pat* which specifies that the individual indicated by that sound pattern performed the action rather than, for example, having the action performed on her. It is our knowledge of the syntax of English that allows us to translate the sound patterns of the sentence into a representation of its meaning. The latter includes the information that it was Pat who performed the action. Thus, it is our knowledge of the language that allows us to translate the sounds the speaker produced into a representation of the message he was trying to communicate to us.

The Nature of Language

We have now seen some aspects of the diversity of language and also some of its important universal characteristics. These are the kinds of characteristics that are important for understanding what language is. For the psycholinguist and the linguist, probably the most important characteristics are the last two universals we discussed—openness and duality of patterning.

The central fact to keep in mind is that the external form of language does not involve representations of meanings. Meaning is conveyed from person to person linguistically only when the speaker translates the meaning he wishes to convey into an external form and the listener translates that form back into a representation of the meaning. Thus, it is the internal and external codes as well as the means by which translations between them are accomplished that constitute language. A language can be thought of as both the two codes and the set of rules or procedures for turning a representation in one of them into a representation in the other. In principle, the procedures must be able to carry out an unlimited number of such translations, each one novel.

To put it slightly differently, what a person knows when he knows a language is how to translate between internal and external representations. The rules and procedures involved in such translations are, as we have already suggested, quite complicated. This in itself would make the task of understanding what a person knows and how he is able to make use of that knowledge a difficult one. Yet as we will soon see, the task is made even more difficult by the fact that we do not have direct access to the knowledge involved. Language users cannot say in any detail what it is they know or how they use that knowledge. But before exploring the implications of this lack of awareness, there are a few additional points about the nature of language that should be touched upon.

A Unique Code and a General Code

Although the external and internal codes will be discussed in detail later, one point of contrast is worth mentioning here. The external code, the highly structured phonological system, is unique to language and serves almost no function other than its linguistic one.[3] Occasionally, the close relationship between the external code and the translation process has led people to speak as if the code itself were language. This is a confusion between speech and language, a confusion about which we will have more to say later.

The internal code, on the other hand, is probably not unique to language. This code appears to serve functions in addition to its linguistic ones. The semantic code involves concepts and propositions of the sorts involved in thought. Language is one way, though not necessarily the only way, of translating these representations into an external code. Language is one means of expressing what we think. Translation from the internal, semantic code to the external code is, of course, not necessary. We often think without speaking. And in some cases a translation can be performed only with great difficulty. We sometimes have trouble finding the appropriate form for expressing what is represented in the internal code. In cases where the translation does occur, we tend to think of the internal code as semantic and a part of language. When translation into the external code of language does not occur, we tend to think of the internal code as a general cognitive code. The semantic and cognitive codes are interrelated, perhaps identical.

Language and the Cognitive System

We have suggested that the internal, meaningful representations may occur in a general cognitive code, the same code involved in thinking. We might think of this code as being the interface between language and thought, the place where the two meet. This implies that the relationship between thought and language is a relationship between forming and manipulating representations in the internal cognitive code on the one hand, and translating some of them into and out of representations in the external phonological code on the other. The

---

[3]This does not mean that the external code must be a phonological system. Other external codes for language are possible, and in fact an alternative code—the manual or hand movement code used in sign language—does exist. However, the sound system is by far the most commonly used and intensively studied external code, and our discussions will focus upon it.

fact that such translations can be performed does not require that they must be. Also, it does not imply that such translations can always be performed easily.

If the internal representations that underlie language are the same kind as those involved in thinking, then it seems likely that there will be close relationships between the kinds of phenomena we observe in language and those we observe in some other kinds of cognitive functioning. This suggests that we might learn a great deal about language and language processing from considering certain other aspects of cognitive functioning. For example, it might be helpful to view the processes involved in a child's acquiring language as reflections of those underlying general cognitive development (see, e.g., Slobin, 1973). We will see later in this book that there are a number of close parallels of this sort.

This view that there are important parallels between the processes of understanding, producing, and acquiring language on the one hand, and other cognitive processes on the other, has not always been a popular one. Many linguists and psycholinguists have thought of language as being special, separate from other human cognitive processes. This latter view has been reflected in a tendency to characterize the universal properties of language as being *linguistic* universals, implying that there is something specifically linguistic about them (see, e.g., McNeill, 1966, 1970). The question of how language is related to other human cognitive processes is, of course, not a matter to be settled by definition. It is an empirical question, a question of what the facts are. We will be concerned throughout this book with trying to determine the appropriate facts and what they imply about this question.

The Nature of Linguistic Knowledge

Usually when we think about what people know, we think in terms of those things they are aware of and about which they can tell us. But most of what people know about language is not of this sort. It is, rather, knowledge of which they are unaware.

It may seem strange to speak of people knowing things that they do not know that they know, but this is a perfectly ordinary situation. What we need when we talk about language, and other systems as well, is a distinction between *explicit* knowledge and *tacit* or unconscious knowledge. Much of what we know we know explicitly, in the sense that we are aware of what we know and can talk about it. For example, we all know explicitly that Paris is the capital of France. But there is also a great deal that we know in a less conscious way. Consider, for example, what you know about riding a bicycle (assuming, of course, that you do know how to ride one). Among other things, you know how to adjust your body's position to keep the bicycle in balance. But this knowledge is tacit, as you will quickly discover if you try to tell someone else how to make such adjustments. The knowledge itself cannot be brought into consciousness.

The distinction between explicit and tacit knowledge is reflected in the different ways we find out what someone else knows. If the knowledge is explicit, we can discover it by asking questions. How a person answers the question, *What is the capital of France?* indicates whether or not he possesses the relevant knowledge. But how a person answers the question, *How do you ride a bicycle?* does not indicate whether he possesses the relevant knowledge. The individual might reply, *You hop on and pedal it* even if he has never been on a bicycle. The best evidence we can get about what someone knows about *how* to ride a bicycle is by watching him try to do it. When knowledge is tacit, we have to infer what the person knows from what he does.

That our knowledge of language is largely tacit quickly becomes apparent if you try to answer questions like the following: What are you doing when you hear and understand an utterance? If you try to reflect upon what you are doing, you will discover that you are not aware of doing anything. You may be aware of the sound of the speaker's voice, and you may be aware of the meaning and of the fact that you have understood what was said. But there is nothing in between. Subjectively it seems as though you haven't done anything at all, as if understanding the utterance just happened.

Of course, understanding doesn't "just happen." There is a great deal of evidence which indicates that you have done something quite complex when you understand an utterance. But the processing that is done in the course of understanding occurs outside of awareness. Similarly, the knowledge of language that underlies your ability to do this kind of processing is not represented in awareness: it is tacit knowledge.

Utterances and Sentences

The fact that people are able to produce and understand utterances indicates that they know how to do these things, even though the knowledge is tacit. But our tacit knowledge of language extends far beyond just knowing how to produce and understand utterances.

Recently, a three-year-old girl told us the story of Cinderella. At one point she said, *And the . . . and the fairy godmother turned her coach into . . . um . . . turned . . . um . . . turned her pumpkin into a coach.* This is not a good English sentence. It contains false starts and improper repetitions of words. This kind of behavior is, of course, not limited to children. We all speak ungrammatically and non-fluently much of the time. We can, however, generally catch and correct our errors if accurate communication is important. Our three-year-old storyteller knew that it was important to get straight just what the fairy godmother had turned into what, and this is reflected in the utterance she produced.

The fact that such "errors" occur and that we often notice and correct them suggests several important things about our knowledge of language. But before we can consider these things, we need to introduce a distinction—the distinction between an *utterance* and a *sentence*. We consider any actual speech performance to be an utterance. As we have seen, utterances are often incorrect in one way or another. But the notion of an utterance is not used solely to characterize those cases we recognize as being flawed. *Any* actual speech episode is an utterance. So, if one says fluently and flawlessly, *The fairy godmother turned the pumpkin into a coach,* that too is an utterance.

A sentence, on the other hand, is a different sort of thing. Utterances are directly observable: sentences are not. You might think of a sentence as that which the speaker intended to say, while an utterance is that which was actually said. Sometimes the actual utterance correctly reflects the intended sentence, but not always.[4] The concept of a sentence is more abstract than the concept of an utterance. In the cases where we notice that an utterance is incorrect, we have noticed that there is a difference between the sentence and the utterance.

Consider now an utterance that most of us would judge to be incorrect or unacceptable: *The boys is going to school.* We know that the utterance *The boys are going to school* (or, perhaps, *The boy is going to school*) would have reflected the speaker's intention more accurately. How do we know this? Clearly, it is not because we have memorized the correct sentence and know what it should sound like. As we saw earlier, our knowledge of English cannot be a list of memorized sentences. In addition, this example is different from the "fairy godmother" example, since here there is nothing wrong with what the sentence means. Since we all know the story of Cinderella, we knew that there was something wrong with an utterance that had the fairy godmother turning a coach into something rather than turning something into a coach. But *The boys is going to school* does not have that problem.

The most obvious explanation for how we know that *The boys is going to school* is incorrect is something like this: we know that subjects and verbs have to agree in number, and in this utterance they do not. That is, we appeal to a *rule* to justify our judgment that something is wrong with the utterance. This is the right move to make: the utterance is unacceptable because it violates a rule of English. It is ungrammatical.[5]

In this particular case there is probably no problem caused by speaking of a rule that the utterance violates, for the rule about subject-verb agreement is one that we all learned in an explicit form in grammar school. But in many cases speakers will find an utterance unacceptable even though they are not able to state the rule that the utterance violates (Gleitman & Gleitman, 1970). As we have seen, a rule may exist even if we cannot state it. The rule that has been violated may be one that is known only tacitly. In fact, the rules which underlie

[4] Later we will see that a sentence is not quite the same thing as an intention, but it is useful to think about it as such at first.

[5] When we speak of an utterance's being "unacceptable" or "ungrammatical" we do not mean that it violates some textbook definition of "good" English, but rather that it is not consistent with a speaker's rules about his own language. Utterances that are ungrammatical for some speakers of English are not for others. In this sense, the rules involved are *descriptive* rules rather than *prescriptive* rules about the way speakers *ought* to speak English.

language, those that are typically involved in our judgments of acceptability and unacceptability, are tacit rules. We cannot explicitly state them, yet we know when an utterance violates one of them.

To summarize, we have made a distinction between utterances and sentences, and have claimed that utterances do not always accurately reflect sentences. We have also said that each speaker of a language has tacit knowledge of a set of rules for the sentences of that language. The judgment that a particular utterance is or is not a sentence is made by using these tacit rules.

Linguistic Competence

We can view the tacit rules of a language as specifying the set of sentences that *could* occur in the language. Thus, the rules that you know determine the set of possible sentences for the version of English you have learned. Your judgments about the acceptibility of particular utterances are essentially judgments about whether or not those utterances accurately reflect possible sentences according to the rules you tacitly know.

The rules that are tacitly known are said to compose or make up the *linguistic competence* possessed by the speaker of a language (N. Chomsky, 1965). One of the major tasks of linguistics is to discover and to state the nature of these rules, to develop a theory of the linguistic competence of speakers of the language. A theory of linguistic competence is called a *grammar* of the language. But unlike the grammar you were taught in school, linguistic grammars are intended to be descriptions of the rules that speakers know and not prescriptions about how they ought to speak.

A theory of linguistic competence states the rules that are tacitly known by the speakers of a language. It is this knowledge that permits each speaker to make judgments about whether or not utterances are grammatical. This knowledge also permits the speaker to make other judgments as well. For example, individuals who know a language can judge whether or not an utterance is ambiguous. They can decide whether the utterance *They are flying planes* has one meaning or more than one. In addition, speakers can judge whether or not two utterances are synonymous—whether, for example, the utterances *Eve kissed Herb* and *It was Herb that Eve kissed* have the same meaning or different meanings.

Developing a grammar is a difficult task. Because knowledge of the rules of language is tacit, linguists cannot simply ask speakers what the rules are. Nor can they sit back and observe the rules operating in themselves. They cannot bring the rules into conscious awareness. Rather, the rules must be inferred from what can be observed. Linguists observe the utterances that speakers are able to produce and understand, and they also evaluate the kinds of judgments that speakers can make about utterances (e.g., ambiguity judgments). These judgments are collectively referred to as the *linguistic intuitions* that speakers have about utterances. Linguistic intuitions are, then, part of the data that linguists use when constructing a theory of linguistic competence. The intuitions are not, of course, the competence itself; they are merely a reflection of it. Competence is the set of tacit rules. Linguists use these various kinds of data to aid in constructing a theory of this linguistic competence—a grammar.

Linguistic Performance

Although our linguistic competence lies at the heart of our knowledge of language, it is clear that we know more than just a grammar. A grammar specifies the rules we know, but it does not state how we make use of that knowledge. That is, a grammar does not say how this knowledge enables us to produce utterances or to understand them, nor does it tell us how we acquired that knowledge. Thus, the grammars which linguists try to construct characterize only a part of a speaker's knowledge.

A theory of the additional knowledge is a theory of *linguistic performance.* A theory of performance describes the psychological processes involved in using our linguistic competence in all the ways that we actually can use it—in producing utterances, in understanding them, in making judgments about them, and in acquiring the ability to do these things. Developing a theory of linguistic performance, a theory of the psychological processes involving language, is the main task of psycholinguistics.

We have already seen that the utterances which speakers actually produce sometimes contain errors—the utterances do not always accurately reflect the speaker's intentions. And hearers sometimes misunderstand, or fail to understand, the utterances they hear. It is an important fact about the nature of linguistic performance that it does not always accurately reflect competence. But more often than not performance occurs without error. Thus, a theory of linguistic performance must be an account of psychological processes that are capable of producing flawless results, but that can sometimes result in errors.

The psycholinguist's task in attempting to develop a theory of linguistic performance is no easier than the linguist's task of developing a theory of linguistic competence, and for the same basic reason. Our knowledge of how we produce and understand utterances, like our knowledge of the rules of language, is tacit knowledge. So, like the linguist, the psycholinguist must make inferences from the observed performances to the processes underlying those performances, hardly an easy task.

Clearly, a theory of linguistic performance is going to be closely related to a theory of linguistic competence. The psychological processes involved in using linguistic knowledge depend upon the nature of that knowledge, and the nature of the knowledge itself is dependent upon the nature of the processes which use it. Given the closeness of the relationship, it is not surprising that the tasks of the linguist and the psycholinguist often overlap. But the two theories are fundamentally different kinds of theories. Essentially, one is a theory of language, a theory of the structure of the language's phonological, syntactic, and semantic systems. The other is a theory of both knowledge and processes. The psycholinguist wants to state how our linguistic knowledge is represented in the cognitive system. In addition, he wants to identify the psychological processes that utilize this knowledge. So, we may expect that the two theories, closely related though they are, will not be related in simple or straightforward ways (see Fodor & Garrett, 1966).

Most of the remainder of this book—except for Chapter 2—is devoted to considering linguistic performance. We will examine the processes involved in understanding language in Section II, and Section III will consider those involved in producing it. Section IV will discuss language acquisition. Finally, Section V will consider related aspects of linguistic performance, such as the reading process and how language is related to thought.

At this point a word of warning is in order. We would like to be able to describe for you a complete and accurate picture of linguistic competence and linguistic performance. Unfortunately, we cannot. Because of the complexity of competence and performance, and because of the difficulty of discovering what they are like, there is simply not enough known yet for us to be able to do this. We will try to lay out those things that are known and will try to make some sense out of them. What follows can best be thought of as our best guess about what linguistic competence and performance are like. It will be apparent by the end of the book that there is a long way to go before we fully understand human language and its use.

Before we continue our discussion of linguistic performance, we need to give some additional attention to the nature of linguistic competence. Given the close relationship between competence and performance, it will be very useful for our thinking about performance to understand something more about the structure of language. Chapter 2 is devoted to a consideration of some of the more important and more relevant aspects of linguistic competence.

Summary

This chapter developed a general view of language and of the approach we will take in studying it. The primary concerns of psycholinguists are to describe what someone knows when they acquire a language, how they acquire that knowledge, and how they put it to use in speaking and listening.

Languages and dialects are diverse in a number of ways, but the ways in which they differ do not make one language or dialect "better" than another. In spite of their diversity there are a number of important commonalities, or universals, shared by all human languages. These include the properties of discreteness, arbitrariness, openness, and duality of patterning. It is these properties that serve to distinguish language from other human and non-human phenomena.

Openness—the fact that speakers of a language are able to produce and understand an unlimited number of novel utterances—is a particularly important universal property of language. It has important implications for how we characterize what speakers know about their language. In particular, this knowledge cannot be represented as a list of utterances that speakers have learned.

Duality of patterning is equally important as a universal property of language. Language involves two forms of representation—an internal, semantic representation and an external, phonological representation—and a means of translating from one of these to the other. The internal code is one that language shares with other cognitive operations; it is, essentially, the interface between language and thought. The external code, however, is unique to language.

A distinction between utterances and sentences was drawn, and it was noted that the former do not always accurately represent the latter. One's knowledge of sentences is best characterized as a system of rules about the phonological, syntactic, and semantic structures of a language; the term linguistic competence is used to characterize this knowledge. Linguistic knowledge is largely tacit rather than explicit. It underlies our abilities to produce and comprehend utterances and to make the kinds of judgments about language that are referred to as linguistic intuitions.

The main task of the linguist is to describe the competence of the speakers of a language. The main task of the psycholinguist is to construct a theory of linguistic performance. A performance theory will state how knowledge of a language is represented in the speaker's cognitive system. It will also characterize the processes by which one speaks, understands, or otherwise makes use of one's linguistic competence. Many of these processes are also involved in other cognitive (mental) activities. Consequently, psycholinguistics can best be viewed as a branch of cognitive psychology.

One's knowledge of language and of linguistic processes is both complex and tacit. Because of this, discovering and understanding linguistic competence and linguistic performance is difficult. Language users cannot tell us what they are doing as they are producing, understanding, or otherwise using language. So we must make inferences about the underlying knowledge and processes from the performances we can observe. We study psycholinguistics by indirection.

SUGGESTED READINGS

The relationship between psychology and linguistics has been the focus of numerous discussions. N. Chomsky (1975) presents one influential position; Pylyshyn (1973) discusses his notion of competence theories; and others occur in Clark and Haviland (1974), Fodor (1968), Stich (1975), and Watt (1974).

2

Aspects of
Linguistic Competence

In Chapter 1 we characterized linguistic competence as the speaker's tacit knowledge of his language—its external form of representation (the phonological system), its internal form of representation (the semantic system), and the relationships between them (the syntactic system). Discovering the nature of this competence is one of the main tasks of linguistics. In attempting to do this, linguists seek to discover those characteristics that are common to all languages and those that are unique to a particular language or family of languages. It is the first of these—the universal properties of language—that most interest the psycholinguist, so here we will be concerned mainly with them.

We can discuss the nature of linguistic competence more easily by breaking the subject into its subtopics, the phonological, syntactic, and semantic systems. But this separate consideration should not give anyone the impression that these three linguistic components are independent of one another. In fact, they are not independent at all. For example, the way in which a theorist characterizes the phonological system often depends upon how he describes the properties of the syntactic and semantic systems. Also, it is important to remember that describing the systems of competence is not the same as describing the psychology of their performance. With these disclaimers, let us begin by briefly considering some aspects of the phonological system of language.

Phonology: The System of Sound

We noted earlier that speakers of a language are able to make judgments about several aspects of their language. One kind of judgment concerns the sequences of speech sounds that *could* be words in that language. For example, consider the phonological sequences *bench, blench,* and *bnench.* Are these English words? You are probably completely certain that *bench* is a word, quite certain that *bnench* is not, and somewhat uncertain about the status of *blench.*

When people are asked why they think that *bnench* is not an English word, they most often answer that the *bn* sequence cannot be pronounced and, consequently, could not be a part of a real word. This sounds like good reasoning, but it is not quite correct. If *bn* were unpronounceable, then *bnench* could not be a word in *any* language. But, in fact, there are languages in which clusters like *bn* do occur. So, it is possible that *bnench* is a word in some other language, and that it has been borrowed by English (just as *clique* and *chalet* were borrowed from French). That the *bn* sequence is pronounceable is also indicated by the fact that English speakers pronounce it whenever they say a word like *hobnob.* So, the reason for being certain that *bnench* is not an English word, barring the possibility of its being a borrowed word, cannot be that it is unpronounceable.

We are confident that *bnench* is not an English word because we know that English does not permit the sequence of sounds *bn* to occur at the beginning of a word or syllable. Knowing this indicates, in turn, that we tacitly know the rules of English phonology which determine the permissible sound sequences in English. It is this same knowledge that leaves most speakers uncertain whether or not *blench* is an English word since *bl* is a sound sequence which the rules permit. The *bl* sequence does occur at the beginnings of a number of English words (e.g., *bleach, blonde, blasphemy*). The uncertainty arises because *blench* could be an English word and because most speakers have never encountered it. As a result, they do not know whether in fact it is a word. (*Blench* actually is a word, though a rare one; the dictionary gives two meanings for it: to flinch, to blanch).

Before considering the nature of the phonological rules that describe the possible English sound sequences, we must first consider the kinds of units which might enter into such rules. That is, rules specifying possible sound sequences must specify sequences of *something.* The question of units is a question about the nature of that something—what is the "stuff" out of which phonological sequences are built?

Phonetic Segments

Consider the sound of the words *pin, pan, pretty,* and *poke.*[1] These words share something that is not shared by *din, can, pretty,* and *bloke.* The words on the first list all begin with the same sound, while those on the second list do not. Similarly, the last sound of *hop* and *jump* seems to be very close to

---

[1] Bear in mind that we are talking here about *sound* units. Sometimes different sounds are represented by the same letters of the English alphabet. Compare, for example, the initial sounds of *cat* and *certain,* both of which are spelled *c*.

the initial sound of *pin* and *pan,* as is the second sound of *spin* and *span.* They all contain the same phonetic segment, *p.* We can conceptualize words as being composed of one or more phonetic segments.

For some segments, the particular way they sound is determined in part by the context in which they occur. For example, the segment *p* does not always sound exactly the same. You can observe a very clear case of this if you say the words *pan* and *span.* For *pan,* there is a puff of air at the beginning of the *p.* For *span,* on the other hand, there is much less of a puff. (You can even feel the difference if you put your hand an inch away from your mouth while saying these two words.) The puff is called *aspiration.* So, we can say that when *p* occurs as the initial segment of a syllable it is aspirated, when it occurs within a syllable, *p* is unaspirated.

We can represent each phonetic segment by a symbol in a *phonetic alphabet.* Because of differences like the aspirated and unaspirated *p*'s, there will be more symbols in this alphabet than in the English spelling system. For example, the aspirated *p* is represented by the symbol [p^h] and the unaspirated *p* by the symbol [p] .[2]

Using a set of symbols sufficient to represent the phonetic segments of English, we could state a rule to explain why *bnench* cannot be an English word: the sequence # [b] [n] . . . # is not a permissible English sound sequence. (The symbol # is used to indicate a word boundary, that is, the beginning or end of a word.) Such a rule would codify our intuition that *bnench* and other sequences beginning with [b] [n] are not possible in English.

However, this rule is not a very efficient way of describing the constraints that the English phonological system places on word-initial sequences. English also does not allow word-initial sequences like *bm, pn, dm, tn, gm* or *kn.*[3] If the rules of English phonology were written in terms of phonetic segments, there would have to be separate rules barring each of these as well as several others like them. This would be acceptable if there was reason to think that English speakers had separate rules of this sort—if, for example, they appeared to learn these restrictions one at a time.

There are, however, several similarities among these cases. The similarities permit us to state a single rule which bars all such sequences. In order to understand these similarities and to state the rule, we must further analyze the phonetic segments.

Features

Although segments like [p] are phonological units, they are themselves built out of other, more basic units. [p] is often referred to as a *stop* consonant.

---

[2] There is a standard phonetic alphabet, the International Phonetic Alphabet (IPA), which is used by linguists for transcribing the phonetic segments of different languages (International Phonetics Association, 1949). IPA contains enough symbols to distinguish all the phonetic segments used by all languages.

[3] Do not be fooled by the existence of English words like *knight* and *knave.* The *k* is silent— it occurs in the words' written form, but not in their spoken form.

This means that in producing [p] the speaker completely closes his oral cavity (roughly, the mouth), stopping the flow of air. When [p] occurs at the beginning of a word, its sound is produced as the closure is released, that is, as the lips begin to open. Thus, one property of [p] is that it is a stop. The property is called a *feature* (Jakobson, Fant, & Halle, 1952).

There are several consonantal sounds that share this feature. In addition to [p], the class of stops includes [b, d, t, g, and k], all of which involve complete closure of the oral cavity when they are produced. Through this feature we can define a class of phonetic segments. We can say that all segments having that feature are members of the class of stops. Other segments, such as [s], do not have the stop feature and therefore are not members of this class. Aspiration, mentioned earlier when we contrasted [p] with [p^h], is also a feature. All segments having the aspiration feature are also members of a class of segments.

The segments [m], [n], and [ŋ] (as in *sing*) are also referred to as stops, but they differ from those described above. [m], [n], and [ŋ] are called *nasal* stops. In producing them there is not a complete closing off of the air flow; air continues to pass through the nasal passages, and only the oral passage is closed. Oral stops like [b] and [p], on the other hand, involve closure of both the nasal and oral passages, a more complete closure. Thus, the feature *nasality* distinguishes between the class of nasal stops and the class of oral stops.

The feature stop is called a *distinctive feature* in English. When two phonetic segments differ with respect to the stop feature, that is, one is a stop and the other is not, English speakers will hear them as two different segments. In contrast, the aspiration feature is not distinctive in English. English speakers do not hear [p] and [p^h] as two different segments. In general, if changing a single feature leads the listener to perceive the segments as different, then that feature is distinctive for the language. Which particular features are distinctive varies among different languages.

We can think of a phonetic segment as being composed of a set of features, features that are all present simultaneously in the sound of that segment. To make an analogy, the segment is the molecule and the features are the atoms from which it is built. We can describe a segment by stating its features; each feature is either present (+ feature) or absent (- feature). For example, we could characterize [p] as including the features [+consonantal, +stop, -nasal . . .], while [m] includes the features [+consonantal, +stop, +nasal, . . .]. All the phonetic segments used by any human language can be described with a set of about 12 to 15 such features. We will see later that features play an important role in both the processes involved in perceiving speech (Chapter 3) and those involved in producing it (Chapters 6 and 7).

Before proceeding further, let us return once more to our earlier example, *bnench,* and ask whether we can better state the rule which bars *bnench* by using distinctive features than we could by using only phonetic segments. In feature terms, the rule is essentially this: English does not allow a word-initial segment with the feature stop (either nasal or non-nasal) to be followed immediately by another stop segment.

Why should this rule be preferred to the one which states that a word-initial [b] cannot be followed immediately by [n]? The answer is, simply, that when the rule is stated in terms of features, it not only bars *bn* but also bars the other sequences we mentioned earlier: *bm, pn, dm, tn, gm,* and *kn.* It also bars a great many other sequences including *mb, kŋ,* and *np* which cannot occur at the beginnings of English words. Thus, stated in feature terms, a single rule accomplishes what would require a large number of separate rules if stated in segmental terms. In addition, the feature rule indicates that all of these cases are barred *for the same reason.*[4]

Underlying Phonological Representations

We have seen so far that we can conceive of a person's phonological knowledge in terms of his knowing a set of features, knowing a set of rules, stating how those features can be combined to form phonetic segments, and knowing a set of rules specifying the permissible sequences of those segments. For each phonological sequence that makes up a word the person knows, we can also assume that there is associated with it a representation of the word's meaning (see Chapters 4 and 5 below). And we can speak of this set of associations between phonological patterns and meanings as being the person's *mental lexicon,* similar in some respects to a dictionary.

Although the phonological system is the most external of all the subsystems of language, we are now discussing an aspect of phonology—its representation in the mental lexicon—that is not external. When we inquire about the properties of the mental lexicon, the answers to our questions may require longer chains of inferences than we have needed up to here. For now we will ask only one question about the mental lexicon, namely, how should we represent the phonological properties of the words in this lexicon? One answer would be that they are represented as sequences of segments, each segment in turn being represented by a set of features. However, a better answer is available. Recall that the segment [p] is not uttered in quite the same way, nor does it sound quite the same, when it occurs in words like *pan* and *span.* Should the first segment of *pan* be represented in the mental lexicon as [p^h][5] and the second segment of *span* as [p]?

In fact, we do not need to represent [p] and [p^h] differently in the lexicon. Which of the two will occur is, in English, determined by the context in which the segment occurs: [p^h] always occurs in word- or syllable-initial posi-

---

[4] The rule also allows us to say why *blench* is a permitted English word: [l] does not have the feature [+stop]. Hence, *bl* is an allowable word-initial sequence.

[5] We are using [p^h] here as a "shorthand" notation for a set of features that includes [+aspiration] and [p] for a set that includes [−aspiration].

tion, and [p] always occurs within a syllable. (Either can occur in word-final position.) Thus, we can state a rule that will determine which segment, [pʰ] or [p], will occur. The rule will specify the choice in terms of the context. In the mental lexicon, then, we can represent [pʰ] and [p] with a single symbol. The symbol linguists use for this is /p/, enclosing the symbol in slashes rather than brackets. This symbol indicates that, in some sense, [p] and [pʰ] are the same.

The level of analysis at which [pʰ] and [p] are represented by the single symbol /p/ is the level of *underlying phonology* or *systematic phonology*. Words are represented in the lexicon in terms of their underlying phonology, not in terms of their phonetic segments. In English, /p/ is always represented by the same set of features in the mental lexicon, regardless of the word in which it occurs. Whether it is to be aspirated or not is determined by applying a rule that converts the underlying phonological segment /p/ into one of the surface phonetic segments [p] or [pʰ]. The rule takes context into account when it applies.

To summarize, we have proposed (following N. Chomsky & Halle, 1968) that words are represented in the lexicon in terms of their underlying phonology. However, not all of the features that occur when a word is produced are represented there. Some, like whether or not /p/ will be aspirated, are determined by rules applied to the underlying representations in the course of preparing to produce the words. Thus, the phonological system of a language involves a representation of speech sounds in terms of segments and features. In addition, several kinds of rules are involved: rules specifying the permissible combinations of features, rules stating the permissible sequences of those combinations, and rules specifying the relationship between the underlying and surface representations of the segments.[6] Recall again that these rules describe the phonological system. It is an open question whether and how they are used by the psychological mechanisms.

It should be apparent by this point that a language's phonological system is, by itself, complex. We have done little more here than to point out the nature of some of the complexities—complexities in the manner in which speech sounds are represented and in the rules involving those representations. We will see later how some of the concepts we have discussed here may be involved in psychological processes, such as perceiving speech, producing it, and reading.

Syntax: The System of Linguistic Structure

In Chapter 1 we noted that the relationship between the phonological and the semantic aspects of language is an indirect one. Some of the relationships between these two systems are provided by the *lexicon* which, as we saw earlier

---

[6]The phonological system also involves rules concerning stress and intonation, properties of the external representation that often involve linguistic units larger than words. For a discussion of these and other properties of the phonological system, see Lehiste (1970).

in this chapter, specifies the meanings associated with the phonological forms of individual words. But language involves units larger than words, units like phrases and sentences, and the organization of these larger units affects the meanings associated with them. Putting the matter very simply, one cannot determine the meaning of a sentence just from the meanings of the words in that sentence. The meaning depends upon the order and organization of the words as well as upon the words themselves. The importance of word order is nicely illustrated by Miller's (1965) comment that a Venetian blind is not the same thing as a blind Venetian.

When we concentrate upon the order and organization among words we are dealing with the *syntactic system*. Syntax is an important aspect of language, both because of its role in determining the relationships between sound patterns and meanings and because certain aspects of the creative use of language can best be accounted for in terms of syntax. The fact that we have the ability to construct and understand an unlimited number of novel sentences is in part explained by the nature of the syntactic system.

Before exploring the nature of the syntactic system, we must note that our approach is considerably different from that taken in grammar schools. One difference is that we are concerned with describing syntax rather than with prescribing correct usage. A more important difference is that we will focus on an aspect of language structure that is usually taken for granted in the schoolroom. The latter approach does not ask why speakers have the ability to produce and understand an unlimited number of sentences. But this is one of the most important facts about language, and our description of the syntactic system must try to deal with it.

The approach to syntax that we will take here is closest to that developed by N. Chomsky (1957, 1965, 1975) and his associates. Other linguists describe some aspects of the syntactic system differently from Chomsky; his system is not universally accepted as the best one. However, Chomsky's ideas have had the most impact on psychology. It would be difficult to discuss psycholinguistics without some reference to Chomsky's system.

Sentences and Structural Descriptions

We saw in Chapter 1 that a person who knows a language has the ability to produce and understand an unlimited number of novel sentences. Knowledge of a language also permits an individual to judge whether or not a particular string of words is a grammatical sentence, to judge whether or not two sentences mean the same thing, to judge whether a sentence is ambiguous, and to do a variety of similar things. The task which Chomsky took up was to provide a characterization of the knowledge that underlies these abilities. To do this he constructed a grammar.

A grammar is a set of rules which, in principle, lists or specifies all of the grammatical sentences of a language and none of the ungrammatical ones. Since there is an unlimited number of sentences, the list can never actually be produced. We will see shortly how the "listing" is accomplished. In addition to "listing" the sentences, a grammar will specify the units that go into each sentence and the relationships that exist among these units. When we state the units of a sentence and the relations among them, we have described the sentence's structure; we have given it a *structural description*. More precisely, then, a grammar is a set of rules that specifies all of the sentences of a language (and only these), and that gives a structural description for each of the sentences. Before looking at the nature of the rules, we will further develop the concept of a structural description.

Consider a simple English sentence, sentence **(1)**.

(1) The boy kissed the girl.

What do we know about this sentence? Among other things, we know that it is a complete, grammatical sentence and that it is composed of words. Further, we could say that each word was a member of a word class (in grammar school terminology, that each belongs to a particular "part of speech"). Thus, *boy* and *girl* are nouns, *kissed* is a verb, and *the* is an article.

Some of the other things we know about this sentence are a little more subtle. Consider, for example, the second *the* in the sentence. Is this word more closely related to the word that precedes it or to the word that follows it? That is, which sounds more natural: *kissed the,* as in (*The boy kissed the*) (*girl*); or *the girl,* as in (*The boy kissed*) (*the girl*)?[7] Almost everyone would agree that *the girl* is the more natural sounding phrase. The word *the* seems to be more closely associated with *girl* than with *kissed.* To describe this intuition, we group *the* and *girl* together into a unit, (*the girl*). Since *girl* is a noun, we can label the resulting unit a noun phrase, symbolized as NP.

We can go through a similar procedure with the word *boy.* Is *boy* more closely associated with *The* or with *kissed*? That is, would it be better to say (*The boy*) (*kissed*) (*the girl*) or (*The*) (*boy kissed*) (*the girl*)? Again, we conclude that (*The boy*) is the more natural phrase, so we group these two words together. And, since *boy* is a noun, the resulting phrase is also an NP. Now the sentence could be symbolized as NP + V + NP, as in the third row of Figure 2.1. The fourth and fifth rows of the figure show the analysis at the level of words and word classes that we have already discussed.

We need not stop at this point, however. We can now ask how the phrases we have already identified are related. Thus, is the verb *kissed* more closely related to the NP that precedes it or the NP that follows it? Which grouping is better: (*The boy kissed*) (*the girl*), or (*The boy*) (*kissed the girl*)? Your intuition may not be quite as clear in this case, but the latter grouping (*kissed the girl*) is generally chosen. We call this grouping a verb phrase and symbolize it as

---

[7]Words are grouped together within parentheses as an indication of how the sentence is segmented into units larger than words.

1	S = Sentence				
2	NP		VP		
3	NP		V	NP	
4	Article	Noun	Verb	Article	Noun
5	The	boy	kissed	the	girl

Figure 2.1. The hierarchical organization of a simple English sentence.

VP. Now the sentence consists of NP + VP, as is shown in the second row of Figure 2.1.

The organization of sentence **(1)** that fits your intuitions is a hierarchical one. This organization bears a resemblance to the sentence parsing often done in grammar schools. But your ability to find such an organization does not depend on the training you may have received in English classes. Rather, it is a reflection of your tacit knowledge of the syntactic structure of the sentence.

Another way of showing the relationships among the units of sentence **(1)** is by a diagram such as the one in Figure 2.2. This diagram shows the words of the sentence and how these words are grouped together into phrases. Thus, it helps to show a part of the structure of the sentence. Such a diagram is called a *phrase-marker* or a *tree-diagram.* By looking at Figure 2.2., one can tell immediately that V + NP is a unit since these two symbols both "come from" a common parent symbol, VP. The diagram also shows that N + V (*boy kissed*) is not a unit since these two symbols do not, by themselves, come from a common parent symbol. Thus, the phrase-marker representation gives us a convenient way of indicating both the units that exist in a sentence and the ways in which they are related to each other. It provides a *structural description* of the sentence. Now we will examine some rules which characterize both sentences and their structural descriptions.

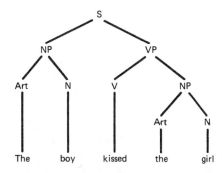

Figure 2.2. The phrase marker for a simple sentence.

Phrase-Structure Rules

The information about sentence structure that is represented in Figure 2.2 can also be represented in terms of a set of rules. Rules R1 through R7 give some instructions for manipulating the kinds of symbols we have already introduced in describing the structure of sentence **(1)**.

(R1)   S → NP + VP
(R2)   NP → Art + (Adj) + N
(R3)   VP → V + NP
(R4)   Art → the, a
(R5)   Adj → happy, sad, . . .
(R6)   N → boy, girl, . . .
(R7)   V → kissed, hit, . . .

These rules, called *phrase-structure rules,* state in an explicit way how we can manipulate the symbols. If we manipulate the symbols in the manner stated by the rules, then we are able to construct, or *generate,* sentence **(1)** and many others besides. In addition, we will not generate anything that is not a grammatical sentence.

The first rule, R1, states that we begin with some initial symbol, S. Rule R1 says that we are to substitute the symbols NP and VP (in that order) for S. Another way to put this is: "Rewrite the symbol S as the symbols NP plus VP." After we have applied rule R1, then the second and third rules can apply. Rule R2 states that whenever we find the symbol NP, it should be rewritten as the string of symbols on the right side of rule R2. Thus, we rewrite NP as Art + N. (Ignore for the moment the symbol within the parentheses on the right side of R2.) Rule R3 states that whenever we find the symbol VP we should replace it with the symbols V + NP. Since applying R3 produces another occurrence of an NP, rule R2 can now be applied again, rewriting NP as Art + N.

All this might seem a bit difficult to follow unless we have some way of keeping track of what we are doing. Fortunately, there is an excellent way to keep track of the applications of the rules, for the rules can be thought of as producing a phrase-marker or tree diagram. When we start by rewriting the initial symbol S as NP + VP, we have gone from Figure 2.3(a) to Figure 2.3(b). When R2 is applied to the NP symbol, rewriting it as Art + N, the tree has branched into Figure 2.3(c). We can continue in this way, applying each rule as it becomes appropriate, until we arrive at the tree in Figure 2.3(f), which is identical to Figure 2.2. By following the rules, we have generated the string of symbols, *The boy kissed the girl,* and we have also generated a phrase-marker which shows the relationships among the symbols in the sentence. Thus, applying the rules generated both a sentence and a structural description of the sentence. Another way of putting this is to say that the sentence has been derived from the rules.

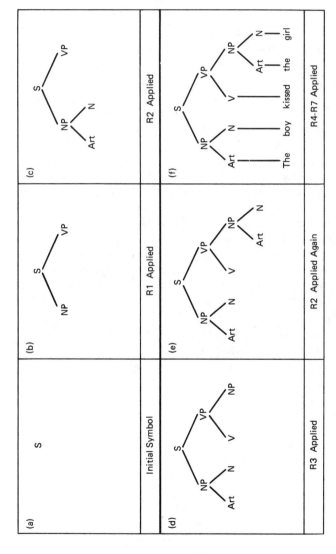

Figure 2.3. Steps involved in deriving a simple sentence from Rules R1–R7.

Note that the application of rules R1 to R7 was completely automatic. We did not have to think about whether some rule applied. Whenever a symbol appeared in the phrase-marker, we looked at the left side of each rule to see if that symbol appeared there. If it did, then the rule containing that symbol applied.

There are two kinds of options allowed by the rules. The first is in R2 where we were instructed to rewrite NP as Art + (Adj) + N. The parentheses indicate an option or choice point. When we rewrite the NP symbol, we can either include the Adj symbol or omit it. Which option is taken determines the particular structure that we generate. If we omit the Adj symbol, the resulting tree is that shown in Figure 2.3(f). If we choose to include the Adj symbol, then R5 will also apply, rewriting Adj as some particular adjective. The resulting phrase-marker will have an additional branch. The existence of the option indicates that the different structures are closely related: Art + N and Art + Adj + N are phrases of the same kind, namely, NP.

A second kind of option is available in rules R4–R7, since there is more than one symbol on the right side of each. These rules permit us to choose any one symbol from the list. The listing indicates that there is more than one member of the classes of articles, adjectives, nouns, and verbs that could appear in sentences with this structure. These are rules of *lexical insertion,* indicating the way in which the words are inserted in a sentence.

Which particular word or lexical item is chosen to replace N (or Art, Adj, or V) is arbitrary. We could have chosen *boy* twice, generating the string *The boy kissed the boy.* Clearly, if we increased the number of words on the right sides of rules R4–R7, the number of sentences that we would be able to derive would increase very rapidly.[8]

To summarize, rules R1–R7 are called phrase-structure rules. A phrase-structure rule always has one symbol on its left side and one or more symbols on its right side. By following the appropriate set of rules we generate, or derive, a sentence and a structural description of that sentence. As each rule applies, it does not cancel out or erase the effects of applying earlier rules. Rather, the rules produce a phrase-marker which preserves the effects of the earlier rules—the effects are cumulative. Thus, the phrase-marker gives us a history of the way in which the sentence was generated.

Rules R1–R3 differ from R4–R7. Rules R1–R3 introduced some symbols that are not directly "seen" when looking at the sentence itself. The symbols S, NP, VP, Art, N, Adj, and V do not appear in the last line of the derivation of the sentence. These symbols are all replaced at some point in applying the rules. For this reason, we can call them *non-terminal* symbols. Such symbols represent abstract entities. We do not perceive them directly in the way we perceive the *terminal* symbols, *boy, the, kissed,* etc. The non-terminal symbols are theoretical

---

[8]We will see later that this is not a very precise characterization of how lexical items are inserted in sentences. For the moment, rules R4 to R7 are close enough.

concepts; they are used to generate the strings of words that make up sentences and to express the relationships among the words. We are led to use such theoretical concepts on the basis of speakers' intuitions about sentence structure. Of course, the rules themselves are also abstract—they do not appear in the sentences. Rather, they are used to generate the structures which, in turn, express speakers' intuitions about sentences.

We can use phrase-structure rules and non-terminal symbols to define some traditional grammatical terms like "subject of a sentence" and "direct object of a verb." The grammatical subject of a sentence is that NP which lies below, or immediately follows, the symbol S. Put technically, the subject of a sentence is that NP which is *immediately dominated* by S (i.e., S is directly above, or dominating, the NP in the phrase-marker). Thus, in sentence (1), the NP *The boy* is the subject. The direct object of a verb is that NP which is immediately dominated by VP. In sentence (1), the direct object is *the girl.* Of course, these definitions express what we already know about such things as sentence subjects, and this is exactly what they should do. The rules and the above definitions are meant to be a statement of our knowledge of the language.

Phrase Structure and Ambiguity. Phrase-structure rules and phrase-markers can be used to characterize and account for some kinds of ambiguous sentences. Sentence (2), for example, has two distinct meanings.

(2) They are broiling hens.

One interpretation is that someone is broiling some hens. Another, different interpretation is that there are some hens of the kind used for broiling (i.e., the kind referred to as "broilers"). The fact that sentence (2) has two interpretations is not indicated by the meanings of the words themselves nor by the order in which they occur. There is one string of four words in a particular order, yet there are two possible interpretations. This arises because there are two different ways of organizing the words in (2), each of which is a grammatical organization.

The difference in organization can be indicated by the different ways you might pause when saying the sentence. To express the first interpretation, the utterance might come out as: *They—are broiling—hens;* to express the second interpretation, it might come out as: *They are—broiling hens.* The difference in intonation would signal which of the syntactic organizations was intended.[9]

The main point here is that word sequences like (2) have two different phrase structures associated with them. In one, *broiling* is part of a V, *are broiling,* while in the other it is part of an NP, *broiling hens.* The set of rules R1–R7 would have to be elaborated to be able to provide the correct structural descriptions for the two interpretations. We will not do that elaboration but will just note that it can be done (see N. Chomsky, 1957, for an example that has been elaborated).

[9] Although intonation *can* be used to disambiguate (remove the ambiguity from) such sentences, it does not always do so. Chapter 4 will take this matter up in more detail.

Sentences like (2) demonstrate the importance of structural descriptions. Clearly, the words of a sentence and their order are not sufficient to determine the meaning of that sentence. We need, in addition, the kind of grouping or organization provided by a sentence's structural description.

Phrase Structure and Complex Sentences. We have seen that several important properties of sentences can be represented with phrase-structure rules and the structural descriptions associated with them. But we have not yet touched upon a property that we earlier described as one of the most important of all: the openness of language, the fact that there are an unlimited number of sentences. To deal with this property we must turn our attention to sentences that are more complex than those we have discussed so far.

Sentence (3) is closely related to sentence (1), which we repeat here for convenience. A part of sentence (3) expresses the same proposition expressed in sentence (1).

(3) The boy kissed the girl who hugged the man.

(1) The boy kissed the girl.

In both, the subject of the verb *kissed* is *the boy,* and its direct object is *the girl.* In (3), however, this same girl is also the subject of the verb *hugged;* the direct object of this new verb is *the man.* Thus, sentence (3) expresses two propositions, the one in sentence (1) and the one in sentence (4).

(4) The girl hugged the man.

These propositions are interrelated since the same NP, *the girl,* is involved in both. (It is, of course, not just the same NP; it is the same girl.)

We can increase the number of propositions by expanding sentence (3) to yield a sentence like (5).

(5) The boy kissed the girl who hugged the man who admired the lady.

Now *the man* also plays a double role; this NP is the object the verb *hugged* and the subject of the verb *admired.* Clearly, we could continue expanding sentence (1) in this way as long as we pleased. The old nursery rhyme about "The house that Jack built" used just such an expansion to build a very long sentence, "This is the farmer that milked the cow that tossed the dog that worried the cat . . . that lived in the house that Jack built." (Parenthetically, note that this simple example could be used to prove that there is, in principle, an unlimited number of sentences in English. Sentences (1), (3), and (5) are three different sentences; each time we added a clause we created a new sentence. Since we never have to stop adding clauses, we never have to stop creating new sentences.)

With a minor adjustment, rules R1–R7 will (almost) be able to generate sentences like (3) and (5). Let us modify rule R2 in the following way:

(R2′) NP → Art + (Adj) + N + (S)

R2′ is the same as R2 except that we have added the initial symbol S as an option. Thus, when we rewrite the NP symbol, we can do so in either of two ways (ignoring for the moment the optional Adj): as Art + N, or as Art + N + S. If we take the latter option, we could generate a structural description like that shown in Figure 2.4(A). But now, since the initial symbol S reappears when we apply R2′ to the direct object NP, *rule R1 applies once again.* Thus, we are in effect generating the two basic sentences labelled S_1 and S_2 in Figure 2.4(A). The second sentence, S_2, is expanded by following the rules again. One possible expansion is shown in Figure 2.4(B) where we have (almost) generated sentence **(3)**.

When we expanded the direct object NP of S_2, we might again have chosen the option of reintroducing the initial symbol S (S_3 in Figure 2.4(B)). Had we done so, and had we appropriately expanded S_3, we would (almost) have gen-

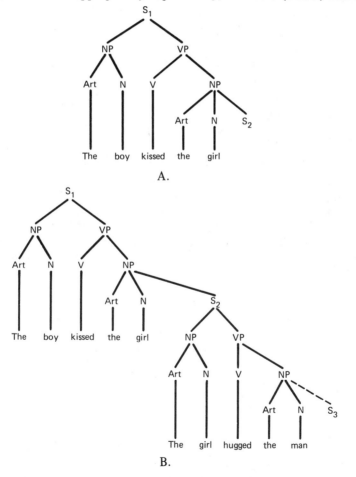

Figure 2.4. Deriving a complex sentence by using Rule R2′.

erated sentence (5). Our modified rule R2′ has given us the ability to continue generating an unlimited number of sentences in this way. Thus, the rule R2′ has provided a partial solution to the problem of openness.

The solution to the openness problem was quite a simple one. All that was necessary was to reintroduce the initial symbol S on the right side of one of the phrase-structure rules. Since S can recur during the generation of a sentence, we may say that rule R2′ is a *recursive rule*. It is through the use of such recursive rules that our grammar acquires the all-important property of openness.

Of course, the strings that are generated by our amended set of rules are not in fact English sentences. In order to have the recursive rule we have paid what seems to be a high price—the grammar has lost its ability to generate actual English sentences. We will soon see, however, that this is really a bargain.

Transformational Rules

Up to this point our grammar has used only one type of rule, the phrase-structure rule. Such a rule operates upon a single symbol, expanding or rewriting it into one or more other symbols. In order to make English sentences out of the strings that such rules generate, we must introduce another set of rules, *transformational rules*.

A transformational rule operates upon a whole string of symbols rather than upon a single symbol. More accurately, a transformational rule operates upon a phrase-marker, changing it into another phrase-marker. To make the contrast between phrase-structure rules and transformational rules a little sharper, we can think of the "input" to a phrase-structure rule as being a single symbol; the rule's "output" is a string of one or more symbols. In contrast, the "input" to a transformational rule is a string of symbols and its structural description; its "output" is another string of symbols and a new structural description. Transformations are a very powerful kind of rule: they can delete symbols from a phrase-marker; they can re-order the symbols; and they can insert new symbols.

To see the way in which transformations work, let us return to the example generated in Figure 2.4(B). The phrase-structure rules generated the string *The boy kissed the girl the girl hugged the man* and the structural description of that string. This is close to, but not the same as, the sentence we wanted to generate: *The boy kissed the girl who hugged the man*. What we need to be able to do is to delete the second occurrence of *the girl* and replace it with *who*.

We can accomplish this goal by using a transformational rule called the "Equi-NP deletion" rule. This rule deletes the second occurrence of an NP like *the girl* if all of the following conditions are met:

(a) the second occurrence must be perfectly identical to the first occurrence (i.e., $NP_2 = NP_1$);

(b) the second occurrence must directly follow the first; and
(c) the second occurrence must be in a sentence that is dominated by the first occurrence.

The last condition says that the second occurrence of the NP must be one sentence "lower" in the tree structure of the structural description than the first occurrence.

All of these conditions hold for the sentence shown in Figure 2.4. The second occurrence of *the girl* immediately follows the first occurrence, and it is in S_2, which is dominated by the first occurrence of *the girl*. When the transformational rule is applied, it deletes the second occurrence of the NP and replaces it with a relative pronoun such as *who*. We will not work through all the technical details of how to state such a transformational rule. The important point is that these rules operate upon structures, changing them into other structures.

The particular transformation that was used to replace the NP with *who* in the example sentence is also used in other, similar sentences. For example, sentence (6) expresses the same propositions as the two simple sentences, (7) and (8).

(6) The man who bought the painting kissed the girl.

(7) The man kissed the girl.

(8) The man bought the painting.

To generate sentence (6), we can use the same set of rules used for sentence (3)—assuming, of course, that we add the necessary words to rules R6 and R7. Figure 2.5 shows the first part of the derivation of sentence (6). The Equi-NP

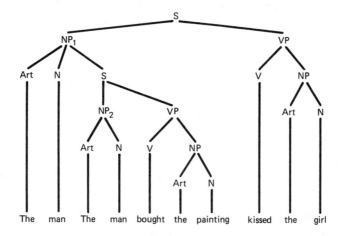

Figure 2.5. The underlying structure of a complex sentence.

deletion transformation will apply to the two NPs marked NP_1 and NP_2, deleting the second occurrence of *the man* and replacing it with *who*. In this case, the second sentence (relative clause) modifies the subject NP of the first; in sentence (3) the relative clause modifies the direct object NP. The Equi-NP deletion transformation can be applied in either case, provided that the necessary conditions (a–c) are met.

The Rationale for Transformational Rules

There are a number of reasons for introducing transformational rules into the grammar. The most basic and important reason is that these rules allow us to explain some facts about language that would be difficult, if not impossible, to explain without them. That is, the addition of transformational rules permits us to give an account of some of the intuitions that English speakers have about their language. We will discuss some of these intuitions and our account of them momentarily. First, however, we will introduce one further distinction that helps in giving these explanations.

Transformations operate upon phrase structures and produce new phrase structures. It follows, therefore, that transformations need an initial phrase structure upon which to operate. The initial structure results from the operation of the phrase-structure rules. In generating a sentence, then, the phrase-structure rules operate before the transformational rules. In consequence, each sentence that is generated by the grammar has more than one structural description. First, there is the structure that results from the application of the phrase-structure rules. This is called the *underlying* or *deep structure* of the sentence. Also, there is the structural description that results after the transformational rules have applied. This is called the *surface structure* of the sentence. Transformational rules start with the underlying structure of the sentence and turn it into the surface structure. (Since more than one transformational rule typically applies in the generation of a sentence, there are also intermediate structures; these do not concern us here, however.)

The distinction between underlying and surface structure is used to help explain a number of facts and intuitions about language. The surface structure is closely related both to the phonological form of the sentence and to its meaning; the underlying form is of importance to the semantic interpretation of the sentence.

Semantic Relations and Underlying Structure. Speakers of English are able to judge when two sentences are expressing the same relationships. Consider, for example, sentences (9) and (10).

(9) It surprised Bob that Vivian arrived on time.

(10) That Vivian arrived on time surprised Bob.

These two sentences are quite different on the surface. Sentence (9) contains a word, *it,* that (10) does not, and the order of the shared words is quite different between the two. And yet speakers of English know that the "real" relationships among the basic terms in **(9)** and **(10)** are the same. In both it is Vivian who arrived on time and it is this fact that surprised Bob. Sentences like **(9)** and **(10)** have almost identical underlying structures. The semantic similarity between them is represented at this underlying level of description. Different transformational rules have been applied to the underlying structure to yield the two different surface structures and word orders in **(9)** and **(10)**.

The above example is not an isolated case. Often, somewhat different transformations can apply to a single underlying structure, resulting in different surface sentences that express the same relationships. Sentences **(11–15)** demonstrate this point.

(11) Chuck gave Helen a microwave oven.

(12) Helen was given a microwave oven by Chuck.

(13) It was a microwave oven that Chuck gave Helen.

(14) Chuck gave a microwave oven to Helen.

(15) A microwave oven was given to Helen by Chuck.

These examples do not exhaust the variety of surface structures that can be used to convey the same underlying meaning.

It would be possible to construct a set of phrase-structure rules that generated **(11–15)**. However, each of these sentences would then be the result of a different set of phrase-structure rules, and the similarities among them would therefore be disguised. According to the present approach, both the similarities and the differences among these sentences are accounted for. The generation of each of them begins with the same phrase-structure rules, showing that their similarity comes from having the same underlying structure. Then somewhat different transformational rules are applied to produce each one, thus accounting for the surface diversity among them. Thus, by adopting the concept of transformational rules we can account for both the similarities and the differences that exist among these sentences.

The distinction between underlying and surface structure permits us to make the further distinction between the underlying and surface subject (or other components) of a sentence. Sentences **(11–15)** have the same subject NP in their underlying structure. In each case, the NP *Chuck* is immediately dominated by the S symbol. Therefore, *Chuck* is the underlying subject of each sentence in the set. Also, the NP *a microwave oven* is the direct object of the verb in the underlying structure of each of these sentences. However, the surface structure subject differs in **(11–13)**. In **(11)** it is *Chuck,* in **(12)** *Helen,* and in **(13)** *a microwave oven.* The surface structure subject corresponds to the grammar school definition of a sentence's subject as "that which the sentence is about." It is often called the topic or theme of the sentence. Although the topic differs across **(11–15)**, in each case we understand that the agent or "giver" was *Chuck,* the underlying subject of the sentence.

Sentences with the same underlying structure will have similar meanings, even if different transformations have been applied to them. Note that this does not imply that sentences with highly similar meanings always have the same underlying structure. The sentence *Peter sold Harvey a car* has nearly the same meaning as does *Harvey bought a car from Peter.* But the two probably do not have the same deep structure (Katz, 1972). This issue will come up again in Chapter 5.

To summarize, we have introduced the concepts of underlying (or deep) structure and surface structure. The former is the structure that results after the application of the phrase-structure rules; the latter results after the application of the transformational rules. Sentences can have very similar underlying structures while differing substantially in their surface structures. We noted that sentences have two subjects, one in the underlying structure and one in the surface structure. By using both of these concepts we can describe similarities and differences among sentences that cannot readily be described using phrase-structure rules alone. In the next section we will describe and try to account for another set of judgments that speakers can make about sentences—whether they are ambiguous.

Ambiguity. The concepts of underlying and surface structure can also help us to understand ambiguity. We should note at the outset, though, that there are several kinds of linguistic ambiguities, some accounted for by other properties of the grammar. Some sentences are ambiguous because a single word has more than one meaning, as in sentence **(16)**.

(16) Tommy found a bat in the attic.

Is the bat Tommy found the kind used in baseball? Or is it a nocturnal flying mammal? Such ambiguities are called *lexical ambiguities.* Because lexical ambiguities involve only the meanings of single words, an explanation of them does not involve structural concepts.

A second kind of ambiguity was mentioned earlier, for example, in sentence **(2)**, which is repeated here.

(2) They are broiling hens.

Such ambiguities arise when there are two different surface structures associated with the same sequence of words (hence the label *surface structure ambiguity*).

There is, however, an additional kind of structural ambiguity. Whereas the two meanings of **(2)** can be distinguished by the way the sentence is pronounced, the two meanings of **(17)** cannot be distinguished in this way. One meaning could be paraphrased by sentence **(18)**, the other by **(19)**.

(17) The chicken is ready to eat.
(18) The chicken is ready to eat (something).
(19) The chicken is ready to be eaten.

Figure 2.6. A figure with two "underlying structures" and one "surface structure": the duck-rabbit.

In contrast to **(2)**, the ambiguity in **(17)** does not derive from differences in the surface structures associated with its two meanings. Rather, sentence **(17)** has two different underlying structures; this is called an *underlying structure ambiguity*. One underlying structure is similar to that of sentence **(18)** and another is similar to that of sentence **(19)**. Different transformations have been applied to the two underlying structures, and the two derivations have resulted in the same surface structure. A visual analogy may help to make this clear. Figure 2.6 is an ambiguous figure. If you stare at it, it sometimes appears to be a duck looking up to the left; then it will switch and become a rabbit looking up to the right. We could say that the drawing has two different "deep structures," one a duck and one a rabbit, which happen to converge on the same surface image. (We borrowed the duck-rabbit from Wittgenstein, 1953). Similarly, sentence **(17)** is "seen" as having sometimes one set of underlying relations among its terms and sometimes another.

The difference between surface structure and underlying structure ambiguities is that for the former there are two distinct underlying structures *and* two distinct surface structures. For the latter, there are two distinct underlying structures, but only one surface structure. This difference is reflected in the fact that surface structure ambiguities can be disambiguated (i.e., have their ambiguity removed) by the manner in which they are pronounced, while underlying structure ambiguities cannot. The difference between the two kinds of structural ambiguities can easily be represented by a grammar that allows two distinct kinds of structural descriptions for each sentence, a transformational grammar. The difference would be difficult, if not impossible, to characterize otherwise.

Lexical Insertion Rules. We noted earlier that rules R4–R7, those that inserted the words into the sentence structure, were oversimplified. In order to be more accurate they must take context into account. That is, not every noun in the language can go along with every verb if we want the rules to produce only grammatical sentences. For example, both (20) and (21) are ungrammatical. (By convention, ungrammatical sentences are marked with an asterisk.)

(20) *The boy frightened sincerity.

(21) *Sincerity was frightened by the boy.

The NP *sincerity* cannot be the direct object of the verb *frighten* in a simple sentence like (20). Likewise, this NP cannot occur as the surface structure subject in a passive sentence with the verb *frighten*. We could make up numerous other ungrammatical sentences (e.g., *It was sincerity that the boy frightened*), and state a rule that keeps each from being correct. However, by using the concept of underlying structure we can state the restriction more economically.

Your intuition tells you that both (20) and (21) are incorrect for the same reason, namely, that sincerity cannot experience fright or anything else. Another way of stating this is to say that the NP *sincerity* cannot be the deep structure object of a sentence with the verb *frighten*. When we have a way to say this within our rule set, then we will rule out (20) and (21) and a host of other ungrammatical possibilities, and we will do it with one rule rather than with dozens of them.

The appropriate rule goes something like this: the underlying object of a sentence with the verb *frighten* must be an NP which refers to either animate objects (e.g., *dog, banker*), or human institutions (e.g., *bank, hospital*). This rule permits just those sentences that we want the grammar to generate and rules out those that we do not want to produce. It is not clear whether this rule is a part of the syntax of the language or its semantics. Concepts like "animate" sound like they have a good deal to do with meaning. We noted earlier that the dividing line between syntax and semantics was not necessarily a sharp one, and this is one instance of its haziness. Nevertheless, the major point remains, namely, that we can make our rules much simpler if we state some of the restrictions at the level of underlying structure.

To summarize, we have seen that a transformational grammar—one that uses both phrase-structure rules and transformations—is capable of accounting for several properties of language that are difficult to account for in other ways. The explanatory power of a transformational grammar comes both from the kinds of rules it employs, particularly transformations, and from its providing two distinct structural descriptions for each sentence in a language. Language properties like synonymy and ambiguity can be accounted for by using the concepts of underlying and surface structures more easily than in any other way.

There is, we should note, considerable controversy among linguists about these structures.[10] One main focus of controversy is the question of whether the

---

[10]In some more recent writings, Chomsky (1975, p. 81 f.) himself has dropped the term "deep structure." Part of his reason for doing so, he says, is that some readers were tempted to treat "deep" as meaning significant and "surface" as meaning trivial and insignificant. Surface structure is far from trivial, and we should not make the mistake Chomsky cautions us against. However, we will keep these terms since they conform to the more common usage in psycholinguistic literature.

underlying structure should be treated as part of the syntactic system of a language or as part of its semantic system. That is, is there a distinct level of syntactic underlying structure which is uniquely linguistic? Or are the underlying structures to which transformational rules are applied part of the internal, semantic code? (see, e.g., Fillmore, 1969; Lakoff, 1972).

It would take us far afield to describe the nature of this controversy and the several others that revolve around similar questions. Undoubtedly the views of linguistic competence that will emerge when these controversies are resolved will profoundly affect future thinking about the nature of a theory of linguistic performance. For example, in a grammar with a semantic underlying structure the transformational rules must be different from those of a grammar with a syntactic underlying structure. But there seems little doubt that *some* form of transformational rules will be required by any grammar. The facts we have discussed demand it, as do many others.

Transformational Operations

Up to this point we have described only one transformational rule—the Equi-NP deletion rule. We will now consider briefly a few other transformations. Doing so will allow us to see some of the properties and functions of such rules. In addition, we will be making use of these particular rules in later chapters.

The Particle–Movement Transformation. In English there are some verbs which consist of two words. An example of this is the pair *call up* as in sentence **(22)**.

(22) Randy called up his wife to ask about the game.

This kind of verb is called a *verb + particle* construction. In certain contexts, we have the option of separating the particle from the verb, as in sentence **(23)**.

(23) Randy called his wife up to ask about the game.

Sentences **(22)** and **(23)** have the same underlying structure; they differ only in one detail of their surface structures. The difference arises because in deriving sentence **(23)** one transformation is applied which is not applied to **(22)**—the *particle-movement transformation*. This rule moves the particle to the far side of the following NP. In this case, it changes *called up his wife* into *called his wife up.* Strictly speaking, the transformation does not apply to the string of words itself. Rather, it applies to the structure that underlies them. The rule can be stated as:

$$V + Particle + NP \; \textit{may be transformed to} \; V + NP + Particle$$

The rule can be applied to any structural description in which the string of symbols on the left occurs. The result is the structure on the right.

The important point here is that the rule applies to the structure of the sentence, not merely to its words. In sentence **(23)** the particle moved two words to the right. But the rule cannot be stated in terms of the number of words involved. Sentences **(24)** and **(25)** also involve particle movement, but in **(24)** the particle has moved three words to the right, and in **(25)** only one word.

(24) Randy called his lovely wife up to ask about the game.

(25) Randy called her up to ask about the game.

The particle is moving over an entire NP, not over a certain number of words. Hence, the particle-movement rule must be stated in terms of non-terminal symbols like NP and V rather than in terms of terminal symbols. This is a general characteristic of transformations: they operate on structures. For this reason, they are characterized as *structure-dependent* rules. Every transformational rule is structure-dependent.

The particle-movement rule must take other aspects of the sentence's structure into account as it operates. For example, the rule must apply if the following NP is a pronoun. Sentence **(25)** is grammatical, but **(26)** is not.

(26) *Randy called up her to ask about the game.

Also, the rule must not apply if the following NP is long and complex, as in **(27)**.

(27) *Michelle called the interesting young fellow with the sandy brown hair, good sense of humor, and sparkling eyes up.

Speakers of English tacitly know the constraints on when the particle can be moved and when it cannot.

Questions. There are several different types of questions that can be formed in English. Two examples are:

(28) Will the boy kiss the girl?

(29) Who will the boy kiss?

Sentence **(28)** is called a *Yes/No question,* since all that is required to answer it is a simple "yes" or "no." Sentence **(29)** is called a *Wh- question.* Any question that begins with *who, what, where, when, why,* or *how* is a Wh- question. Answering a Wh- question requires more than "yes" or "no." To answer **(29),** we must supply at least an NP, such as *the girl.* There are other types of questions in English, but we will concern ourselves with these two.

The Yes/No question **(28)** is related to a simple declarative sentence, sentence **(30).**

(30) The boy will kiss the girl.

The underlying structure of the declarative sentence contains the sequence NP – Aux – V – NP, where the symbol Aux stands for an Auxiliary or "helping" verb like *will, may, can,* etc. (Our earlier rules ignored the Aux, but now we need it.) To form a Yes/No question, a transformational rule is applied to this structure, moving the Aux to the front of the sentence. If there is more than one Aux (as in *The boy should have kissed the girl*), then the first Aux is moved and the rest are not (e.g., *Should the boy have kissed the girl?*). Forming a Yes/No question thus involves moving one item over a preceding structure. In this respect the rule involved is much like the particle-movement rule.

Forming a Yes/No question is not always so straightforward, however, for there are many declarative sentence structures in which there is no Aux, as in sentence **(31)**. In this case, the corresponding Yes/No question is sentence **(32)**.

(31) The boy kissed the girl.

(32) Did the boy kiss the girl?

When the underlying structure does not contain an Aux, some form of the verb *do* is inserted. (The "do-insertion" rule is not used just for questions; the same rule is used in the derivations of several other constructions as well.)

Accounting for the structure of Wh- questions like sentence **(29)** is a bit more complex. First, we need to modify the phrase-structure rules presented earlier so that an optional symbol, Wh, can occur with the NP. Rules R1 and R3 then become Rl′ and R3′, respectively.

$$(R1') \quad S \rightarrow (Wh)NP + VP$$
$$(R3') \quad VP \rightarrow V + (Wh)NP$$

The Wh symbol indicates that the NP with which it occurs is unknown and that the sentence is asking for information about that constituent. For example, sentence **(29)** is asking about the identity of the direct object of *kiss.* We can characterize its underlying structure as: NP - Aux - V - WhNP. A question asking for information about a sentence's underlying subject, e.g., sentence **(33)**, would have the underlying structure: WhNP - Aux - V - NP.

(33) Who kissed the girl?

There is a transformational rule that moves the WhNP symbol to the front of the sentence, called the rule of Wh- fronting. Another transformation, which applies after Wh- fronting, changes WhNP into the appropriate Wh word, *who, what,* etc. Thus, for the underlying structure of sentence **(29)**— NP - Aux - V - WhNP—applying the Wh- fronting rule will yield: WhNP - NP - Aux - V. However, the Wh- fronting rule and the rule that inserts the correct interrogative pronoun are not enough. Applying just those rules yields sentence **(34)** which is clearly ungrammatical and sounds rather childlike.

(34) *Who the boy will kiss?

(Children do produce such questions, as we will see in Chapter 8.)

The problem can be solved, however, by also moving the Aux term in front of the NP, resulting in **(29)**. And, nicely enough, for this we can use the same Aux movement rule that we used for Yes/No questions. But Aux movement must occur *before* Wh- fronting if we are to arrive at the correct sequence: WhNP - Aux - NP - V. If Aux movement occurred after Wh- fronting, we would have the sequence: Aux - WhNP - NP - V, which corresponds to the ungrammatical sentence **(35)**. (Children do not produce questions like this.)

(35)   *Will who the boy kiss?

It is a general characteristic of transformational rules that their application is ordered.

We have seen that question formation involves the ordered application of several transformational rules. Furthermore, some of the same rules are involved in generating both Yes/No and Wh- questions, and in generating other structures as well. The characteristics of the transformations we have seen here are general ones. Most sentences, even apparently very simple ones, require several transformations to derive their surface structures.

The Structure of a Transformational Grammar

Some of the important characteristics of a standard transformational grammar are shown in Figure 2.7. The grammar is divided into four major components, two of which correspond to the two major rule types that we have discussed, the phrase-structure and the transformational rules. The phrase-

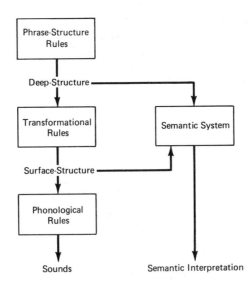

Figure 2.7. The structure of a transformational grammar.

structure rules (along with the lexical insertion rules) generate what we have called the deep structure of the sentence. The transformational component of the system takes the output of the phrase-structure component and produces a surface-structure representation of the sentence. The phonological component takes the surface structure and the lexical items and converts them into a phonetic representation. It also assigns stress and intonation to the string of lexical items. Finally, there is a semantic component which assigns a meaning to the sentence. This component makes use of information both from the underlying form of the sentence and from its surface form.

Chomsky has proposed that all languages can be correctly described using this general framework. That is, he has hypothesized that every language has a phrase-structure component and a transformational component, that the transformations are structure dependent and ordered with respect to each other, etc. This is to claim that these features are universal among languages. Recall that in the first chapter we discussed some possible universals of language, such as displacement and openness. The generative grammar framework, if it is a universal, is a universal of quite a different sort. The framework does not describe some readily observable characteristics of language; instead, it offers an explanation for some of them. It is the basic principles of this explanation that are suggested to be universal. That is, while the particular rules will not be the same for all languages, the types of rules and their overall organization are hypothesized to be universal. This is obviously a very strong claim.

As we have noted, however, there are several controversies about the form and content of a transformational grammar. Many linguists argue that the underlying structure is a semantic representation itself and, hence, that there is no separation between the semantic and syntactic systems. There are, in fact, very few details of the grammar that are not controversial. But the major points that we have been outlining here are relatively unquestioned. One is that the meaning of a sentence is only indirectly related to its phonological representation, that there is a highly complex system of linguistic structure, syntax, intervening between them. We have seen that it is necessary to attribute to sentences a complex structure with at least two levels of representation in order to account for what speakers know about their language. And for our present purposes, these are the characteristics of an account of linguistic competence that are important.

Before turning our attention to the nature of the semantic system, there is one last point that should be mentioned. In describing the syntactic system we have frequently used terms like "generate" and "derive," and we have spoken of such things as the ordered application of transformational rules. It would be easy to think of these processes as a model of the steps a speaker goes through in constructing an utterance. It would also be a mistake. The sense of "generate" and "derive" used in describing a grammar is the sense used by mathematicians and logicians when, for example, they speak of deriving theorems of geometry from a set of axioms. We will see later that the actual processes involved in producing and comprehending utterances are probably quite different from the rules described here. But for the moment we can do no better than to quote Chomsky on this point:

> ". . . although we may describe the grammar as a system of . . . rules that apply in a certain order to relate sound and meaning, we are not entitled to take this as a description of the successive acts of a performance model—in fact it would be quite absurd to do so" (N. Chomsky, 1967, p. 399).

Semantics: The System of Meaning

The semantic system of language forms the interface between language and thought. It is an internal system of representation, and this fact makes it difficult to study and to understand. Thus, although semantics—the problem of meaning—has been studied very extensively by philosophers, linguists, and psychologists, we are still far from being able to offer anything like an adequate account of meaning. Anyone who tries to survey the field of semantic studies will find a bewildering array of approaches to the topic and a lot of disagreement, not only about the form of semantic theory but also about the problems to be addressed by such theory. To quote Kalish (1967), "A single rubric [semantics] for these diverse disciplines is perhaps warranted by their common concern with signs and meanings, but in some instances the differences are more striking than the similarities . . ." (p. 348). How, then, are we to characterize meaning? What does a person know when he knows the meaning of a word or a sentence? We can perhaps learn a bit about the nature of meaning by briefly considering two popular but incorrect characterizations of this knowledge. Examining some of the reasons why these views are wrong will help us to see the problems somewhat more clearly.

Two Misleading Approaches to Semantics

Like many approaches to semantics, both of these focus mainly upon the meanings of words. As we will see, they do not deal adequately with even this aspect of meaning.

Meaning = Reference. According to this theory, the meaning of a word is the word's referent (that to which it refers). Words are "names" for things; we can define a word by pointing to the thing which it names. This view is reflected in the classroom approach to meaning which says that nouns are the names of persons, places, or things; verbs are the names of states or actions; adjectives are the names of properties or qualities, etc. The meaning of *snow*, for example, is that white stuff that often falls during the winter.

Much of the appeal of the reference theory of meaning is its simplicity—the meaning of the word is, simply, the thing named. But despite its appeal, there are a large number of arguments against it. Some of these arguments can be presented informally and quite briefly, and we will sketch them here.

The reference theory seems most plausible when applied to simple, concrete nouns, e.g., *snow, boy, table,* etc. But there are many other nouns whose meanings cannot be dealt with so simply. What, for example, is the meaning of *elf*? Most people would agree that there is no such thing as an elf; therefore, there is nothing for the word *elf* to refer to. Is the word then meaningless? Clearly it is not; we all know what the word means and are able to converse quite knowledgeably about elves even though they do not exist. Much the same could be said about the words *unicorn, gorgon, Zeus,* and a great many more. A similar problem arises with "abstract" nouns like *truth, beauty, love,* etc. What are the things to which such terms refer? There is, in fact, nothing "thinglike" about truth, beauty, and love. But the words are hardly meaningless.

The problem with the reference theory of meaning goes far beyond the fact that there are many words for which there are no referents. Even words that can have referents do not always have them. Consider, for example, the word *tiger* in sentences (36) and (37).

(36) Jerry shot a tiger.

(37) Jerry hunted a tiger.

In (36) the phrase *a tiger* refers to a particular tiger, the one that was shot. But in (37) the same phrase may not refer to anything. There may not *be* any tiger, even though Jerry was hunting for one (Fodor, 1975). Sentence (37) is surely a meaningful one even if there was no tiger. It makes no sense to say that *a tiger* means something different in (36) and (37). Rather, the meaning stays the same even though in one case the phrase has a referent and in the other it does not. Meaning is not equal to reference.

Meaning = Image. The image theory of meaning is closely related to the reference theory. But whereas the reference theory says that the meaning is the thing the word names, the image theory says that the meaning is an image of the thing. Thus, the meaning of *snow* is not snow itself, but rather a mental image of snow; likewise, the meaning of *dog* is a mental image of a dog.

The image theory of meaning has many of the same problems as the reference theory. For example, both have difficulty in dealing with abstractions. It has been well-known for at least two centuries that the image theory cannot account for the meanings of abstract words. What kind of image represents the meaning of *truth* or, indeed, of *image*? Also, the theory has difficulty in specifying the meaning of general (common) nouns. What kind of an image represents the meaning of *dog*? The noun *dog* can be applied to any dog. But any image you form is of a particular dog, perhaps a German sheperd you have known, perhaps an Irish setter. That is, the image is particular—it is an image of *a dog* (and of a dog seen from a particular view, a dog either wagging its tail or not, etc.). There is no image that corresponds to dog, the general concept expressed by the word *dog*.[11]

We have suggested some of the reasons why two popular views of meaning are incorrect. What remains is to try to say what a better view might be.

The Problems of Meaning

One helpful attitude to take when approaching the topic of semantics has been expressed by Jerrold Katz (1972). Katz notes that we are often too simple-minded when we ask, *What is meaning?* in that we are expecting a simple answer to the question. If someone asked, *What is an ecdysiast?* we could give a simple reply, namely, a strip-teaser. But if the question instead was, *What is an electron?* a simple answer could not be given. In order to answer the latter question we might have to introduce numerous concepts from physics (atom, charge, proton, etc.) and to state how these concepts interrelate with one another. In other words, we would have to state a theory and explain how the term in question (*electron*) fits into the theory. In order to give an answer to the question, *What is meaning?* the analogy of the electron is more appropriate than is the analogy of the ecdysiast.

Katz argues that the question *What is meaning?* can be broken down into a number of sub-questions. As we answer each of these we will be contributing pieces to the solution of the semantic puzzle. The answer to the question is a theory, not a simple statement. Of course, Katz also argues that the pieces must make a coherent picture. Furthermore, the theory should relate to the syntactic system.

One of Katz' sub-questions is, *What is a paraphrase?* By this he means that we have to state why the sentence *John loves Mary's only sister* and *John loves the female sibling of Mary* mean the same thing. Another of his questions is *What is semantic similarity?* Here Katz has in mind finding an explanation for the fact that such terms as *aunt, sister, nun, actress, filly,* and *mother* are semantically similar in one respect, similar in a way that *shadow, afterimage,* and *reflection* are not, though the latter are also similar to one another. Likewise Katz would like to explain why *Uncles are males* is uninformative, and *Babies are adults* is necessarily false. In all, Katz lists fifteen preliminary questions for his investigations of semantic phenomena. Rather than stating all of these questions, we will briefly discuss two issues: word meaning and sentence meaning.

Word Meaning

The meaning of a sentence is built from the meanings of its parts. In order to state the meaning of *Jerry hunted a tiger,* we must state the meaning of *tiger,*

---

[11]Numerous other arguments against the view that meanings are images could be raised, some of which will be considered in Chapter 5. For a general discussion of mental images and why they cannot be the same kinds of things as meanings, see Pylyshyn (1973).

among other things. We already know that the meaning of this word is neither a tiger nor an image of a tiger. Rather, we will say that the meaning of *tiger* is a concept. But now, of course, we must say what a concept is. Although we do not have an explicit definition or theory of *concept,* we have some relevant observations.

A concept is, first, a theoretical entity. This entity is related both to other concepts and to certain actions that can be carried out by individuals who possess the concept. With respect to actions, for example, someone who knows the meaning of *tiger* can make judgments about whether something is or is not a tiger; that is, he has a rule which specifies what counts as being a tiger. Essentially, the rule defines the properties of tigers. As you might imagine, stating such a rule in detail is quite a difficult task. We will have a bit more to say about some possible ways of approaching this task in Chapter 5.

As was the case with the theoretical term *electron,* the concept expressed by *tiger* must be stated in terms of its relations to other concepts, such as those expressed by *animal, cat, ferocious, lion,* etc. These relations fall into various groups. For example, both lions and tigers are big and tawny (sensory properties). They are both animals and cats (class membership). Concepts such as animal, big, etc., have sometimes been called *semantic features.* Some theorists have tried to devise systems in which the meaning of lexical items was stated largely in terms of such features. According to such approaches, concepts that share a large number of features are closely related (Katz, 1972). The words *aunt, sister, actress,* etc. all share the feature "female." Again, we will have more to say about these ideas later.

To summarize, the meaning of a word is a concept. A concept, in turn, is a theoretical term. In order to understand any one concept (e.g., that expressed by *electron*), we must state (a) a rule for specifying what counts as an instance of that concept, and (b) the relations between that concept and others. These tasks are difficult to carry out since they are equivalent to solving many of the problems of cognitive psychology.

Meanings of Sentences

The meaning of a sentence involves both the meanings of the words in the sentence and the organization of those words. Syntactic structure is an important determiner of meaning.

Syntax and Sentence Meaning. Earlier in the chapter we noted that sentence (2), *They are broiling hens,* has two syntactic structures and that the two structures have different meanings associated with them. We should also point out that even though the organization among words is an important determiner of sentence meaning, syntax and semantics are not always in perfect agreement. The syntactic aspects of a sentence are not always reliable indicators of its meaning. To take a commonly cited example, there is an imperfect correlation between the syntactic concepts of singular and plural and the semantic distinction between those concepts. The terms *wheat* and *oats* both refer to collections of objects; in that sense they are semantically plural. But in **(38)** the verb following the noun is singular, while in **(39)** it is plural. Syntactic number does not always reflect semantic number.

(38) The wheat is almost ready to harvest.

(39) The oats are almost ready to harvest.

Even when we have the syntactic structure of a sentence, constructing its meaning is not a simple task. To take just one small problem, consider how the meaning of an NP is constructed from the meanings of a noun and its modifying adjective. The phrase *red squares* refers to those things that are both red and square. But the phrase *large fleas* does not refer to those things that are both absolutely large and fleas. A large flea is smaller than a small elephant. The interpretation of a relative-concept adjective such as *large* depends upon the noun that it occurs with. The rules for interpreting an adjective + noun pair like *large fleas* are somewhat different from those for interpreting *red squares*. The complexity becomes even more obvious when we consider a phrase like *a Picasso painting*. This phrase is definitely not used to refer to something that is both Picasso and a painting. And *a fake Picasso painting* may refer to a painting, but Picasso had nothing to do with it. As can be seen, rules for semantically interpreting even such simple constructions as adjective + noun are complex. Such rules have not been completely worked out, although a considerable amount of work has been done on finding an appropriate form in which to express such rules (e.g., Lewis, 1972). Much of this work is beyond our present scope.

To summarize, the syntactic organization of a sentence is an important determiner of the sentence's meaning. Each syntactic structure (e.g., adjective + noun) does not, however, always contribute to meaning in a uniform way.

Propositions, Entailments, and Truth. Every sentence in a language has a meaning associated with it. A theory of meaning will describe how meaning gets assigned to each sentence. Such a theory will no doubt say that the particular words and their syntactic structure play a large role in determining the meaning of any individual sentence. If the theory of meaning is relevant to psychology, it will also state the internal code in which the meaning of a sentence is represented. For now, let us assume that the internal representation is in terms of *propositions*. A proposition expresses the relationships that exist among a sentence's concepts. Of course, all that now remains is to specify the concepts and relationships. Chapters 4 and 5 will address these issues further. Here we will simply note that relationships are usually expressed by verbs, as when, in **(37)**, *hunting* expresses the relationship between *Jerry* and *a tiger*. A proposition is more abstract than a sentence. The same proposition can be expressed in different sentences (e.g., sentences **11–15**) and even in different languages.

The view that sentences are internally represented as propositions permits us to make two further observations about sentence meaning. First, the meaning of a sentence is related to its *entailments;* second, the meaning of a sentence is related to its *truth conditions.* Looking first at the notion of entailment, note that the two sentences **(40)** and **(41)** entail sentence **(42)**. The latter "follows from" the former two.

(40) Susan is a red-headed psychologist.

(41) Susan is an ice-skater.

(42) Susan is a red-headed ice-skater.

However, sentences **(43)** and **(44)** do not entail sentence **(45)**. Even though **(43–45)** are similar in form to **(40–42)**, the entailment relations among the two sets are different.

(43) Susan is a skillful psychologist.

(44) Susan is an ice skater.

(45) Susan is a skillful ice skater.

The meanings of *red-headed* and *skillful* affect the kinds of entailments that can be made from sentences containing them. A theory of meaning must specify how and why the entailments are different in such cases.

In addition to having entailments, propositions have *truth values* associated with them; that is, they can be either true or false. The proposition expressed by **(37)**, *Jerry hunted a tiger,* is true if and only if there actually was a person, Jerry, who at some past time engaged in the activity of hunting a tiger. As we noted above, there need not have been an actual tiger—sentence **(37)** could be true without one. We will only credit someone with understanding **(37)** if that individual agrees with the statements in the previous two sentences. If the person thinks that **(37)** is true when, in fact, he knows that Jerry wasn't even looking for a tiger, that Jerry was seen running from a tiger, etc., then he does not know the meaning of **(37)**.

Thus, when an individual knows the meaning of a sentence, then he knows (among other things) what conditions would have to exist for the sentence to be true; he knows, in other words, the sentence's *truth conditions.* If you know what *Jerry hunted a tiger* means, then you know what the world would be like *if* the sentence were true. Whether it *is* true, whether, in fact, Jerry actually *was* out hunting a tiger is irrelevant. To be credited with knowing the meaning of a sentence, you only need to know what conditions would be like if it *were* true. You must know its truth conditions. Unless you know what these conditions are, you do not know what the sentence means. Finding a way to state the relationship between a sentence and its truth conditions is one of the chief problems for semantics.

To summarize, we have briefly discussed two of the many problems of sentence meaning, specifying entailments and truth conditions. A complete psychological account of language will have to address these problems, though as we will see, primarily in Chapter 5, our psychological theories about language cannot yet solve them. But now it is time to explore in more detail some of the processes that are used when we comprehend sentences. The next section begins by studying some of the better known aspects of language, those closer to the external code. By the end of the section, however, we will also have given considerable attention to the internal code.

Summary

The language system can be divided into three broad areas of study: the phonological, the syntactic, and the semantic. Although these areas are treated separately, they are not independent of one another—especially the latter two.

Phonology is the study of the sound system of the language. Each word is made up of one or more sound (phonetic) segments. Each segment is, in turn, composed of a bundle of phonetic features such as stop, nasality, etc. Some features are distinctive in a language, others are not. Rules that state the permissible sequences of sounds in a language can be expressed in terms of segments and features. In addition, each word has two phonological codes—a surface and an underlying representation.

The syntactic system describes the order and organization among words in a sentence. The description is given by a set of rules. These rules permit one to generate an unlimited number of sentences, and they assign a structural description to each sentence that is generated. Two main rule types were discussed, phrase-structure and transformational rules, and a rationale for each type was presented. Although controversial, the concepts of transformational grammar have had an important impact on studies of both linguistic competence and linguistic performance.

The semantic or meaning system is best thought of as a set of problems to be solved. Some of the problems were noted and two unsuccessful semantic theories—the reference and image theories—were described.

A successful theory of semantics will state how the meanings of words are to be characterized and how these meanings combine when they appear together in sentences. Also, when one knows the meaning of a sentence one knows something about what the sentence entails and about its truth conditions. Clearly, the internal code, meaning, is the least understood aspect of linguistic structure.

SUGGESTED READINGS

Further discussions of phonology can be found in Hyman (1975) and Schane (1973). The topic of syntax is well covered by Akmajian and Heny (1975) and by Baker (1977). The development of Chomsky's thoughts about syntax can be traced by looking at his 1957, 1965, and 1975 books. His 1972 book, *Language and mind,* is perhaps the best place to start reading his original works. Lyons (1970) also provides an overview of Chomsky's system.

The topic of semantics is introduced by Bierwisch (1970), Leech (1974), and Lyons (1977). More advanced readings on the topic can be found in Steinberg and Jakobovits (1971).

II

Understanding Language

INTRODUCTION

What is it that a person is doing when he hears an utterance and understands it? Intuitively we might say that understanding an utterance means something like "getting out the meaning that the speaker intended." This seems reasonable as a rough, general statement of the goal of understanding language. But here we are concerned with a more detailed answer to the question. In particular, we want to know what happens between the time a listener hears the sound a speaker has produced and the time he has discovered the underlying meaning of the utterance.

If you try to consciously reflect upon what you are doing during understanding—to observe it with your "mind's eye"—two things become clear fairly quickly. First, whatever is happening, it is something that does not take very long. Usually there is no interval at all between when the speaker stops and when you feel that you have understood what he said. To be sure, there are exceptions, cases in which you may have to work hard and long before you feel that you have understood what was said. But such cases are notable just because they are exceptions—usually understanding comes very quickly.

The second thing that becomes clear when you try to reflect upon the process of comprehension is that there is nothing there. The speaker spoke; you understood; and that is all there is to it—no feeling of effort, no feeling of having done anything. So it appears to you that your understanding of what is said simply emerges, quickly and effortlessly: there is nothing in between. But the appearance of a lack of effort is a bit misleading. Even though there is no apparent effort, there is abundant evidence to suggest that, in fact, a great deal of extremely complex perceptual processing intervenes between the sound of an utterance and your understanding of what it meant.

The process of comprehension begins with a sound wave arriving at the hearer's ears. As we will see, the sound waves involved in human speech are quite complex. But one thing that is immediately apparent if we examine the sound waves a speaker produces is that they are nearly continuous. That is, the sound does not come in nice neat chunks that correspond to the words that the speaker is saying. Instead, we generally cannot tell from looking at the sound itself where one word ends and the next begins. If fact, it is often difficult to tell even where one sentence ends and another begins.

What this means is that, in order to be able to find the meanings of the utterance's words in his mental dictionary, the hearer must be breaking the continuous sound wave into word-like chunks. Furthermore, he must be identifying the series of units, or phonemes, that occur within each of those word-like chunks. We can think of the process of translating sound into a sequence of linguistic units as the process of *speech perception*. In perceiving speech one begins with a continuous sound pattern and ends with something like a written text. Of course, the output of the speech perception process is different from a text in a number of ways. For example, rather than having letters as units, the units seem to be much more like phonemes or sets of distinctive features. In addition, the output contains information about the stress pattern of the utterance and the intonation of the speaker's voice that is difficult to represent in a written text. Still, the analogy to text is close enough to be useful. The process of speech perception is the topic of Chapter 3.

We may conceive of comprehension processing as a series of processing stages, each of which transforms, or changes, the form of an utterance, moving from its form as a sound pattern toward a representation of its underlying meaning. Speech perception is the first stage. The output from this stage, however, contains little or no information about the syntax of the utterance or the meanings of its words. Clearly, these are important omissions.

First of all, the meaning of the utterance depends upon the meanings of the words it contains. A hearer who knows the words has something equivalent to a mental dictionary—a storehouse in which information about the meanings of the words he knows—is associated with the phonological forms of the words. So at least one part of the process of comprehension must be something equivalent to looking up the meanings of the utterance's words in the mental dictionary. Until this has been done, the hearer does not even know whether the words are nouns, verbs, or some other parts of speech. In the second place, as we saw in Chapter 2, the meaning of an utterance, or sentence, depends not only upon the meanings of its words, but also upon the way in which those words are arranged, that is, upon the sentence's syntax. So, another part of the process of comprehension must involve discovering the syntax of the heard utterance.

These kinds of information emerge during the second processing stage, one which might be labelled the stage of *syntactic and lexical processing*. Although the analogy is far from exact, we might think of the output of this stage as being a representation of the utterance corresponding to the sort of deep-structure tree diagram discussed in Chapter 2. Describing the processes of syntactic and lexical processing is the topic of Chapter 4.

Finally, there must be an additional processing stage in which representations of this sort are transformed, or interpreted, semantically, a stage whose output is a representation of the utterance's meaning. It is difficult to determine exactly what such a representation should look like or even where the process of semantic interpretation ends. Suppose, for example, someone came up to you and asked, *Do you know what time it is?* In its literal meaning this is a request for information about the state of your knowledge, and at some stage of processing the utterance would probably be represented this way. This is what is often referred to as a Yes/No question, a kind of question to which *Yes* or *No* would be an appropriate answer. But it is clear that the person who asks this particular Yes/No question is unlikely to be interested in hearing a *Yes* or *No* answer; he does not really want to know only whether you know what the time is. (If you have any doubts about this, the next time someone asks you a similar question try answering *Yes* and then saying nothing more.) Rather, what he wants to know is what time it is. He wants an answer like *5:25* or *Half-past three,* not an answer like *Yes.*

There is, then, a difference between a sentence's literal meaning and what we may call its "conveyed" meaning. But how do we decide which it is that the speaker intended? When should we take him literally, and when should we look further for a non-literal conveyed meaning? And, if we do decide to look further, how do we find the appropriate conveyed meaning?

The answers to these questions are complicated, and as yet no one has complete answers. But in simplified form the answer seems to be that the hearer arrives at the sentence's literal meaning and then evaluates that meaning in terms of the situation in which it occurred. That is, he combines information about the literal meaning with information about the speaker, the occasion on which the utterance occurred, etc., and bases a decision on that. Often, our best information about what the listener understood a sentence to mean comes from studies of his memory for what he heard. Chapter 5 will take up the issue of memory for sentences.

Before proceeding further, a word of warning is in order: the sketch we have presented of the processes of comprehension is misleading in at least two ways. First, it would be incorrect to think of the processing stages we have mentioned as occurring in a strict sequence. A hearer does not wait until the speech perception processing of an entire utterance has been completed before starting to search out its syntactic structure and lexical content. Rather, it appears that these processes overlap in time, syntactic and semantic processing beginning almost simultaneously with speech perception processing.

Second, the processes we have mentioned are not independent. That is, decisions made by the speech perception mechanisms are affected by the operation of the lexical and syntactic mechanisms. The process of understanding is, then, far more complex than simply one of first perceiving the speech signal, then decoding its syntax and retrieving its lexical content, and then finding a semantic interpretation for the utterance. With this in mind, let us turn to consider the process of comprehension in more detail.

3

Perceiving Speech

One of the most obvious facts about perceiving speech is that we usually do it quickly and effortlessly. Only occasionally, when there is a great deal of noise along with the speech, do we have to pay much attention to the sounds the speaker is producing. More generally, our attention is focused on what the speaker is saying, on the meaning, rather than on the sounds themselves.

If we do focus our attention on the sounds of speech, the impression is that we hear a series of words and that each of them is composed of a series of sounds, corresponding roughly to phonological segments, coming one after another. If the same phoneme occurs several times in different contexts, it seems to sound very much the same each time it occurs. If the speaker says *dog,* and then sometime later says *bad* or *day* or *under,* all the different /d/s sound pretty much the same.

The appearance, then, is that each phoneme has a distinctive sound, much the same regardless of the context in which it occurs and different from that of any other phoneme. To be sure, there can be a good deal of variation in the pronunciation of a given phoneme. A /d/ spoken by one person does not sound exactly like that spoken by someone else, and even in a single speaker a /d/ spoken quietly is noticeably different from one shouted loudly. But even so, all these sounds seem to have a quality of "/d/-ness" that distinguishes them from any other phoneme a speaker produces, and that quality seems quite invariant.

It also appears in listening to speech that there is a simple relationship between the order in which sounds occur and the order in which we hear them. In listening to the word *dog,* for example, it seems that the first part of the sound corresponds to the consonant /d/, the next part corresponds to the vowel, and the last part corresponds to the consonant /g/.

If this is the case, then we should be able to find the acoustic cues for the phonemes by cutting up a word into segments corresponding to each of its phonemes. Having done so, we should also be able to examine segments from several words that all correspond to a particular phoneme and, by looking for what they have in common, find the invariant speech signal cues for that phoneme.

A simple way to go about this would be to take a tape recording of a word or syllable, say, the syllable /do/ (*doe*), and start cutting off parts of the tape. If we cut off bits from the beginning, we should eventually reach a point where all traces of the consonant had vanished, leaving us with only the vowel. In fact, this is what would happen. If we try to isolate the consonant in the same way, cutting off bits of tape from the end, we would find something quite different. When we had removed enough of the tape to eliminate the vowel, we would find that we had also eliminated the consonant. What is left would not even sound like speech; it would sound more like a "chirp."

This is characteristic of many speech sounds and illustrates an important fact: there is no simple one-to-one correspondence between the segments of a speech signal and the phonemes we hear. Information about a particular phoneme often overlaps with that about other phonemes, a phenomenon referred to as *parallel transmission.*

In addition, if we examine several syllables or words that start with /d/ and compare them with ones starting with other consonants, there seems to be little that is common to all the /d/s that is not also shared by one or another of the other consonants. That is, there is no part of the speech signal that is always present for a /d/ and never present for any other phoneme. For many phonemes, there are no invariant cues, a phenomenon known as *lack of invariance.*

What, then, do we use to identify a phoneme? If there is nothing in the speech signal that is unique to a particular phoneme and common across all the contexts in which it occurs, why does it always seem to sound the same? Before we can answer such questions, we must first gain some understanding of what speech sounds are like. It is to that task that we now turn.

The Sounds of Speech

There are several ways of representing speech sounds. The most useful one is a *sound spectrogram,* a three-dimensional visual representation of the sound. Figure 3.1A presents a spectrogram of the utterance, *the dog snapped,* spoken slowly and distinctly. Because it is difficult to see what is important in a spectrogram made from real speech, Figure 3.1B presents a schematic spectrogram of the same utterance. The schematic spectrogram includes most of the important properties of the real spectrogram.

The vertical dimension, or ordinate, of the spectrogram represents the frequency of the sound in cycles per second or Hertz (Hz). As Figure 3.1 shows, speech sounds tend to be complex in that there is sound energy at several different frequencies at the same time. The horizontal dimension, or abscissa, represents time. The utterance's phonemes are printed beneath the abscissa in their approximate locations. The spectrogram's third dimension is darkness and represents intensity, or loudness. The darker a portion of a spectrogram, the louder the sound at that frequency and time.

At any point in time, the sound is not equally loud at all frequencies. Throughout much of the utterance the sound appears as bands of high intensity, called *formants*. These can be seen clearly in the vowels in *dog* and in *snapped*. Notice that the formants tend not to remain at the same frequencies for very long: they vary almost continuously. For convenience in referring to the formants, we will number them in order from low to high frequency. The lowest formant, F_1, is in the vicinity of 300-700 Hz. The second formant, F_2, is in the neighborhood of 1000-1800 Hz; and the third formant, F_3, is in the vicinity of 2500-3000 Hz. Notice in Figure 3.1A that the higher formants tend to be lighter, and thus less loud, than the lower ones.

Most of the information useful for identifying different phonemes is concentrated in the range from 100 to 4,000 Hz, a range that includes F_1, F_2, and F_3. Formants higher than F_3 are usually quite weak and are unimportant in identifying which phonemes occurred. The higher formants are, however, important for giving the voice its distinctive human quality. Without them speech tends to sound "tinny" and artificial.

To understand why speech sounds look the way they do, we must understand a bit about the ways in which they are produced. Figure 3.2 presents a side view of a human vocal tract. Speech is produced by forcing air out of the lungs, past the vocal folds, and out through the oral cavity (and sometimes also through the nasal cavity as well). If the vocal folds are drawn together, as they are for all vowel sounds, the air being forced past them causes them to vibrate. The rate, or frequency, of this vibration is the *fundamental frequency* (F_o) of the speaker's voice, which varies with the rate of air flow and with the tension on the vocal folds.

When the vocal folds are vibrating, the sound is a regular, or periodic, one. Sounds produced this way are referred to as *voiced*. The fundamental frequency appears in a spectrogram as a voice bar, indicated in Figure 3.1B below F_1. It also appears as the "stripes" in the formants themselves as, for example, in the vowel in *dog* (see Figure 3.1A).

The vibration which produces the fundamental frequency also produces a set of higher frequency sounds, called overtones or harmonics. If speech sounds were emitted directly into the open air from the vocal folds, these harmonics

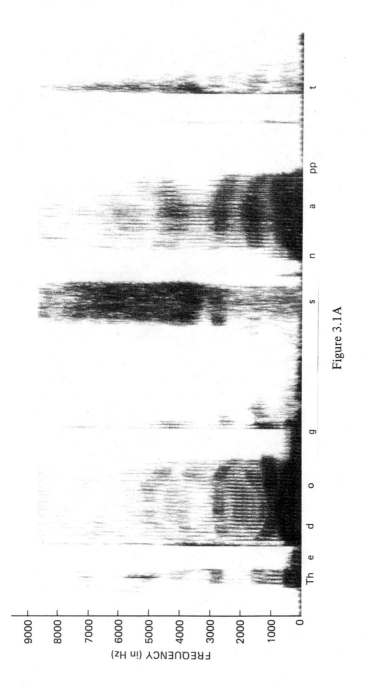

Figure 3.1A

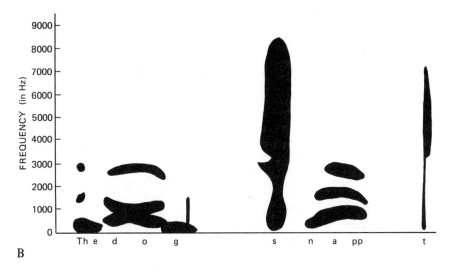

Figure 3.1. Spectrograms of the utterance, ***The dog snapped.*** (A) shown on the facing page is a real spectrogram. (B) is a schematic spectrogram showing the perceptually important noise and formant patterns of (A).

would be part of the resulting sound. But before speech emerges into the open air, the sound must pass through the rest of the vocal tract. And this acts as a resonator, much like the sounding box of a violin or guitar. The effect of passing a sound through a resonator is to shape it, reinforcing and increasing the intensity of some harmonics, and cancelling and lowering the intensity of others. The result is the formants. Their frequencies are determined by the fundamental frequency and by the size and shape of the vocal tract, and they can be varied in complicated ways by changing the shape of the vocal tract. We will discuss later how this variation is accomplished (Chapter 7).

Before turning away from speech production, there is one more thing that should be mentioned. We have described the manner in which voiced speech sounds are produced with the vocal folds drawn together so as to vibrate periodically. It is also possible to produce speech sounds when the vocal folds are relaxed and too far apart to vibrate. Such sounds have a different character, as they result from turbulence created by air rushing rapidly past the vocal folds. Sounds produced in this way are aperiodic (i.e., irregular) and have no clear fundamental frequency or formant structure. These are referred to as *voiceless* sounds and tend to have their energy smeared across the frequency range, giving them a "noisy" quality. This can be seen in Figure 3.1 in the interval between the /ɔ/ and /g/ of *dog*; it is particularly clear at the beginning of the /s/ in *snapped*.

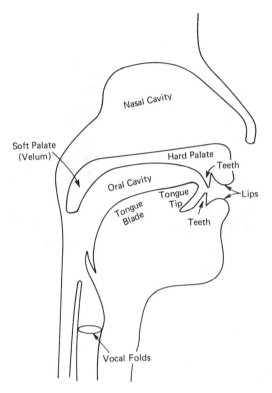

Figure 3.2. The human vocal tract showing most of the articulatory structures important in the production of speech.

With these few facts about speech production and the representation of speech sounds in mind, we can begin to consider the perceptually important properties of speech sounds.

Speech Perception Phenomena and Speech Cues

One major aim of research on speech has been to discover the acoustic cues in speech sounds. The most fruitful research technique for this has involved creating artificial, or synthetic, speech and studying how listeners respond to it. The electronic circuitry and programming needed to produce clear synthetic speech are highly complicated, but for research purposes speech produced in this way has several advantages over natural speech. One important advantage is that with synthesized speech we can vary a single property of the sound at a time, something very difficult for a human speaker to do. For example, the frequencies of F_1, F_2, and F_3 and the ways they change over time provide important cues for perceiving many phonemes. But with a human speaker all the formants vary together in complex ways, leaving us no way of deciding which formant or formant change is the most important or even whether any one is more important than the others. Using synthesized speech, we can vary one formant without varying the others; and by studying how listeners' judgments of the sounds are affected by such variations we can discover what variations are important.

This approach, supplemented by a variety of other kinds of research, has led to a considerable (though hardly complete) understanding of the cues involved in perceiving speech. As we have already noted, there are few cases in which a phoneme can be identified by any simple property of the speech signal—complexity and lack of invariance are the rule, not the exception. With this thought in mind, let us turn to considering the kinds of speech signal cues which listeners use to identify phonemes and to distinguish between different phonemes. We will begin with vowels, since the cues for these phonemes are somewhat simpler than those for many consonantal phonemes.

The Perception of Vowels

Vowels are generally characterized as having formants which maintain the same frequencies for at least a short period of time. The relative values of the formant frequencies serve to distinguish between different vowels. Figure 3.3 presents schematic spectrograms of the vowels commonly occurring in English, all in the context /d/_. The initial portion of each pattern where the formant frequencies are changing rapidly provides some of the cues for identifying the consonant and could be removed without altering the vowel.

Comparison of the patterns in Figure 3.3 indicates that it is the relationship between F_1 and F_2 that distinguishes the vowels. Neither formant alone is sufficient for identifying vowels. For example, F_1 is nearly identical for /de/ (*day*) and for /do/ (*doe*); these differ only in their F_2s. On the other hand, F_2

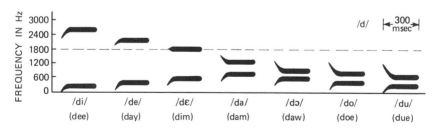

Figure 3.3. Schematic spectrograms showing the first 2 formants of the stop consonant /d/ followed by several different vowels. The vowels are identified phonetically in slashes and as they sound in English syllables in parentheses. (From Liberman, A. M., Cooper, F. S., Shankweiler, D. P., & Studdert-Kennedy, M. Perception of the speech code, *Psychological Review,* 1967, *74,* 431–461. Copyright 1967 by American Psychological Association. Used by permission.)

is nearly identical for /dɔ/ (*daw*) and /do/ (*doe*); these differ primarily in their F_1 s. This indicates that it is the relationship between F_1 and F_2 that is important. The specific frequencies could be different, as they would if the syllables were spoken by a female or a child. But if the relationship remains the same, the vowels remain the same.

The formant patterns presented in Figure 3.3 contain only the first two formants. This does not mean that F_3 plays no role in vowel identification. The relationship between F_1 and F_2 is usually the most important cue for identifying vowels, but the F_3 frequency contributes more to some distinctions than to others.

The Perception of Consonants

Most languages, English included, have more consonants than vowels. In addition, the sound properties that serve to distinguish among the different consonants are more varied and often more subtle than those distinguishing among vowels. We will limit ourselves here to considering a few of the more important classes of consonants.

Stop Consonants. We saw in Chapter 2 that stop consonants are characterized by the manner in which they are produced. They involve closing off the airflow through the vocal tract. When a stop consonant occurs at the beginning of a word or syllable, the sound begins when the closure is released. The consequence of this can be seen in the formants at the beginning of *dog* in Figure 3.1 and at the beginnings of the syllables in Figure 3.3. There are rapid changes in the frequencies of the formants, referred to as *formant transitions*. There is also a short burst of noise spread across a wide range of frequencies just before the formant transitions. This is clearly visible in the /d/ in the real speech spectrogram in Figure 3.1A, but it has been omitted from the schematic spectrograms in Figure 3.3.

Examining the patterns that are heard as /d/ before different vowels (Figure 3.3) reveals that, in all of the vowel contexts, /d/ has a rising F_1 transition lasting about 50 msec[1] (though the transition may last as little as 10–20 msec in rapid, fluent speech). However, the frequencies of the F_1 transition differ in the different vowel contexts. More important, the F_1 transition for /d/ before a particular vowel is nearly identical to the F_1 transition for /b/ or /g/, also stop consonants, before the same vowel. Thus, the F_1 transition is not constant for /d/ in different contexts and also fails to distinguish /d/ from other stops.

The F_2 transitions for /d/s in different contexts are no more constant than the F_1 transitions. Most of the /d/ patterns do have F_2 transitions, but their magnitude and even their direction varies. Thus, as is the case with F_1, there is

---

[1] A millisecond (msec) is one-one thousandth of a second (1/1000 sec). Thus, for example, 250 msec is 1/4th of a second.

no aspect of F_2 that is invariant across all occurrences of /d/. This is particularly surprising since, as we noted earlier, /d/ sounds like the same sound pattern in all of these contexts. Why should we perceive it as invariant when clearly it is not?

There is, however, one characteristic of /d/'s F_2 transition that serves to distinguish /d/ from /b/ and /g/. As the dashed line in Figure 3.3 indicates, the F_2 transitions for all the /d/s "point toward" the frequency of 1800 Hz. That is, if the F_2 transitions are projected backward in time—about 50 msec—they would all meet at 1800 Hz. There is no easy way to describe why this is so, but it results from the shape of the oral cavity involved in producing /d/. (We will discuss this more fully in Chapter 7.) The 1800 Hz frequency is sometimes referred to as the *locus* for /d/.

If we were to examine spectrographic patterns for /b/ and /g/, we would find that each has a locus different from that for /d/. For /b/, the locus is at about 720 Hz. Since this is a frequency lower than the F_2 of most vowels, /b/ generally has a rising F_2 transition preceding a vowel. An F_2 locus for /g/ is more difficult to specify, because there is no single locus frequency for /g/ in all contexts. For most cases the locus is at about 3000 Hz. Since this is higher than the F_2 for any vowel, /g/ will tend to have a falling F_2 transition before any vowel.

The rising or falling character of an F_2 transition is, by itself, not sufficient for distinguishing among /b/, /d/, and /g/. For /b/ it is always rising, and for /g/ it is always falling. For for /d/ it is sometimes rising, sometimes falling, and sometimes nearly unchanging. This suggests that the problem of distinguishing among these stop consonants is a complex one for the listener. It appears that the transitions in the F_3s for the different stops contribute some additional information to help in the task of distinguishing them (see Stevens & House, 1972). And in fact the relationships among the F_1, F_2, and F_3 transitions seem to provide all the necessary information.

An additional, secondary cue for distinguishing the stop consonants is the burst which occurs before the start of the formant transitions. These bursts tend to be short, of relatively low intensity, and spread across a wide range of frequencies. The frequency range tends to be lowest for /b/, intermediate for /d/, and highest for /g/. But these differences between bursts appear to be less important cues than the formant transitions.

The three consonants we have discussed so far, all stops, are generally said to differ from each other in *place of articulation*. This refers to the fact that in producing them the point in the vocal tract at which the stop closure occurs is different for the three. For /b/ the closure is produced with the lips, and /b/ is called a *labial* stop. /d/ is produced by touching the tongue tip to the alveolar ridge behind the upper teeth; hence its designation as an *alveolar* stop. /g/ is produced by touching the body of the tongue to the velum at the back of the roof of the mouth and is referred to as a *velar* stop. We will discuss these differences more fully in Chapter 7 when we consider the nature of speech

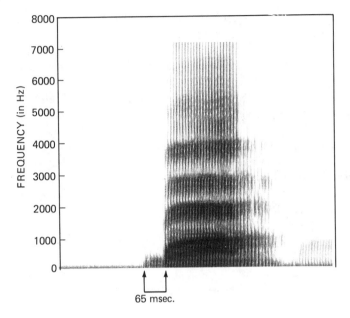

Figure 3–4A

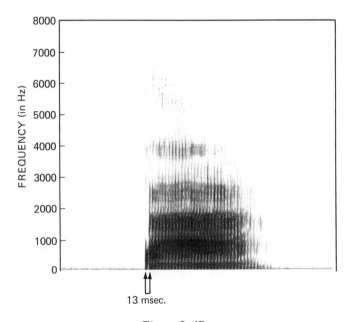

Figure 3–4B

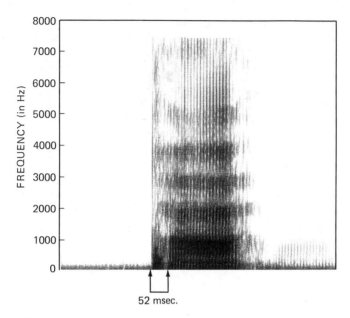

Figure 3–4C

Figure 3.4. Spectrograms of stop consonants varying in voice onset time (VOT): (A) is a prevoiced stop with 65 msec of voicing lead; (B) is a voiced stop with 13 msec of voicing lag, the English syllable /di/; (C) is a voiceless stop with 52 msec of voicing lag, the English syllable /ti/.

production. For the moment it is sufficient to have labels for the three places of articulation.

In addition to all being stops, /b/, /d/, and /g/ share another characteristic. They are all *voiced* stop consonants. When such a sound is produced, the vocal folds begin vibrating at nearly the same time that the closure is released. This property distinguishes the *voiced* stops, /b/, /d/, and /g/, from the *voiceless* stops, /p/, /t/, and /k/. For the voiceless stops, the onset of voicing (vocal fold vibration) is delayed until after the release of the closure. We can describe the difference between voiced and voiceless stops in terms of the timing relationship between the release of closure and the onset of voicing—the *voice-onset-time* (VOT) relationship. The way in which this difference is reflected in the speech sounds themselves is shown in the spectrograms in Figure 3.4.

The spectrogram in Figure 3.4B shows a voiced stop like the English /d/. Notice that the sound has a clear formant structure almost from its beginning and that the "striping" characteristic of voicing is also present nearly from the beginning. The spectrogram in Figure 3.4C shows a voiceless stop, /t/. This differs from the /d/ in that following the burst there is a long period (52 msec) during which there is no voicing apparent. In addition, the formant transitions are much less clear in /t/ than in /d/, and there is also less energy throughout the frequency range.

A number of experiments (e.g., Abramson & Lisker, 1968) have found, using synthetic stop consonant-vowel (CV) syllables that varied only in VOT, that listeners classify ones with VOTs less than +30 msec[2] as being voiced (i.e., /b/, /d/, or /g/, depending on the formant transitions). Ones with VOTs greater than +30 msec are identified as voiceless (i.e., /p/, /t/, or /k/). Thus, VOT appears to be a sufficient cue for distinguishing voiced from voiceless stops.

In fact, however, the listener's problem in distinguishing voiced from voiceless stops is rather more complex than this suggests. The boundary varies with the place of articulation, being closer to 0 VOT for labial stops (/b/ and /p/) and greater than +30 for velar stops (/g/ and /k/). In addition, in rapid speech, the boundaries all move closer to 0 VOT. Thus, interpreting the VOT value of a particular speech sound requires taking into account the sound's place of articulation and also the speaker's rate of speech.

In general, though, stop consonants can be divided perceptually into voiced and voiceless classes on the basis of their VOT properties. In addition, they can be divided on the basis of their places of articulation. /b/ and /p/ share the burst and formant transition properties associated with the labial place (though the transitions are less clear in the voiceless /p/). Similarly, /d/ and /t/ share the burst and transition properties of the alveolar place, and /g/ and /k/ share those of the velar place.

Before turning away from the stop consonants, we should note that there is a third category on the VOT dimension. Stops in this category have the same place properties as the stops we have already described. But while voiced stops are produced with a small voicing lag (e.g., 0 to +30 msec) and voiceless ones with a long voicing lag (+30 to +150 msec), this third category involves voicing lead. That is, voicing starts at least 40 to 50 msec before the closure is released. These are characterized as *prevoiced* stops and have negative VOT values, as in the spectrogram in Figure 3.4A. English does not treat the prevoiced stops as separate phonemes, but a number of other languages do (e.g., Thai, Hindi, and Arabic). The existence of this third voicing category poses some interesting perceptual problems, as we will see shortly.

We have discussed stop consonants in considerable detail because they are the class of speech sounds that contrasts most sharply with vowels in both their production and the perceptual cues they provide. In addition, much of the research which has revealed the properties of speech perception has involved stop consonant stimuli. We can summarize the properties of the stops in terms of two dimensions, as shown in Table 3.1. The columns differ in voicing—prevoiced,

---

[2]A + VOT is one for which voicing starts after the closure release; a – VOT is one for which voicing starts before the release.

voiced, and voiceless. The rows differ in place of articulation—labial, alveolar, and velar. Perceptually, the voicing differences can be characterized according to differences in VOT, differences in the properties of the sound when it begins. The place differences can be characterized in terms of differences in formant transitions, particularly of F_2 and F_3, and in burst frequency.

Among stop consonants there is wide variation among the sounds that are heard as being the same phoneme. The formant transitions that allow us to categorize different stops according to their place of articulation vary greatly within each category, depending upon the following (and preceding) phonemes. The same is true of the VOT differences that allow discriminating among voicing categories. This lack of invariance within phonemic categories reflects the role of context: the actual sounds that convey a particular phoneme are greatly influenced by the phonemes that are adjacent to it. Thus, the vowel following a particular stop consonant affects the extent, and even the direction, of the formant transitions. We will later consider some other ways in which context affects speech sounds and the problems this creates in the perception of speech.

To summarize briefly, we have seen that there are several kinds of cues that underly the perception of vowels and stop consonants. The relationships between the frequencies of the formants provide important information. So, too, do patterns of formant transitions and the noise bursts that occur in stop consonants. A different kind of information is provided by the timing relationship (VOT) between different aspects of the speech signal. These same kinds of cues are also involved in distinguishing among other phonemes, as we will see when we describe some of the other kinds of consonantal phonemes.

Fricative Consonants. Fricatives include such sounds as /f/, /s/, /v/, /ʃ/ (the "sh" in *shop*) and /ð/ (the "th" in *the*) and are produced without completely closing off the air flow through the vocal tract. They involve a partial closure which produces a turbulence in the air flow (see Chapter 7). This turbulence results in a noisy sound, without clear formant structure, which spreads over a broad frequency range. Although this frication noise is much like the burst of a stop consonant, it may last over 100 msec, while a stop consonant burst lasts only 10–15 msec. When a fricative occurs at the beginning of a word

Table 3.1

Characteristics of Stop Consonants

Place of Articulation		Voicing	
	Prevoiced	*Voiced*	*Voiceless*
Labial	(b)	b	p
Alveolar	(d)	d	t
Velar	(g)	g	k

the frication noise occurs first, followed by formant transitions much like those of the stops. Two fricatives can be seen in the spectrograms in Figure 3.1: the /ð/ at the beginning of *the,* and the /s/ at the beginning of *snapped.*

Some fricatives are voiced like /v/, and others are voiceless like /f/. The differences here are similar to those between voiced and voiceless stops, the main one being a difference in VOT. For many fricatives, the frication noise is the main cue, both for discriminating one fricative from another and for discriminating fricatives from other classes of speech sounds. The fricatives differ in the frequency ranges of their frication noises and also in the distribution of their energy across the frequency range. Thus, many fricatives can be identified by the frication noise alone (Harris, 1958). It appears, however, that the formant transitions of the fricatives contribute something to their identifiability, and for some fricatives the transitions are quite important.

Since the frication noise of a fricative is relatively unaffected by the context in which the fricative occurs, fricatives have more nearly invariant cues than do stops. But this invariance is only relative. This is shown by the fact that a fricative's formant transitions affect how it is identified; these formant transitions are influenced by their context in the same way that a stop's transitions are.

Cues for Other Classes of Consonants. The duration and rate of formant transitions allow discriminating among a variety of consonant phonemes. For example, a stimulus with the formant transitions characteristic of /ba/ can be changed to /wa/ simply by slowing down the rate at which the transitions occur. The change occurs when the duration of the transitions reaches about 100 msec. If the rate of change is slowed still further so that the transitions last over 150 msec, the stimulus is now perceived as a "vowel of changing color," a diphthong such as the vowel in *how* as it is pronounced in most dialects. And if the rate is slowed still further, a simple or pure vowel is perceived.

The nasal consonants—/m/, /n/, and /ŋ/ (the "ng" in *sing*)—have the formant transition characteristics of stops. They are produced like stops, in that the oral cavity is completely closed and then opened. But they are unlike other stops in that air continues to flow through the nasal passages during the closure. This results in a distinctive set of nasal resonances or formants that occur just before the formant transitions. These nasal formants serve to distinguish nasals from stops; but again, it is the nature of the formant transitions themselves that allow distinguishing one nasal from another.

There are many other consonantal phonemes, but we will mention just one last variety—the liquids /r/ and /l/. Like the fricatives, these are produced with a partial rather than a complete obstruction of the vocal tract. Their formant transitions are somewhat slower than those of stops and more like those of semi-vowels (e.g., /w/). These transitions are preceded by short duration steady-state formants that allow distinguishing /r/ and /l/ from several other kinds of phonemes. However, /r/ is distinguished from /l/ mainly by a difference in the F_3 transition—for /r/ it tends to rise, while for /l/ it tends to fall. Since F_3 is generally much less loud than either F_1 or F_2, a distinction between phonemes that is based only on an F_3 difference will be difficult to detect. This may be one reason why many languages do not treat /r/ and /l/ as separate phonemes, and why children learning languages that do differentiate them tend to have difficulty with them.

Our survey of the cues involved in discriminating one phoneme from another is hardly exhaustive. In describing the cues that listeners use, we have dealt exclusively with vowels occurring in isolation and with consonants appearing at the beginnings of words and preceding vowels. Even so, it is apparent that the listener's task is a difficult one. Many of the perceptual cues are subtle ones—small changes taking place in a speech signal that is continuously changing in many other ways simultaneously. But the listener's problem is even more complex than this would indicate. We have already seen that the sound cues involved in identifying stop consonants vary with the following vowel. They are also affected by other aspects of a speech sound's context.

Speech Cues in Context

A phoneme's context may vary in many ways, each of which carries its own difficulties for the listener trying to identify the phoneme. For example, we described /b/ as being identified by a relatively low frequency burst followed by rising F_1, F_2, and F_3 transitions. This is the case when /b/ occurs at the beginning of a word and precedes a vowel. But when it follows a vowel the formant transitions are falling rather than rising; and whether or not the transitions are followed by a burst is determined by the next phoneme after it. Thus, the cues for /b/ depend upon whether it precedes or follows a vowel, as well as by which vowel it precedes or follows. (The situation becomes still more complex if we consider cases in which /b/ occurs in a consonant cluster as in *blonde* or *blench.*) This context dependence of the sound cues is also characteristic of most other phonemes, including vowels.

We described vowels earlier in terms of the relationship between steady-state formants. It is generally assumed that vowels are best characterized in this way, as patterns of formants that maintain fixed frequency values for at least short periods of time. But if we examine vowels that occur in speech contexts rather than in isolation, we find that they generally do not have this steady-state character. Rather, the formant transitions associated with a preceding consonant are often not completed before those associated with a following consonant begin. The steady-state of the vowel may be so short as to be non-existent. In some cases, the context effects are sufficiently great that the formants never reach their steady-state values at all, but instead "undershoot" them. Thus, in context, vowels cannot be identified solely in terms of their steady-state formant frequencies.

Shankweiler, Strange, and Verbrugge (1977) have shown that vowels are actually identified more accurately when they occur in consonantal contexts than when they occur in their "ideal" steady-state form. This suggests that the formant transitions themselves are used in identifying vowels. Since the nature of the transitions is affected by the nature of the preceding and following consonants, even vowels are perceived in a context-dependent manner.

Still another way in which context affects the sounds of speech is through variation in stress. When a syllable is spoken in isolation, it tends to receive stress. During rapid, fluent speech, however, many syllables are relatively unstressed. Stress variation is useful in differentiating between different words (compare the noun *súbject* with the verb *subjéct*) and in discovering the syntactic structure and meaning of an utterance (see Chapter 4), but it also affects the sound pattern itself. Vowels in unstressed syllables, for example, have formant structures which differ far less from each other than they would when the vowels are stressed. In addition, unstressed syllables tend to be lower in intensity and shorter in duration than stressed ones, with the result that the formant structures of both their consonants and their vowels are considerably less distinctive. These effects may be seen by comparing Figure 3.5 with Figure 3.1A. Both represent the same utterance—*the dog snapped*—produced by the same speaker. Figure 3.1 represents the utterance when spoken slowly and distinctly; Figure 3.5 represents it when spoken as part of a longer utterance in normal conversation.

Parallel Transmission. One fact about speech that is emphasized by the dependence of a phoneme's sound on those surrounding it is that information about phonemes is transmitted in parallel. The formant transitions that are so essential for identifying stops and other consonantal phonemes also carry information about the vowels that precede or follow consonants. In the syllable presented schematically in Figure 3.6, for example, the information necessary for identifying the initial consonant is distributed across at least the first half of the syllable. Also the information necessary for identifying the final consonant is distributed across at least the last half of the syllable. And, as we saw earlier, the formant transitions also carry information for identifying the vowel.

Thus, we cannot treat speech sounds as being like beads on a string, the sound for one phoneme following that for the preceding phoneme. There is no way in which we can segment the speech signal so that a single segment carries all the information about one phoneme and no information about other phonemes. But while this kind of parallel transmission makes the listener's task a difficult one, it also allows the speaker to transmit information at the rate of about 15 phonemes per second.

Thus, speech is communicated by a complex and varying pattern of sound, one which transmits information at a high rate. Stressed syllables last 200–350 msec, and transmit information about anywhere from one to six phonemes. Unstressed syllables may last less than 100 msec. Thus, much of the speech

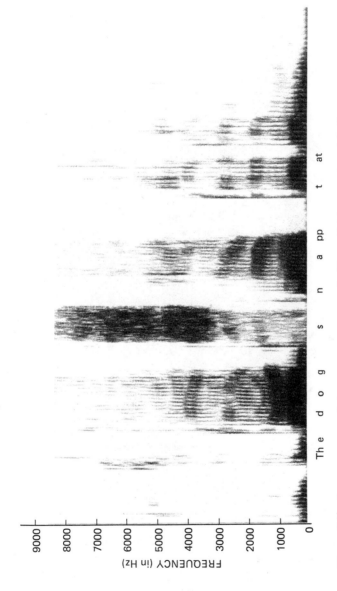

Figure 3.5. A spectrogram of the same utterance as in Figure 3.1 but produced in fluent conversation as part of the utterance, *John said that the dog snapped at him* . . . .

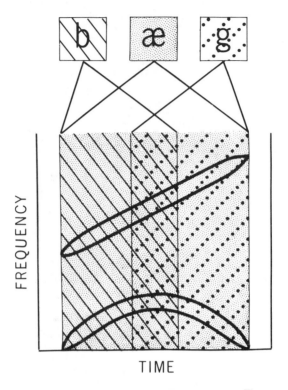

Figure **3.6.** Parallel transmission of phonetic segments: The translation from phonemes to sounds. (From Liberman, A. M. The grammars of speech and language. *Cognitive Psychology,* 1970, *1,* 301–323. Copyright 1970 Academic Press, Inc. Used by permission.)

signal the listener hears is a rapidly changing blur in which the cues necessary for recognizing the phonemes are not represented very distinctly. Examining spectrograms of rapid, fluent speech leaves one wondering how a listener is able to perceive its linguistic content at all.

Yet listeners do perceive speech as language, and generally do so rapidly and without effort. How are we to reconcile the speed and efficiency of speech perception with the complexity of the task the listener faces? One clue comes from the observation that we are unaware of much of the variability and complexity of speech sounds themselves. While a phoneme such as /b/ may be represented by quite a variety of sounds, we hear them all as /b/. And this suggests that part of the answer to how listeners cope with the complexity of speech sounds lies in the nature of the process of speech perception itself.

The Nature of Speech Perception

In order to understand the nature of speech perception let us first consider the general problem of how perceivers identify stimuli. For most kinds of stimuli, a person's ability to discriminate among stimuli is much better than his ability to identify them (i.e., to classify them as belonging to one or another category). In the perception of color, for example, people can reliably identify colors only as members of one or another of a relatively small number of categories—red, orange, yellow, etc. But they can discriminate among individual colors much more finely than this. That is, when colors that are physically very similar are shown to people, they can readily tell them apart. Interestingly, there is no relationship between how people categorize colors and how they discriminate them from each other. Two slightly different hues that people identify as both being red can be discriminated as accurately as two that are physically just as close but one is identified as red and the other as orange.

This lack of a relationship between identification and discrimination is characteristic of the perception of most kinds of stimuli and is often referred to as *continuous* perception. In continuous perception a person can reliably identify stimuli as belonging to only a relatively small number of categories, but can make a great many fine discriminations, both among stimuli from different categories and among stimuli from the same category. Continuous perception is, however, *not* characteristic of the way in which many speech stimuli are perceived. And the difference is important in accounting for why listeners are not bothered by the variability of speech sounds.

Categorical Perception. Many speech sounds are perceived in a categorical manner, not a continuous one. The phenomenon of categorical perception plays a central role in much theorizing about the process of speech perception. Many theorists (e.g., Liberman, 1970) have argued that it is a distinctive characteristic of the perception of *speech,* a characteristic not shared with the perception of other kinds of stimuli. If this is the case, it suggests that speech perception involves a special perceptual mechanism, one not shared with the perception of other auditory stimuli. For this reason, it is important for us to understand the nature of categorical perception and the role it plays in speech perception.

Suppose we construct a series of synthetic consonant-vowel syllables that differ from each other only in their F_2 starting points and transitions. At one end of the series is a syllable with the steeply rising F_2 characteristic of /ba/; at the other end is one with the steeply falling F_2 characteristic of /ga/. Between these are syllables with gradually rising F_2s, a level F_2, and gradually falling F_2s (see Figure 3.7). Now, suppose we present these syllables, one at a time and in random order, to a group of listeners and ask them to identify each one as /ba/, /da/, or /ga/. How well can they perform this task?

This experiment was actually performed by Liberman, Harris, Hoffman,

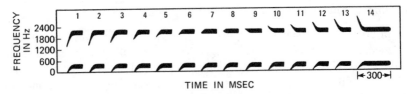

Figure 3.7. Spectrographic patterns from which the /b, d, g/ stimuli used in the identification and discrimination tasks (see text) were produced. All stimuli except 14 have been shortened by omitting part of the vowel. (From Liberman, A. M., Harris, K. S., Hoffman, H. S., & Griffith, B. C. The discrimination of speech sounds within and across phoneme boundaries. *Journal of Experimental Psychology,* 1957, 54, 358–368. Copyright 1957 American Psychological Association, Inc. Used by permission.)

and Griffith (1957). The results for one of their subjects are presented in Figure 3.8. Not surprisingly, like most of the subjects in the experiment, this person was able to identify most of the stimuli with great consistency. In a few cases (e.g., nos. 9 and 10) he expressed some uncertainty, calling the stimuli sometimes /da/ and sometimes /ga/. These stimuli are close to the points where the curves for the different responses cross. We may identify these cross-over points as the perceptual boundaries between the phoneme classes.

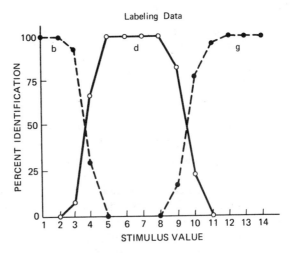

Figure 3.8. Identification (labeling) data for one subject for synthetic stimuli varying from /b/ to /g/. (From Liberman, A. M., Harris, K. S., Hoffman, H. S., & Griffith, B. C. The discrimination of speech sounds within and across phoneme boundaries. *Journal of·Experimental Psychology,* 1957, 54, 358–368. Copyright 1957 American Psychological Association, Inc. Used by permission.)

Liberman et al. also arranged their stimuli in triads. The first and second syllables of a triad were always different, and the third was either the same as the first or the same as the second. These are called ABX triads, A and B referring to two different stimuli, and X referring to a stimulus that could be either an A or a B. These triads were presented to the same subjects who had taken the identification test, and they were asked to say whether X was the same as A or the same as B in each triad. This is a discrimination test, since a subject's performance is determined by how well he can discriminate between the A and B syllables. If the difference between A and B is easy to perceive, then the listener should have little difficulty in deciding which of them is identical to X. His performance should be close to 100% correct. If, on the other hand, A and B are so similar that they sound the same, there is no way a subject could decide which was identical to X. Since all three stimuli would sound the same, he would have to guess. His performance would be only about 50% correct.

The results for the discrimination test are presented in Figure 3.9 for the same subject whose identification data were presented in Figure 3.8. For some of the triads performance was excellent. For others, however, discrimination was little better than chance. Overall, there are marked "peaks" and "valleys" in the discrimination curve. Furthermore, there is a relationship between the discrimination data and the identification data. The peaks in the discrimination curve correspond to the cross-over points in the identification curves. That is, the stimuli that were best discriminated were ones which were identified as being

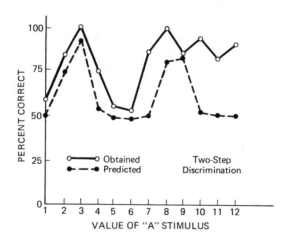

Figure 3.9. ABX discrimination data for one subject for synthetic stimuli varying from /b/ to /g/. (From Liberman, A. M., Harris, K. S., Hoffman, H. S., & Griffith, B. C. The discrimination of speech sounds within and across phoneme boundaries. *Journal of Experimental Psychology,* 1957, 54, 358–368. Copyright 1957 American Psychological Association, Inc. Used by permission.)

different phonemes. When the stimuli in a triad were identified as belonging to the same phonemic category, discrimination among them was quite poor.

This relationship between discrimination performance and identification performance defines categorical perception. Discrimination is good among stimuli that are identified as members of different categories; discrimination is poor among stimuli identified as belonging to the same category. This contrasts with continuous perception where discrimination is as good among stimuli belonging to the same category as it is among stimuli belonging to different categories. Categorical perception data seem to suggest that in a discrimination task a listener is unable to hear the acoustic differences among stimuli that he identifies as belonging to the same category, and can discriminate well only among stimuli he identifies as belonging to different categories.

Since Liberman et al. first demonstrated categorical perception, a number of experiments have shown that many speech sounds are perceived categorically. The differences in place of articulation among stop consonants (e.g., /b, d, g/) tend to be perceived this way. In addition, voice onset time differences in both stops and fricatives are perceived relatively categorically, as are the laterals /l/ and /r/ (see Studdert-Kennedy, 1976, for a review of much of this research).

However, speech stimuli are not perceived categorically in all cases. Vowels tend to be perceived continuously when they are presented in isolation. That is, under that condition listeners can discriminate among steady-state vowel sounds that they identify as being the same phoneme. But when vowels are presented in a speech context, such as a consonant-vowel-consonant syllable, they tend to be perceived more categorically.

Thus, under most circumstances most speech sounds are perceived categorically. As we noted earlier, this fact, taken together with the fact that non-speech stimuli are perceived continuously, has been adduced as evidence that speech perception involves a specialized speech processor. Recently, however, a number of experiments have cast doubt upon this view by showing that categorical perception effects can be obtained with some non-speech auditory stimuli (Cutting & Rosner, 1974; Miller, Wier, Pastore, Kelly & Dooling, 1976) and with some visual stimuli (Pastore, Friedman, Baffuto & Fink, 1976).

Since categorical effects can be obtained with non-speech stimuli, it appears that there is no need to hypothesize the existence of a specialized *speech* processing mechanism to account for the effect. But this does not diminish the importance of the generally categorical nature of speech perception. In the first place, this phenomenon helps explain why listeners are not distracted by variations in the speech sounds that signal a particular phoneme: they perceive the sounds categorically and do not even hear the variations. Of course, the question of why this should be so remains open. In the second place, even though categorical perception may not be unique to speech perception, it does raise several important questions about the nature of that process. One is the question of *which* speech sounds are perceived categorically. This is in part a question about the effects of linguistic experience upon speech perception.

Effects of Experience on Categorical Perception. Speakers of a particular language often experience difficulty in listening to another language. No doubt there are several reasons for this, but one reason is suggested by data on categorical perception. For example, Strange and Halwes (1971) collected identification and discrimination data from English-speaking listeners on stimuli varying in VOT from a strongly prevoiced /ba/ to an extremely voiceless /pa/. They found a peak in the discrimination curve at about +20 msec, a VOT value corresponding closely to the /b/–/p/ category boundary in the identification data. But their subjects gave no evidence of a second discrimination peak in the prevoiced range. English, of course, does not distinguish prevoiced from voiced stops, but many other languages do. And the English-speaking subjects appear not to have been able to hear the difference.

There is no reason to suppose that children exposed to one language start out life any different from those exposed to a different language: any child can acquire any language. And adults that have been exposed from childhood to languages that distinguish prevoiced from voiced stops are able to make this discrimination (Strange, 1972; Streeter, 1975). Thus, the fact that English speakers cannot suggests that their perceptual abilities have been affected by their having been exposed only to English.

Similar results have been obtained by Miyawaki, Strange, Verbrugge, Liberman, Jenkins, and Fujimura (1975). They have found that a stimulus series that varied from /ra/ to /la/ is perceived relatively categorically by English-speaking subjects. But the same series is not perceived categorically by speakers of Japanese, a language that does not treat /r/ and /l/ as different phonemes. The Japanese subjects' performance at the /r/–/l/ boundary was like that of the English-speaking subjects within the phoneme categories. That is, the Japanese showed poor discrimination all along the continuum, with no peak at the category boundary.

Thus, being exposed exclusively to a particular language affects perception. Listeners discriminate sound differences that represent phonemic differences in their own language, but they do not discriminate other differences, even though those differences may be phonemic in some other language whose speakers can distinguish them easily. There are at least two possible explanations for this. One is that exposure to a language makes a listener sensitive to the sound differences which that language uses to signal phonemic differences. If this were the case, then we would expect that before being exposed to any language a young infant's ability to discriminate any speech sound differences would be very poor—their discriminations would all be like the within-category discriminations of adults.

The other possibility is that infants are capable of making all the discriminations that could be phonemic in any language. If so, then the effect of exposing them to a particular language would be to decrease their sensitivity to those distinctions that are not phonemic in that language. Clearly, the way to evaluate these possibilities is to examine the speech perception abilities of young infants.

Categorical Perception in Infancy. Recently, it has become possible to study speech discrimination in very young infants. The techniques are fascinating in themselves, but it would take us far afield to discuss them here. Let us instead focus on the results that have been obtained. Most of the research has been directed to the question we just raised: do infants discriminate sound differences that are linguistically significant (i.e., phonemic), and do they discriminate differences that are not linguistically significant? In general, the results that have been obtained suggest that even 1-month-old infants perceive speech in a remarkably adult-like manner.

For example, Eimas, Siqueland, Jusczyk, and Vigorito (1971) have shown that young infants discriminate among stimuli differing in VOT when the stimuli lie across the /b/–/p/ boundary. But the infants appear not to discriminate between two sounds lying within either the /b/ category or the /p/ category, even when these stimuli differ as much as those lying across the /b/–/p/ boundary. Similar results were obtained when infants were tested with several other kinds of speech stimuli that adults perceive categorically (see Eimas, 1975; Morse, 1974, for discussions of the research techniques and results).

Since infants, who as yet have no language of their own, show categorical perception effects much like those of adults, it seems reasonable to suppose that infants could discriminate all phonemic sound differences, even those present only in languages other than the one they are going to acquire. The few studies that have examined this question suggest that this is so. Streeter (1975), for example, has examined the effect of stimulus variation in voicing on Kikuyu infants. Kikuyu is a language that discriminates prevoiced stops from voiced stops, but does not discriminate voiced from unvoiced stops. It therefore lacks the voicing contrast that is phonemic in English. Streeter found that the Kikuyu infants discriminated both the prevoiced and unvoiced stops from voiced stops, but did not discriminate among stops that are phonemically similar in all languages. Similar results have been reported by Lasky, Syrdal-Lasky, and Klein (1975).

The data suggest, then, that infants begin life with a kind of generalized categorical perception. They seem not to discriminate sound differences that are not phonemic in any human language. But they do discriminate differences that are phonemic in some languages, even if those differences are not phonemic in the language to which they are being exposed. The effect of linguistic experience on people appears to be a loss of the ability to discriminate those differences that are not phonemic in the language they acquire. The questions that remain are, what is the nature of this loss, and why does it occur? To answer those questions properly we must begin with the question of why categorical perception effects arise in the first place. Why, that is, are listeners apparently unable to hear sound differences that for them are not phonemic differences?

Mechanisms Underlying Categorical Perception. There are two aspects of the phenomenon to be considered. First is the fact of categorization itself. There must be some mechanism which identifies a speech sound as belonging to one or another phonemic category. Such a categorization mechanism need not be unique to categorical perception, for even stimuli that are not perceived categorically can be categorized (e.g., vowels, colors, etc.). Second, there must be some aspect of the processing of speech sounds that accounts for the poor discrimination within phonemic categories. It is this that is responsible for the difference between stimuli that are perceived categorically and those that are not.

The most widely accepted account of the difference is one proposed by Fujisaki and Kawashima (1968, 1969). We can assume that the process of categorizing a speech sound takes at least a small amount of time. Thus, the hearer's perceptual system must be able to retain information about the physical properties of the sound at least long enough for the sound to be categorized. The memory involved in this is of the sort often identified as a "sensory register" or "echoic memory," a very short-term memory retaining detailed information about the physical (sensory) properties of a stimulus.

Fujisaki and Kawashima proposed that the difference between categorically and continuously perceived stimuli is a difference in the length of time that information about the physical properties of the stimuli remains available in the echoic memory. Consider what is involved in the kind of discrimination test used for demonstrating categorical perception. Since the stimuli are presented sequentially, the comparison between them can only be based on information about the first stimulus that is still available at the time the second stimulus occurs. If the echoic trace of the physical properties of the first stimulus has been lost by this time, then the only basis for comparison would be its phonetic category identity. That is, the two stimuli could be discriminated only if they were identified as belonging to different categories, when they would be perceived categorically.

For continuously perceived stimuli, on the other hand, information about the stimuli's physical properties remains available longer. Because such information is still available at the time the stimuli are compared, the comparison can be in terms of whether or not the two have detectably different physical properties as well as whether or not they have the same categorical identities. Thus, even when the stimuli are identified as belonging to the same category, they can often be discriminated on the basis of their physical differences. Hence, for continuously perceived stimuli, within-category discrimination is relatively good. For categorically perceived stimuli, the discrimination must be based on the category identities of the stimuli, and when they are identified as belonging to the same category they cannot be discriminated. This stems from the difference in the kind of information available at the time the stimuli are compared.

Evidence for Memory Effects in Categorical Perception. If differences between categorical and continuous perception are attributable to differences in the length of time over which information about physical properties remains available, it should be possible to affect discrimination performance by varying the time interval between the stimuli. That is, for stimuli which are perceived continuously when the inter-stimulus interval is short, perception should become more categorical as the interval is lengthened because their echoic traces should fade. Pisoni (1973) performed this experiment, presenting steady-state vowels for discrimination at intervals varying from 0 to 2000 msec. Listeners' category discrimination between vowels was quite good when the interval between them was short, but became worse as the length of the interval increased, suggesting that echoic memory for the physical properties of speech sounds does decay over time. Pisoni performed the same experiment using stop consonant plus vowel syllables and found that the listener's perception of the consonants was unaffected by the length of the inter-stimulus interval—even at the shortest interval within-category discrimination was poor. This suggests that for categorically-perceived stimuli the echoic memory decays extremely rapidly; physical property information is not available even when there is no interval at all between the stimuli.

There are other kinds of evidence to suggest that information about the physical properties of categorically and continuously perceived stimuli decays at different rates (see, e.g., Crowder, 1972). But there is also evidence which suggests that the difference in the availability of physical property information may *not* result from differences in the rates at which echoic traces fade. For example, Barclay (1972) presented subjects with synthetic stop consonant-vowel syllables varying from /b/ through /d/ to /g/ (see Figure 3.7). The stimuli were presented individually, and one group of subjects was asked to identify each stimulus as being *b, d,* or *g.* This, of course, is the normal identification task. However, a second group of subjects was presented the same stimuli and asked to identify each as being either *b* or *g*; they were not allowed to identify any stimulus as *d.* Barclay reasoned that if these latter subjects had available no information about the physical properties of the /d/ stimuli, these would be randomly classified as *b* or *g.* However, if they did have information available about the stimuli's physical properties, then some of the /d/s should sound more "*b*-like" than others, presumably those whose formant transitions were more like those of /b/ than those of /g/.

The results showed that the subjects who were forced to use only *b* and *g* as responses did not respond randomly to the /d/ stimuli. Rather, the stimuli closest to the /b/—/d/ boundary were more likely to be identified as *b* than as *g,* and the ones closest to the /d/—/g/ boundary were more likely to be identified as *g* than as *b*. Thus, there was apparently some information detected about the stimuli's physical properties in spite of the categorical identification.

If this is the case, then the question of why such stimuli tend to be perceived categorically remains. If information about the physical properties of speech stimuli is available to the listener, why is it not used as a basis for within-category discrimination in the discrimination task? The likely answer is that such information is unnecessary to the mechanisms that categorize speech stimuli, and in fact is ignored as irrelevant to identifying the stimuli. Attending to it would only make the process of identification more difficult for the hearer. But if information about the physical properties of categorically-perceived stimuli is available, it should be possible to train listeners to attend to it and to use it in discrimination tasks.

Training Studies and Categorical Perception. Doty (1970) attempted to train listeners to discriminate among VOT differences within the voiced and voiceless categories of stop consonants. His results indicate that after long and intensive training there was some improvement in discrimination performance near the voiced-voiceless boundary, but little improvement elsewhere. Similar results were obtained by Strange (1972), who used a variety of training and test procedures in attempts to improve the prevoiced-voiced discrimination of English-speaking adults. There was some improvement, but the English-speakers' performance did not approach that of Thai speakers whose language distinguishes prevoiced and voiced categories.

More recent studies have used a more effective training procedure than the Doty and Strange studies. Carney and Widin (1976) trained English-speaking adults on same-different discriminations of stimuli varying in VOT. For each block of 40 training trials, one of the stimuli in the pairs remained constant. The stimulus with which it was paired was either identical, a stimulus within the same phonemic category but with a different VOT, or a stimulus differing both in category and in VOT.

Following each block of training trials, the subjects were retested on the same discrimination pairs, but now without feedback about whether or not their responses were correct. The pre- and post-training discrimination performance for the trial block in which the constant stimulus had VOT = +80 (i.e., a stimulus clearly within the voiceless /pa/ category) is shown in Figure 3.10. The improvement is considerable, one of the subjects performing perfectly on all within- and between-category discriminations. In addition, Carney and Widin tested their subjects at the end of the experiment on the more usual discrimination task involving stimulus triads. Here, too, their subjects performed considerably better than chance in within-category discrimination. Cooper and Nager (1975) report that Eimas and Cooper have obtained a similar result.

These results suggest that the physical properties of categorically-perceived speech sounds are available for detection and can be attended to by a listener with appropriate training. The within-category physical properties, also detected

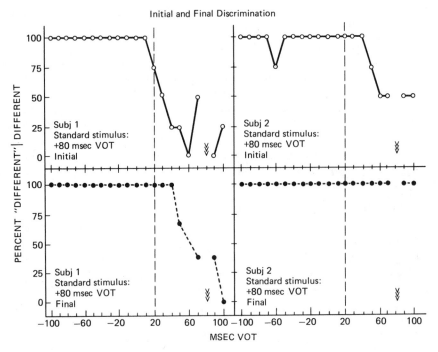

Figure 3.10. Initial and final (i.e., post-training) discrimination of stimuli varying in VOT for two subjects (From Carney & Widin, 1976. Used by permission.)

well after training, are not normally discriminated even by infants with too little linguistic experience to have learned that such differences can be ignored. Thus, the fact that infants can make discriminations which many linguistically-sophisticated adults do not may indicate that the adults have learned to ignore the very subtle physical differences on which the discriminations are based. But, as these tests indicate, this effect of linguistic experience may be reversible. (See Strange & Jenkins, in press, for further discussion of these topics.)

To summarize, it appears that the poor within-category discrimination characteristic of categorical perception occurs because listeners ignore the physical differences between stimuli, not because they cannot hear them. As we have suggested earlier, it is probably useful for listeners to be able to do this. The normal concern when listening to speech is to discover the phonemic identity of the speech sounds, to categorize them. Attending to the within-category sound differences is not relevant to this end. But though such differences are ignored, even without linguistic experience, with proper training they can be attended to. Furthermore, since categorical perception effects can be obtained with non-speech stimuli, these effects are probably not unique to speech and may not involve any specialized speech perception mechanisms.

Models of Speech Perception Processes

The processes by which speech signals are identified begin with a highly complex, continuously varying acoustic signal and end with a simple output: a representation of the phonological features and segments encoded in that signal. One kind of process involves the analysis of the speech signal itself. But the speech signal is often not sufficiently distinct to allow its features to be unambiguously identified. It appears that identifying the signal's phonological features also involves a second, synthetic process, one that integrates information from the speech signal with information from other sources. We will consider these two kinds of processes in turn.

Analytic Processes in Speech Perception: Categorization

The categorization process yields a representation of the speech signal's phonological features. Apparently the process is not greatly affected by any variability in the signal that is not relevant to categorization. Thus, the process is essentially all-or-none—a feature is either present or absent, regardless of how it is represented physically. This fact has suggested to many speech researchers (e.g., Abbs & Sussman, 1971; Stevens, 1973) that the mechanism underlying the identification of phonological features might be similar to the system of visual feature detectors uncovered by neurophysiological research.

In a now classic paper entitled "What the frog's eye tells the frog's brain," Lettvin, Maturana, McCulloch, and Pitts (1959) reported a series of experiments in which they recorded the neural activity in single fibers in the optic nerves of frogs while they presented the frogs with a variety of visual stimuli. Their results indicated that a certain number of varied stimuli had the same effect on a particular fiber's activity, while many other stimuli had no effect at all. That is, the response of the fiber was essentially all-or-none, apparently based on the presence or absence of a particular property or feature in the stimulus. For example, some fibers responded only when a rounded dark area entered the frog's visual field, a response highly useful to the frog in identifying potential food objects. (This kind of detector has come to be known as a "bug" detector, though it responds to anything with the appropriate shape regardless of whether or not it is edible.)

Since that time a considerable body of knowledge has developed concerning the nature of such visual feature detection mechanisms (see Lindsay & Norman, 1977). The interesting property of such feature detectors is that they respond to particular features of a stimulus—sometimes to quite complex features—while they remain unaffected by its other properties. This behavior is quite similar to the all-or-none manner noted in the categorizing of speech sounds according to phonological features.

The problem for speech researchers has been to find a technique that would determine whether such feature detector mechanisms were involved in speech perception. The neurophysiological techniques of the vision researchers are not suitable, for they involve implanting electrodes in the relevant areas of the brain. Clearly, one cannot do that to humans. The alternative of performing such experiments on lower animals is also unavailable, for we do not yet know whether other organisms perceive speech in the same way as humans (but see Kuhl & Miller, 1975a, 1975b; Morse, 1977). Researchers had to wait for the development of a behavioral research technique to explore the possibility that detectors exist that identify phonological features in speech sounds.

Such a technique was reported in 1972 by Eimas and his colleagues (Eimas & Corbit, 1972; Eimas, Cooper, & Corbit, 1972). Eimas reasoned that if feature detectors underlie the categorization of speech sounds it should be possible to fatigue the detectors. Neural mechanisms can generally be made less responsive by repeatedly presenting stimuli to which they respond. After repeated and frequent responses the mechanism's fatigue may reach the point where it does not respond at all to a stimulus sufficient to bring a response from it in its rested state.

Suppose, for example, that the distinction between voiced and voiceless stop consonants results from the existence of two feature detectors, one, called A, responsive to stimuli with VOTs characteristic of voiced stops, and the other, B, responsive to ones characteristic of voiceless stops. If the ranges of VOTs to which the two respond overlap slightly, then a stimulus whose VOT is very close to the category boundary (e.g., the +20 msec boundary for labial stops) will activate both detectors. Which way such a stimulus is perceived—as /b/ or as /p/—will depend on which detector is more strongly activated. Figure 3.11A illustrates what the response characteristics of such a pair of detectors might look like.

If this is the case, then repeatedly presenting a voiced stop consonant, e.g., a /b/ with 0 VOT, should fatigue detector A far more than detector B. One result of this adaptation would be to shift the category boundary toward /b/. With detector A thus adapted, stimuli on the /b/ side of the boundary but close to it would now have a greater effect on detector B than on detector A, the situation illustrated in Figure 3.11B.

Eimas and Corbit (1973) reported two experiments testing this prediction. In the first, the subjects first took an identification test on a series of stimuli varying in VOT from /b/ to /p/. They then listened for 2 minutes to repeated presentations (a total of 150) of either a /b/ or a /p/. Following this initial adaptation they received a series of 14 trials, each trial consisting of 70 more presentations of the adapting stimulus followed by a stimulus to be identified. In other conditions of the experiment, subjects identified and were adapted by stimuli on a VOT continuum from /d/ to /t/. And, to determine if adaptation effects were specific to the particular stimuli on which the subjects had been adapted, the experiment also included conditions in which the adaptation and the identification testing were on different stimuli, e.g., identification of the /b/—/p/ stimuli after adaptation with /d/ or /t/ (cross-series test).

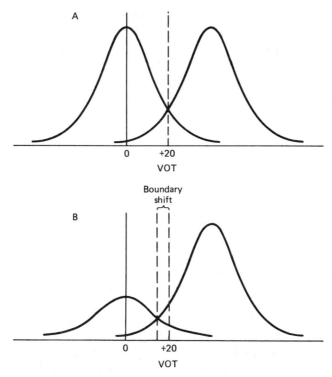

Figure 3.11. Hypothetical sensitivity functions for detectors sensitive to VOT values for /b/ and /p/: (A) before adaptation with a repeated /b/ stimulus; and (B) after adaptation.

The results for a single subject are presented in Figure 3.12. The predicted adaptation occurred in all conditions. That is, the category boundary shifted in the direction of the adapting stimulus so that some stimuli which were initially identified as being in the same category as the adapting stimulus were, after adaptation, identified as being in the other category. The effects are not equally large for all conditions, but it does appear that the cross-series effects are as large as those when both identification and adaptation involve the same series.

The second experiment was similar, except that discrimination tests were substituted for the identification tests. The results of this corresponded to the boundary shift found in the first experiment, as they indicated that the peak in the discrimination function also moved in the direction of the adapting stimulus. Eimas and Corbit's results, then, are consistent with the assumption that a system of feature detectors underlies the perception of speech stimuli as being voiced or voiceless.

After Eimas introduced the adaptation procedure a large number of experiments were performed using it to uncover properties of the categorization process for speech sounds. Results similar to those we have described were

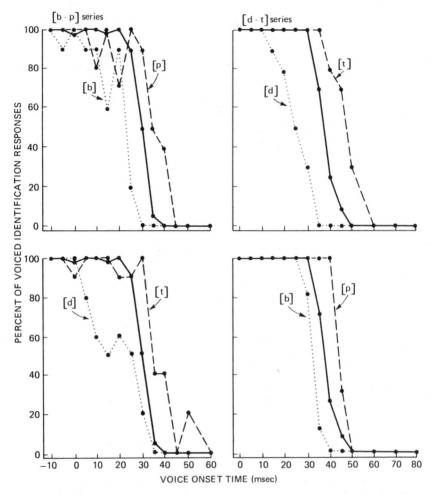

Figure 3.12. Percentages of voiced identification responses ([b or d]) obtained with and without adaptation for a single subject. The functions for the [b, p] series are on the left and those for the [d, t] series are on the right. The solid lines indicate the unadapted identification functions and the dotted and dashed lines, the identification functions after adaptation. The phonetic symbols indicate the adapting stimuli. (From Eimas, P. D., & Corbit, J. D. Selective adaptation of linguistic feature detectors. *Cognitive Psychology,* 1973, *4,* 99–109. Copyright 1973 Academic Press, Inc. Used by permission.)

obtained for a number of other phonological feature distinctions. Several experiments have shown, for example, that the place of the articulation distinctions between /b/, /d/, and /g/ can be shifted by adapting the mechanism with a stimulus having the formant transitions characteristic of one or another place of articulation (e.g., Cooper, 1974a). But information on the nature of the detector mechanisms is still quite sketchy, leaving many questions unanswered.

Synthetic Processes in Speech Perception

A system of feature detectors is apparently involved in mapping speech inputs into an output consisting of a representation of the input's phonological features. If the phonological features were translated into phonemic or alphabetic symbols, such an output would look much like a written transcript of the message.

The process of perceiving speech cannot, however, be as simple as this would suggest. In normal fluent speech many parts of the acoustic signal are obscured. Unstressed syllables are reduced in intensity, duration, and the clarity of their formant structure. The result is that much of the speech signal is so degraded that the problem of perceiving its phonological content is more difficult than simply detecting the phonological features. There is often too little information in the acoustic signal to allow the features to be identified unambiguously.

The nature of the problem is illustrated by a result obtained by Lieberman (1963). Lieberman removed the word *nine* from the spoken sentences, *A stitch in time saves nine* and *The number that you will hear is nine,* and asked subjects to identify the isolated words. When taken from the second sentence, the subjects identified *nine* correctly 90% of the time. But the *nine* taken from the first sentence was identified only 50% of the time even though it was clearly heard when it occurred in the sentence. Lieberman argued that the word *nine* in the first sentence is so highly predictable from its context that the speakers did not articulate it as clearly as they did in the second sentence, where *nine* is not so predictable.

Thus, the processes that analyze the acoustic signal frequently do not have sufficient information to identify its phonological features. We would expect, therefore, that there would be a great many blanks in the transcript produced by the speech perception processor. But this does not generally happen. We hear what the speaker said even when the acoustic signal is quite degraded. The output of the speech perception process is clearer and more complete than the input would allow. If the information necessary to construct a phonological representation of the message is not always present in the acoustic signal itself, where does it come from?

Analysis-By-Synthesis. The sort of theory usually suggested as a solution to this problem includes a process of analysis-by-synthesis. We might think of this process in the following way. The output from the feature detector system that analyzes the acoustic signal is not the final output from the speech perception processor. It is, rather, a preliminary series of hypotheses, or guesses, about the phonological content of the signal. These hypotheses are the input to a second component of the processor, a synthesizer, which evaluates the hypotheses in the light of other information and decides what constitutes the best guess about what the speech signal contained.

Many versions of this theory emphasize the listener's use of his knowledge about possible combinations of phonological features and about the phonological structure of his language (see, e.g., Stevens & House, 1972). For example, suppose that the analysis process yields an output in which it is certain that the first segment has the features characterizing /b/ and the third segment has those of a vowel, but in which it is unclear what the second segment is. The listener knows that the second segment cannot be a stop consonant or a nasal and that it probably is not a vowel. He can consider how the segments that could occur in that position would sound and select the one that matches the acoustic signal most closely.

If a listener can use analyses of the context surrounding an unclear portion of the input in this way, there is no need for him to "hear" all of the signal. The unheard parts—whether they are too degraded to be analyzed unambiguously or simply went unnoticed—can be filled in on the basis of what the heard portions imply about them. The suggestion here is that speech perception processing interacts with other aspects of comprehension processing in such a way that information about the phonological, lexical, syntactic, and semantic properties of the utterance all enter into determining the final phonological representation constructed by the speech perception processor.

It is not yet clear exactly how a listener brings contextual information to bear on the synthesis of a phonological representation of an utterance. But there is evidence that something of this sort does occur. Warren (1970; Warren & Obusek, 1971) presented listeners with tape-recorded sentences from which speech segments had been removed and replaced it with extraneous sounds. For example, from the sentence *The state governors met with their respective legislatures convening in the capital city,* Warren removed the first /s/ from *legislatures* and enough of the preceding and following context to insure that there were no acoustic cues to the /s/. He then added a cough in the blank interval.

The listeners had little difficulty determining what the missing sound was. More interesting is the fact that most of the listeners were completely unaware that any sound was missing. That is, they actually *heard* the /s/ that was not in the acoustic signal at all. The illusion of hearing the missing sound persisted even when the listeners knew in advance what sound had been removed and even if they listened to the sentence repeatedly.

The interpretation of this phenomenon, which Warren has called "phoneme restoration," seems fairly clear. Since there are no acoustic cues to the sound, the listener must be inferring what the sound should have been on the basis of the preceding and following context. Since knowing that the missing segment is /s/ requires knowing that the word containing it is *legislatures,* this implies that the listener has consulted his mental lexicon on the basis of information about the word's other segments to discover this fact. The fact that the missing sound is actually heard suggests that what we hear when we listen to speech is a representation based on an analysis of the signal itself, on analyses of the signal's surrounding context, and a synthesis of the two. What we hear is not only what is physically present.

Warren and Sherman (1974) have demonstrated the amount of processing that can intervene between the acoustic input and the speech sound that is actually heard. They constructed sentences in which the context that indicated what the missing phoneme should be came several words after the missing phoneme itself. Until the context was processed, the missing phoneme was ambiguous, there being two or more different phonemes that could have been inserted to produce a word. For example, the sentence, *The #eel was on the* _____, could end with either *car* or *table.* When it ended with *car,* listeners tended to hear *wheel;* when it ended with *table,* they tended to hear *meal.*

It appears that listeners can make quite extensive analyses of parts of an utterance in order to synthesize other parts that are unclear or missing. To know that the missing phoneme should be /m/ when the sentence ends with *table* requires discovering the meaning of *table* and also analyzing the sentence's structure sufficiently to know how *table* is related to the word from which the phoneme is missing.

Thus it is apparent that the process of perceiving speech is not simply a passive process of analyzing the phonological content of the acoustic signal. Instead, it is an active process involving both analysis and synthesis. In addition, although perceiving speech is the first stage of comprehension processing, it is not the case that comprehension proceeds in a step-by-step manner. Phonological analysis of an utterance is not completed first and followed by the looking-up of stored lexical information and a syntactic and semantic analysis. Rather, these processes interact in such a way that information about the results of higher-level analyses can be used to resolve uncertainties at the phonological level.

The active character of speech perception and comprehension processing is nicely illustrated by research indicating that the listener attends selectively to the acoustic signal and actually tries to predict in advance what parts are likely to be the most informative. As we have seen, the parts of the signal most likely to contain high quality information about their phonological contents are the parts of the utterance that are stressed. Martin (1972) and Cutler (1975) have found that the phonological content of stressed syllables is discovered more quickly and easily than that of unstressed syllables. The data from these experiments are complicated, but they suggest that listeners use the anlyses they have performed on the early parts of an utterance to try to predict where the stressed syllables are going to occur.

There is still a great deal to be learned about this active, synthetic aspect of speech perception. And there is also much that remains to be learned about the analytic processes involved in extracting phonological information from the acoustic signal. But having seen how dependent speech perception is upon other aspects of comprehension processing, we should consider the nature of some of those other, higher-level processes.

Summary

The process of speech perception begins with a highly complex and continuously varying acoustic signal and ends with a representation of the phonological features and segments encoded in that signal. The speech signal itself is characterized by bands of energy, called formants, occurring simultaneously in different frequency ranges.

Many of the cues to the phonological content of the signal are carried by the patterns of formants and by the ways in which the formants change over time. Stop consonants like /b/, /d/, and /g/ are identified primarily in terms of changes in the formants, called formant transitions, with particular patterns of transitions distinguishing these consonants from one another. Other consonantal sounds, such as fricatives and nasals, also involve formant transitions. But they involve other cues as well, such as the distinctive noises lacking formant structure that occur for fricatives and the distinctive nasal formants that precede the transitions for nasal consonants.

An important fact about the cues for different phonemes is that the cues themselves change as the phoneme's context changes—the cues are context-dependent. This means that many phonemes do not have an unvarying and characteristic pattern that is exclusively their own. Thus, identifying a particular phoneme also involves identifying the ones preceding and following it. This points to the fact that the speech signal transmits information about more than one phoneme at a time, a phenomenon referred to as parallel transmission.

Even vowels, which are often characterized in terms of unvarying, steady-state formant patterns, are affected by the contexts in which they occur. In fluent speech there is rarely any great amount of time during which a vowel's formants maintain a steady state. In some cases, the steady-state frequencies are never even reached. Consequently, vowels are also identified by the changing formant patterns of the phonemes that precede and follow them.

Although speech signals are extremely variable, the presence of this variability does not affect the listener as he pursues the goal of identifying the signal's phonological content. Generally, listeners are quite unaware of the variability of speech signals except when it has phonemic significance. This phenomenon has been referred to as categorical perception—listeners tend to hear speech signals as different only when they identify them as different phonemes.

Categorical perception has been the subject of much research and theorizing in speech perception, in part because it was believed to be a unique phenomenon, implying that speech is perceived by processes different from those used in perceiving other, non-speech stimuli. Several important and intriguing characteristics of categorical perception have come to light as a result of this extensive research. For one thing, it appears that adult, linguistically sophisticated listeners do not hear speech sound differences that are not phonemic in their language, even if those differences are phonemically important in other languages. For another, infants who are too young to have received much exposure to any language also show categorical perception effects, but with a difference—they respond to all sound differences that are phonemically important in any language, but not to equally large sound differences that are not phonemically important.

The most popular theory of categorical perception has been that information about the physical properties of speech signals remains available for too short a time to be attended to and used by listeners. But recent research has cast doubt both on this theory and on the claim that categorical perception is uniquely a speech perception phenomenon. Categorical perception effects have been obtained with non-speech stimuli, suggesting that the phenomenon results from the particular physical properties of stimuli rather than from the fact that they are speech. It has also been found that listeners can be trained to discriminate categorically-perceived stimuli on the basis of their physical properties. This suggests that categorical perception arises because listeners *do* not attend to the physical properties of speech stimuli, not because they *can*not attend to them.

The categorization, or identification, process for speech stimuli appears to involve a system of feature detectors, mechanisms that respond in an all-or-none manner to the presence or absence of a particular property in the speech signal. The evidence for the existence of feature detectors for speech signal properties is mainly indirect—no one has yet obtained neurological evidence for such detectors. A great deal remains to be learned about how such detector mechanisms might operate in identifying the phonologically important features of speech signals.

Speech signals often contain too little information to allow their phonological features to be identified unambiguously. This suggests that speech perception involves more than just the phonological analysis of the speech signal itself. It appears that listeners are able to bring other kinds of information to bear on their analyses of speech signals—information about the phonological properties of the language, its lexicon, and its syntactic and semantic properties. Thus, the phonological analysis of speech signals involves synthesizing information from a number of different sources. The speech we hear depends not only on the information actually present in the speech signal but also on information about what could have occurred in the signal. As yet, the manner in which this synthesis is carried out is not well understood.

SUGGESTED READINGS

Denes and Pinson (1973) provides a good introduction to the nature of the speech signal and the acoustic cues involved in speech perception; see also Ladefoged (1971). General reviews of speech perception research and theorizing may be found in Darwin (1976), Pisoni (1977), Stevens and House (1972), and Studdert-Kennedy (1976). Research on many interesting topics has begun too recently and is accumulating too rapidly for there to be good reviews as yet. Cooper (1975) provides a preliminary review of work on selective adaptation and feature detector mechanisms; and Eimas (1975) and Morse (1974) provide reviews of much of the work on speech perception in infants.

4

The Process
of Comprehension

Imagine two students listening intently to a lecture. The first understands what is said, but the second does not. What, then and there, is the difference between them? This question, posed by Ziff (1970), is a disarmingly simple one at first glance. We all know what it is to understand someone; the experience happens to all of us hundreds of times every day. And yet it is easier to recognize when we have understood something or when we haven't than it is to define or explicitly characterize what understanding is. In this chapter we will try to describe some of the processes that are involved in understanding. Before we begin this attempt, however, we must state in more detail the nature of the problem itself.

The Problem of Comprehension

The meaning of a sentence is dependent upon the meanings of its words. So a part of the process of comprehension must involve getting from phonological representations of the sentence's words to representations of their meanings. We may conceive of this as a process of "lexical lookup." In lexical lookup a word's phonological representation is used as a basis for retrieving stored information about the semantic (and syntactic) characteristics of the word. The meaning of a sentence also depends upon its syntactic structure. Therefore, another part of the process of comprehension involves inferring or "building" that structure from the sentence's phonological and lexical representation. Finally, the lexical and syntactic information must be integrated into a representation of the sentence's meaning.

Describing the process of comprehension in this way does not imply that these three aspects of comprehension are independent. They are not. Nor are they independent of the processes of speech perception *per se.* As we saw earlier, the phonological representation is sometimes incomplete. In such cases, the missing information tends to be filled in by processes that use the lexical and syntactic characteristics of the surrounding context. Thus, the various processes involved in comprehension are *interactive* processes. Each depends upon the others.

The main focus of this chapter is on the processes involved in comprehension—lexical lookup, inferring of syntactic structure, and integrating these into a semantic representation. In order to discuss these processes intelligently, it is useful to consider briefly the question of just where the process of comprehension ends. The decision about how one gets somewhere is not independent of the question of where one is going.

The Products of Comprehension

What is the nature of the mental representation that results from understanding an utterance? Some suggestions about how this question might be answered were made in Chapter 2, but there are really several other ways of answering it. To begin with, we can describe our understanding of an utterance at three levels: structural, intentional, and motivational.

The first level is the one we characterized in Chapter 2 as involving a representation of the propositions that a sentence expresses. It is representations at this level that are most directly dependent upon the sentence's syntactic structure and lexical content. But not all of the information that is important for understanding an utterance at this level is explicitly present in the utterance. Suppose, for example, someone said to you, *Close the door, please.* Since the utterance was directed to you, you would probably infer that *you* were the implied subject of the request. That is, you would represent the utterance as being equivalent to, *You close the door, please.* Filling in such gaps is part of the process of arriving at a structural representation.

But there is more to comprehension than just forming the structural representation. Suppose someone remarked to you, *It's too cold in here.* Under some circumstances (e.g., the door being open, the room actually being cold, etc.), you would probably interpret the utterance as a request to close the door, not just a comment upon the room's temperature. In this case the speaker's intention was less directly incorporated in the utterance than it was in *Close the door, please.* His intention—his desire to have you close the door—must be inferred from the statement along with a great deal of contextual information. We can call the meaning resulting from this kind of inference as the *conveyed meaning,* as opposed to the *literal meaning* of the statement itself. Making the inference from a literal meaning to a conveyed meaning is a further step in the comprehension process.

The process need not stop here, however. Once we have made the inference from the speaker's literal meaning to his conveyed meaning, there is a further inference that we can make—an inference about the speaker's motivation for expressing his intention in the way he did. In the case of *Close the door, please,* the speaker's motivation is fairly obvious. He wanted the door closed, and he wanted to be direct and polite. But in the case of his saying, *It's too cold in here,* the motivation is less obvious. Why did the speaker phrase his request in the form of a statement? One possibility is that the social status of the speaker and that of the hearer were such that the speaker did not wish to make his request directly. Making such an inference about the motivation underlying an utterance clearly requires taking into account a good deal of information about the speaker. But a listener can make such inferences only after he has discovered both the literal and the conveyed meanings of the utterance.

These three ways of analyzing comprehension—in terms of syntax and semantics (structure), conveyed meanings or intentions, and motivations—give only a crude idea of its products. But they do suggest that there is no simple way of establishing where the process of comprehension ends. Does it end with the discovery of a sentence's literal meaning? If so, then we could consider the inferring of conveyed meaning and motivation as things the listener can do after he has comprehended the utterance. Or does the process of comprehension include discovering the conveyed meaning and motivation?

It probably makes little difference where we say the process of comprehension ends, but it is useful to divide it up in this way. The vast bulk of the research and theorizing that has been done in psycholinguistics has concerned itself with the first-level products of comprehension—the literal meanings of utterances—and with how these are discovered. For this reason, we will focus on those processes.

States and Processes

To understand an utterance one must at least construct a representation of its literal meaning. We will understand understanding when we can characterize both that mental representation and the construction process itself. Although we discussed this issue in Chapter 2, we want to expand upon it here. To help us understand it, let's make a simple analogy. Imagine that we want to understand someone's ability to multiply. In order to understand the multiplication ability we might do two things. First, we might try to characterize the state that the person is in both after he has heard the problem and after he has completed it. Initially the individual may have the numbers *17* and *19* represented in some internal code. After some time he may have the number *323* represented in an analogous code. Characterizing the code is one of our tasks. (Example problem:

Is the code for a three-digit number like *323* psychologically longer and more complex than the code for a two-digit number? If so, shouldn't we be able to remember more two-digit numbers than three-digit numbers?)

Another task is to say how the person got from one state to the other. We want to describe the process that intervenes between the two codes. It is clear that the process cannot be one of looking up the answer in some table that the person has stored in his head. He can do so many multiplications that he could not possibly have memorized all of them. In this respect multiplication is like sentence comprehension. Instead of looking up the result in some table stored in the head, the individual must calculate the answer. We want to give a characterization of the steps that the person goes through in making the calculations. We also want to know how the knowledge about making calculations is represented in the individual. We will understand the process of mental multiplication when we can describe the state that the person starts in, the state that he ends in, and the processes and states that occur in between. In the same way, we will understand sentence comprehension when we can characterize the initial state of the listener, the state that the listener arrives at, and the processes (calculations) that intervene. Furthermore, we will want to describe the psychological mechanisms that are involved in executing the calculations. Thus, "understanding" is the name of a problem. Psycholinguists will solve the problem when they provide a theory which describes the states and processes involved in understanding.

To summarize briefly, we have said that a theory of the processes involved in comprehension will describe how a listener gets from a representation of an utterance in the phonological code to a representation of the sentence's literal meaning. In order to describe these processes, we must also describe the nature of such literal meanings—the way in which listeners mentally represent them. A comprehension theory could also involve a description of the processes involved in inferring conveyed meanings and in inferring the speaker's motives. However, our discussion will focus on the processes leading to representations of literal meanings, primarily because more is understood about them. Detailed consideration of the nature of semantic representations will be deferred until the following chapter. But it is impossible to separate completely a consideration of comprehension processes from a consideration of comprehension products. Consequently, both this and the following chapter will consider both questions, though with a difference in emphasis.

Comprehension Processes

In this section we will examine some of the steps that the listener goes through as he comprehends a sentence. The first step, speech perception, was discussed in the previous chapter. But since the output of the speech perception mechanisms is used by the remainder of the comprehension system, we must be clear about the nature of that output.

Information Available in the Phonological Representation

The speech perception process yields an output that represents the phonological segments and their features. Roughly, this is a representation containing information comparable to that in a printed text. There are, however, some differences. As we saw in the previous chapter, many phonological segments, particularly unstressed ones, are incompletely represented. Their identities are somewhat uncertain, as though the print were blurred in spots. In addition, the phonological representation often fails to indicate the boundaries between the utterance's words. Generally, then, there is less information in the phonological representation than there is in a printed text. The phonological representation is closer to: JohnanMarywenttothéstoretabuyaloafabréadbuttheymetsómeotheŕchildrenonthéway . . .

The above representation does not include information about the stress and intonation pattern of the utterance. It often seems to listeners that stress and intonation provide a considerable amount of information about the segmentation of the input into words and about the syntactic structure of the utterance. Is this correct?

Stress and Intonational Cues to Structure. There is little doubt that stress and intonation cues are useful in analyzing the structure and meaning of utterances. These cues are often available to listeners. Speakers sometimes give extra heavy stress (contrastive or emphatic stress) to a word in order to signal a particular meaning. This information aids the listener in correctly interpreting the utterance. In sentence (1), for example, the meaning changes depending upon whether the speaker gives emphatic stress to *Anne* or *job* or *England.*

(1) Anne got a job in England.

In general, though, the role of stress and intonation cues is more limited than one might expect. Three examples will demonstrate the limitations of these cues. The first example has to do with the perception of pauses during speech. Listeners often believe that speakers pause at the ends of sentences, and they also believe that the pause is used as a cue to the fact that a sentence has ended. But, as we noted in Chapter 3, in fluent discourse there is often no pause between sentences. Martin (1967) has found that listeners tend to "hear" pauses even in cases where there is no pause in the speech signal itself. What is "heard" does not correspond to what is physically present. Most likely, the heard pause is based on an inference by the listener that the sentence has ended. We will explore this process later in the chapter.

The second example of the limitation of intonation has to do with whether an utterance is perceived as a statement or a question. The same string of words can often be spoken as either a statement or a question—sentence (1) is an example. The intonation of the speaker *can* indicate to the listener which of these is intended, and it is commonly believed that intonation is the major cue for deciding whether an utterance is a statement or a question. The basis for this belief is not secure, however. If utterances that vary in intonation are presented in isolation (i.e., without any contextual information) then a listener's accuracy in telling whether the utterance was intended to be a statement or a question is not very good, especially when hearing several different speakers (Greenberg, 1969, cited in Cutler, 1974). Greenberg found that different speakers use different intonations to signal the same meaning. In ordinary speech the listener usually has a lot of contextual information which helps to determine whether he hears the utterance as a statement or as a question. This contextual information may be more important than the intonation.

The third example has to do with perceiving ambiguous sentences. We saw earlier that some ambiguous sentences can be disambiguated by grouping the words. For example, sentence (2) can mean (*Steve or Ron*) *and Bill will come*; or it can mean *Steve or* (*Ron and Bill*) *will come*.

(2) Steve or Ron and Bill will come.

If we pause after *Ron,* then the former interpretation is conveyed, while if we pause after *or* the latter interpretation is signaled. Do speakers typically provide such cues to their listeners? Clearly, it would be a great aid in inferring syntactic structure if they did. Evidence gathered by Lehiste (1973), however, strongly suggests that speakers do not usually provide such cues. She had one group of subjects read ambiguous sentences like (2) aloud and then asked them which interpretation they had in mind when they were speaking. The readers had not been told about the ambiguity prior to reading the sentences aloud. Next Lehiste played the sentences to a second group of subjects. The listeners could not tell which interpretation the speakers had in mind while reading the sentences. In other words, even when a sentence was highly ambiguous, and even when a straightforward intonational cue such as a pause could have been used to convey the appropriate syntactic structure to the listener, the speakers did not use this intonational cue.

In general, then, it appears that speakers do not typically supply their listeners with the kinds of intonational cues that could be used to infer an utterance's structure. Such cues can be used when they are available, but speakers often fail to provide them. To summarize in more technical language, the output of the speech perception mechanisms is a string of phonological segments, some of which are incompletely specified. In addition, some information about stress is represented in this output, but the information is not completely reliable.

With these general characteristics of the phonological representation in mind, let us consider the nature of some additional comprehension processes. Next we will examine some aspects of lexical lookup. Some of the information that is retrieved from the mental lexicon seems to be used by the processes which construct a sentence's syntactic structure. In this sense, lexical lookup is prior to other comprehension processes.

Lexical Access

In order to discover the structural relationships among the words in a sentence, the listener must discover some information about the words themselves. The process by which such information is obtained is often thought of as analogous to searching a "mental dictionary," using the phonological representation of a word to look up the information stored under that representation. Until this information is found, the word has no meaning for the listener and hence can contribute little to the understanding of the sentence in which it occurs. Having found the appropriate entry in the mental dictionary (or mental lexicon), the listener then has available information about the syntactic and semantic characteristics of the word.

One of the striking aspects of the process of lexical lookup is the speed at which it occurs. It is possible to listen to speech at the rate of 250 words per minute with no appreciable loss of comprehension (Foulke, 1971). Since this rate includes the time taken by speech perception processing and by other aspects of comprehension processing, it is clear that lexical lookup occurs extremely rapidly. A number of experimenters who have tried to measure the amount of time it actually takes (Rohrman & Gough, 1967; Sabol & DeRosa, 1976) have obtained estimates in the range of 150–200 msec. Whatever the precise time may be, this is an astonishingly quick process.

Word Frequency and Lexical Access. One variable that seems to affect the time required to retrieve or access a lexical item is the frequency with which the word occurs in English. In general, as word frequency goes up, the word is retrieved more rapidly. One study that manipulated word frequency in a sentence context was conducted by Foss (1969). The subjects in Foss' experiment heard a list of 60 unrelated sentences and were asked both to comprehend the sentences and to listen within each sentence for a word that started with the segment (or phoneme) /b/. The subjects were told to push a button as soon as they heard such a target word. A timer was started when the word beginning with /b/ occurred; it was stopped when the subject pushed the response button. This is called a phoneme-monitoring task. Sentences like **(3)** and **(4)** were presented.

(3) The traveling *b*assoon player found himself without funds in a strange town.

(4) The itinerant *b*assoon player found himself without funds in a strange town.

These two sentences are identical except for one word, the word that immediately precedes the target phoneme /b/. In **(3)** the preceding word *traveling* is a word of relatively high frequency while in **(4)** the word *itinerant* is a word of relatively low frequency. The words *traveling* and *itinerant* are intuitively similar, though not identical, in meaning.

Foss reasoned that reaction time (RT) in the phoneme-monitoring task directly reflects the difficulty that listeners are having with sentence processing at the time when the target phoneme occurs. That is, when a sentence is relatively easy to process the listener should be able to devote more of his processing capacity to listening for the target phoneme than when the sentence is difficult to process. Perhaps an analogy will help. Imagine yourself driving down a freeway on a clear day with no traffic. It would be possible to play a game of mental tic-tac-toe with your passenger, and the game would go relatively quickly. Now imagine that the traffic is nearly bumper-to-bumper at 55 mph and that it is dark and rainy out. It would probably not occur to you to play mental anything at that point (at least we hope not). However, if you did decide to play mental tic-tac-toe, then the time that you would take for each move would be longer than under the good driving conditions. Thus, when driving (sentence processing) is easy, RT is faster.

In the experiment under discussion, Foss found that the average RT to respond to the target phoneme was significantly longer when the target was preceded by a relatively infrequent word than when it was preceded by a relatively frequent one. Given the above reasoning, it follows that the sentence processing mechanism is taxed more in the presence of low frequency words than it is in the presence of high frequency words. This conclusion was tempered somewhat by the results of some further studies (e.g., Cairns & Foss, 1971), but for now we will stay with the simple view that lexical access is affected by word frequency.

A number of models of lexical access have been proposed to account for the frequency effect. One model states that the primary organizing principle of the mental lexicon is word frequency. Those items that are frequent in the language are toward the "front" of the dictionary, i.e., they are examined first to see if they match the input item. This view has a number of defenders (e.g., Forster & Bednall, 1976), and of course it accounts for the frequency effect since it was originally devised for that purpose. However, the model is not very plausible since it says that the mechanism of lexical access makes no use of the phonological information that has been extracted by the speech perception mechanisms.

Other models for lexical access assume that information about the word's phonological code can be used to guide the search through the mental dictionary. A very simple example of such a model would say that the mental dictionary was just like Webster's in that items starting with /a/ were stored in one location, those starting with /b/ were stored in another location, etc. Thus, when we know the phonological "spelling" of the input item we know where to go to look for the word and the information associated with it. We noted earlier that the "spelling" may be incomplete, that *bread,* for example, may be represented as *b/ead.* In this case the phonological code would still guide the search through the mental lexicon, although occasionally an incorrect entry might emerge. The listener will usually discover that the entry is incorrect, since the item will not make sense in context.

One problem with a phonologically-oriented model of lexical access is that apparently it cannot account for the frequency effect at all. If we can go directly from the phonological code to the item in the mental dictionary, why should the frequency of the item have any impact on our speed of comprehension? One reason might be that frequency affects the time it takes the listener to convert the input into a phonological representation. This suggests that lexical access is a two-stage operation, in which the first stage involves constructing a phonological representation and the second involves gaining access to the lexical item. The word-frequency effect may operate upon the first stage and not the second. There is a good deal to say for this as a model of how we read; we will discuss it further in Chapter 11. There is also another alternative to examine when discussing speech comprehension.

The last and perhaps best idea about lexical access that we will pursue here suggests that the word frequency effect is not really due to frequency at all. Instead, the effect is due to another factor that is correlated with frequency, namely, the recency with which the word has been heard. According to this hypothesis, words that have been heard (or read) recently are retrieved more rapidly than words which occurred longer ago. Since frequently heard words are also generally more recent, their degree of frequency will appear to predict their lexical access speed even if the important factor is actually their recency.

The results of an experiment by Scarborough, Cortese, and Scarborough (1977) support the recency hypothesis. They presented their subjects with printed strings of letters and asked them to decide quickly whether each string was a word or not. The time it took to make this decision was measured. Some of the words they used occur with high frequency in normal speech while some occur with low frequency. Scarborough et al. found that the RTs to say that the letter strings were words did vary with frequency, high frequency words leading to faster responses. But this was only true for the first presentation of the words. When the words were presented a second time, later in the experiment, the difference between the high and low frequency words almost disappeared. The rare (but now recent) words were responded to nearly as quickly as were the common (and also recent) words. This result suggests that the frequency effect is largely a recency effect.

In order to account for the above results, we might speculate that information in the mental lexicon stays in a state of readiness or excitation for some time after it has been retrieved. The access time for a word whose internal representation is in the "excited" state may be less than that for an "unexcited" word. The phonological information would still be used during the retrieval process. We will expand upon this model later in this chapter.

Morpheme Structure and Lexical Access. Until now we have been treating each word as though it were like every other word except for its phonology and its frequency. Other aspects of words may also affect lexical access. For example, consider two words like *telegraphy* and *temerity*. Both of these are rare words in English; each occurred only once in a sample of over one million words of naturally occurring text (Kucera & Francis, 1967). The words differ greatly in how familiar they seem, however. *Telegraphy* seems to be a much more familiar word. This might simply be due to a sampling error in the word count, but there is another, more plausible reason for this difference. *Telegraphy* has many related words (e.g., *telegraph, telegrapher,* etc.), while *temerity* has none. The sum of the frequencies of the items related to *telegraphy* is 38, a very large difference from a frequency of one. Does the frequency of such related items influence the access time of *telegraphy,* and is this the source of the difference in familiarity that we feel exists between the two example words? There seems to be no clear demonstration in the literature to prove that this is the case, though it seems a reasonable hypothesis.

If this hypothesis is correct, then words might be broken down into their components before lexical access occurs. What this means is that a word like *telegraphy* may be represented as something like *telegraph* + *y* at some stage of the access process. If so, the listener could then look up the "stem" word *telegraph.* The basic syntactic and semantic information might be listed there, together with a rule specifying how that information is affected when the affix *-y* occurs (see N. Chomsky & Halle, 1968).

What we are suggesting here is that the phonological representation may be segmented into *morphemes.* Morphemes are the smallest units that have syntactic functions. Thus, the verb *singing* is composed of two morphemes, a verb stem *sing,* and the ending *ing.* The latter is a morpheme since it plays a syntactic role, e.g., it signals the progressive tense of the verb. To take another example, the adjective *unlovely* consists of three morphemes: *un* + *love* + *ly.* There is some evidence (e.g., Taft & Forster, 1975) that the phonological representation is segmented into morphemes during lexical access.

Analyzing the phonological representation of an utterance into morphemes may provide a part of the solution to the problem of segmentation. For example, given the phonological string, . . . *quicklyfadinglight* . . . , the knowledge that *-ly* is a morpheme that generally occurs at the ends of words would allow segmenting the string into *quickly fadinglight.* Similarly, the *-ing* suffix on *fading* allows tentatively segmenting that word from *light.* Thus, affixes like *un-, -ing, -ed, -ly,* etc., may serve two functions. First, they often provide important cues to the utterance's syntactic structure; and second, they may aid in segmenting the phonological representation into units appropriate for lexical lookup.

Information in the Mental Lexicon

Whether or not the process of lexical access is affected by the morphological structure of words, it seems very likely that information about morpheme structure is stored along with the phonological code in the mental lexicon. That is, the word *juggling* will be represented as *juggle* and *ing.* One reason for this is that morphemes like *ing* are potentially of great use to the mechanism that builds the syntactic structure of the sentence. Whether or not a verb is in the progressive or past tense is important to the understanding of a sentence containing it. When presented with a word like *juggling,* the listener can determine that this item is *juggle* and *ing,* a fact that makes a difference in the representation of the sentence he is constructing. We have not yet presented any psychological evidence that words like *juggling* are represented in the mental lexicon as *juggle + ing.* Such evidence is available. But, since the most compelling data come from studies of sentence production, we will postpone discussing this evidence until Chapter 6.

Once we have gained access to a word's representation in the mental lexicon we have available the information that is stored with that word. As we have just noted, one type of information may be the morpheme structure of the word. Another important type of information concerns the part of speech of the word, its syntactic category (or categories). It clearly makes a difference to our understanding of a sentence whether a word is a noun, verb, adverb, etc. (The number of such categories used to build the structure of sentences is not a settled question, so we will not try to list them all here.) Essentially, the category of a word specifies the place that the word can occupy in the structure of the sentence. Hence, categorical information is really relational information; it is information about how that word relates to others in the sentence.

The information stored in the mental dictionary will also tell us more about the kind of structures into which the word can fit. To see why this is so, consider two common verbs, *hit* and *sleep.* These verbs are quite different in terms of the tree structures within which they grammatically function. The verb *hit* can fit into a tree structure that has an NP direct object in its underlying representation. Something must be the object of the verb *hit.* On the other hand, *sleep* cannot fit into such a tree; it cannot take a direct object. While we *hit a ball,* we do not *sleep a bed* or sleep anything else. The verb *hit* is listed in the lexicon as one that must have a direct object, while *sleep* is listed as a verb that cannot have a direct object. In grammatical terms, *hit* is a transitive verb, and *sleep* is an intransitive verb. The categories of transitive and intransitive identify the tree structures within which the verbs will normally function. (This kind of categorization is sometimes referred to as "subcategorization," since it specifies subcategories within the category of verbs [N. Chomsky, 1965]). If we encounter a sentence that violates one of these subcategorization specifications, we regard the sentence as being ungrammatical, like example (5).

(5) *The boy slept the bed.

Although there are some verbs that can fit into only a single kind of tree structure, there are many more that allow several possibilities. *Surrender,* for example, can be used as either a transitive verb, as in sentence (6), or as an intransitive verb, as in sentence (7).

(6) The bookkeeper surrendered the ledgers to the grand jury.

(7) The bank robber surrendered to the police.

When the listener gains access to the representation of some words, he also gets an additional type of information that restricts the kinds of structures within which these words can fit. To demonstrate this, let us again consider the verb *sleep*. Not only are there restrictions like those just discussed, i.e., the verb cannot have a direct object, there are also restrictions on the kinds of nouns that can be the subject of this verb. Thus, (8) is perfectly grammatical while (9) is not, at least when we interpret *sleep* literally.

(8) The canary slept.

(9) *The cage slept.

The verb *sleep* only fits with certain classes of subject nouns. This is true of other verbs also; there is a restricted class of nouns that can be the underlying subject (or object, if there is one) of each verb in the mental lexicon. Hence, the class of nouns that can go with each verb must be specified in the lexicon. The exact manner in which this is to be done is controversial. For our present purposes it is enough to note that such specification is necessary. We will see later how such information may be used in the process of constructing the syntactic structure of an utterance.

There are several other kinds of information available in the mental lexicon. Some of these will be discussed in Chapters 5 and 6. However, let us now go on to consider what happens after the information in the mental lexicon has been retrieved.

Comprehension and Short-Term Memory

One of the fundamental facts about comprehension is that it occurs piecemeal while we listen to utterances. That is, we do not store each incoming utterance in some unanalyzed form and then operate upon it all at once. We can demonstrate the fact of piecemeal comprehension with sentence (10).

(10) The shooting of the prince shocked his wife since she thought that he was an excellent marksman.

As you read (10) you probably understood the first five words to mean: Somebody shot the prince, i.e., that *the prince* was the underlying object of the verb *shoot.* When you got to the end of (10) it then became apparent that this interpretation was incorrect, that the prince was the one who was doing the shooting and that he had probably done poorly at it. The fact that you make an interpretation of part of a sentence becomes obvious when that interpretation is incorrect, when you have to redo it. The misunderstanding shows us that the process of understanding is well under way during the presentation of the sentence. Each word and phrase triggers some operations which contribute to the understanding of the sentence. This is not to say that we have a conscious understanding of each word as we hear it. If you pay attention to your own process of understanding, you will note that the meanings of individual words do not appear as separate conscious events.

One reason for the piecemeal aspect of comprehension is that utterances are strung out in time; hence, they put a significant demand upon the memory of the listener. As you are aware, we do not have unlimited memory for events. It is fairly common for someone to look up a telephone number and then forget part of it during the time that it takes to dial the number. There is also plenty of evidence that our memory for the exact sequence of words in an utterance is highly limited. Typically we cannot exactly recall an utterance by the time we have finished processing the next one. What, without looking, was the exact form of the sentence before this one? Stop and try to recall it.

This limitation on our memory capacity strongly suggests that at the same time we listen to an utterance we are recoding its strings of words into some other structured representation, and that this recoding occurs at a very rapid rate. The original form of the utterance is typically lost in the process.

Sachs (1967) conducted the best known demonstration of this phenomenon. She presented listeners with paragraphs describing some historical event. Embedded within a paragraph would be a sentence like **(11)**.

(11) He sent a letter about it to Galileo, the great Italian scientist.

A short time later—either immediately, 80 syllables, or 160 syllables after the sentence—she presented a test sentence and asked her subjects whether or not they had heard it. She found that they could reliably recognize changes in meaning, but could not recognize changes that involved only the surface structure. For example, after 80 syllables her subjects were over 80% correct when asked if they had heard **(12)**, but they were less than 60% correct when asked if they had heard **(13)**.

(12) Galileo, the great Italian scientist, sent him a letter about it.
(13) A letter about it was sent to Galileo, the great Italian scientist.

Sachs concluded that the "original sentence which is perceived is rapidly forgotten, and the memory then is for the information contained in the sentence" (1967, p. 443).

An even more dramatic demonstration of the rapid decay of information about the exact form of the input sentence was carried out by Wanner (1974). He was able to show that listeners had lost the exact wording of a sentence when only 16 syllables intervened between the presentation of a sentence and its test. We may conclude, then, that in the normal course of comprehension the information about the exact surface form of a sentence vanishes very quickly. This implies that the input is analyzed very rapidly and changed into some more abstract form of representation. The new representation does not include a specification of the input words or their exact sequence, but may incorporate instead some of the structural information extracted from the sentence—information about the deeper relationships among the words.

It has been known for a long time that the limitations of the short-term memory for structured material, such as sentences, are different from those for unstructured material. Miller (1951) cites a 1924 study by Reed in which students had a memory span of 6.55 for disconnected words but a span of 25.36 for words in ordinary sentences. A nice demonstration of the difference between structured and unstructured material has been carried out by Gough and Mastenbrook (cited in Gough, 1972). They presented subjects with strings of ten words and asked for verbatim recall of the string. Two types of strings were presented, one of which was like (14), the other like (15).

(14) radio arm chief test window melting snows cause sudden floods

(15) melting snows cause sudden floods radio arm chief test window

The subjects were able to recall more words from lists like (15) than from lists like (14). Gough interpreted this finding to mean that the first five words of (15) are understood as a sentence and then removed from the short-term memory, thus permitting the final five words to be stored there with relative ease. In contrast, the first five words of (14) cannot be removed from the short-term memory because they do not constitute a linguistic unit. Since linguistic recoding cannot occur, the words must be held in short-term memory. While there they interfere with the processing and storage of the final five words.

To summarize, we have found that subjects rapidly decode words into some structural representation, thus freeing their short-term memories to deal with new incoming material. We have also found that the exact form of the utterance is lost during this recoding. We will examine what happens to the words during the recoding after we discuss the theory that syntax is not always involved in the recoding process.

Semantic Relations and Sentence Comprehension

We noted in Chapter 2 that sentences do not wear their entire meanings on their surfaces. In order to understand (16) a listener must determine, among other things, who was excited, the boy or the girl.

(16) The boy who loves the girl was excited about the party.

Of course, (16) asserts that the boy was excited. But the way in which one comes to this conclusion is not obvious. The noun closest to the verb *excited* is *girl*. The last seven words of the sentence taken alone are *the girl was excited about the party*. Listeners cannot interpret the meaning of the sentence in terms of simple surface relations such as: The noun immediately prior to the verb is the subject of that verb. Such a procedure would yield misunderstanding. The appropriate structure associates *excited* with the more distant noun *boy*. Hence, at some point during the comprehension of (16), it appears that the listener must have figured out, or computed, the appropriate syntactic structure.

It may sometimes appear that the structural phase of understanding can be short-circuited. Imagine a sentence constructed with these three words as its nouns and verb: *girl, flowers,* and *watered.* What sentences could we construct from these terms? Among the sentences that we could make are **(17)** and **(18)**.

(17) The girl watered the flowers.

(18) The flowers were being watered by the girl.

We would not consider making a sentence like **(19)**; **(19)** is nonsense and could only be true in a cartoon.

(19) *The flowers watered the girl.

Sentences like **(17)** and **(18)** are called "non-reversible" sentences, for the roles played by the two nouns are fixed. The term *girl* must be the underlying subject of the sentence, and the term *flowers* must be the underlying object. If we try to use *flowers* as the underlying subject, a strange sentence like **(19)** results. In comprehending **(17)** or **(18)** perhaps listeners can ignore the voice of the sentence (i.e., whether it is active or passive). Since the terms can go together in only one way, maybe listeners can simply take the terms and put them together in that way. The structural phase of understanding would thus be omitted. (We will see in Chapter 9 that children not yet old enough to be sensitive to the structural relationships actually proceed in very much this way.) But the possibility of ignoring sentence structure does not arise when the sentence is "reversible," that is, when either of the two nouns in a simple sentence could play the role of underlying subject. Sentence **(20)** is a reversible sentence, therefore **(21)** is perfectly all right too.

(20) The dog chased the cat.

(21) The cat chased the dog.

Hence, if a listener is presented with the terms *dog, chased,* and *cat,* it makes a big difference whether they are in the passive voice or not. Sentence **(22)** is clearly different from **(20)** even though the three terms are in the same left to right order.

(22) The dog was being chased by the cat.

The above observations suggest something like the following as a comprehension strategy: *Assign the roles of underlying subject and object to the nouns that can possibly have these roles. If more than one noun can be the underlying subject then (and only then) compute the syntactic structure.* This strategy assumes that active and passive sentences are equally comprehensible if they are non-reversible, as in the case of sentences **(17)** and **(18)**. When we deal with reversible sentences the picture may change. Then passive sentences may take longer to comprehend than actives because the surface structure of the passive is quite different from its underlying structure.

There are data to argue both for and against the above strategy as an accurate model of the comprehension process. On the supporting side, Slobin (1966) conducted an experiment in which subjects were asked to determine whether a picture shown at the end of a sentence correctly depicted the meaning of that sentence. His subjects first heard a sentence like (17) and then were presented with a picture. They pressed one button if the picture correctly showed what the sentence said, and a second button if it did not. The time it took each listener to make these judgments (verification time) was recorded and provided the measurement of interest. Slobin reasoned that longer verification times would mean that the listeners were having a harder time comprehending the sentences. He found a difference in verification time between active and passive sentences, but only if they were reversible sentences like (20) and (21). There was no difference in verification time between active and passive non-reversible sentences like (17) and (18). Slobin concluded that something like the above strategy was operative. Similar results have been reported by Herriott (1969).

On the opposing side are some experiments conducted by Forster and Olbrei (1973). These authors were critical of the verification task since, they argued, it reflects the time to evaluate the picture and therefore is not a very direct measure of the time required to comprehend the sentences *per se.* (Gough, 1966, and Tannenhaus, Carroll & Bever, 1976, have also argued that verification time is not a good measure of comprehension.) In some of Forster and Olbrei's experiments, the subjects were presented with strings of words and were asked to judge as quickly as possible whether or not each string constituted a sentence. Some of the word strings were nonsense while others were, in fact, sentences. The decision time was assumed to reflect the difficulty of comprehending the string. Here we will concern ourselves with only the positive responses, those made when the string actually was a sentence. Forster and Olbrei presented four types of sentences, reversible actives and passives and non-reversible actives and passives. Example sentences and the results from their study are shown in Table 4.1.

As can be seen, passive sentences took longer than active sentences, even when they were non-reversible. Thus, sentences whose surface form was complex (passives) always took longer to understand than did those whose surface form was simple (actives). Forster and Olbrei concluded that these data lent no support to the idea that syntactic or structural analyses of sentences can be short-circuited by semantic strategies of the sort described above.

The weight of evidence suggests, then, that comprehension involves constructing an internal representation of the syntactic structure of the utterance. The data on adult comprehension are consistent with this view, and the data on children's comprehension suggest that children, once they begin attending to the syntactic structures of sentences, also construct such structural representations.

We must use care in interpreting the above claim that "comprehension involves constructing an internal representation of the syntactic structure of the utterance." The claim says that the listener extracts the same kinds of informa-

Table 4.1

Example Sentences and Reaction Times to Respond (in seconds) as a Function
of Sentence Type and Voice.

Sentence Voice	Sentence Type	
	Reversible	*Non-reversible*
Active	The parents dismayed some teachers. 1.436	The essays dismayed some teachers. 1.361
Passive	Some teachers were dismayed by the parents. 1.709	Some teachers were dismayed by the essays. 1.668

(Modification of Table 3 from Forster, K. I. & Olbrei, I. Semantic Heuristics and syntactic analysis. *Cognition*, 1973, *2*, 319–347. Copyright 1973 by Academic Press. Used by permission.)

tion that are represented by the linguist in a tree diagram. This is not the same
thing as saying that there is some psychological representation exactly like a tree
diagram that is built up by the listener as he comprehends the utterance. In the
next section we will look at evidence on exactly what structural information is
extracted as the listener processes the incoming utterance.

Sentence Structures in Comprehension Processing

We have concluded that the listener cannot by-pass a sentence's syntactic
structure en route from its phonological representation to its meaning. Still
remaining, though, is the question of which structures the listener actually constructs during comprehension. We saw in Chapter 2 that two kinds of structures
play important roles in the syntactic description of language, surface structures
and underlying structures. Now we must ask if both of these are involved in
comprehension. Does the listener first build a representation of the input in
terms of its surface structure and then, by the application of some rules, arrive
at the underlying structure?

Ideally, we would like to state the exact sequence of structures that the
listener constructs as the utterance is translated from the phonological code to
the meaning. If we knew what structures the listener actually came up with, this
would tell us a lot about the processes that are being used. To return to our
earlier analogy, if we knew the sub-totals that were computed while someone
did a mental multiplication problem, then we could more easily determine the
method that was being used to come up with the answer. In this section we will
examine some of the evidence that has been gathered on the question of which
structures listeners actually construct, that is, which ones are "psychologically
real."

Intuitive Judgments of Sentence Structure

There are several ways to get evidence about the structures built up by the listener while interpreting an utterance. One of the most straightforward ways of obtaining data on this question is simply to ask the listeners. You may recall that this is what we did in Chapter 2 when we asked for your intuitions about which words in the sentence *The boy kissed the girl* were most closely related to each other. We decided that we would segment the sentence as ((*The boy*) (*kissed the girl*)). That is, if we take the basic subject-verb-object (SVO) components of a simple sentence, we segment them as (S(VO)).

A number of investigators have asked listeners to segment complex sentences. The segmentations that resulted were affected by factors other than those that we have discussed up to now. Furthermore, these segmentations do not always agree with the one we gave in Chapter 2. For example, E. Martin (1970) presented subjects with sentences like (23) and asked them to arrange the words of each sentence into "natural groups." No constraints were put on the subjects as to the number of groups that they should come up with.

(23) Politicians were spending the year's tax money.

By the use of a statistical analysis Martin was able to determine the typical tree structure that described his subjects' responses. The main syntactic break in sentence (23), according to Martin's analysis, was between the words *spending* and *the*. That is, the sentence was broken down like this: ((*Politicians were spending*) (*the year's tax money*)). The verb was more closely associated with the subject NP than with the object NP. In all sentences like (23) the organization was ((SV)O) rather than (S(VO)).

In another study in which subjects were asked for their intuitions about the grouping of words, J. Martin, Kolodziej, and Genay (1971) found that the grouping was influenced by the length of the sentence and of its various parts. For example, when the subject NP was relatively long, the judges were very likely to use the grouping that we used earlier, (S(VO)). On the other hand, when the subject NP was short and the object NP was long, then J. Martin et al. found the same groupings as E. Martin, ((SV)O). Hence, the intuitive analysis of the sentence into hierarchical units appears to be affected by the length of the components of the sentence.

In other, related work, Levelt (1970) showed that the clusters or groupings subjects give are influenced by the underlying relations among the words of the sentence. Levelt presented sentences like (24) to some of his subjects. (The sentences were actually in Dutch, (24) is Levelt's translation of the sentence.)

(24) John eats apples and Peter pears.

He found that the subjects' intuitive organization of this sentence was identical to that of (25).

(25) John eats apples and Peter eats pears.

Levelt concluded that the missing word in (24) was influencing the representation that his subjects were constructing. (The word *eats* is missing at the surface of the sentence, but is, by Levelt's hypothesis, present in the underlying representation of the sentence.)

The lesson to be learned here is that the intuitive tree structure that individuals will give for a sentence is influenced by many of its aspects, including its underlying structure. If we want to discover what listeners extract from an utterance it may be unwise to construct a single structural representation from their data; for listeners may compute more than one structure. A part of the problem with this technique arises from the fact that the intuitive judgments of structure are made *after* the sentences have been comprehended. For this reason they probably are not an accurate reflection of the structural representations constructed *during* comprehension.

"Click" Studies

One approach to the goal of determining the structures actually created during comprehension involves using the "click" methodology. The click technique was popularized by Fodor and Bever (1965), and has been used in dozens of experiments since then. Fodor and Bever began with the hypothesis that the listener segments the input utterance into its surface-structure constituents during sentence comprehension. According to this view, the utterance is organized according to its surface structure tree. Thus, the surface NP is a unit, as is the VP. In other words, Fodor and Bever claimed that the listener computes the surface structure as one of the "sub-totals" during the comprehension process.

In developing their method, Fodor and Bever supposed that perceptual units are relatively immune to the interrupting effects of an extraneous stimulus. Put the other way around, they conjectured that an extraneous stimulus was more likely to be detected if it occurred between the perceptual units of an utterance than if it occurred within a perceptual unit. Thus, if someone softly calls your name while you are engrossed in reading, you are more likely to attend to this stimulus if it happens to occur between sentences than if it occurs within a sentence. In order to test this idea they presented listeners with sentences like (26) in one ear. At some time during the presentation of the sentence a very brief click was presented to the other ear. Each subject was instructed to listen to the sentence and the click, and then, after the sentence was completed, to write it down, indicating where the click had occurred.

(26) That he was happy was evident from the way he smiled.

In some sentences the click actually occurred at the major syntactic break in the surface structures, that is, between the words *happy* and the second *was*. In other sentences the click occurred just prior to or after this position. According to Fodor and Bever's hypothesis the listeners should have noticed the click and recalled its location best when it occurred at the major syntactic break. And that is what they found. Furthermore, Fodor and Bever reported that the clicks which had actually occurred in places other than the major boundary were perceived as being located closer to the boundary. That is, clicks occurring earlier in the sentence tended to be displaced to later positions, while those occurring after the boundary were reported as having occurred earlier in the sentence.[1] Fodor and Bever concluded from these results that their major hypothesis had been supported. If we are willing to assume that units of perception resist interruption, then *That he was happy* is one major unit of **(26)** and *was evident from the way he smiled* is another major unit of that sentence.

In an important extension of the click work, Garrett, Bever and Fodor (1966) later showed that perception of the clicks was influenced by the structure of a sentence even in the absence of intonational cues. These investigators presented sentences like **(27)** and **(28)** to their subjects. The two sentences were identical from *hope* onward.

(27) In her hope of marrying Anna was surely impractical.

(28) Your hope of marrying Anna was surely impractical.

The common portions of each sentence were made acoustically identical by tape splicing. A click was placed in the word *Anna* or in the word *was,* and listeners were asked to judge where they had heard the click.

The results indicated that the listeners perceived the clicks as occurring earlier than *Anna* in **(27)** and later than *Anna* in **(28)**. These locations correspond to the major syntactic breaks of the two sentences. Thus, the syntactic organization that the listener imposes upon the sentence appears to influence his click location judgments. The results do not appear to reflect rhythmic or intonational cues because these were acoustically identical over the important part of the sentences. This is an interesting finding. It suggests that click location accuracy can be used to determine the results of the structure building process. Furthermore, it argues that the results of this process are not due simply to acoustic factors in the stimulus. The listener is actively engaged in constructing the sentence structure for himself.

The sentences used in the click studies reviewed so far have been complex sentences, that is, sentences with two or more clauses in them. From the perspective of transformational grammar this means that each complex sentence has two or more sentences in its underlying representation, one for each clause (see Figure 2.5). The accuracy of click location appears to be affected most when the click occurs near the clause boundary. That is, accuracy is high (and reaction time to a click is fast; see Holmes & Forster, 1970) when the click occurs at the point in the surface structure of the sentence that reflects the boundary between

---

[1]There was also a general tendency to report that clicks occurred earlier than they actually did, so the data were not quite as clean as we are making them out to be.

the two underlying sentences. Bever and some of his associates (e.g., Bever, Lackner, & Kirk, 1969) have conjectured that this is the *only* place where click location accuracy will be affected. In other words, Bever has hypothesized that click location is not influenced by surface structure (as was first supposed by Fodor and Bever, 1965), but rather by the underlying structure that the listener extracts from the utterance.

Bever's claim is controversial; it has been challenged by Chapin, Smith, and Abrahamson (1972), who argued that clicks were in fact affected primarily by aspects of the surface structure. This issue has been discussed in some detail by Fodor, Bever, and Garrett (1974). Unfortunately, the arguments have not been conclusive. In part this is because they depend upon the linguistic analyses given to particular sentences, and not all linguists agree on which analyses are correct. Another reason for the inconclusiveness is that click location accuracy may be affected by such variables as the length of sentence constituents, regardless of whether the constituents correspond to the boundaries between underlying sentences. Consequently we cannot be sure whether the click location results are affected by surface structure alone, underlying structure alone, or by a mixture of surface and underlying structure. Our inferences about the structures that are constructed and the processes that do the job are somewhat improved because of the click studies, but these studies have not by any means answered all of the questions about them.

Probe Latency Studies

A probe latency technique has also been used in trying to identify the structural representations that people construct during comprehension. In studies using this technique, listeners hear a sentence and immediately afterwards are asked to make a judgment about a probe word. For example, Caplan (1972) presented sentences like **(29)** and **(30)**, followed by a probe word that either had or had not occurred in the sentence.

(29) Whenever one telephones at night, rates are lower.

(30) Make your calls after six, because night rates are lower.

The subjects' task was to decide quickly whether the probe word had occurred in the sentence. (The probe for sentences **(29)** and **(30)** was *night,* so the correct response was "yes.") By using tape splicing, Caplan made the last four words of each sentence acoustically identical. The words were physically identical, but not, of course, the syntactic relationships among them. In **(29)** the words *night* and *rate* are in different clauses, while in **(30)** these words are in the same clause. Caplan found that the average time to respond "yes" to *night* was longer for **(29)** than for **(30)**. The probe latency was affected by the clausal structure of the test sentence. He concluded that clause boundaries are important units in the perception of an utterance; people segment an utterance into clauses as one of the first stages in comprehension.

Walker, Gough, and Wall (1968) presented further evidence that a listener's reaction time to a probe is affected by the underlying grammatical relations of a sentence. These investigators presented sentences like (31) to their subjects, and then presented a two-word probe. In this study the subjects' task was to say whether or not both of the probe words had occurred in the sentence. The time it took to make this "yes" or "no" response was measured.

(31) The scouts the indians saw killed a buffalo.

Two of the probes that were presented were *scouts-killed* and *indians-killed.* In the former case the two words come from the same underlying proposition, *The scouts killed a buffalo.* In the latter case the probe words are not members of the same underlying sentence, although they are closer together in the actual sentence, i.e., *indians* is physically closer to *killed* than is *scouts.* Walker et al. found that the time to respond positively to *scouts-killed* was less than the time to respond to *indians-killed.* Thus, the reaction time was affected more by the underlying relations among the words than it was by their physical proximity. Evidence for a similar conclusion can be found in the work of Ammon (1968).

The results of the probe latency experiments suggest that listeners construct representations of the underlying syntactic organization of sentences during comprehension processing. These experiments do not make clear whether surface structure properties are represented during comprehension. Caplan's results can be interpreted as reflecting either surface or underlying structure since the surface structure clause boundaries in (29) and (30) are also divisions between underlying sentences.

In this respect, then, these experiments suggest conclusions similar to those obtained with the click technique and from listeners' intuitive judgments. While we have plenty of evidence that listeners quickly structure the input into groups of items during the comprehension process, we do not have strong evidence that they construct the kind of surface structure representation provided by a transformational grammar. Later in this chapter we will discuss a theory of comprehension which says that comprehension processing is indeed closely related to the linguistic levels of syntax that have been proposed by linguists such as Chomsky. For now, however, we must suspect that comprehension processing does not closely follow the linguistic models which stimulated most of the original research into the problem—a somewhat ironic situation, to be sure.

In the next section we will discuss a different aspect of comprehension processing, putting aside for now the question of whether a sentence's surface structure is an actual product of the process.

The Problem of Ambiguity

Many English words have multiple meanings; in consequence, many of the utterances that we hear every day are ambiguous. The word *sentence* is itself ambiguous—it may mean a jail term or a linguistic object. From a linguistic point of view, then, the sentence *The sentence was long* is ambiguous. Sentences which are ambiguous because of the presence of an ambiguous word are called lexically ambiguous sentences. We noted in Chapter 2 that ambiguity can also arise from structural sources, as in *The chicken is ready to eat.*

Typically, listeners are not aware of the potential ambiguity that lurks within many of the utterances they hear. They generally come up with only one conscious interpretation of the input, and in the vast majority of cases it is the appropriate one. This poses an interesting problem. In a lexically ambiguous sentence, for example, how does the listener arrive at the correct meaning for the ambiguous word? The choice cannot be made either by chance or by magic. There must be some principles that guide comprehension processing in such a way that the correct meaning is chosen.

When the problem of ambiguity is pointed out, most people first say that an utterance is not "really" ambiguous since the context within which it occurs will tell the listener which interpretation of the ambiguous word is the correct one. Such an observation does not, however, solve the problem; it merely restates part of it. We have to find out how context has its effect before this observation can have much interest. Since listeners typically do not notice that sentences are ambiguous, perhaps we should ask if the ambiguity only exists in the abstract, never influencing what happens during sentence processing. Is there any evidence to suggest that ambiguity has an effect on comprehension? In fact, there is.

MacKay (1966) found evidence that the presence of ambiguity slowed sentence processing. He gave written sentence fragments to his subjects and asked them to make complete sentences by orally completing the fragments. Some fragments contained ambiguities and others did not. Here is an example of each kind.

(32) After taking the right turn at the intersection, I

(33) After taking the left turn at the intersection, I

MacKay found that the time needed to complete a sentence fragment was significantly longer when the fragment contained an ambiguity (*right turn*) than when it did not (*left turn*). He argued that the two possible interpretations of the ambiguity interfered with one another, delaying the processing until one interpretation was chosen.

Other evidence in support of the hypothesis that ambiguity slows comprehension comes from a phoneme-monitoring experiment carried out by Foss (1970). He presented sentences like **(34)** and **(35)** to his subjects and asked them to monitor for the phoneme /b/. In **(34)** the ambiguous word *drill* occurs just before the target, while in **(35)** the relatively unambiguous *march* occurs at that point.

(34) The men started to drill *b*efore they were ordered to do so.

(35) The men started to march *b*efore they were ordered to do so.

Reaction time to respond to the target was longer for the ambiguous sentence (34) than for the unambiguous one (35). In a subsequent experiment, Cairns and Kamerman (1975) manipulated the distance between the ambiguous word and the word carrying the target phoneme. They found an increase in RT for ambiguous sentences when the target occurred immediately after the ambiguity (thus replicating the earlier finding). However, they found no increase in RT when the target phoneme occurred two words after the ambiguity. The presence of an ambiguity appears to increase the difficulty of comprehension, but this effect is short-lived. Garrett (1970) has suggested that the effects of an ambiguity, lexical or structural, only persist throughout a single clause of the utterance; but this claim has not been fully documented.

Lexical ambiguity seems to add a burden to the comprehension process. One way that this could happen is if the process of lexical access was slowed down or interfered with by the existence of the ambiguity. It appears that deciding between two interpretations does take longer than finding a single interpretation, but such a conclusion may be premature. So far the ambiguity studies that we have looked at have used sentences with no relevant context. Perhaps the ambiguity effect is limited to these unnatural circumstances. A few experiments have been conducted in which listeners were provided with relevant context before the ambiguous word. For example, Foss and Jenkins (1973) added various types of contexts to their sentences and had listeners do the phoneme monitoring task. Examples of their sentences are shown in Table 4.2. The target phoneme was /b/ in these sentences. Half of the sentences were ambiguous, and half were not. In addition, half of the ambiguous sentences had neutral contexts and half had biasing contexts; the same was true for the unambiguous sentences. Let us suppose that a biased prior context (the word *farmer*) effectively removes the ambiguity from *straw*, leading the listener to retrieve only the barnyard interpretation. If so, then the ambiguous sentence in effect becomes an unambiguous one, and it should be just as easy to process as an unambiguous sentence. This view predicts that there should be no difference between ambiguous and unambiguous sentences in a biased context (bottom row of Table 4.2), but that there should still be a difference between them when the context is neutral (top row of Table 4.2).

The results of the study are also shown in the table. While relevant context led to faster RTs overall, it did so for both ambiguous and unambiguous sentences. The difference between ambiguous and unambiguous sentences was just as great in the biased sentences as it was in the neutral sentences. On the basis of these results Foss and Jenkins proposed that listeners always retrieve both interpretations of an ambiguous word from the mental lexicon and that the context then operates to help decide among them. They argued, in other words, that the ambiguity effect is due not to slower lexical access for ambiguous words, but instead to the necessity of choosing among the interpretations that are (unconsciously) looked up.

Table 4.2
Examples of the Materials used by Foss and Jenkins (1973); and Reaction Times in msec.

Context	Sentence Types	
	Ambiguous	*Unambiguous*
Neutral	The merchant put his straw beside the machine. RT = 564	The merchant put his oats beside the machine. RT = 525
Biased	The farmer put his straw beside the machine. RT = 549	The farmer put his oats beside the machine. RT = 513

(Modification of Table 1 from Foss, D. J., & Jenkins, C. M. Some effects of context on the comprehension of ambiguous sentences. *Journal of Verbal Learning and Verbal Behavior*, 1973, *12*, 577–589. Copyright 1973 by Academic Press. Used by permission.)

Subsequently, however, Swinney and Hakes (1976) carried out some work using similar experimental techniques which did find evidence that context reduced the number of interpretations that the listener considers. Swinney and Hakes modified the Foss and Jenkins experiment, improving the materials to make sure that the bias produced by the context was very strong. They found that the difference between ambiguous and unambiguous sentences disappeared in the biased sentences. This result suggests that the presence of context can actually make an ambiguous word into an unambiguous one, a conclusion that contradicts the "choice" theory proposed by Foss and Jenkins.

The results of the Swinney and Hakes experiment argue that lexical access is affected by information that the listener has recently processed. That is, lexical access is not only influenced by such variables as the frequency or recency of the word in question, but also by what the whole processing system has done recently. This conclusion squares quite well with our commonsense impression of what is involved in retrieving a word from the mental lexicon.

To make this somewhat more precise, we could assume (following Morton, 1969) that the internal representation of each word in the lexicon—its meaning—has a certain "threshold" of response associated with it. When its threshold is exceeded, the meaning becomes available to the listener (is activated). The meaning is sensitive to two sources of input, one from the senses (e.g., phonological information) and one from semantically-related words. Input from these two sources sums. So if a semantically-related word has recently occurred, then the amount of sensory information required to activate the meaning is less than if no such word had preceded the new one.

Evidence in support of such a threshold model of lexical access comes from an experiment carried out by Meyer and Schvaneveldt (1971). They showed their subjects two strings of letters simultaneously, one above the other, and asked them to respond "yes" if both strings were words and "no" otherwise. The times required for the subjects to make the decision were measured. In one experimental condition the words were semantically related, as in *Doctor-Nurse, Bread-Butter.* In another condition the words were unrelated, for example *Doctor-Butter* or *Bread-Nurse.* Meyer and Schvaneveldt found that the RTs were faster when the words were related than when they were not. They assumed that when the meaning of the first word of the pair was made available, it also activated the meanings of words semantically related to it. Since the second member of a pair like *Doctor-Nurse* already has been activated by the occurrence of the first member of the pair, less sensory information is required to gain access to the second word, and the RTs are faster.

Theories of Comprehension Processing

In this section we will look briefly at two proposed theories of sentence processing. Since this problem has stimulated a lot of work, it is important to note at the outset that the approaches we will discuss are only a small sample of those that have been suggested. At the present time there is no one theory of comprehension that is entirely satisfactory, and there may be none for a very long time. Theories of comprehension processing borrow from linguistic theory to varying degrees. We will begin by looking at a model which is heavily in debt to linguistic theory; then we will discuss an approach that has been mined from other lodes.

Transformational Models

Although Chomsky has stated many times that his theory of language is not a theory of language performance, models of comprehension which directly incorporate some aspects of transformational grammar have often been proposed. According to one version of such a model, each transformation in the grammar will have associated with it a "reverse transformation"—a set of operations which "detransform" a structure. If there is a transformational rule which, say, exchanges the positions of two NPs as the underlying structure is changed into the surface structure, then the "reverse transformation" will put them back in their original order. The reverse transformational model proposes that, after lexical lookup, the input string is represented as a surface structure (the way in which this occurs is usually not stated). Then the reverse transformations apply. For example, if the surface structure contains the sequence *NP was V by NP'* (e.g., *The boy was kissed by the girl*), then the "reverse passive" transformation will apply resulting in the underlying sequence *NP' V NP* (e.g., *The girl kissed the boy*). Specific morphemes in the surface structure trigger the application of the reverse transformation rules. For example, when the sequence *was V by* occurs, the "reverse passive" is applied.

One of the most important implications of this model is that sentences which undergo more transformations should take longer to comprehend than those which undergo fewer transformations. If we assume that each inverse transformation takes some amount of time, then the more of them that need to be applied, the longer it should take before the meaning of the sentence can be determined. Thus, a passive sentence should take longer to comprehend than its corresponding active sentence since the inverse of the passive transformation has to be applied to it. This point of view has been called the *Derivational Theory of Complexity* or DTC (Fodor & Garrett, 1967).

The assumptions of DTC are: (a) the underlying representation of a sentence is extracted; (b) this is accomplished by first constructing the surface structure of the sentence; (c) then reverse transformations are applied until the underlying form of the sentence is obtained; (d) furthermore, each reverse transformation takes time to apply. In general, the more transformations used to generate the sentence in the grammar, the more reverse transformations will be required to comprehend the sentence. Thus, according to DTC, there is a direct correspondence between the transformational rules of the grammar and the number and complexity of the mental operations that are required to understand the sentence.

A good bit of the psycholinguistic work of the 1960's was guided, either explicitly or implicitly, by DTC, and some evidence was obtained which appeared to support this model. You may recall that Forster and Olbrei (Table 4.1) found that passive sentences took somewhat longer to comprehend than active sentences. This is just the result predicted by DTC. Since the passive requires an additional inverse transformation, it should take longer to comprehend. Other studies, using primarily memory tasks, found further evidence that was interpreted as supporting DTC. However, there are also problems with this model.

One of the problems is that the DTC model proposes that sentences are first cast into their surface structure form. This suggests that we should find evidence for a surface structure way-station during the comprehension process. The evidence that we have already reviewed (e.g., the click experiments) does not strongly support this hypothesis. Therefore, this aspect of the model is weak. Also, some transformations which should have led to differences in comprehension time did not do so (Fodor & Garrett, 1966). Furthermore, no satisfactory set of reverse transformation has ever been developed; this idea was never really carried beyond the formative stages.

This last criticism is an important one, for it is not as easy as we may have made it appear to construct such reverse transformations. Even our earlier example was oversimplified. If we have *The boy was kissed by the tree* as our input utterance, it fits the *NP was V by NP'* format. However, it is not correct to apply the reverse of the passive transformation to this configuration, thereby arriving at a structure that corresponds to *The tree kissed the boy*. It is clear that the phrase *by the tree* is meant to signify a location and not an underlying subject. We could adjust the reverse passive transformation for this case so that it only applied when the surface object referred to an animate object. However, other problems of this sort abound when one tries to actually construct the reverse transformational rules (see Fodor, Bever, & Garrett, 1974, for further discussion of DTC).

Although we could try to modify DTC in an attempt to save it, that is not what most psycholinguists have done. Since it did not look as though DTC was going to be a fruitful theory of comprehension, most psycholinguists abandoned it. They agreed with Chomsky that the theory of performance should not directly incorporate aspects of the theory of competence. Instead, independent theories of performance were constructed, theories that did not bear such a close relationship to the grammatical rules proposed by linguists. We will now look at a model of comprehension which replaces the reverse transformational rules with a set of more independent "strategies."

Strategy Models

The reverse transformational model of structure building assumed that the psychological complexity of a sentence was related to the transformational "distance" between the underlying and surface forms of the sentence. We will now examine a model which also assumes that comprehension involves discovering the underlying structure of the input utterance. However, the new model does not also assume that the listener constructs a representation of the utterance's surface structure. In addition, its assumptions about the way in which the underlying structure is recovered are different, and it therefore has a different way of calculating what qualifies as a psychologically complex sentence.

According to the strategy model, each lexical item is associated with certain information in the mental dictionary that can be used to construct the deep structure of the input. (Recall our earlier discussion about the information in the mental dictionary.) Of particular importance are verbs. In order to see this, consider sentences **(36–38).**

(36) The girl met the man.

(37) The girl knew the man.

(38) The girl knew that the man was tall.

Sentences **(36)** and **(37)** have very similar structures, differing only in their verbs. The verb *know* is very different from the verb *met,* however, not just in terms of its meaning, but also in the kinds of sentence structures in which it can appear. Thus, *know* can have a simple NP direct object, as in **(37)**, and it can also have as its object an entire sentence, as in **(38)**. In **(38)**, for example, what the girl knows is not *the man,* but the entire proposition, *the man was tall.* But the verb *met* cannot appear in a sentence structure that is parallel to **(38)**, and so example **(39)** is clearly ungrammatical.

(39) *The girl met that the man was tall.

According to the strategy model, information stored with the verb *met* will indicate that this verb can go along with a simple direct object (i.e., the verb can have an NP as its object), but that it cannot have an entire underlying sentence as its object. On the other hand, information stored with the verb *know* will indicate that this verb can occur in both kinds of structures. Verbs of the latter sort, those that can appear in more than one kind of basic sentence structure, are considered to be more complex than verbs which can occur in only one structure.

The strategy model assumes that the listener gains access to information about the kinds of sentence structures in which the verb can appear. As a result, the listener is less certain about the kind of sentence structure he is hearing when the sentence contains the complex verb *know* than when it uses the simpler verb *met*. This aspect of the strategy model has been called the *Verb Complexity Hypothesis* (VCH). It predicts that a sentence like **(37)**, in which the verb allows two hypotheses about the structure that follows, requires more processing than one like **(36)**, the additional work being necessary to decide which structure is correct.

The Verb Complexity Hypothesis was proposed by Fodor, Garrett, and Bever (1968), and they and others have provided some evidence in its support. For example, Holmes and Forster (1972) showed their subjects sentences which contained either simple or complex verbs and asked them to recall each sentence after it was presented. The ten-word sentences were presented very rapidly, one word at a time, so that recall errors occurred. The average number of words recalled was 7.87 for the sentences which contained the simple verbs and 7.63 for the sentences that had the more complex verbs. Though small, this drop was statistically reliable and in the direction predicted by VCH.

Although the Holmes and Forster experiment obtained results that were consistent with VCH, the recall task is not a very direct measure of comprehension difficulty. A somewhat more direct test of VCH was carried out by Hakes (1971). He constructed sentences in which either a simple or a complex verb could occur, as in example **(40)**, and he asked his subjects to paraphrase the sentences and to monitor each for a target phoneme. Example **(40)** represents two sentences, one with the simple verb *suspended* and one with the complex verb *suspected*.

(40) The manager (suspended/suspected) the bookeeper when he discovered that $5000 was missing.

The target phoneme occurred either in the verb itself or in the next noun following it. The reasoning behind the monitoring task should be clear. If the complex verbs add to processing difficulty, then RTs to respond to the target phonemes should be longer for these verbs.

The results that Hakes obtained were mixed. On the one hand, he found that paraphrase accuracy was poorer after complex verbs than after simpler ones. On the other hand, he found no differences at all in the RT data. This was a somewhat surprising outcome, and one that gives little comfort to VCH proponents. The phoneme-monitoring task would seem to be a more direct measure of comprehension complexity than the paraphrase task. Hence, if VCH is true, positive results in the monitoring task should be expected. (However, we cannot be certain of this until we thoroughly understand the monitoring task.) Subsequently, Hakes carried out four more experiments testing VCH. It is relatively easy to summarize the results of all this work: RTs in the phoneme-monitoring task were never predicted by verb complexity, though the paraphrase data typically were affected by this variable. It seems fair to conclude, then, that the effect of verb complexity (and it does have an effect) may be one that does not occur *while* the sentence is being processed.

A second aspect of the strategy model has received stronger experimental support. Some words are useful in that the information which they convey restricts the possible sentence structures that contain them. Consider, for example, sentences **(41)** and **(42)**.

(41) The girl the man met was tall.

(42) The girl that the man met was tall.

At the beginning, sentence **(41)** is less informative; it might continue on to say, *The girl the man and the boy were tall.* In **(42)** the word *that* signals that *the man* is not the second of a string of NPs which share the same verb. It restricts the possible ways that the sentence can continue. According to the strategy theory, then, the listener knows that *that* operates in this way, that it restricts the relationships among the NPs in the sentence. Hence, when we hear a sentence like **(42)**, we are getting extra information as compared to when we hear **(41)**. As a result, we can figure out the underlying relationships among the phrases in the sentence more rapidly; **(42)** should be easier to comprehend than **(41)**.

Fodor and Garrett (1967) provided some evidence in support of this aspect of the strategy model, as did the present authors (Hakes & Foss, 1970). We reasoned that RT in the phoneme-monitoring task should be shorter in sentences which contained *that,* since comprehension would be aided by the presence of this cue word. The results supported this line of reasoning. Subsequently, Hakes (1972) conducted a test of the strategy model which used quite different materials, such as sentence **(43)**.

(43) The blind student felt (that) the material in the art course would be too difficult for him to understand.

Sentence **(43)** contains a verb, *felt,* which is complex in the sense that we discussed earlier. That is, *felt* may have either a simple NP direct object as in *felt the material,* or an entire proposition as its direct object as in **(43)**. If we omit the word *that* in sentence **(43)**, then it is momentarily unclear which type of sentence is being presented. That is, when presented with *The blind student felt the material* the listener cannot know whether the sentence's direct object is complete, or whether it will continue as it does in **(43)**. However, when the word *that* is presented immediately after the verb, then the listener knows that the sentence will not stop after a simple direct object; it must continue on in the manner of **(43)**. Hakes presented several sentences like **(43)**; in half of them he omitted the word *that,* and in the other half he included this word. The strategy model predicts that sentence comprehension should be easier in the case where the word *that* is included, as it provides a signal about the sentence structure. The subjects in the experiment were asked to paraphrase each sentence and to monitor for a target phoneme which occurred after the verb (e.g., the /m/ beginning *material* in **(43)**).

Hakes found that the word *that* had a strong effect on the time it took to respond to the target phoneme. As predicted, RTs were shorter when the cue word *that* was present in the sentence. He also observed some effect of the word *that* on paraphrase accuracy, though in this case the effect was a weak one. Taken together, the results of Hakes' experiments support this aspect of the strategy model. We have evidence that certain cue words like *that* aid in the comprehension of a variety of sentences.

So far we have examined only a few comprehension strategies. Each one has been based upon the information that is supposedly associated with the internal representation of words. Other sorts of strategies have been proposed. For example, Bever (1970) has stated a variety of strategies which, he conjectured, govern the operation of comprehension. He did not propose specific mechanisms by which these strategies were carried out; his first attempt was to state the strategies themselves. One example of the kind of strategy proposed by Bever is this: *The first N . . . V . . . (N) . . . word sequence is the main clause of the sentence unless the verb is marked as subordinate.* This says that listeners assume that the first verb they hear is going to be the verb of the main clause of the sentence. This assumption is changed if there are certain specific cue words that occur before the verb. One such cue word is *because*. This word signals that the first verb is not the main verb in sentences like *Because the food was gone, the dog bit the cat* (Bever, 1970, p. 294).

Bever listed over a dozen strategies in his 1970 paper. One problem with the list is that the relationships among the strategies are not very clear. For example, sometimes two separate strategies might be applicable to one sentence. In that case the order of application would have to be specified, and this was not done.

One interesting feature of the strategy model was pointed out by Bever himself (p. 294): "Note that such strategies capture generalizations which are not necessarily always true. That is, there are exceptions to every strategy—the validity of each strategy is that it holds for most cases." This property of the model predicts that certain kinds of sentences, those for which the generalizations do not hold, are very likely to be misunderstood. Sentence **(44)**, taken from Bever (1970), is one such sentence.

(44) The horse raced past the barn fell.

Listeners tend to interpret *the horse* as the subject of *raced* until they come to *fell.* Only then is it possible to discover that **(44)** has the same structure as sentence **(45)**.

(45) The horse that was raced past the barn fell.

The strategies proposed by Bever account for why **(44)** should be misunderstood and also for many of the sentences which children misunderstand. Since the set of strategies proposed is far from complete, it is not clear whether a strategy model will do as well in accounting for other misunderstood sentences.

The proposed strategies are not only incomplete, many of them are also vague. There have been numerous attempts to build more specific and precise models of comprehension processing which incorporate something like the concept of strategies. For example, Kaplan (1972, 1975) has explored the psychological implications of one model which has been stated precisely enough so that it has been implemented on a computer. Kaplan argues that many of Bever's strategies have been included in this system and that they have been clarified in the process. The development of such detailed strategy models is an important one, one which will almost certainly have an impact on our understanding of linguistic comprehension in the next few years. However, the outlines of an appropriate theory of strategies are still quite fuzzy. It seems highly likely that whatever model proves best, it will credit the listener with making a large contribution to his own comprehension.

Summary

The chapter began by discussing the nature of the problem of comprehension. We noted that understanding can occur at a number of different levels, structural, intentional, and motivational, the first of which has been the focus of our discussion. Only someone who has carried out the activities involved in constructing a structural representation of an utterance can understand it. The problem of comprehension will be solved when we can state the internal representations that are constructed by the listener as he hears an utterance, and when we can state the processes by which he constructs these representations.

The phonological processing mechanisms yield an output which is not complete. For example, the boundaries between words are not all marked, nor are all of the phonological segments identified. Stress and intonational information is present in the input, but this information is not fully reliable as a cue to the structural aspects of the utterance. The listener gains access to the information stored in his mental lexicon by using the phonological code, even though the code may not be complete. We noted that lexical access is a process that takes time (150-200 msec), and that it is influenced by word frequency or recency. The morphological structure of the words may also affect both lexical access and the segmentation of the utterance into words.

When the listener gains access to the information in the mental lexicon, he learns about the part of speech of the input word, the structures in which it can occur, and the types of words that it can occur with (e.g., *sleep* only occurs with certain types of subject nouns).

The comprehension processes operate rapidly upon the individual words and morphemes. Information about the exact sequence of words that is heard fades very quickly during the course of comprehension. The comprehension processes operate upon the words and build a structural representation of them. The evidence suggests that listeners do not skip this structural stage and go directly to the meaning of the sentence even when the semantic relationships among the words permits only a single interpretation of the utterance.

In the section on "Sentence structures in comprehension processing," we saw that the listener translates the input words into a structured representation. We reviewed studies which relied upon subjects' intuitive judgments and experiments using both the "click" method and the probe latency technique. We concluded that there is little evidence that both surface and underlying structures (as in transformational grammars) are extracted by the comprehension process.

Listeners typically perceive only one interpretation of an ambiguous sentence. We discussed the role of context on the processing of ambiguity and touched upon some models of the process.

Two general theories of comprehension were discussed. The first relies heavily upon the organization of transformational grammar. According to this model, listeners construct a surface structure of the input and then "de-transform" it to construct the underlying structure of the sentence. We concluded that there was little support for this model.

We called the second approach the strategy model. According to this approach, the listener has a stored set of strategies that he applies to the input in order to determine its structure. Many of these strategies are triggered by information that is associated with lexical items. The studies that we reviewed gave support to some of these lexical strategies, but not to all of them. We also saw that some of the strategies can account for miscomprehension as well as for comprehension. Comprehension models are still in their infancy.

SUGGESTED READINGS

The role of stress in comprehension is further discussed by Cutler (1976), while many of the issues involved in lexical access are described by Forster

(1976). The topic of short-term memory is covered by Wanner (1974). Many of the issues involved in the click studies, as well as others covered in the present chapter, are discussed in greater detail by Fodor, Bever, and Garrett (1974).

Readers should also note that the issues of comprehension (and memory) are regularly discussed in such journals as the *Journal of Verbal Learning and Verbal Behavior, Cognitive Psychology, Cognition, Journal of Experimental Psychology: Human Perception and Performance, Memory & Cognition,* and *Perception & Psychophysics.*

5

Memory
and Comprehension

Ever since 1885, when Hermann Ebbinghaus first published his investigations of forgetting, the study of memory has been an area of active interest to psychology. Ebbinghaus and many other theorists in the succeeding years studied the memory for nonsense materials; they did not want their results "contaminated" by the structures of language. Today, students of memory are intensely interested in memory for structured material of all sorts, particularly linguistic materials. More specifically, they are interested both in how we represent the units (e.g., words) that are used by the comprehension mechanisms, and in how we represent the products of comprehension (e.g., sentences). In addition, many theorists are concerned with the manner in which the comprehension processes themselves are stored in our memories. For example, if one thinks that sentence comprehension involves the use of strategies, then one should specify the form in which these strategies are stored in memory.

The connection between models of processing and those of memory is an intimate one. As we noted earlier, assumptions about the nature of memory—including those about the form in which linguistic units are stored—have large implications for comprehension processing models. The processor must make use of the units that are stored in the memory system. Because of this close relationship the topics of comprehension and memory cannot be sharply separated. In this chapter we focus our attention upon memory issues, but we will also be frequently discussing comprehension. In addition, both of these topics will call our attention to the closely related problems of inference making.

In the previous chapter we said that listeners "calculate" their own mental representation of input sentences, that they are involved in constructing their own perceptions. We also talked about some factors, mostly linguistic ones, that are involved in such calculations. In the present chapter we will continue to focus on the activity of the language user as we discuss memory. The listener is not a passive recipient of information who simply stores it like a recorded tape or an exposed photographic film. Such analogies with human memory are grossly misleading. (The fast decay of surface information that we discussed in the previous chapter is already strong proof against the photographic memory analogy.) We assume instead that what gets stored in memory depends, to a certain extent, upon the information already there and upon the mental activities that the listener carries out at the time of comprehension. We will elaborate upon this idea later.

In the present chapter we will discuss (again) the storage code, the manner in which a sentence (more accurately, the information conveyed by it) is stored in memory. We will also discuss how the information conveyed by a sentence interacts with information already in the listener's memory, and how it interacts with other information that has occurred in the conversation (the role of context). The mental code in which certain linguistic units are stored will also be touched upon. For example, the question of how morphemes (or words) are represented in memory will be taken up again. Before we attempt to say more about the representation of sentences in memory, however, it may be useful to ask what the representation is for. That is, knowing some of the functions served by the mental representations of sentences may help us to characterize these representations correctly.

Sentences and Mental Logic

Among the most important functions of understanding is that of supporting inferences. Thus, from comprehending and believing one sentence we are able to make inferences concerning the truth or falsity of many others. Sentences are generally not treated as isolated bits of information. One new sentence may have very important implications for our system of knowledge; it may change our picture of the world in a drastic way.

To take a simple example, imagine that someone truthfully says sentence (1) to you. As a speaker of English you will then be able to determine the truth of sentence (2); you will be able to infer that (2) is also true.

(1) John sold the car to Debbie.

(2) John no longer owns the car.

On the other hand, you cannot decide anything about the truth of (3), given that sentence (1) is true.

(3) Debbie owns a book.

Sentence (1) does not bear on sentence (3) in anything like the same way that it bears on (2). From information concerning the selling of X we can infer information about the ownership of X, but not the ownership of Y. Likewise, from sentence (1) we can infer the truth of sentence (4).

(4) John and Debbie transacted some business together.

Sentence (4) is quite different from (2) in terms of content, yet both follow from the truth of (1).

By saying that (2) and (4) both follow from (1) we do not want to give the impression that the listener always makes such inferences at the time of understanding (1). In order to understand (1), it is not necessary that representations of (2) and (4) arise in the mind of the listener. The point is that the listener, by virtue of understanding (1), has built a mental representation which *permits* him to make inferences of this sort. He is able to carry out such mental logic, and our theory of how sentences are represented must also permit this to occur. Of course, a complete theory would also have to provide the inference rules that are actually used. The "psychologically real" inference rules are not necessarily those that are logically correct (e.g., Henle, 1962). People often make logically faulty inferences.

In Chapter 4 we discussed some of the information that is stored with each verb in the mental lexicon (e.g., which sentence structures the verb can fit into). Note that the inferences that are permitted from sentence (1) depend upon the verb in that sentence, among other things. If we change the verb, we change the set of inferences that one can appropriately draw from the sentence. Therefore, we must expand our view of what information is stored with the verbs in the mental lexicon. In particular, we will say that information about the kinds of inferences that are permitted is associated with the verbs. Much of this information is of a highly systematic nature. For example, consider the verb *outweighs*. This verb is transitive, but in a somewhat different sense than we used in Chapter 4. In this context we are using transitive in its mathematical sense. The symbol ">" (is greater than) is one that expresses a transitive relation. If $a > b$, and if $b > c$, then it follows that $a > c$. The verb *outweighs* (and others) permits a similar inference. If (5) and (6) are true, then so is (7).

(5) Jerry outweighs Tom.
(6) Tom outweighs Merrill.
(7) Jerry outweighs Merrill.

On the other hand, the verb *helped* (among others) does not permit such inferences; it is not transitive in this sense. If we know that (8) and (9) are true, we cannot conclude anything about the truth of (10).

(8) Jerry helped Tom.

(9) Tom helped Merrill.

(10) Jerry helped Merrill.

The mental lexicon must contain information specifying whether the verb is transitive or not. For the present we are not concerned with the manner in which this information is represented; we simply want to note that it must be there.

Let us look at one more example. From the truth of sentence **(11)** we can infer the truth of sentence **(12)**.

(11) The chicken is ready to eat.

(12) The chicken has been cooked.

So far, so good. Note, however, that if we interpret sentence **(11)** in a different way it permits an inference to sentence **(13)**.

(13) The chicken is hungry.

Sentence **(11)** has two separate interpretations; it is ambiguous. The two interpretations are quite different from one another, and they therefore permit different sets of inferences to be made (essentially that is what we mean when we say that the sentence has two separate interpretations). We cannot infer the truth of **(13)** from the truth of **(12)**. The importance of examples like **(11)** is this: the set of inferences that follows from a sentence depends upon the meaning of the sentence and not upon its surface form. This observation supports the conclusion we came to in Chapter 2; namely, that the surface form is not an appropriate way in which to characterize the mental representation of a sentence. We cannot just directly translate the words, or their order, or even the entire surface structure of a sentence into some mental representation and consider that to be the code into which sentences are translated when they are understood. Instead, we must suppose that the representation of a sentence includes information about the underlying relations that it expresses.

Models of Memory Representation

The information conveyed by a single sentence gets much of its importance from its relationship with other information possessed by the listener. This fact has one simple but very important implication, namely, that the code in which sentence information is stored must be compatible with the way in which the rest of our knowledge is represented. That is, the linguistic information must be represented in such a way as to make contact with information that is not linguistic. For example, if you are asked whether a certain odor smells like coffee, you can answer the question. The memory representation for the odor of coffee is not linguistic (such sensory qualities are notoriously hard to describe in words), but the question itself is obviously formed via language. Hence linguistic and non-linguistic information must be able to interact. It is often suggested that there is an abstract mental code (not equal to language) into which both linguistic and non-linguistic information is translated.

Imagery

A number of candidate codes have been offered as the universal code—the one in which all kinds of information from numerous sources (such as vision, language, etc.) is stored. One such code is that of imagery. What is meant by the term "image" is usually a hypothesized internal representation which corresponds to some external object in a one-to-one relationship. That is, for each significant point of the external object there will be a corresponding point in the internal representation. This does not mean that the image itself (in its neurological code) concretely resembles the external object. To make an analogy, when pictures are transmitted to earth from a space satellite they are coded into radio pulses. The pulses do not resemble the photograph; but they are, in our sense, an image, since there is a direct correspondence between each segment of the photograph and some segment of the radio signal.[1]

Paivio (1971), Shepard and Chipman (1971), and others have made "image" a respectable term in psychology, showing that a concept of image can be used in trying to explain a number of memory phenomena. For example, Shepard and his associates (e.g., Metzler & Shepard, 1974) have shown that the internal representation of three-dimensional objects can, at least in some circumstances, be adequately represented as an image.

Many people will say that they store linguistic information in an image-like form. That is, they use linguistic information to construct an image bearing a one-to-one relationship to the situation that is being described. The image is then stored in their memory. Such reports are not convincing, however. We don't doubt that one can form an image of an event that was only linguistically described. But note that it is possible that the information is stored in some other format which, in turn, permits an image to be generated from it. That is, just as we can generate a visual image of a scene when it is described in words and not presented pictorially, so too we might construct images from the information that is stored in our memories even if the storage code is not itself an image. This suggests that we can construct an image which is both consistent with the information stored in memory and, at the same time, inconsistent with aspects of the original situation that gave rise to the memory representation.

A number of facts argue against the notion that images are the form in which linguistic information is coded. The arguments have been discussed in some detail by Pylyshyn (1973), and we will not review them all here. To take just one example, Pylyshyn notes that when an image we construct is incom-

---

[1]We have used the term "image" here to mean visual image, although this is not a necessary interpretation of the term. We do not think that this simplification oversimplifies the issues under discussion.

plete, it is always missing some structured or wholistic information, not just some arbitrary part. For example, when imaging the last party we went to, we might forget to include some of the people who were there, or where they were standing, or what they were wearing. Our image in this case would be missing something significant, not at all comparable to missing, say, the upper left hand corner of an old torn photograph. Pylyshyn's arguments suggest that we store the information we obtain from sentences not as images but in some other form.

Sentence Representation: Underlying Structure and Beyond

If we assume that the information conveyed by a sentence is not stored as images, then one alternative is that it is stored in a form analogous to the underlying structure of the sentence. According to this hypothesis, the propositions that are expressed by the sentence (and the relations between them) are each explicitly represented in the listener's memory system. Some theorists in fact have proposed that the underlying structures of sentences are stored in long-term memory. They have suggested, in other words, that the underlying structure representation itself is identical with or similar to the form in which the information expressed by sentences is stored in memory. This is a reasonable first guess, for the underlying representation of a complex sentence does break the sentence down into its constituent sentences, and these might be said to represent the propositions it expresses.

Wanner (1974) is one of the investigators who has suggested that sentences are stored in a form similar to their underlying structure. Wanner ignored many of the details of the linguistic structures of sentences and focused upon the *number* of propositions that the sentences expressed. He tried to show that the number of propositions that are expressed by a sentence, and the relations among them, are coded into the listener's long-term memory. In order to test this hypothesis, Wanner presented sentences like **(14)** and **(15)** to his subjects and later asked the subjects to recall them.

(14) The governor asked the detective to cease drinking.

(15) The governor asked the detective to prevent drinking.

Although sentences **(14)** and **(15)** are superficially quite similar, they differ in the underlying relationships that they are expressing. Wanner made use of this fact to make his predictions about sentence recall. According to Wanner's analysis, both **(14)** and **(15)** express three underlying propositions. To a close approximation, these are:

(14a) The governor asked the detective something.

(14b) The detective ceased something.

(14c) The detective drinks.

(15a) The governor asked the detective something.

(15b) The detective prevented something.

(15c) Someone drinks.

The important thing to note is that in sentence **(14)** it is the detective who is doing the drinking, while in **(15)** it is someone else (unspecified) who is imbibing. The word *detective,* which occurs in all three of the propositions underlying sentence **(14),** occurs in only two of the three propositions underlying **(15).**

Wanner reasoned that the word *detective* would be a better recall aid for sentence **(14)** than for sentence **(15)** because this word occurs in more of the underlying propositions of the former sentence. He assumed, in other words, that the effectiveness of a recall aid or prompt word would be directly related to the number of propositions in which the prompt word occurred. Therefore, he gave his subjects the word *detective* as a prompt or recall cue and tested to see whether it was more effective in stimulating recall of **(14)** than of **(15).**

Although Wanner's results were not absolutely clear-cut, he did find evidence that the effectiveness of the prompt word was greater in sentences like **(14)** than in those like **(15).** Wanner cautiously concluded that the more propositions a prompt word is involved in, the greater the effectiveness of that word as a prompt. This conclusion is consistent with the view that the underlying propositions of a sentence are stored in memory, even if all of the details of its underlying structure are not.

Even before Wanner's results were published (they had been circulating in an unpublished form for some time), Lesgold (1972) provided some evidence that the number of propositions in which a prompt word occurs is not the only predictor of the effectiveness of that prompt word, that other factors can more strongly influence prompt effectiveness. Lesgold presented sentences like **(16)** and **(17)** to his listeners and then gave them a prompted recall test.

(16) The aunt ate the pie and she was senile.

(17) The aunt ate the pie and Alice was senile.

According to Lesgold, each of the two example sentences contains two propositions, one on either side of the conjunction. The word *ate* is involved in one of these propositions in each of the two sentences. When Lesgold used this word as a prompt in the recall test, it was more effective for sentences like **(16)** than for sentences like **(17).** Subjects were able to recall 57% of the total sentences in the former case and only 34% in the latter.

Lesgold argued that the pronoun in **(16)** causes its two propositions to be integrated in the memory of the hearer. This claim certainly makes sense; the pronoun *she* in **(16)** stands for the NP *the aunt.* That NP is therefore represented in both of the sentences underlying **(16).** As a result, when one retrieves a part of **(16)** the information expressed by both propositions is likely to be retrieved. On the other hand, the two propositions in **(17)** are, as far as we can tell without further context, independent of one another; the listener does not have a tendency to integrate these two into one memory representation. Lesgold's results demonstrate that a prompt's effectiveness is determined more by the relationships among the underlying sentences than by their sheer number. Nevertheless, these results are still compatible with the view that what is stored in memory are the underlying propositions expressed by the sentence.

Further work on sentence memory, however, has called the above viewpoint into question. These studies suggest that the eventual memory representation of a sentence or set of sentences is not well characterized by its underlying structures. Some of the relevant research was carried out by Bransford and Franks (1971; Franks & Bransford, 1972). They presented a set of sentences to subjects and asked them to answer questions about each sentence. For example, they presented *The ants in the kitchen ate the jelly,* and then asked, *Did what?* Subjects were to respond by answering the question. A set of sentences on the same topic was presented to the subjects (see Table 5.1), although other sentences on three other topics were also intermixed with these. Take a moment to read each sentence in Table 5.1 and to answer the question after it.

Following this acquisition phase of the experiment, the subjects were given a recognition test (see Table 5.2) in which they were shown some old sentences and some new ones. The subjects were asked to say which were old and which were new and to state how confident they were in these judgments. Can you tell, without looking back at Table 5.1, which of the sentences in Table 5.2 are new?

The subjects in Bransford and Franks' experiments could not, in general, tell which sentences were old and which were new. As long as the sentences were on the same topic and were consistent with the information they had heard, the subjects were poor at discriminating old sentences from new ones.

There is one other aspect of Bransford and Franks' results that is of interest. The last sentence in Table 5.2 contains all of the information conveyed by the others. It can be broken down into four propositions: The ants were in the kitchen, The ants ate the jelly, The jelly was on the table, and The jelly was sweet. Some of the test sentences (e.g., *The jelly was sweet*) expressed just one of the four propositions (call them ONES). Other test sentences (e.g., *The sweet jelly was on the table*) expressed two of the propositions (TWOS), still others

Table 5.1

Sentences Presented During the Acquisition Phase of the Experiment

The ants ate the sweet jelly which was on the table.	Did what?
The ants were in the kitchen.	Who was?
The ants ate the sweet jelly.	What jelly?
The jelly was on the table.	Was where?
The ants in the kitchen ate the jelly which was on the table.	Ate what?
The ants in the kitchen ate the jelly.	Where were they?

Table 5.2

Test Sentences Presented for Recognition

1. The ants in the kitchen ate the sweet jelly.
2. The ants ate the sweet jelly.
3. The jelly was sweet.
4. The sweet jelly was on the table.
5. The ants were in the kitchen.
6. The ants ate the jelly which was on the table.
7. The ants in the kitchen ate the jelly which was on the table.
8. The ants in the kitchen ate the sweet jelly which was on the table.

(The second, fifth, and seventh sentences are old; the rest are new)

expressed three of them (THREES). The last test sentence of Table 5.2 is the FOUR, as it incorporates all four of the underlying propositions. Bransford and Franks found that the more propositions a test sentence contained, the more likely subjects were to say that it was old (that is, that they had seen it during the acquisition phase of the experiment). Thus, although the FOUR was *not* presented during the acquisition phase of the experiment, it was the sentence that the subjects were most confident that they had seen before. The results are shown in Figure 5.1. The recognition scores do not differ between the old and new sentences, but they do differ between the FOUR, THREES, TWOS, and ONES. The authors concluded that "Individual sentences lost their unique status in memory in favor of a more wholistic representation of semantic events" (1971, p. 348).

In Chapter 4 we saw that the surface form of sentences is not represented for long in the listener's memory. The Bransford and Franks findings argue that the underlying structure of sentences has a similar fate. While the listener may construct the underlying representation of an individual sentence, it is soon lost. The information conveyed by individual sentences contributes to a larger, more integrated mental representation of the event described. The subjects use this latter structure when they make their judgments about whether test sentences are old or new.

In a related study, Barclay (1973) presented listeners with sentences like the following: *The lion is to the left of the bear, The moose is to the right of the bear,* etc. The set of sentences expressed the positional relationships among five animals standing in a row: *lion, bear, moose, giraffe,* and *cow.* During the acquisition phase of the experiment some, but not all, of the possible sentences expressing the left-to-right relationships were presented to the subjects. The subjects were told simply to understand the sentences and to get a mental image of the information conveyed by them. They were not told that there would be a recognition test. During the test phase of the experiment some old and some new sentences were presented, and the subjects were asked to tell which were old and which were new. Among the new sentences were some that correctly expressed the left-to-right relationships (e.g., *The bear is to the right of the lion*)

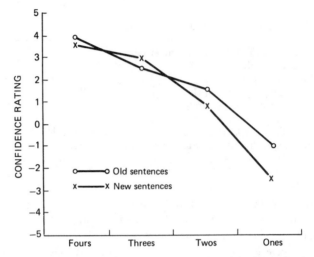

Figure 5.1. Recognition scores for the sentences used by Bransford and Franks. Positive scores indicate that the sentence was recognized as "old." (From Bransford, J. D. & Franks, J. J. The abstraction of linguistic ideas. *Cognitive Psychology,* 1971, *2,* 331–350. Copyright 1971 by Academic Press, Inc. Used with permission.)

and some that incorrectly expressed these relations (e.g., *The bear is to the left of the lion*).

The results of Barclay's experiments showed that the subjects could not tell the difference between old and new sentences which correctly expressed the left-to-right relationships in the line of animals. On the other hand, the subjects were very good at saying that a sentence was new if it expressed a relationship that was incorrect. Barclay summarized his results as follows, "Thus, in the recognition tasks subjects drew a sharp line only between true and false sentences thinking they were distinguishing old from new" (1973, p. 251). What this means is that the memory representation incorporated information about the left-to-right relationships among the animals in the array; it did not incorporate information about the underlying structure of the particular sentences from which the subjects learned about the array. This is not to say that the listeners didn't figure out the underlying structure relationships for each sentence that they heard: they must have. But such information is not stored for long in the memory systems of the listeners. If the underlying structure is computed, it is used to construct a mental representation in a somewhat different code and is then discarded.

Propositional Models of Sentence Memory

Historically, most theories of memory assumed that one can describe the memory system in terms of associations among either mental elements ("ideas") or more objective elements such as stimuli and responses. Furthermore, the associations between two elements were thought to be the result of a few basic principles, most of which were set out by Aristotle. For example, one principle of associationism was that two elements would become associated if they occurred together in space and time. Another said that two items would be associated if they were "similar" to one another; a third stated that an association between elements occurred if one was the cause and the other the effect. Up to the twentieth century only a few other principles were proposed. Complex thinking or complex responding was typically viewed as being constructed out of chains of simpler associations. Reviews of this "classical" tradition can be found in Humphrey (1963) and Mandler and Mandler (1964).

Present memory theorists differ from classical associationists in a number of ways. They assume that the relations among elements in memory are considerably more complex than the "chain of ideas" concept of the classical theorists. In addition, they do not restrict the relations among the mental elements in the way that older theorists did. Many recent theories permit (indeed, require) new relationships among mental elements within the memory system. For example, one item (concept) may be associated with another by the relationship of *agency* (e.g., in *The man opened the door,* the concept expressed by *man* is the agent of *opened*), or by something similar. Different theorists propose different sets of basic relationships by which concepts can be tied together in memory.

Let us entertain the idea, then, that part of our knowledge is represented in terms of concepts (we introduced this notion in Chapter 2). Concepts are theoretical terms; they are abstractions that specify important, meaningful information. Both English speakers and French speakers probably have some highly similar concepts—for example, they will share the concept expressed by the word *book* in English and by the French word *livre*. The concept is distinguishable from the linguistic term or phrase used to express it.

A *proposition* is an abstraction that specifies relations among concepts. For example, the phrase *to the left of* expresses the relation between two concepts in the sentence, *The lion is to the left of the bear.* Some propositions involve relations among more than two concepts (this happens in the sentence *The man hit the nail with a hammer*) and some involve specifying a property of a concept (e.g., *The book is red*). The same proposition can be expressed in many ways: *The book is red, Le livre est rouge, Red is the color of the book,* etc. Armed with the notion of propositions we can make a distinction between a sentence and the proposition that the sentence expresses. It is propositions that have truth values (are true or false) and that can be used in making inferences.

There are a large number of propositionally oriented models which attempt to characterize our memory for sentences and the way that information in memory is retrieved. It would take a book to survey this topic alone. We will look at some aspects of a few such models without examining any of them in detail. Our aim here is to introduce the assumptions behind some of the present models and to state some of their virtues and faults. The work that we are referring to has been carried out by Anderson and Bower (1973), Norman and Rumelhart (1975), Frederiksen (1975), Kintsch (1974), and others.

Propositional theories hypothesize that memory consists of a set of interconnected propositions, each of which consists of a set of concepts and the relationships among them. To get a feel for this kind of system, look at Figure 5.2. In it we have represented the proposition that corresponds to the sentence, *The boy hit the landlord.*

The diagram expresses the fact that a certain relation holds between the boy and the landlord, namely that of hitting. Furthermore, it shows that the boy is the agent and the landlord the object of the action. There are many ways in which we can diagram this relationship, so one shouldn't take too seriously the particular diagram used here. But a few features of the diagram are notable. The term boy appears twice, once as *boy* and once as BOY. Likewise landlord and hit also occur twice. The sentence *The boy hit the landlord* is used to express a relationship among a certain boy, a certain landlord, and a certain act of hitting. The representation of the particular event is given by the filled circles or nodes of the figure and by the italicized words. The particular boy is a member of the class of boys, of course. This information is expressed by the relation *is.* The boy *is* a member of the class of boys.

Information about boys in general will be found associated with the unfilled circle labeled BOY. In other words, information about the concept boy is stored only once in the memory system. Each time the word *boy* appears in any given sentence, a relation between that particular occurrence of the word and the concept BOY will be established. The distinction between a concept and any particular instance of it is sometimes called the type-token distinction. The particular boy is a token of the type BOY. The information that is associated with the concept is available for interpreting the sentence further, e.g., for making inferences. Thus in Figure 5.3 we see expressed the information that a boy is a human, as is a landlord; that both are male; that hitting is a physical act, etc. From the truth of *The boy hit the landlord,* we could infer the truth of *A human hit a human.* As you can already see from Figure 5.3, networks of interrelationships among concepts can get very big and complex very quickly. Trying to add, say, 100 verbs and 500 nouns to the system would make it very formidible in-

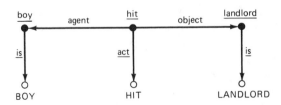

Figure 5.2. A propositional representation of a simple sentence.

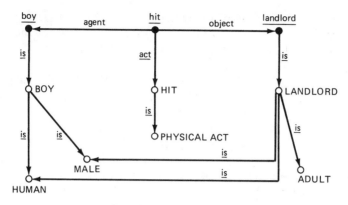

Figure 5.3. A propositional network for a simple sentence.

deed. (We should note, then, that the example networks given here are quite primitive and incomplete.)

According to the propositional theorists, when a subject comprehends a sentence he constructs a propositional representation such as the ones shown in Figures 5.2 and 5.3, and these propositional representations are integrated into his overall network of propositions (i.e., into his memory). Another aspect of some propositional memory models (e.g., Norman & Rumelhart, 1975) is shown in Figure 5.4. That figure is meant to represent the sentence *The quarterback threw the ball.* The propositional representation breaks down terms like *threw* into what may be their conceptual parts. Thus, the diagram expresses the notion that to throw something is to cause it to change from one location to another.

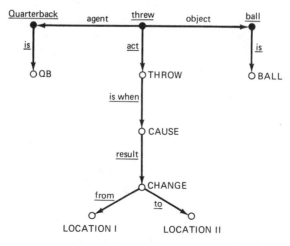

Figure 5.4. A network representation showing some conceptual components of *throw.*

So underlying the concept of *throw* is a set of more primitive concepts such as *cause, location,* etc. These representations can get quite complex and, if they are to be complete, essentially would be stating the basic semantic atoms and their relationships.

As we have indicated, propositional theories result in complicated conceptual networks. A simple model will not be able to do the job. How do we know that the theorists who are building such models are not constructing skyscrapers without foundations? This is a problem that the theorists care about. They want to construct theories which correspond to the structure of knowledge possessed by speakers of human languages. However, such complex theories tend to be very difficult to test because an experimenter must typically make dozens of assumptions about how the system will perform in any particular circumstance. If the model does not stand up to the test, we don't know if the entire model is wrong or merely some of those assumptions.

Tests of Propositional Models. There are, however, some experiments in the literature that attempt to test some important aspects of network models. For example, Kintsch (1972) proposed a model of memory for sentences in which their representations are constructed from propositional building blocks. In one test of his theory, Kintsch and Keenan (1973) constructed sentences that were of approximately equal length in words but which differed in the number of propositions they expressed. Kintsch and Keenan hypothesized that sentence **(18)** contained four propositions, while **(19)** contained eight. In one experimental task, Kintsch and Keenan had their subjects read such sentences at their own rate and then, after each one, give a written recall of it. The experimenters measured both recall accuracy and the amount of time that the subjects spent reading each sentence.

(18) Romulus, the legendary founder of Rome, took the women of the Sabine by force.

(19) Cleopatra's downfall lay in her foolish trust in the fickle political figures of the Roman world.

Kintsch and Keenan found that their subjects' reading time increased as the number of propositions contained in the sentence went up. For each additional proposition, approximately one second was added to the reading time. Thus, **(18)** took about four seconds less to read than did **(19)**. These times reflect both the time required to comprehend the sentences and the time required to store them in memory. Kintsch and Keenan felt that this result and others like it strongly support the idea that semantic memory is based upon propositions.

While the above results are certainly consistent with the theory, they do not provide compelling support for it. For one thing, Kintsch and Keenan did not provide a procedure for deciding how many propositions are contained in any sentence. Without such a procedure, we cannot be sure that they have correctly counted the propositions. What is required is a system of parsing a sentence which results in the correct propositional representation, and it is just this that was not provided. Another difficulty with the experiment is that the task puts a premium upon accurately recalling the sentences. To accomplish this the subjects almost certainly adopted the strategy of holding onto the surface structure information as well as the propositional or semantic information. So, since the sentences with many propositions differed syntactically from those with only a few propositions, this syntactic difference could account for much of time difference recorded in the data.

In other tests of the propositional view of memory, Anderson (1974) and Lewis and Anderson (1976) had their subjects learn varying numbers of "facts" about individuals; for example, *A hippie is in the park, A hippie touched the debutante,* etc. The subjects were then presented test sentences and asked whether or not each was one that they had learned earlier. The time it took to make these decisions was measured. The RT to decide about a sentence containing *hippie* depended upon how many propositions about the hippie had been acquired in the earlier phase of the experiment. More propositions led to slower decision times. Anderson argued that in order to answer the question the subject searched the information that is stored with the concept HIPPIE. As more propositions are stored with that concept, the time that it takes to answer a question about it goes up. Thus, the RT results are consistent with the view that the information extracted from sentences is stored in terms of propositions.

Although the above results are consistent with the propositional view of memory, there is one aspect of them and of Anderson's theory that is troubling. If it is correct that the more one knows about a concept the longer it takes to answer an inquiry about it, then this suggests that **(20)** should take longer to answer than **(21)**.

(20) Are you the President of the U.S.?

(21) Is Chomsky the President of the U.S.?

It seems unlikely that answering a question about yourself (about whom you must know tens of thousands of propositions) would take longer than answering a comparable question about someone about whom you only know a few propositions. Thus, although the results of the studies were quite impressive, it is not clear that they will generalize to knowledge about real world events.

Another aspect of some propositional theories (e.g., Anderson & Bower, 1973; Norman & Rumelhart, 1975) that is worth looking at concerns the assumptions that the memory representation for a sentence includes the conceptual components of the lexical items as in Figure 5.4. Anderson and Bower (1973, p. 159) state that sentence **(22)** is stored in memory as **(23)**.

(22) John gave a book to Mary.

(23) John transferred a book causing Mary to possess it.

Breaking down complex concepts (like *give*) into their components suggests that the memory representation for sentence **(24)** is very complex compared to that of a superficially similar sentence like **(25)**.

(24) John gave Mary a book.

(25) John gave Mary a headache.

Example (25) might be represented by the conceptual components of (26); but clearly (25) does not involve the verb *transfer.* Nothing is transferred when John gives someone a headache.

(26) John caused Mary to have a headache.

The existing evidence that bears on this problem (e.g., Kintsch, 1974) suggests that sentences like (24) are not more difficult to comprehend and store than ones like (25). Therefore, this aspect of the model has not received support.

So far we have seen that propositional theories of semantic memory have their strong points, but that they are far from worked out. For one thing, the procedures for translating the input into propositional representations are not complete. In addition, the idea that words are decomposed into their components has little support in the literature. And finally, many problems of representation remain to be solved. One of the aims of propositionally based theories of semantic memory is to represent the meaning of sentences in a psychologically valid way. This is hard to do. It is even difficult to grasp the concept of "meaning" since, to quote Woods (1977, p. 770), "you can never present the meaning of a sentence on a silver platter—all you can ever produce is various representations of it. The meaning itself is something abstract and nebulous . . ." What we want to do, of course, is to find a representation of meaning that captures our everyday intuitions about it and that also has psychological validity.

Procedural Models

One alternative to the propositional representation of sentences is what has been called a *procedural* representation. According to this approach, at least some of our knowledge is in the form of procedures—instructions for carrying out certain activities. These activities can themselves be mental; they need not be overt and directly observable. The distinction between propositional and procedural knowledge can be introduced by a distinction between "knowing that" and "knowing how" (e.g., Winograd, 1975). We know *that* Tirana is the capital of Albania (a proposition); we know *how* to tie our shoes (a procedure). Thus, some of our knowledge may consist of a set of procedures that we have acquired for carrying out certain activities. For example, adults can quickly decide whether 807 is larger than 328. They do not make this decision by inspecting a stored list of propositions but by applying some procedures to the information about numbers that is stored in their memories.

In order to understand the question posed in (27), the listener need not, of course, actually come up with the answer to the question.

(27) Is 807 larger than 328?

Understanding a question occurs prior to the attempt at answering it. Therefore, in order to understand the question, the listener need not actually apply the appropriate procedures for answering it to his stored information about numbers. Instead, the listener can be said to understand the question when he activates the procedures (gets them ready to be applied). According to this point of view, then, the representation of sentence (27) is in terms of the actions or procedures that could be applied in trying to answer it. Whether or not those procedures are in fact applied is a separate decision. The sentence's meaning is represented as a set of procedures, independent of whether they are actually carried out.

Procedural models of sentence representation are closely related to some of the semantic issues that we briefly discussed in Chapter 2. Recall that one problem in the study of semantics involves the relationship between linguistic objects (words, morphemes, sentences) and the things to which they refer. From a more psychological perspective, this problem has to do with the relationship between our representation of words and sentences and our representation of the world. In order to see the relevance of the procedural approach to this relationship, we need to be aware that the meaning of a declarative sentence is also closely related to the concept of *truth*. To understand this, consider how we can tell whether or not someone knows the meaning of sentence (28).

(28) The cat is on the mat.

One simple test is this: the individual can be said to know the meaning of (28) if he says that it is true when the cat is in fact on the mat, and that it is false otherwise. If someone cannot accurately make such judgments (e.g., he says that (28) is true when, in fact, the cat is under the mat), we do not credit him with knowing the meaning of (28).

Let us translate the above remarks into the procedural framework. First, we assume that the listener has some representation of the situation. That is, he has the perceptual information about the cat and the mat, and about which is on top, represented in his cognitive system (the form of the representation does not concern us here). When presented with (28), the listener activates or makes ready a set of procedures that he can apply to the perceptual representation. If actually applied, these procedures will tell the listener that the sentence is true if the cat is on the mat. If it is not true, if instead the cat is under the mat, then the procedures will say that sentence (28) is false. The procedures need not be actually applied to the perceptual representation for the listener to understand the sentence. All that is necessary is that the listener has in principle the ability to tell, for any possible perceptual situation, whether the cat is on the mat.

To summarize, according to the procedural approach (sometimes referred to as procedural semantics), the representation of a sentence in memory is in terms of a set of procedures. For questions, the procedures specify a way of trying to answer the question. For declarative sentences, the procedures specify a way of determining whether the sentence is true, relative to some perceptual or cognitive state of affairs. Furthermore, the procedure is applicable, in principle, to any possible state of affairs.

There are some existing computer programs which attempt to "converse" in English. To do so they must represent the meaning of the sentences that are given to them. Some of the most successful of these programs use a procedural approach (e.g., Woods, Kaplan, & Nash-Weber, 1972). A few psychologists have also adopted this approach, or a variant of it. Suppes (1974) has addressed these issues, and Anderson (1976) provides a review of some of the work. (Anderson's model uses both propositional and procedural representations.) Miller and Johnson-Laird (1976) have used these ideas extensively. Discussing any of these attempts in detail is beyond our present scope; they have not yet had much influence upon experimental work.

Some Effects of General Knowledge on Comprehension and Representation

We have now looked at some evidence which argues that listeners integrate information from a number of sentences into an abstract representation (e.g., Bransford & Franks, 1971). Furthermore, we have seen that the representation does not preserve the underlying structures of the particular sentences that conveyed the information. Now we will examine some evidence which suggests that both the comprehension process itself and the memory representation that results from it are affected by other knowledge possessed by the listener.

Memory Affects Comprehension

The process of comprehension itself may be affected by the memory structures that are active when the sentence is being processed. In other words, not only does comprehension change the memory representation, but the existing memory representation can also affect the course of comprehension. One casual observation consistent with this notion is the fact that ambiguous sentences are rarely perceived as ambiguous by the listener. When the topic of conversation is the psychology of language, then the word *sentence* is interpreted as a linguistic object and not as a jail term.

Another example (Winograd, 1972) which points out the influence of our general knowledge on comprehension is given in (29–30).

(29) The city council refused the women a parade permit because they feared violence.

(30) The city council refused the women a parade permit because they advocated violence.

In **(29)** everyone interprets the pronoun *they* as referring to the city council while in **(30)** *they* apparently refers to the women. This difference arises because of what we know about city councils, not because of some linguistic rule for interpreting pronouns.

Dooling and Lachman (1971) devised a clever demonstration of the fact that activating the appropriate information in memory is necessary for good comprehension. They had subjects read a prose passage such as that shown in Table 5.3. The subjects were informed that they were in a memory experiment and that they would be given a recall test. The subjects were asked to write down all of the words that they could remember after reading the passage once. You should now read the passage in Table 5.3 through once at your normal reading rate.

As you probably noted, it is very difficult to make sense of the passage on one quick reading. How much of it can you recall? Now re-read the passage, but this time we will give it a title. It is called "Christopher Columbus Discovering America." You will probably have quite a different response to the passage now. Whereas the first time you were probably quite confused, now you readily understand the paragraph. In the Dooling and Lachman experiment some of the subjects were given the thematic title before they read the passage the first time, while others were not. The recall scores were significantly better for those who had been given the title before they read the passage. Bransford and Johnson (1972) conducted a similar experiment with similar results. The latter investigators included a third condition, however, one in which the subjects were given the title of the passage after they had heard it but before they recalled it. In this condition the subjects performed just as poorly as did those subjects who were given no title at all. In other words, the value of the title was in helping the listeners comprehend the sentences of the passage in the first place. After the passage was over, the title was of little or no help to the listener.

The results from the Dooling and Lachman and the Bransford and Johnson experiments (and numerous others like them) are, then, quite consistent. When listeners can activate a topic or theme for the input sentences, they can comprehend and remember them much better than when the topic is missing

Table 5.3
Prose Passage Used by Dooling and Lachman (1971)

With hocked gems financing him, our hero bravely defied all scornful laughter that tried to prevent his scheme. Your eyes deceive you, he had said, an egg not a table correctly typifies this unexplored planet. Now three sturdy sisters sought proof, forging along sometimes through calm vastness, yet more often over turbulent peaks and valleys. Days became weeks as many doubters spread fearful rumors about the edge. At last, from nowhere, welcome winged creatures appeared, signifying momentous success.

---

or when it is given after the listener has been exposed to the passage. Activating an appropriate memory into which the input can be integrated has a large effect on the immediate comprehension of the input sentences.

Effects of Knowledge about the World
on Sentence Representation

In the previous section we saw that comprehension is affected by memory. In this section we will argue that memory is also affected by memory—that is, the representation of a sentence in the listener's memory is affected by other knowledge he possesses. Earlier we described Sachs' experiment which found that subjects could not tell whether they had heard an active or passive version of a sentence shortly after hearing it. Sachs' work has been replicated and extended by Offir (1973). She presented paragraph-length stories to her subjects and then tested the subjects' recognition of one critical sentence from the paragraph. In one comparison, Offir contrasted active and passive sentences again. Thus, sentence (31) might appear in the paragraph while either (31) or (32) might appear in the test, which asked whether the sentence had been in the paragraph.

(31) Mr. Smith ordered the coffee.

(32) The coffee was ordered by Mr. Smith.

In another comparison, Offir contrasted sentences like (33) and (34), one of which had appeared in the paragraph.

(33) It was Mr. Smith who ordered the coffee.

(34) It was the coffee that Mr. Smith ordered.

The latter two sentences would typically be uttered in two quite distinct situations. Sentence (33) answers the question, *Who ordered the coffee?* It presupposes that someone ordered the coffee, and it states that that someone was Mr. Smith. On the other hand, sentence (34) would typically be used to answer a question like *What did Mr. Smith order?* Example (34) presupposes that Mr. Smith ordered something, and it states that what he ordered was coffee. Thus, (33) and (34) have different presuppositions and would typically occur in different sets of circumstances (i.e., as answers to different questions). In contrast, (31) and (32) do not differ in their presuppositions.

Using a recognition test, Offir found that her subjects were not very clear about whether they had been presented with (31) or (32); just as Sachs had found, these two were confused with each other. The subjects were quite good, however, at telling whether they had heard (33) or (34). These two were not confused with each other. This suggests that information derived from the presuppositions of sentences, that is, information about the likely situation in which the sentence would have occurred, has an effect on the way in which the sentence is represented in the listener's memory.

Other work exploring the representation of sentences in memory has shown that it is affected by the inferences that the listener is likely to draw from the sentences he hears. These inferences are in turn affected by the listener's general knowledge. For example, Harris (1974) was interested in whether inferences affect the information in memory and in whether the representation changes over time. He presented sentences like **(35)** to some subjects, and sentences like **(36)** to others.

(35) Miss America realized that she played the tuba.

(36) Miss America said that she played the tuba.

After the subjects had heard the sentences Harris asked them whether or not it was true, from what they had heard, that Miss America played the tuba. If we say sentence **(35)** truthfully (and if we assume that *she* stands for *Miss America*), then it follows that Miss America does in fact play the tuba. However, if we truthfully say sentence **(36)**, then it does not necessarily follow that Miss America plays the tuba; she might have been lying.

Harris' subjects were divided into two test groups. One group was tested immediately after each sentence (the Comprehension group), and the other was not tested until an entire set of 32 sentences had been presented (the Memory group). For sentences like **(35)**, over 90% of the subjects in both the Comprehension and the Memory groups said it was true that Miss America played the tuba. However, after hearing **(36)**, only 36% of the subjects in the Comprehension group said it was true that Miss America played the tuba, while fully 69% of the subjects in the Memory group said she played it. Thus, the majority of the Memory group made an inference that did not, strictly speaking, follow from the information presented. When one hears a sentence like **(36)** there is an "invited inference" to the effect that what was said was true, but strictly speaking this does not logically follow. Yet after some time it appears that the memory representation includes the invited inference.

Once again, Harris' results are consistent with the idea that listeners do not store the exact underlying structure of the sentences that they hear for long, if at all. In Harris' study the subjects' memories included reasonable inferences. They are reasonable, that is, if we assume that the subjects integrated the sentences into their overall knowledge systems, which probably included the belief that Miss America would not lie about her talents. It appears that after a short period of time the subjects were unable to discriminate between the actual information that they were presented and the information that they contributed. Here again, then, is evidence that the listener is an active participant in both the comprehension and memory processes. To the extent that the listener has the time and the inclination to process a sentence fully, he may change his initial representation of it by bringing to bear related information also stored in his memory.

The above conclusion is also supported by some work on sentence memory performed by Bransford, Barclay, and Franks (1972). They presented a list of sentences to their subjects and told them that they would be asked questions about the sentences later. Among the sentences was one like (37).

(37) Three turtles rested on a floating log and a fish swam beneath it.

Later the subjects were presented a longer list of sentences and asked to identify the ones that had been on the original list. Among the test sentences was (38).

(38) Three turtles rested on a floating log and a fish swam beneath them.

The subjects in the experiment were willing to say that they had heard (38) in the original list of sentences, when in fact they hadn't; that is, they could not accurately discriminate whether they had originally heard (37) or (38). In (37) the pronoun *it* stands for the NP *a floating log,* while in (38) the pronoun *them* stands for the NP *three turtles.* The sentences thus have distinct meanings. However, the situation that is described by both sentences is almost the same: turtles above log above fish. (Strictly speaking, this would not have to be true, but apparently most subjects took it to be true.)

It appears that the listeners were making their judgments about whether a sentence was old or new in terms of the situations described by the sentences. The mental representation they formed of the situation described by (37) was influenced by what the subjects knew about the normal geometry of the physical world—if A is above B, and B is above C, then A is above C. Since this made the situations described by (37) and (38) seem the same, the subjects were willing to say they had heard (38) when in fact they had heard something different. As a control for the similarity among the sentences, Bransford et al. also presented sentences like (39) in the original list and sentences like (40) in the test. These two sentences are, on the surface, just as close to each other as the earlier pair. They do not, however, describe the same situation, and the subjects in the experiment were not confused. They did not say that (40) was an old sentence.

(39) Three turtles rested beside a floating log and a fish swam beneath it.

(40) Three turtles rested beside a floating log and a fish swam beneath them.

Higher-Level Structures

In the previous sections we have argued that the knowledge stored in one's general memory affects both comprehension of and memory for sentences. When we discuss general or "global" memory we must face the fact that tremendous amounts of information about the physical and social worlds must be stored within it. One large and unsolved problem concerns how this vast quantity of information is stored and how new input interacts with it. In recent years a number of psychologists, computer scientists, and linguists have tried to create the outlines of a theory of global memory, identifying some of the principles which guide its organization.

Kintsch (1976), for example, has been concerned with the organization of simple stories or narratives. He conjectures that the listener has what he calls a *narration schema* to guide the processing of a story. The narration schema consists of a set of expectations about the structure of a typical story. Thus, one expects to receive (a) information about the main character(s), his or her situation and background; (b) some unusual episode that complicates the hero or heroine's life; and (c) some resolution of the complication. Kintsch suggests that each of the particular events in the story will be organized under one of these headings. The headings guide the comprehension, allowing the listener to fill the appropriate "slots" in the narration schema as new information arrives. Thus, rather than approaching each story naively, the listener has the narration schema in mind to guide his listening or reading. The narration schema also helps to determine which of the propositions in the story are the important and central ones (those that fill in some important aspect of the pre-existing narration schema).

A similar idea has been proposed by Minsky (1975) under the term *frames*. We have a frame (set of expectations) for a number of common and familiar activities. For example, we have a frame for "eating out at a good restaurant." We know that between the time we sit down and the time the food arrives we will give our order to the waiter. This aspect of the frame need not be explicitly stated. If a listener is told that the speaker ate a delicious steak at a restaurant, he will assume that the speaker ordered steak. If asked, the listener might agree that he had actually been told that the individual ordered steak. In other words, the listener might not be able to tell which parts of the standard frame he had actually heard, and which he had filled in himself. In contrast, the frame for eating out at a friend's home does not include the episode of ordering. If the listener is told that the meal was at the Jones' and that the steak was delicious, he will not assume that the speaker ordered steak. If later asked whether he had actually been told that the individual ordered steak, the listener will not be confused. Thorndyke (1977) carried out an experiment to test whether listeners in fact show the pattern of confusions suggested above. His data came out just as predicted.

As we noted earlier, Kintsch argues that sentences are represented in propositional form. Not surprisingly, he also says that the narration schema is hierarchically organized into sets of propositions. Numerous other organizational schema have been proposed, e.g., Rumelhart (1975), Mandler and Johnson (1977). A procedural approach can also incorporate the idea of a narration schema or frame. Much current research attempts to separate the fruitful ideas along these lines from those that have no psychological validity.

We have now discussed some ways in which sentences and larger units might be represented in memory. These units are, of course, constructed from the building blocks that are permanently stored in the mental lexicon. In the next section we explore further the memory's representation of these important units.

Representation of Lexical Items

When thinking about how words are represented in the mental lexicon we must keep in mind the primary use to which those representations are put, namely, to aid the comprehension (and production) systems. The comprehender is using information retrieved from the mental lexicon to aid in constructing the internal representation of the sentence. These representations are in turn used to make inferences and to change the "global" memory system. Since there are many theories about comprehension and sentence representation, it is not surprising that there are also many points of view about how lexical information is represented in the memory system of the language user. Thus, while it is reasonable to discuss the mental representation of words or morphemes before one discusses higher-level comprehension processes, we have chosen to move this topic out of that neat order. We do this to underscore the fact that lexical information is used in the service of higher order processes.

In the previous chapter we did discuss some of the information that is stored in the lexical memory (e.g., categorical information such as whether the word is a noun or a verb, and some information about the noun types that can go with each verb). Here we will expand upon that discussion, concentrating upon semantic information, though not limiting ourselves to it. We will divide the discussion into sections which more or less correspond to the theories of sentence representation that we have looked at earlier in this chapter.

Featural Models of the Lexicon

What is "A navigational instrument used in measuring angular distances, especially the altitude of sun, moon, and stars, at sea"? Brown and McNeill (1966) read brief definitions such as this to a group of subjects and asked them to give the word defined. About 10% of the time Brown and McNeill stimulated a "tip-of-the-tongue" (TOT) state in their subjects. The listener knew that he knew the word but could not quite recall it. The subjects were then asked to state how many syllables the word had, its initial letter, and what words came to mind instead of the target word. The subjects' responses were better than chance on the first two of these categories. Also, about 30% of the time the words that the subject thought of were similar in meaning to the target word, and about 70% of the time they were similar in sound. TOT subjects wrote things like *compass, astrolabe,* or *protractor* (words similar in meaning); or they wrote *secant, sextet,* or *sexton* (words similar in sound to the target word *sextant*).

The Brown and McNeill results are interesting for a number of reasons, the one closest to our present concern being its demonstration that information about words is not represented in a listener's mental lexicon as an indivisible concept. The representation appears instead to have discrete parts, since in the TOT state both phonological and semantic aspects of the words were partially recovered.

When we studied the sound system of the language we noted that the obvious units, the phonemes, are actually not the most basic units of the sound system. They are the molecules built of the phonological atoms (the features). Many theorists across the centuries have tried to analyze meaning in a similar fashion. They have taken the obvious units (the word or the morpheme) and tried to find the semantic "atoms" that combine to form the meaning of the word. Psychologists, who are interested in how to represent the meaning of words, have also been concerned with the basic units of meaning and the way they are organized.

Traditionally, psychologists, linguists, and philosophers have conceptualized the meanings of words by listing the properties that go to make them up. It is sometimes assumed that there is a list of fundamental properties—for example, sense qualities such as color, and inborn qualities such as the concept of a straight line—and that the meaning of a word is some combination of these basic properties. At other times the properties themselves are thought to be complex. These properties are often referred to as *features,* somewhat parallel with the featural notion of phonology. Thus, in one well-known semantic theory, that of Katz and Fodor (1963), the meaning of the word *bachelor* is composed of a set of features such as ANIMATE, HUMAN, etc. By proposing that the meanings of words are built out of features, certain aspects of our everyday notion of "meaning" can be accounted for. Thus, all English speakers will agree that the words *uncle, brother, bull, rooster,* and *lad* all have something in common—they refer to males. Feature theory may propose that there is a feature MALE which is associated with each of the above words in the mental lexicon of the English speaker. The above words then do have something in common—that semantic feature.

Certain other aspects of language can also be clarified by using features. For example, it seems odd to say *My brother is a male.* The word *brother* has the semantic feature MALE associated with it, as does the word *male.* (Note that there is a difference between words and the theoretical, abstract notion of semantic features. The word *male* is not the same as the semantic feature MALE.) In saying *My brother is a male,* we are asserting that a MALE is a MALE—we are saying something redundant and totally obvious to any speaker of the language. In saying *My brother is not a male,* we are in effect saying that a MALE is not a MALE—asserting a contradiction. It is the ability of a feature-based semantics to account for such intuitions that Katz (1972) takes as one of the strong points of this approach.

The features said to constitute the meaning of a word are not simply arranged in a list; a more complex organization is usually proposed. For example, some features may be interrelated so as to permit inferences to be made. Anything that is HUMAN is also ANIMATE (as opposed to *tree* which is IN-ANIMATE), and is also CONCRETE (as opposed to *grammar* which is AB-STRACT). Therefore, from the truth of *A girl is hiding in the closet* we can infer the truth of *An animate being is hiding in the closet.* .

In addition, not all of the features interact with their contexts in the same way. Thus, the feature YOUNG does not convey the same age range when it is applied to *President* as it does when applied to *boy*. Furthermore, Clark (1969), following numerous linguists, has argued that some semantic features can be "neutralized" by the context. For example, the word *better* does not necessarily convey the feature GOOD. The sentence, *Peter is better at tennis than Joe,* does not necessarily imply that either of them is good relative to the general population. They both might be weekend hackers. (It is all right to say, *Although both are horrible, Peter is better than Joe.*) On the other hand, the word *worse* cannot be neutralized by its context. If *Joe is worse at tennis than Peter,* then neither of them can be GOOD. (It is quite odd to say, *Although both are world champions, Joe is worse than Peter.*) Information about which terms can be neutralized and which cannot must be represented in the lexicon and, according to Clark, will have an effect on the memory representation of sentences containing these words.

Representing Features. There are a number of ways to represent lexical information by features. One influential way of doing this is via a network, similar in form to the networks that we used to represent propositions. Figure 5.5 shows one example of a simplified lexical network. Each node in the network stands for one of the concepts, and the labeled lines state the relations between concepts. The network permits us to represent some hierarchical relations. For example, we see that CANARY and ROBIN are members of the class BIRD. Since all birds have wings and feathers, we can store this information (presumably in the form of features) along with BIRD; and we therefore need not store it with each concept, CANARY, ROBIN, etc. The information that is specific to CANARY can be stored directly with it. Similarly, since all birds, dogs, mice, and indeed all animals eat and breathe, we can store this information with the concept ANIMAL. We need not, then, repeat it for every animal in the lexicon.

Collins and Quillian (1969) proposed that the mental lexicon is organized according to the same principles as Figure 5.5. In a test of this model they presented sentences like (**41–43**) to their subjects and measured the time it took the subjects to push a button signifying that the sentences were true. A set of false sentences was also presented, so the subject did have to make a choice for each sentence.

(**41**) A canary can sing.

(**42**) A canary can fly.

(**43**) A canary has skin.

According to the model, the feature SING is stored directly with the concept CANARY, FLY is stored with BIRD, and SKIN is stored with ANIMAL. Thus, the information required to verify (**41**) is more directly accessible than is the information required to verify (**42**) and (**43**). Collins and Quillian found that

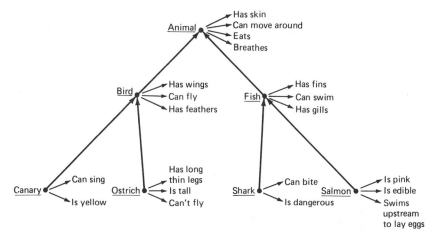

Figure 5.5. A proposed hierarchical organization of the mental lexicon (From Collins, A. M., & Quillian, M. R. Retrieval time from semantic memory. *Journal of Verbal Learning and Verbal Behavior,* 1969, **8,** 240-247. Copyright 1969 by Academic Press, Inc. Used by permission.)

the RTs were fastest in the case of **(41)** and slowest for **(43)**, just as their network model predicted.

A number of investigators have assumed that words which share a large number of semantic features, such as DOCTOR and NURSE, are conceptually "near" each other in the lexical network. This assumption is used to account for the fact that first presenting *doctor* leads to a fast response to *nurse* in the word-nonword judgment task (see the Meyer et al. experiment discussed in the previous chapter).

Although many theorists support it, the network conception of lexical memory has been challenged on a number of grounds. Some experimental results do not readily fit into this conception. For example, Rips, Shoben, and Smith (1973) showed that subjects were faster in verifying the truth of **(44)** than that of **(45)**.

(44) A cat is an animal.

(45) A cat is a mammal.

They argued that MAMMAL is closer to CAT in the hierarchy than is ANIMAL. Therefore, the hierarchical network model should predict that **(45)** is faster to verify. Since it was not, Rips et al. took their results as evidence against the network representation of lexical information.

Another experimental result that does not readily fit into the network representation is obtained if one asks subjects to verify sentences like **(46)** and **(47)**.

(46) A robin is a bird.

(47) A duck is a bird.

A number of investigators have observed that subjects are faster in responding to items like **(46)**, even though both sentences are testing the same level in the hierarchy and even though *robin* and *duck* occur with approximately equal frequency in the language (e.g., Rosch, 1973). It appears that subjects are faster in responding to "typical" or representative members of a category than to atypical ones.

It is possible to modify the network model so that the results of the above two experiments can be accounted for. Collins and Loftus (1975) do this by assuming that, within the network, the strength of the connection between nodes is variable. However, not all of the problems of the network representation can be solved in this way, as we will note below.

Some investigators have adopted the feature system of representing lexical information without adopting the network model. For example, Smith, Shoben, and Rips (1974) have argued that features are listed more directly with the entries in the mental dictionary. These authors have proposed that each word has a set of features directly associated with it. The features vary as to how much they define the word's meaning, some features being more essential than others. For example, the feature WINGED is more essential to the word *robin* than is UNDOMESTICATED. The theories of direct feature representation and the network models are very similar; in fact, it has been shown that the two models are mathematically equivalent to each other (Hollan, 1975). Therefore, the two make the same kinds of predictions. Of course, they also face the same kinds of problems.

Some Problems for Featural Models. The critical words used in the experiments reported above were nouns which refer to concrete objects. Stating semantic features for abstract nouns, adverbs, verbs, and other classes of words appears to be a much harder task than stating them for words which refer to concrete objects (though no adequate set of features for the latter class of words exists either). Some features must really be relations. The word *good* has to be interpreted relative to some object. As Katz (1972) remarks, *a good knife* has different properties from *a good meal.*

One of the potential advantages of the featural system is that it permits us to state the selectional restrictions on the verbs in the language. A selectional restriction is a rule that tells us which nouns can go along with which verbs as subject and object (a problem area we discussed earlier). Thus, the verb *appeased* requires an object noun that has the feature ANIMATE: sentence **(48)** is okay, while for most people **(49)** is nonsense.

(48) The soldier appeased the colonel.

(49) *The farmer appeased the kernel.

Some verbs require a direct object that has the feature FEMALE.

(50) The doctor hysterectomized the actress.

(51) *The doctor hysterectomized the actor.

And so on.

However, many of these restrictions are relative to the world within which our discourse is taking place. Thus, if we move to cartoon worlds, a sentence like **(52)** makes sense, as does **(49)**.

(52) The ant decided to invent the laser.

Given this, no attempt to account for the selectional restrictions with a fixed set of features is assured of success.

We noted earlier that words serve the needs of the comprehension and inference systems. A theory of word representation must account for the role of words in aiding these systems. We also mentioned earlier that some words (e.g., *faster*) express a transitive relation. If Tom is faster than Bill, and Bill faster than Joe, then it follows that Tom is faster than Joe. It is part of the meaning of *faster* that it permits such transitive inferences. A word like *close* does not. If we tell you that, by Texas standards, Austin is close to Waco, and that Waco is close to Dallas, you cannot conclude that, by the same standards, Austin is close to Dallas. Thus, *faster* and *close* are different in the inferences that they permit. Any competent adult speaker of English tacitly knows these differences, and they must be represented in our mental semantics. Some theorists (e.g., Bar-Hillel, 1969, 1970) have argued that information about the kinds of legitimate inferences that are permitted by *faster* (and other comparatives) cannot be represented in anything like a dictionary (mental or otherwise) of features.

To explore this a bit further, let us consider some other words and the relations among them, for example, *buy* and *sell*. These two are "converses" of one another. If **(53)** is true, so is **(54)**.

(53) The women bought the store from the agent.

(54) The agent sold the store to the women.

Likewise such pairs as *precede* and *follow* are converses (if *John precedes Bill*, then *Bill follows John*), as are many others. Bar-Hillel argued that the speaker's competence must include such knowledge as "*buys from* is the converse of *sells to*," "*precedes* is the converse of *follows*," and many other such relations. A specification of the rules of transitiveness, conversion, and so on would exist in the speaker's competence. Such specifications are not features in the sense discussed earlier. (The rules that specify the converse have been understood by logicians for some time. In effect, Bar-Hillel proposed that there is an intimate connection between logic, linguistics, and psychology.) In reply, Katz (1972, p. 296) has argued that the sorts of information discussed by Bar-Hillel can be stored in a dictionary format; but in order to do so he clearly modifies and makes more complex the entries in his proposed semantic dictionary. The "features" are now quite different.

The feature or network models proposed by Collins and Quillian (1969), Collins and Loftus (1975), and other psychologists do not adequately represent the kinds of relations discussed by Bar-Hillel. There is some truth to the idea that the meanings of words can be captured by properties, but it is by no means the whole truth.

Schema or Prototype Models

We will now briefly discuss two alternatives to the feature and (simple) network concepts. One alternative has been argued comprehensively by Cassirer (1923) and by Putnam (1975, especially chapters 8 & 12), and finds some reflection in the psychological work of Rosch (1973, 1975) and others. According to this alternative, a very important consideration is ignored by the view that the meaning of a word can be captured by a set of features. Putnam argues, for example, that many properties of an object can be abnormal while the object is still an instance of the same category. A red lemon is still a lemon, a three-legged tiger is still a tiger, etc. Thus, the meaning of *lemon* cannot have the feature YELLOW as one of its necessary components. Putnam does agree that there is a special relationship between yellow and lemons, since lemons are usually yellow. He introduces the concept of the "natural kind" or "stereotype" and says that part of the meaning of *lemon* is that (*a*) it is a word used to refer to a natural class of objects and that (*b*) the normal members of this class (or the stereotypical members of the class) are yellow, tart, have such and such a shape, etc. Thus, while Putnam does not get rid of semantic features (the concepts of "yellow," "tart," etc. are analogous to features) he adds the idea of stereotype. (We will use the term prototype, since it is more common.) A speaker acquires the meaning of the word *tiger* only when he acquires the prototype. One doesn't know the meaning of *tiger* unless one knows that the stereotypical or prototypical tiger has stripes, lives in the jungle, is ferocious, and so forth.

The concept of a prototype is similar to that of a schema.[2] The latter concept has been a topic of frequent discussion in psychology since the time of Bartlett (1932). Schema theorists typically equate the meaning of a word with a mental concept, so their views on concepts are also their views on meaning. The basic premise of schema theory is that the memory representation of a concept has two components, a core central representation (sometimes called the prototype), plus rules for generating other exemplars of the concept. The rules operate upon the prototype, deforming it in various ways while still representing the concept.

---

[2] The concept of schema is closely related to that of narration schema discussed earlier in the chapter. They share the idea that there is a standard or prototype which underlies and guides our interpretation of events.

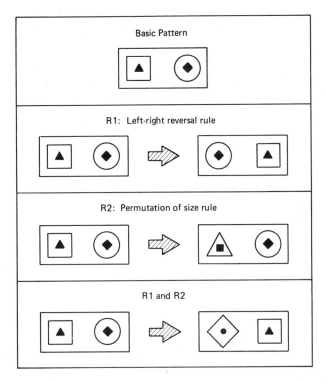

Figure 5.6. A basic pattern (prototype) and the rules for changing it. (Adapted from Franks, J. J., & Bransford, J. P. Abstraction of visual patterns. *Journal of Experimental Psychology,* 1971, *90,* 65–74. Copyright 1971, American Psychological Association. Used by permission.)

The "prototype plus rules" approach is thought to describe the representation of many different inputs. For example, there is a supporting experiment conducted by Franks and Bransford (1971) in which visual materials were used. They devised a "basic" visual pattern and some rules for distorting the basic pattern, as shown in Figure 5.6. One rule (R1) switched the left and right figures, and another (R2) interchanged the larger and smaller figures on one side of the basic pattern. More than one rule could apply, yielding a pattern like that shown at the bottom of the figure.

Franks and Bransford generated a set of example pictures by applying such rules to the basic pattern. Then they showed these examples (those on the right side of Figure 5.6), one at a time for five seconds each, to a group of subjects, asking them to reproduce each figure after it had been shown. They did *not* show the basic pattern or prototype to the subjects, nor did they tell them that there would be a later test. After 16 various patterns had been shown, the subjects were given a recognition test to see which items seemed most familiar to them. The results were quite clear. The item that the subjects were most certain that they had seen was the prototype—an item that had never been presented. In general, the fewer rules that were applied to the prototype in generating the test item, the more certain the subjects were that they had seen the test item before. Franks and Bransford concluded that the subjects had learned and stored a prototype—the basic underlying pattern—as the "best representative" of what they had seen.

Those who favor the "prototype plus rules" approach do not think that concepts or meanings can be adequately represented by a set of features or by the network models that follow from featural models. Some psychologists have explicitly adopted schema theory as a model for semantic memory. For example, Rosch (1973, 1975) has argued that such terms as *furniture, bird,* and other category terms are represented in memory in terms of their "best examples" (e.g., *chair, robin*), with other members of the category "surrounding" the central representative. Those items that are less similar to the prototype, and those that only marginally belong to the category (e.g., *stove, turkey*) are said to be farther from the central term. In order to provide support for this notion, Rosch and others have shown that people agree on what constitutes a "good" bird (a robin, not a duck) and that they are faster in agreeing that a robin is a bird than they are in agreeing that a duck is (see examples **46–47** above). Likewise, these theorists argue that such phrases as "technically speaking" can only be used with marginal members of the category, not with central ones, making sentence **(55)** all right, but **(56)** very odd.

(55) Technically speaking, a penguin is a bird.

(56) Technically speaking, a robin is a bird.

This demonstration is used to argue that various examples of the BIRD category do not hold equal membership in that category. Penguins, turkeys, and ducks are not as birdlike as robins, sparrows, and canaries. The representations of these concepts in memory reflect this continuum of membership in the category. Rosch (1975) conducted an experiment to verify the idea that some words are better members of categories than others. The experiment used a "priming" technique. In the priming task the subjects were first given (primed with) a category name (e.g., *bird*). Then, after a short delay, the subjects were shown two words. They were instructed to push one button if both words were from the *same* category (two birds or two furniture words, etc.), and another button if the words come from *different* categories (e.g., a bird and a furniture word.) Half of the word pairs were primed and half were not.

Rosch reasoned as follows. Presenting the priming word will facilitate making the *same* response if and only if the primer calls to mind information that is closely associated with the test items. If feature theory is correct, then the word *bird* will lead to a speeded decision for all bird words since they all have this feature closely associated with them. If, on the other hand, prototype theory is correct, the priming word *bird* should only speed up decisions concerning the "good" or prototypical birds. Priming will lead to faster responses for good examples of a category, while priming won't matter for the poor examples.

The results of the experiment supported the predictions drawn from the prototype model, but only in part. When the two category members were identical, then the good members (*robin-robin*) were aided by the priming and the poor members (*turkey-turkey*) were not. This result was predicted by the prototype model. However, when the category members were not identical, then the good members (*robin-sparrow*) were not helped by the priming any more than the poor members (*turkey-penguin*). Rosch added some other hypotheses in order to explain this latter finding, and so, overall, she concluded that the study strongly supported schema or prototype theory and did not support feature theory.

Schema theory has some attraction as an alternative to feature theory. One important asset is its acceptance of the idea that the range of application of our concepts is often not clearly defined. Many everyday concepts are vague. Just what is a chair or democracy? There seems to be some looseness in the meanings of our words. On the negative side, schema theory as it exists does not tie in at all with the rest of the language processing system. This is a very serious problem. The meanings of sentences are built from the meanings of words, syntax, and other factors. It is necessary for a theory of semantic memory to state how the meanings of words interrelate with syntax and with each other. So far no schema theorist has tried to do this, and so the theory exists off by itself, separate from the rest of psycholinguistics. This criticism must be taken for what it is, not for a blanket dismissal. We mean only that no one has yet integrated schema theory into the larger system, not that such an integration is impossible. Time will tell whether it can be done.

Procedural Models

The second alternative to the featural model of word meaning is that of procedural semantics, introduced earlier in our discussion of sentence representation. Recall that the proponents of procedural semantics believe that the meaning of a declarative sentence is closely related to the concept of truth. The representation of a declarative sentence in memory is in terms of a set of procedures for determining whether the sentence is true relative to some state of affairs.

Now imagine that we devise a set of procedures to evaluate the truth of sentences relative to sets of circumstances. In this case we will have a procedural semantics. In it the representation of lexical items will not be in terms of a set of features or a network. Instead, each lexical item would be thought of as containing a set of instructions for how that word combines with others to aid in the evaluation process. To make this more concrete, consider (57).

(57) The tall man is carrying a steel anvil.

Let us first examine the phrase *steel anvil*. The referent of this phrase is the "intersection" of the referents of the two component words. That is, the phrase can be appropriately applied to any objects that are both anvils and steel. The entry for the adjective *steel* must indicate that this combination rule applies to it. Sentence **(57)** is false in all circumstances in which the thing carried is either not made of steel or not an anvil.

Now consider the phrase *tall man*. The combination rule associated with the adjective *tall* cannot be the same as that associated with *steel*. The word *tall* is a relative one. Sentence **(57)** can be true even if the man carrying the anvil is only 1.73 meters (about 5'8") tall. In this case the man is not tall relative to all men; but if he is the tallest man in the set under discussion, then **(57)** can be true. So the rule combining *man* and *tall* is not the "intersection" rule. The new rule must be associated with the lexical entry for *tall*.

An even clearer case of the difference in rules for combining adjectives with nouns is shown in sentence **(58)**.

(58) The alleged criminal sold a fake antique.

Consider the phrase *fake antique*. When we modify the noun *antique* with the adjective *fake*, then the referent of the resulting phrase is not an antique. This certainly violates the intersection rule; the referent of *fake antique* is not the intersection of fake things and antiques! Sentence **(58)** is false whenever the individual is selling a genuine antique. Also, the referent of *alleged criminal* may or may not be a member of the set of criminals; sentence **(58)** can be true in either case.

We have not stated the rules for combining the adjectives *tall, fake,* or *alleged* with the nouns they modify. The examples are simply meant to show that the rules of combination are not semantically uniform and that they will have to be stated as little "recipes" in the mental lexicon. At least this is one of the implications of a procedural approach to semantics. Is this how words are stored—as little recipes for carrying out mental actions? If so, then the way in which we represent lexical information will be quite different from the systems proposed by either the feature or the network theorists.

We cannot resolve the issue of which lexical representation is correct, for the exact way in which information about words is stored in our mental lexicon is still unknown. Even though the models that we have discussed are fairly complex, they are probably not yet complex enough to do justice to our knowledge of words. Unfortunately, the study of language and its psychological representation does not seem a rewarding field for those who love simplicity. We will have some more to say about the representation of linguistic information (including some high-level information) in the next chapter when we consider sentence production. For the moment let us summarize what we have done in this chapter.

Summary

Some of the information that results from comprehending a sentence is stored in the listener's memory. This chapter discussed some of the functions of such information as well as models of how it is represented. The manner in which lexical items are represented in long-term memory was also discussed.

One function of the memory's representation of sentences is to support inferences. Information that is associated with the sentences—primarily in their verbs—specifies the appropriate kinds of mental logic that one can carry out.

A number of theories were reviewed concerning the form in which sentences are represented. One theory is that images form the basis for representing sentences. Although the concept of an image is a respectable one in cognitive psychology, this concept is insufficient to represent sentences. There is evidence that some aspects of the underlying structure of a sentence are stored by the listener—in particular, the number of propositions in the sentence seems to affect memory. However, an even more compelling case can be made that the representation of sentences is in a form more abstract and integrated than the underlying structure of single sentences. The work on sentence integration (e.g., Bransford & Franks) supports this conclusion.

Propositional and procedural models of sentence representation were described. A propositional model states that the information conveyed by sentences is represented in terms of a set of interconnected concepts and the relations among them. Numerous propositional models have been proposed and some of the tests of these models were described. Not all of the results are consistent with the most popular propositional models. A procedural model states that some of our knowledge about a sentence consists of a set of procedures or activities that we could carry out in order to verify the sentence (or answer the question). It is not necessary that the procedures actually be carried out, only that they can be planned. In discussing this model, we noted that there is a close relationship between the meaning of a declarative sentence and the concept of truth.

The present chapter also noted that the process of comprehension is affected by the listener's memory structures. Our knowledge of the world affects comprehension just as comprehension can change our knowledge of the world. Some higher-level memory structures, such as narration schema or frames, can affect both what is stored in memory and the inferences that are made by the listener.

The final section of the chapter discussed the memory's representation of lexical items. Among the approaches reviewed were the featural, prototypical, and procedural. Feature models say that the representation of a word is in terms of a set of properties or features such as HUMAN, ANIMATE, etc. While the featural model can account for some facets of meaning, there are many that it cannot handle without substantial modification.

A prototype model says that the meaning of a lexical item is not solely in terms of features. Instead, the meaning is represented as some common or stereotypical instance, plus some rules for saying how uncommon instances relate to the common ones. There is evidence to suggest that some members of a category are "better" or more central than others. This point of view has not been well integrated into a general semantic and syntactic theory, however.

Finally, it was noted that, in contrast, procedural models of the lexicon can be integrated with a model of sentence memory. However, the appropriate framework within which to represent lexical items is still a subject of theorizing and debate.

SUGGESTED READINGS

The topic of imagery and sentence memory is reviewed by Pylyshyn (1973). Kosslyn and Pomerantz (1977) have replied to Pylyshyn. Propositional models of memory are further described in Norman and Rumelhart (1975), Kintsch (1976), and, at a more advanced level, Anderson and Bower (1973). Procedural models are described by Winograd (1972) and are discussed in great detail by Miller and Johnson-Laird (1976). The prototype models are described in the papers by Putnam and by Rosch, referenced earlier.

III

Producing Language and Speech

INTRODUCTION

We began the last section with a question: What is it that a person is doing when he hears an utterance and understands it? We will begin this section with a similar question: What is it that a person is doing when he thinks of something to say and says it?

Intuitively we might say that the process of producing an utterance begins with the speaker formulating some idea or thought that he wishes to communicate. This idea need not be fully formed and completely specified before the speaker begins translating it into an utterance, but of course he must at least have started to formulate it. Somehow, the idea is translated from its original form into a linguistic form—a sentence to be uttered. This linguistic form must then be translated into a plan for executing a series of movements of various parts of the speech musculature. Finally, that plan is put into operation; a pattern of sound is produced which represents the speaker's utterance.

In thinking about all this activity, it is necessary to make a distinction between the processes involved in the production of language (i.e., sentences) and those involved in the production of speech. Sentence production includes the formulation of an idea that initiates an act of speaking and the choice of an appropriate linguistic framework into which to cast it. These, what we might term the "planning" aspects of production, include such things as finding appropriate lexical items to use and arranging them in a suitable semantic and syntactic framework. Very likely, these sentence production processes are much the same whether the thought is eventually expressed in speech or in writing.

Speech production processes, on the other hand, are peculiar to speaking, for they involve the construction of a program of skilled motor movements to produce the speech sounds corresponding to the intended sentence and, of course, the realization of that program, the actual generation of a sound pattern.

The processes of production, according to this view, involve a series of translations: first, from the code of the thought or intention into a linguistic code; later, from that linguistic code into a physiological, motor movement code. Unfortunately, we cannot observe the code of thought directly; it is not available to our introspection. As a result, we know very little about its nature. We do know that it must be capable of representing anything about which we can talk, and some psychologists believe that it is also capable of representing things about which we cannot talk. At the very least, this suggests that the code is immensely complex. But beyond that we know very little about its nature. This lack of knowledge creates a serious problem: how can we understand the process of translating thoughts into a linguistic code if we do not know what it is a translation from?

There is another problem that arises in trying to understand the processes for the production of sentences and speech. Not only do we know very little of the initial thought code, there also appears to be no way of gaining control over it without distorting it. This makes it extremely difficult to perform experiments dealing with production processes. That is, since we cannot control what a speaker is thinking, we are never certain what the input to the production processes is. If we try to control the input to the processes, we are in effect telling our speaker something like *Please say a sentence about* . . . or *Please produce the following utterance.* In doing so, we ourselves, not the speaker, would be directing the initial stages of production processing.

As a result, most of what we know about the production of sentences in its initial stages comes from observations of spontaneous speech. Such observations provide us with rich and intriguing data about the nature of the processes even though they are difficult to interpret. Chapter 6 describes many of the issues surrounding sentence production and offers an interpretation of the available data.

The kind of problem we have described would seem to present less difficulty when we study the later stages of production processing, those that have to do with speech production. But here we encounter all the problems that are inherent to the study of any complex neurological and physiological process, the difficulties of trying to observe and record neurological and muscular activities as they occur. Since it is the production of *speech* in which we are interested, we do not have the option of studying these processes in lower animals. The ones that produce speech-like sounds (e.g., mynah birds) do so in ways very different from humans, and organisms that are more like humans (e.g., chimpanzees) are not at all adept in producing speech sounds.

Still, there are some models of the speech production processes to work with, and the available evidence does permit an assessment of these models. Chapter 7 reviews these models and the evidence. Thus, the two chapters of this section stress sentence planning and speech production respectively.

6

Sentence Production

Most people would probably agree with the following informal model of the communication process: a speaker has an idea, encodes it into a linguistically structured message, and "sends" this message via the airwaves to a receiver who then decodes it into the same—or a highly similar—idea. In the past few chapters we have been primarily concerned with the decoding process, the operations performed by the listener. In this chapter and the next we are concerned with aspects of the encoding process, the operations performed by the speaker.

It is widely believed that encoding an idea into a linguistically structured message is an imperfect process, that the speaker does not have foolproof techniques for translating thoughts into words. Every teacher has heard a student say, "I know what I mean, but I'm just not able to say (write) it." A few years ago a popular song written by Leon Russell included the line, "we tried to talk it over but the words got in the way . . ."* a lyric expressing the same sentiment. Others, however, believe that any thought can be put into words. Harold Ross, the late founding editor of the *New Yorker* magazine, was famous for holding the opinion that nothing is indescribable. *New Yorker* prose, like that of many novelists, is wonderful to read, in part because the writers are able to paint marvelously accurate word pictures of seemingly indescribable events. But, as such writers will attest, such prose is not easily produced. Much rewriting goes

*From *This Masquerade* by Leon Russell, Copyright 1972, 1973 by Skyhill Publishing Co., Inc. Used by permission.

on before the final product is printed. It is apparent to anyone who listens that much normal, non-edited, speech consists of false starts, hesitations, backtracking, and hemming and hawing; and that it generally does not mirror underlying propositions with great accuracy. What is going on when one talks?

In what follows we will discuss three aspects of the encoding process. First, we will look at the problem of what speakers say. Here we will describe some principles of effective conversation and, in general terms, some of the knowledge that the speaker uses in constructing sentences. Second, we will discuss the internal code in which information is represented before it is encoded into a linguistically-structured message. And third, we will consider the operations involved in translating the message from its internal to its external form. Most theorizing and empirical work on speech production has been concerned with the last of these topics, and our discussion of it will carry over into the next chapter.

What Speakers Say

A speaker's utterances are determined by many factors. Analogous to our discussion of comprehension, we could group these factors into three classes: motivational, intentional, and structural. Sometimes a speaker may utter, *It's cold in here,* when what he intends to communicate is *Close the door.* Although we could try to determine the speaker's motives for putting the command in this oblique way, the study of such motives is beyond our present scope. We will, however, discuss some of the intentional and structural factors involved in producing sentences. In discussing the intentional aspects of the utterance, the conveyed meaning that lies behind the literal meaning, we will stress the idea that the speaker must take the listener's knowledge into account if the appropriate meaning is actually to be conveyed. The speaker's assumptions about the listener's present knowledge affect both what he says and his choice of structures for saying it. In addition, we will describe a set of assumptions about certain rules of conversation (conversational maxims) that are shared by the speaker and the listener. We will take up this last topic first.

Conversational Maxims

When we encode our thoughts into language we often, though not always, do so in order to communicate them to others. When this is the case, it is important for the speaker to take the listener's cognitive state into account if the communication is to be successful. For example, the speaker must not omit crucial information from his utterance unless he is sure that the listener already has this information in mind. Likewise, the speaker must not give too much detail, or the conversation will bog down in trivia. Thus, even if the speaker knows in detail where Dennis is right now, it is not appropriate to answer the question, *Where's Dennis?* by saying something like, *Dennis is leaning against the doorframe in the southeast corner of room 320, Mezes Hall, University of Texas at Austin. His left foot is six inches north and eight inches west of the doorframe,* etc., etc. Even if all of the above is true, it is typically inappropriate, and speakers know it. The speaker should answer at the "right" level of detail. If the conversation were taking place in New York, the right answer might be, *He's in Texas.* If it were occurring on the second floor of Mezes Hall, then the right answer might be, *He's in room 320.* The speaker knows that the listener will draw appropriate inferences from the utterance; he knows, in this case, that the listener will assume that the room number refers to the building that they are presently in.

Discussions of the "logic" of conversations and of appropriate things to say in them have been greatly stimulated by the work of the philosopher H. P. Grice (1975). Grice has tried to formulate a logic of conversation, and some of his observations are clearly relevant to the psychologist speculating on the decisions speakers make about what to say. Grice distinguishes between two types of inferences that listeners can draw from the speaker's utterances. On the one hand, there are the "conventional" inferences that logicians have studied for years. Thus, if a speaker says to you that it is true that Dennis is in Mezes 320, and if you know it to be true that Mezes Hall is on the campus of the University of Texas, then you can correctly infer that Dennis is on the campus too. Inferences of this type have been studied extensively, and it is clear that people often make errors in applying them.

On the other hand, there are the "conversational" inferences. These are not necessarily logical inferences. For example, if the speaker tells you *Dennis is either in Mezes Hall or in Benedict Hall,* you will infer that he does not know in which of the two buildings we could find him. In fact, the speaker may know that Dennis is in Mezes Hall. If, knowing that, he says that Dennis is either in Mezes or in Benedict, the speaker will, strictly speaking, be telling the truth. Dennis is in one of the two buildings. But you could accuse the speaker of being misleading. You infer from the speaker's statement that he has given you just the right amount of the information that is in his possession. He has *conversationally implied* that he does not know which of the two buildings Dennis is in.

Grice has tried to work out some of the principles of conversational implication. His basic principle is that of *cooperation.* Grice assumes that the participants in a conversation are committed to achieving a maximally effective communication (one that exchanges information toward some mutually acceptable goal). Naturally, this assumption does not always fit the facts; occasionally the hidden goal of one of the participants in the conversation is to mislead the others. Let us ignore these cases, however; matters are already complex enough. Grice develops a number of maxims which help to clarify the principle of cooperation. One of these, the maxim of *quality,* is simply that the contribution that one makes to the conversation ought to be true. Another, the maxim of *quantity,* is that the contribution to the conversation ought to be "appropriately" informative—that is, neither too precise nor too general. If the speaker says that Dennis is either at location A or location B, then these two maxims permit us to infer that he doesn't know which. We assume that the speaker cannot be more precise without violating the maxim of quality. According to Grice, both speaker and listener tacitly know these maxims, and furthermore the maxims guide the speaker in his choice of what to say.

Occasionally, of course, a speaker may violate the maxim of quality without the listener being misled. The speaker can do this in good faith if he knows that the listener will recognize his utterance as an intentional violation of the maxim. Thus, after coming out of a movie during which you fell asleep, you might say to your companion, *That sure was an exciting film.* Since your companion knows that you fell asleep during the film, you are not really violating the maxim of quality. Given the cooperative principle, your companion will correctly infer that you are being ironic.

In general, what your remarks convey to a listener depends greatly upon the listener's knowledge. What you convey by saying *That sure was an exciting film* depends on whether or not your friend knows that you fell asleep. If he doesn't know it, then the attempt to be ironic may end up being misleading. One of the determinants of what a speaker says, therefore, is his assumptions about the listener's knowledge. To take just one final example of this idea, recall the way in which your speech changes when you talk to a 2- or 3-year-old child as compared to your manner of speaking with an adult. You know that the child does not have the same inference-making capacity as does the adult, and your speech is modified accordingly.

Although it is easy to note that one's speech changes when talking to a 2-year old, it is not so easy to describe, in general, what determines the content of one's utterances. Of course, in some ways it seems easy to predict what someone will say. If we hold a pencil up to a friend and ask *What's this?*, we are not surprised if we get the common answer. But we are not surprised if we don't, either. Since our friend must assume that we already know what the thing is, he may reply by giving a detailed description (thinking that we are trying to test his powers of observation), or by saying that it is a writing tool, or a cultural artifact, or any one of innumerable other descriptions that can appropriately be given for the pencil. Alternatively, our friend may simply give us a strange look, say that the object is a fire hydrant, and walk away. The existence of this range of possibilities makes two points. First, there is a huge number of ways in which one can react to or describe any stimulus. Second, the way in which a speaker does react to a stimulus depends upon the assumptions that he makes concerning what is *really* the object of the question. The internal state of the speaker makes an enormous contribution to the content of the utterance. Until we have a theory which sets forth in great detail the internal state of the speaker at the time of the utterance, predicting the content of what is said will, in general, be impossible.

Some Determinants of Sentence Structure

Attempts to predict the content of utterances have not been generally successful. However, there have been a few small successes in discovering what determines the structure of simple utterances. For example, Osgood (1971) has reported the results of some demonstrations in which he asked a group of graduate students to describe each event in a series by giving a single simple sentence. For example, he might roll a black ball across a table. On the next "trial" he would again roll the ball across the table, but more slowly. The listeners were told to observe each event and to write a description of it.

Among the observations made by Osgood was the frequency with which the observers referred to the ball with the indefinite rather than the definite article. When the ball first made its appearance, 73% of the sentences produced referred to it with the indefinite article *a*. On the next trial only 54% of the sentences used *a*, while the remainder used *the;* and on the third trial, the percentage of *a* had dropped to 35%. The indefinite article is used when the speaker assumes that the listener or reader is not familiar with the object; the definite article when such familiarity can be assumed. Note that when we first mentioned the ball in the previous paragraph we used the indefinite *a*. The next mention used *the*.

In another of his demonstrations, Osgood found that the occasions on which the speaker produces a sentence like **(1)** differ systematically from those when he produces a sentence like **(2)**.

(1) The black ball is on the table.

(2) The cup on the table is green.

Sentence **(1)** occurs when the black ball has already been introduced into the situation; it describes its present location or activity. Sentence **(2)** occurs when the speaker knows that other cups might have been put on the table, that is, he knows that Osgood had, say, a red cup that he might have put there. In both **(1)** and **(2)** the informative part of the description occurs late in the sentence. The sentence structure is apparently chosen so that this will happen. Thus, even a simple distinction like *the adjective noun* vs. *the noun is adjective* is one that carries information about the speaker's assessment of what the listener knows at the time of the utterance.

The idea that the informative part of a sentence is saved until last has been further discussed by Clark and Haviland (1974), who called it the "Given-New Strategy." According to Clark and Haviland, each sentence produced by a speaker contains some old, "given" information, and some that is new. The old information serves as an indication of where, in the listener's memory, he will find information related to that conveyed by the present sentence, and thus as "an instruction specifying where the new information is to be integrated into the previous knowledge" (p. 105). In other words, the given information specifies a "location" in memory, so that the new information can be integrated with the old information that resides at that memory location.

It is not the case, however, that the "given" information must be presented first in the sentence. Thus, in **(3)** the given information is that someone stole the art treasure, and the new information is that the guilty party is the man in the black hat.

(3) It was the man in the black hat who stole the art treasure.

Clark and Haviland recognize this fact; they do not insist that the given information come first, only that the listener be able to determine what is given and what is new. This means that the speaker must provide some standard cues signalling which information is given and which is new.

There are many limitations on the Given-New Strategy, many situations in which all of the information in a sentence is old or all of it is new. The theory has not been fully worked out. However, it is clear that speakers do often take the listener's state of knowledge into account, and that they structure their utterances accordingly. The speaker's assessment of the listener's present state has a lot to do with what he says. We should point out before leaving this topic that speakers are free to ignore their listeners. Not all speech fits into the framework provided by Grice. Sometimes one speaks to destroy a conversation, to make a joke, etc. (see N. Chomsky, 1975, for further criticisms of the framework). Conversational goals are not always shared by the parties conversing.

From Thought To Language

We assume that the process of speaking involves translating or encoding a message (idea) from a nonlinguistic code into a linguistically-structured message. Very roughly, we can divide the translation process into three parts. The speaker must decide about the content of the sentence, its structure, and the particular lexical items that will appear in it. We have a good idea about the final output of the translation process since we can record speech quite objectively. It is much more difficult and speculative to discuss the input to the translation process and its intermediate stages. In this section we will touch upon two aspects of the input: first, the mental code in which the input might be represented; and second, some effects of content decisions on measurable aspects of the utterance.

The Mental Code

The content of what the speaker is going to say must be internally represented, at least in part, prior to his beginning the utterance. Furthermore, the mental code in which the message is formed must include all of the information that is going to be represented in the utterance. If the utterance is going to have, say, both direct and indirect objects, then the internal representation must make an analogous distinction. William James made a similar point in 1890: he called the internal representation "the intention."

And has the reader never asked himself what kind of a mental fact is his *intention of saying a thing* before he has said it? It is an entirely definite intention, distinct from all other intentions, an absolutely distinct state of consciousness, therefore; and yet how much of it consists of definite sensorial images, either of words or of things? Hardly anything! Linger, and the words and things come to mind; . . . the intention . . . welcomes them successively and calls them right if they agree with it, it rejects them and calls them wrong if they do not (p. 253).

What is the nature of the code in which the intention is represented? In the previous chapter we described the general character of some propositional models of memory. These models, according to many theorists, represent the information derived from a comprehended sentence. Some aspects of certain propositional models were presented via graph structures (see Figure 5.1, 5.2, and 5.3). We noted that inferential processes operate upon these structures to derive new propositions.

It seems reasonable to turn things around and suggest that a similar abstract propositional models were presented via graph structures (see Figures 5.1, 5.2, which are eventually expressed linguistically. According to this view, the representational system underlying sentences is based upon propositions—relations among concepts—and upon the processes that operate upon them to produce new propositions. Although this is a reasonable approach, very little in the way of evidence can be cited either for or against it. The propositional model and the early stages of the translation from thought to speech would have to be elaborated in much more detail before we could carefully evaluate them.

Decisions that we make about the structure of the mental code have implications for our view of the production process. To see this, consider the following problem. In the previous chapter we discussed the idea of a semantic feature. We noted that there is a controversy over whether such terms as *bachelor* are represented in the underlying system of thought as being composed of a set of concepts corresponding to the words *unmarried, adult, male,* etc. If the concept of bachelor is constructed from other concepts, then the speaker would actually have to construct the concept underlying *bachelor* out of its conceptual components before using it. This construction would be an early stage in the production process.

Detailed theories of the early stages of the translation process have not been worked out and tested. There have been, however, a number of investigations into the effects that certain decisions about sentence content have on observable aspects of sentence production. Before we review some of these investigations, we should point out that the types of data gathered in sentence production studies are often different from those we saw in earlier chapters. Some investigations do use somewhat familiar measures, such as the time taken (latency) to begin speaking. Others, however, measure such factors as hesitations and other speech disfluencies and speech errors. We will describe each of these sources of data in more detail as we introduce experiments or claims based upon them.

More on Content

It seems reasonable to suppose that the difficulty of the topic under discussion will have a measurable impact on sentence production. In one demon-

Table 6.1
Effects of Topic Word on Latency to Produce a Sentence. Latencies in Seconds.
(Examples of topic words are shown in parentheses.)

	Topic Word Frequency		
	High	*Low*	*Mean*
Concrete Topic	2.27 (car)	3.49 (kaleidoscope)	2.88
Abstract Topic	2.71 (joy)	3.76 (affluence)	3.24
Mean	2.49	3.62	3.06

(Modification of Table 1 from Taylor, I. Content and structure in sentence production. *Journal of Verbal Learning and Verbal Behavior,* 1969, *8,* 170–175. Copyright 1969 by Academic Press, Inc. Used by permission.)

stration of this, Taylor (1969) gave her subjects a single word which was specified as a topic word. The subjects were told to make up a complete sentence using the word; they were also instructed to begin producing the sentence as soon as the topic word was presented. Four basic categories of topic words were used: topic words were either high or low frequency words and, within each of these categories, they referred to either concrete or abstract objects (see Table 6.1). Taylor measured the amount of time from the presentation of the topic word to the time when the subject started producing the sentence. She found that the topic word had a significant impact on the production latencies. Concrete words led to shorter times than did abstract words; frequent words led to shorter times than did infrequent words. These results square pretty well with common-sense expectations.

Taylor did not find that sentence structure had any effect. Passive sentences took no longer than active ones; even long sentences did not differ from short ones. The long reaction times (they varied from .5 to 48 seconds) suggest that the speakers had usually formulated what they were going to say before they began speaking. That is, they may have explicitly rehearsed all or part of the sentence to themselves before speaking. This is not, of course, what normally happens during sentence production, and it may have hidden the effects, if any, of sentence structure.

Another set of studies has investigated the complexity of sentence content by examining its effects on hesitations and pauses during speech. Levin, Silverman, and Ford (1967) began their experiment by showing children some unusual events. In one case, two balloons of different colors and sizes were filled with gas, the larger with helium, the smaller with air. The experimenter then held both balloons in one hand and released them. The large one floated up, the small one fell. Then the children were asked a series of questions, including *What happened*? and *Why do you think that happened*? The experimenters recorded the children's replies to these questions and analyzed them for several types of speech disfluencies: filled pauses such as *uh, um, er;* grammatical corrections such as *The balloons go - went up;* repetitions such as *Then-then-you put them together;* and others. They also noted where unfilled pauses of greater than 80 msec duration occurred.

Levin et al. hypothesized that descriptive speech is easier to construct than explanatory speech. They reasoned as follows. First, they assumed that the speaker makes some choices about sentence structure and lexical items while the utterance is occurring (i.e., the entire utterance is not planned before it begins). Second, they assumed that there is a relationship between the ease of constructing the content of the message and the ease with which the structural and lexical choices are made. When content is relatively easy to form (as in descriptive speech), then speech will be more fluent than when content is relatively harder to form (as in explanatory speech). If this line of reasoning is correct, then descriptive speech should be more fluent. And that is what they found. Both the number of hesitations and the number of filled pauses went up dramatically in answer to the *why* (explanatory) questions as compared to the *what* (descriptive) questions. For example, there was an average of about one hesitation every twelve words while answering the *what* questions. But in answering the *why* questions there was a hesitation every seven words.

Earlier Goldman-Eisler (1962) had found similar results when she asked adults to describe and then interpret *New Yorker* cartoons. We may quote the conclusion reached by Levin et al. "To search one's memory, to accept or reject an idea that comes to mind, to put ideas together—in short, to think—is not automatic and results, as we have seen, in slow, pause-filled, hesitant, speech" (p. 564).

Once again, the above results correspond quite well to our common sense beliefs about what happens during the construction of a sentence. There is some tension, however, between the results we have just cited and the earlier quotation from William James. Recall that James said that our intentions were formed before we spoke and that the words and structures were welcomed when they fit the intention and rejected when they did not. The Levin et al. results suggest that the intention is not totally formed before the onset of normal spontaneous speech. At the limit this is obvious; we do not have the entire paragraph, with all of its detailed structure, in mind before we begin holding forth on some topic. But we seem to have some pieces of it. What pieces? How far ahead do we plan? These are questions having primarily to do with structural matters.

Structural Factors in Sentence Production

We have noted that one difficulty in looking at the problem of sentence production as a translation process is that we do not know the input to the translation mechanism. We assume that some portion of the message is formulated in an abstract propositional code before the utterance begins; we do not know how much. In order to discuss the "size" of the planning unit for sentence production, it will help to recall that each sentence has both a hierarchical structure and a particular sequence of words or morphemes. There are some elementary models of production which emphasize one of these or the other. Neither is a complete model, but both merit attention since they have stimulated experimental work in the area.

Elementary Production Models

One elementary approach to sentence production emphasizes the fact that the words or morphemes in an utterance occur one after another. For that reason, this is sometimes called the "*left-to-right*" model of production. Assume for the moment that the basic unit of production is the word. Then, according to the left-to-right model, the single word is also the planning unit for production, and the choice of the next word in the utterance is solely determined by those preceding. Sometimes the context restricts this choice severely, as in the greeting sequence, *How do you____*? We know with near certainty that the next word is *do.* At other times the decision about the next unit is more difficult because the context does not so strongly determine it. Consider, in this light, sentence fragments **(4)** and **(5)**.

(4) The present experiment was based _____

(5) The results showed that the _____

In **(4)** the next word is probably one like *on* or *near;* it seems as though it would be easy to guess what the next unit will be. In **(5)**, on the other hand, it is not so clear what will occur next; the decision about the next word will be relatively difficult since there are many alternatives.

Figure 6.1 is meant to show this aspect of left-to-right models of production. Each circle or node represents a state of the production system. In Figure 6.1 we start at the initial state (S_1). At that point there are three possible continuations. As we move to the next state (say, S_2), the system produces the word on the branch of the network that we travel (e.g., it produces *a*). At state S_2 there are more possible continuations (five) than there were at S_1; thus, the decision here is more uncertain because of the greater number of alternatives. By the time we are in state S_4 we have only two alternatives; the choice is relatively easy. Left-to-right models of production emphasize this "one after the other" aspect of sentence production; they assume that the production process consists of a series of decisions about what the next output unit will be. Such models do not strongly emphasize the structural character of sentences.

In contrast, the second elementary model of production does emphasize the structural or hierarchical nature of sentences. According to this second model, the units "high up" in the surface-structure tree diagram are chosen before those lower in the tree. Such models are often called "*top-to-bottom*" models of production. According to a top-to-bottom model, the production system may already "know" before it chooses the first word that the sentence is going to have, let us say, an indirect object NP. Therefore, to some extent the

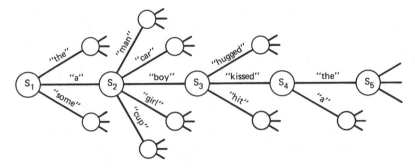

Figure 6.1. A simple left-to-right model of sentence production.

(surface) structural description of the sentence is made use of by the production procedures.

Consider, for example, the initial structure shown in Figure 6.2 In a top-to-bottom production model the first decision concerns the expansion of the S node into, for example, the NP and VP nodes. In one version of a top-to-bottom model we might store the VP node in memory while the NP node is expanded

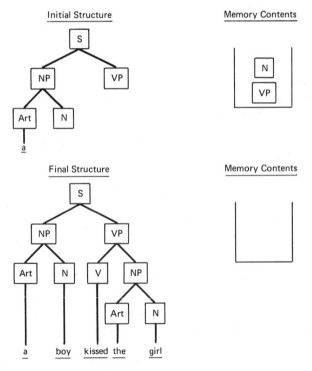

Figure 6.2. A simple top-to-bottom model of sentence production.

into the Art and N nodes. The N is also stored in memory while the Art *a* is produced. This is the momentary picture represented by the top half of Figure 6.2. Both the VP and the N structures are being held in memory at this point. The next step in the process is to recover the last item stored in memory (in this case, the N) and to produce the noun *boy*. Next, the other item in memory, the VP, is recalled, and it is then expanded into its constituents, the V and the NP. The latter is stored in memory and the former is produced as *kissed*. And so on. According to this procedure, the sentence is generated more or less in accordance with a set of phrase-structure rules, with the various high-level nodes of the sentence occupying the short-term memory as the production proceeds. The resulting structure is shown by the bottom half of the figure.

The top-to-bottom model definitely takes the surface structure of the sentence into account—it directly incorporates it into the model, in fact. The model does not, however, say anything about which surface structure is to be produced. That is, it does not provide for a choice between, say, the active and passive versions of a sentence. Therefore, it cannot be the entire story. We will look at some other types of production models shortly. Before then, however, we will review some of the evidence that was stimulated by the question of whether left-to-right or top-to-bottom models are closer to the truth. These studies are concerned with the units of speech planning; most of them also have in common the use of speech disfluencies as evidence for their conclusions.

The Planning Unit: Evidence from Hesitations and Other Disfluencies

In the early 1950's Lounsbury (reprinted, 1965) hypothesized that the left-to-right model had implications for hesitation pauses during sentence production. If words are the units of encoding, he reasoned, then hesitations should increase before words that require difficult decisions, as in those places where the possibilities for continuing the sentence are not restricted to just one or two words. As Lounsbury put it, "Hesitation pauses correspond to the points of highest statistical uncertainty ..." When the speaker is relatively certain of his choice of words, speech should be fluent; when he is uncertain, speech should be disfluent. In terms of Figure 6.1, there should be more disfluencies before *boy* than before *kissed*.

Goldman-Eisler (1958) tested Lounsbury's hypothesis and found some evidence supporting it. She looked at a small sample of spoken utterances and calculated the relative amount of "uncertainty" at each point in the sentence. This can be done by using a guessing technique. In this technique we take sentence fragments like (4) or (5) and ask subjects to guess the next word. They are to continue guessing until they get the word. We can do this for each point in the sentence. Words which require a large number of guesses are at the points of high uncertainty. Typically the points just before "content" words (e.g., nouns, verbs, adjectives) will have more uncertainty than points just prior to "function" words (e.g., articles, prepositions, conjunctions). Goldman-Eisler found in her speech sample that words which had been preceded by a pause were more difficult to guess than words which had not been preceded by a pause. That is, the pauses occurred at the points of uncertainty. Related studies by Maclay and Osgood (1959) and Martin (1971) also found more disfluencies before content than before function words. These findings are consistent with the idea that word choices are made as the speaker goes along during sentence production; that is, they support a left-to-right model of production with words as the unit of encoding.

The idea that single words are the planning units and that speaking is a left-to-right choice process has not gone unchallenged. In a now classic paper called "The problem of serial order in behavior," Karl Lashley (1951) noted that the order in which speech segments are produced must be imposed by some high-level organizational principles or schema. He argued that the order of sounds within words and of words within sentences cannot be determined by simple habitual (left-to-right) connections between them. The same sounds (approximately) that constitute the word *right* also constitute the word *tire,* but in reverse order. The order that occurs on any particular occasion must be imposed by some higher-level planning system which has chosen the word to be uttered. Lashley noted that the problem of order among elements is a general one, affecting all skilled movements.

Some researchers have questioned the evidence which seems to support the left-to-right model of production. Boomer (1965, 1970), in particular, has been critical of the claim that the hesitation data support the left-to-right model. For example, he has pointed out that the speech samples used by Goldman-Eisler were both small and highly selective. Only twelve grammatical, well-constructed sentences were used in Goldman-Eisler's (1958) experiment. Also, the samples of speech used by Maclay and Osgood were somewhat atypical. They only analyzed utterances from monologues longer than 80 words. And Martin (1971) and others have shown that hesitations still occur when the speaker knows in advance the content words of the utterance that he is going to produce. If hesitations are due to the problem of choosing content words, such hesitations should not have occurred in Martin's experiment.

Boomer (1965) proposed that the encoding unit was not the single word but, rather, a sequence of several words roughly corresponding to a surface structure phrase. He argued, "If the encoding unit is a sequence of several words then the hesitations should predominate at the beginnings of such sequences, rather than occurring randomly wherever a difficult word choice occurs" (p. 148). Boomer found that hesitations occurred much more frequently than chance allowed at the beginnings of phrases, but only at chance levels in the middles and at the ends of phrases. He also argued that the point of major uncertainty typically occurs toward the end of a phrase; his results show no increase in hesitations at those points. Boomer concluded, therefore, that his data implied "a rather more complex process in which planning ranges forward to encompass a structured 'chunk' of syntax and meaning. As a given clause is being uttered the next one is taking shape and focus" (p. 157). He went on to propose that speech is suspended at the clause boundary until the entire clause has been subjectively formulated. Hesitations primarily reflect this latter process, not that of individual word choice. This model has, therefore, more elements of the top-to-bottom view than did Goldman-Eisler's.

We might note at this point that hesitations need not spring from a single source. When one reads aloud one does not suppress all of the pauses. These pauses can be used to signal structural information to the hearer. It is also worth keeping in mind the finding of Levin et al., cited earlier, that hesitations are more numerous when the utterance is on a difficult topic than when it is on a simple one. It may be that the ease of planning ahead is a function of the topic difficulty, and that difficulties due to content decisions as well as structural ones will show up at clause boundaries. Thus, clause boundary hesitations may reflect content decisions as well as structural or lexical ones.

Boomer's hypothesis concerns itself with phrase boundaries in general. Recently there has been some work on hesitations which looks more closely at the type of clause or phrase boundary. For example, Rochester and Gill (1973) analyzed the speech disfluencies of 20 subjects as they spoke about current events in either a monologue or a dialogue with another subject. Rochester and Gill were interested in whether disfluencies would be more common in syntactically complex sentences than in simple ones. They compared disfluencies such as filled and unfilled pauses in these two types of utterances. In addition, they looked at two types of complex sentences, those like **(6)** which contain relative clauses, and those like **(7)** which contain what are called noun-phrase complements.

(6) The book [which was written by Millet] was lauded by all.

(7) The fact [that the woman was aggressive] threatened the professors.

They chose these two types because they occurred with high frequency in the spontaneous speech of their subjects. In addition, they suspected from linguistic analyses that relative clauses are more closely tied than complements to the noun phrases they modify. As a result, they expected that there would be fewer disruptions at the clause boundaries for the relative clause sentences.

Rochester and Gill found that there was a relationship between sentence complexity (as measured by the number of subordinate clauses in a sentence) and speech disfluencies. The more complex the sentence, the greater the likelihood that a disfluency occurred. They also found fewer disruptions in sentences with relative clauses than in sentences with complements, as they expected. These findings suggest that the speaker may be engaged in some fairly complex planning at the points where he pauses or otherwise disrupts the flow of his speech. This planning may be affected by the fact that some clauses are more closely related than others, though it is not clear what determines the degree of relationship. In any event, the simple left-to-right model of production cannot account for data such as these.

Up to this point, then, we have seen evidence that sentence planning can extend considerably past the next word, and that such aspects of production as hesitations and other disfluencies can be affected by the syntactic structure of what is to come as well as by the conceptual difficulty of what is being spoken. This evidence does not support any model which says that only the next constituent has an effect on speech disfluencies.

A Direct Incorporation Model

Let us now consider a hypothesis that is at once simple and unintuitive: namely, that the translation system utilizes something analogous to the transformational component of the standard generative grammar. According to this theory, the intention of the speaker during the translation process is represented for a time in a form equivalent to the underlying structure of the sentence. At this point the main and subordinate clauses of a complex sentence both assume their mental representation. The translation procedure would then consist of operations that are equivalent to transformational rules. According to this view, sentence production processes directly incorporate part of the grammar of the language. We will call this the *direct incorporation* model of sentence production.

A direct incorporation model of sentence production is, as we said, simple and unintuitive. It is simple because it permits the psycholinguist to borrow whatever transformational rules are linguistically sound, so the linguist must do all the work. (Of course, it isn't quite that simple, since linguists hotly dispute which rules and rule schema are the correct ones.) The model is not intuitive for a number of reasons. For one thing, it seems to say that the entire underlying sentence is present in the mind of the speaker before he even utters its first word. This must be so, because some transformational rules require that the entire underlying structure be present before we can tell whether the rule applies. We have seen, of course, that speech is full of disfluencies. According to the direct incorporation model, some of them might arise when an underlying structure was not developed enough for the appropriate transformational rules to apply. Thus, the model really claims only that a fully developed underlying structure is required whenever we observe fluent speech. Perhaps this is intuitive after all; fluent speech is not the rule.

There is some evidence that is consistent with the direct incorporation model of sentence production. For example, Valian and Wales (1976) have argued that speakers do know the underlying structures of their utterances, and that they can produce either relatively simple or relatively complex versions of them. A simple version is a sentence whose surface form is close to the underlying form and so does not require many transformations in its derivation. A complex version is a surface form which differs greatly from the underlying form.

In order to demonstrate that speakers know whether their utterances are simple or complex versions of the underlying sentence, Valian and Wales had speakers first read a sentence from a card. A listener would sometimes ask, *What?*, and the speakers were instructed to act as they would in real life, either repeating the sentence verbatim or changing it in any way that they chose, whichever seemed most natural.

Some of the sentences on the cards required relatively few transformations; others required more. For example, **(8)** requires fewer transformations than does **(9)**; and **(10)** requires fewer than **(11)**.

(8) The spy divulged the secret to Emma.

(9) The secret was divulged to Emma by the spy.

(10) Ginny persuasively argued her case.

(11) Ginny argued her case persuasively.

Valian and Wales counted the number of times that the sentences were repeated verbatim and the number of times that one form was changed into another, e.g., how often **(9)** was changed to **(8)** in response to *What?*

Usually the subjects repeated the sentence verbatim in response to *What?* However, this tendency was much stronger for the transformationally simple sentences (69% verbatim responses) than for the transformationally more complex sentences (42% verbatim responses). The subjects were more likely to simplify the complex sentences than they were to complicate the simple ones. Valian and Wales concluded that speakers "have knowledge of deeper levels of syntactic representation than the surface level" (p. 69). Furthermore, they argued that speakers interpret a *What?* question as a request to simplify the sentence when it is transformationally complex. Since speakers have knowledge of the deeper level of representation and can, when asked, give a simpler sentence, it seems reasonable to conclude that transformational operations correspond fairly closely with some of the operations of normal sentence production.

Other arguments in favor of the direct incorporation model have been put forward by Hausser (1971) and by Fay (e.g., Foss & Fay, 1975). Fay argues that there is a class of speech errors which can be explained if we assume that there has been an error in the application of a transformational rule. Consider, for example, sentence fragment **(12)**:

(12) And when they chew coca, which they chew all day long, they . . .

In the underlying structure of this sentence, the second clause contains the word *coca*. It would be something like **(13)**:

(13) . . . they chew *coca* all day long . . .

During the course of the transformational derivation of **(12)**, the NP *coca* is deleted from the second clause. Fay proposed that this deletion operation might sometimes fail to take place. In case it did fail, then one would observe utterances in which the NP occurred twice, once correctly and once because it had not been properly deleted. In fact, Fay observed utterance **(14)**, which fits this description.

(14) And when they chew coca, which they chew *coca* all day long, they . . .

Menyuk (1969) has also observed utterances by children which appear to support Fay's hypothesis that some required deletion operations are occasionally omitted. For example, Menyuk observed **(15)** and **(16)**.

(15) Put on some rouge on.

(16) How can he can look?

Of course, the existence of such speech errors does not prove the direct incorporation model. But they at least suggest that some elements are moved from one location to another after the message is formulated but before the utterance makes its appearance.

Among the evidence bearing on the direct incorporation model there is some running contrary to it, such as that arising from a sentence production experiment carried out by Tannenbaum and Williams (1968). The subjects in their experiment were presented with a picture (e.g., a train hitting a car) and were asked to make up quickly a sentence describing the picture. Each picture had either an *A* or a *P* in the corner. The letter specified whether the sentence should be spoken in the active or the passive voice (e.g., *The train is hitting the car; The car is being hit by the train*). Tannenbaum and Williams measured the total amount of time that the subject took to speak the sentence after the picture was shown. There was one additional variable in their experiment. Each picture was preceded by a short paragraph which focused on either the agent (the train) or the object (the car) of the picture or on neither of them (neutral focus condition). The investigators hypothesized that if a subject had just been reading about cars it would be more natural to say that the car is being hit by the train than it would be to say that the train is hitting the car.

The results of the Tannenbaum and Williams experiment are shown in Figure 6.3. In the neutral focus condition it took the speakers longer to say the passive than the active sentence. This is what the direct incorporation model would predict, since the passive sentence requires more transformational operations to produce. The advantage of the active was even greater when the focus of the previous paragraph was on the actor (the train). However, as can be seen in Figure 6.3, the difference in production time between active and passive sentences essentially disappeared when the previous paragraph had focused upon the object (the car). This result argues against a simple direct incorporation model of production.

So far, as we have discussed the planning units of speech, we have seen that these units are larger than single words. The word-by-word, left-to-right model of production is not correct. The data argue that the next phrase or

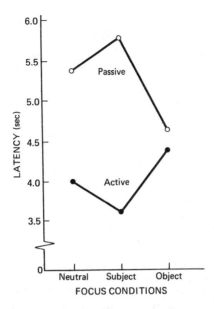

Figure 6.3. The time (latency) required to produce active and passive sentences under various conditions of focus. (From Tannenbaum, P. H. & Williams, F. Generation of active and passive sentences as a function of subject or object focus. *Journal of Verbal Learning and Verbal Behavior,* 1968, *7,* 246–250. Copyright 1968 by Academic Press, Inc. Used by permission.)

clause is in a state of readiness before it is uttered. However, this does not necessarily mean that the speaker has chosen all of the lexical items for a phrase before he begins to utter it. Rather, it means that the sentence's structure and semantic interpretation have been prepared. The speaker may still occasionally have to grope for a word at the time when the concept is due to be expressed. We will expand upon this view later. In the next section we will look at some additional evidence concerning the units of speech planning and at some other models of production. Most of the work that we are going to examine derives from analyses of speech errors. Therefore, we will briefly detour and consider in somewhat more detail this method of collecting production data.

Speech Errors and Sentence Production

For a long time there has been at least some interest in speech errors as a source of relevant data for models of sentence production. Fromkin (1973) cites Meringer as the "father" of the linguistic interest in speech errors: in 1895 and 1908 he published over eight thousand speech, reading, and writing errors. However, since most linguistic research in the intervening years has been concerned with the structure of language and not with the process of producing it, interest in speech error data was fairly slight until the past fifteen years or so. Up to 1968 there had been fewer than a dozen systematic studies of slips of the tongue; now there are many papers on the topic (some of the important ones have been collected by Fromkin, 1973).

Slips of the tongue have long been thought to reveal some of our inner thoughts, including those that we would rather keep hidden; the Bible says, "But the tongue can no man tame; it is an unruly evil, full of deadly poison" (*James* 3:8). In his *Psychopathology of Everyday Life,* Sigmund Freud speculated that some of the sources of errors come from outside the word or sentence context; come, in fact, from sources that we had not intended to reveal. Freud analyzed many slips, making psychodynamic interpretations of them. For example, a young woman at a social gathering "uttered with fervor and under the pressure of a host of secret impulses: 'Yes, a woman must be pretty if she is to please men. A man is much better off; as long as he has his five straight limbs he needs nothing more!'" Freud speculated that the slip was a fusion between "four straight limbs" and "five wits about him." Interesting as such speculations are, it turns out that most slips (though perhaps not all) can be accounted for by more homely linguistic hypotheses. One of the interesting discoveries that has been made about speech errors is that the errors themselves follow rules. Before we get to such rules, however, let us look at what speech errors can tell us about the linguistic units that are actually utilized during sentence production.

Errors and Linguistic Units

Recall from Chapter 3 that the speech stream is continuous; there aren't any neat breaks in the speech signal which correspond to linguistic units. Theorists have devised the units as part of the theory of language organization and use. Speech errors can be found to support most of the units that have been hypothesized as underlying the speech stream: phonological segments, features of segments, syllables, words, morphemes, etc. Let us consider some errors for what they tell us about the units of speech, for a model of production must make use of such units.

Many speech errors involve phonological segments (e.g., phonemes). For example, if a speaker is attempting to say *a reading list* and instead says *a leading list,* it is plausible that the error resulted from the /l/ in *list* being anticipated by the speaker. In addition to anticipation errors, there are perseveration errors at the level of the phoneme. In a perseveration error an earlier phoneme reappears at a later, incorrect, point, e.g., *a phonological rule* comes out as *a phonological fool.*

One of the most interesting types of segmental errors occurs when two segments change places. These have come to be known as "spoonerisms," named after Rev. Wm. A. Spooner (1844-1930), who served as dean and warden of New College, Oxford. Spooner is famous as the source of many excellent speech errors. Examples: instead of saying the intended *our dear old queen,* Spooner said *our queer old dean;* he said *you have hissed all my mystery lectures* instead of *you have missed all my history lectures;* and when Spooner intended to say *he dealt a crushing blow,* he came out with *he dealt a blushing crow.* Two more: Spooner is reputed to have spoken of the *noble tons of soil,* and to have said that *Work is the curse of the drinking classes.* Actually, there is some question as to whether all of these errors were spontaneous; Spooner may have planned many of them for their humor value. Nonetheless, many such reversals do occur as spontaneous speech errors.

In the above examples we can already see some regularities in the errors: initial phonemes of words change places with initial phonemes of other words; initial phoneme clusters such as /cr/ and /bl/ change locations; and entire words shift positions. There are also examples in which vowels change places. A famous example, available in Kermit Schaeffer's recorded collection of radio and TV bloopers, occurred when a radio announcer was making an introduction; he said, *Ladies and gentlemen, the President of the United States, Hoobert Heever.* Then, too, the vowels have shifted position in the error, *The Duck and Doochess of Windsor.* Final consonants can also switch with each other as when *hash or grass* becomes *hass or grash.*

There are also speech errors that can be neatly accounted for if we assume that phonological features such as voicing have switched positions. Consider this example, borrowed from Fromkin (1971, 1973). A speaker intended to say *clear blue sky,* but instead said *glear plue sky.* In this example we cannot simply say that two phonemes have switched places. Perhaps the occurrence of the /g/ and the /p/ are just randomly occurring errors. However, Fromkin has a more interesting hypothesis. She suggests that the feature [+voiced] has been dropped from the /b/ in *blue* and has appeared earlier in the /k/ in *clear.* Recall that if we add [+voiced] to /k/ we get /g/, thus *clear* will change to *glear.* And if we drop the voicing feature from /b/ we get /p/, thus *blue* will become *plue.* So *glear plue sky* might not be just a random error, but the result of a Spoonerism at the level of phonological features. One other example of this kind of error: a speaker intended to say *big and fat* but came out with *pig and vat.* Once again we can account for this error by assuming that the voicing feature has vanished from /b/, leaving *pig,* and has reappeared later on /f/, yielding *vat.* Since we can tell such a coherent story about speech errors by appealing to phonological features, it bolsters our confidence that this concept is psychologically valid.

We have now looked at enough errors to begin to see some emerging patterns. One generalization about slips, called by Wells (1951, reprinted in Fromkin, 1973) the "First Law of Tongue Slips," is that each error results in a phonetically possible noise. That is, when we err we do not produce some bit of linguistic hash that could not be English. We might say *scrill* as an error; it is a possible English word. We (almost) never say something like *ktin* which is not a permissible English syllable. The rules of English syllable formation carry over into our errors. It is important to note that there is nothing humanly impossible about a work like *ktin;* words in ancient Greek can begin with *kt.* (Note that English words can end in *kt* as in *picked.*) This sequence is forbidden at the beginning of a word by the rules of English syllable formation, not by some inherent biological limitation. This suggests that some editing of phonetically illegal sequences occurs during the production process. If an error results in an "impossible" sequence for English, it may be blocked by the "editor," thus causing a speech disfluency. Of course, suggesting that there is an internal editor raises as many problems as it solves, since we must then ask why the editor does not catch all the errors. We will discuss this problem more fully later.

A second generalization about speech errors, agreed to by everyone who has studied the problem, was nicely stated by Boomer and Laver (1968): "Segmental slips obey a structural law with regard to syllable place; that is, initial segments in the original syllable [the syllable actually spoken] replace initial segments in the target syllable [the intended syllable], nuclear replace nuclear, and final replace final." All of the above examples fit this generalization. If a Spoonerism occurs with *well made,* it will come out as *mell wade,* not as *wem lade.* That is, the last phoneme of the first syllable does not interchange with the first phoneme of the second syllable. Such errors are simply not made. This fact attests to the psychological reality of the syllable as a planning unit in speech production. We cannot even state the generalization without appealing to the concept of the syllable.

To summarize, we have seen that the error data support the hypothesis that speech has many planning units: words, syllables, phonological segments, and even phonological features. We also noted that there are rules or generalizations about the types of errors that can occur.

Later we will examine some of the implications of these generalizations for models of the production process. First, however, let us look at some other kinds of errors.

Errors and Sentence Stress

Speech errors in which segments are exchanged usually involve two words that receive fairly high stress in the utterance. Thus, in an utterance like *He saw the boy,* interactions between *the,* which receives fairly low stress, and *boy,* which receives fairly high stress, are uncommon. We will not often see errors like *He saw thoy ba,* with the ends of these two words interchanged. On the other hand, we do observe errors like *Children interfere with your nife lite* (night life). In this example, taken from Garrett (1975), the words *night* and *life* were both meant to receive stress in the intended utterance. This example also demonstrates another generalization: exchange errors tend to involve words that are phonologically similar to one another.

Perhaps more importantly, speech errors show the following general tendency: the stress pattern of a sentence stays the same even when syllables or words are transposed. For example, among the sample of 3400 speech errors collected by Garrett and his colleagues was this gem: *Stop beating your brick*[1] *against a head wall.* The main stress of the sentence fell on the work *brick,* not on the word *head.* (The superscript [1] shows the point of highest stress.) The intended utterance, clearly, was *Stop beating your head against a brick wall.* If said with normal intonation, the main stress will fall on *head.* When the error occurred, the words *head* and *brick* were interchanged, but the stress remained in its originally intended place; the stress did not move along with *head.* Fromkin, too, has observed many examples of this phenomenon. To cite just one, the speaker intended, *Hey, Mike, have you heard the joke about . . .* but instead said, *Hey, joke, have you heard the Mike about . . .* Again, the stress stayed in the original location and did not move with the word that was intended to carry it.

Let's look at the last error type for what it might tell us about a model of the production process. Following Fromkin and others, we might speculate that, at some point during the internal preparation of the sentence, the speaker translates the message from its non-linguistic code into one that is syntactically structured. Stress is then assigned to the sentence on the basis of its syntax and the concepts that are meant to be its focus. If a word transposition error occurs, it does so after this stage of the production process. However, since stress is still determined by the syntactic organization that was given to the message at the earlier stages, the stress will occur at its proper location and not on the proper word. We are proposing, then, that production consists of a series of stages, and that speech errors can help us to understand the stages and the order in which they occur.

Errors and Production Adjustments

There is another kind of error which also sheds some light on the stage analysis of sentence production. Consider the error that occurred when a speaker was attempting to say *an eating marathon.* In this case the /m/ was anticipated in the immediately preceding word and was dropped from the word *marathon.* The result was *a meeting arathon.* What is notable about this error is that *an* has also changed: it is now *a.* Other examples show the same phenomenon. Thus, the intended *an ice cream cone* came out as *a kice ream cone.* In this example the /k/ phoneme was anticipated, and, again, the *an* changed to *a.* It is possible to tell an interesting story about why this happens.

Whether or not an English speaker says *a* or *an* depends upon the initial phoneme of the following word. If the next phoneme is a vowel, then *an* is used; if it is a consonant, *a* is used. This is a general rule of English. Now suppose that when the sentence is being planned, all that is specified is that there will be an indefinite article before the noun or adjective; the form of the indefinite article (*a* or *an*) is not specified. Thus, the planning code might look something like this: *[indef art] eat + ing marathon.* In addition, suppose that during the course of sentence production there is a rule which applies to the segment *[indef art*] ; this rule looks at the next phoneme and specifies whether [*indef art*] should be *a* or *an,* depending upon whether that phoneme is a consonant or a vowel. Now, when the anticipation error occurs—when the /m/ moves into position in front of *eating*—the resulting code will then be: [*indef art*] *meet* + *ing arathon.* Note that exactly the same rule will apply to the segment [*indef art*] but the result of applying the rule will be different. Since the next phoneme is a consonant, the word *a* will be chosen. Once again the speech error data suggest that there are specific stages to the production process, and that the stages are defined by the rules or operations that occur in them. This particular example (from Fromkin, 1971) suggests that phonological adjustments to terms like [*indef art*] occur quite late in the production process.

You may have noted that we represented the word *eating* in the above example as *eat* + *ing;* that is, we broke it down into its morphemes. The speech error data suggest that words like *eating* are not single entries in the speaker's mental dictionary. Many speech errors occur in which the stem of the word (e.g., *eat*) gets separated from the prefix or suffix (e.g., *ing*). Thus, in the Rev. Spooner's creation, cited earlier, we observed *Work is the curse of the drinking class.* In this case the *ing* stayed in the intended position while *work* and *drink* shifted positions. And *McGovern favors pushing busters* (busting pushers) shows the same thing. These data suggest, then, that at least some suffixes are added to the basic morphemes by rules. For example, at one point during the assembly of the message to be produced, the verb may be marked as occurring in the progressive tense, that is, the code may be [*bust* + *prog tns*]. When an exchange error occurs and, e.g., *bust* and *push* are transposed, the resulting code would be [*push* + *prog tns*], which will end up as *pushing* after the rule for turning *prog tns* into -*ing* is applied. There is room for a lot of discussion about which forms are stored in the mental lexicon and which are formed by rules (recall our discussion of the mental lexicon in Chapter 4); this is a topic upon which linguists are currently working. Overall, however, the speech error data are consistent with the notion that at least some forms are constructed by rules which come fairly late in the production process.

There is also evidence that some "editing" occurs late in the production process. Baars, Motley, and MacKay (1975) have described a clever technique for stimulating spoonerisms. The subject is shown a number of word pairs, and on some pairs is given a signal to pronounce the words as quickly as possible. For example, the subject may be asked to quickly pronounce *dumb* - *seal.* If this word pair is preceded by three pairs, each of which starts with /s/, there is a tendency for the speaker to spoonerize the target pair, yielding *some* - *deal.* Baars et al. used target pairs like *dumb* - *seal,* which yield two new words if spoonerized, and others like *dump* - *seat,* which do not lead to two real words if spoonerized. The subjects were much more likely to spoonerize *dumb* - *seal* than *dump* - *seat.* That is, they made more production errors when such errors gave new words than when the products were not all words. This result suggests that errors which do not yield words are typically edited out at a late stage in the production process. That is, we may assume that the probability of internally making an error is the same in each case, but only the errors which pass lexical inspection are permitted to occur. Those that fail this inspection rarely make it all the way through the production system.

Semantic Errors

The most Freudian-sounding speech errors occur when the meaning of a lexical item is changed. It sounds suspicious when someone says *I've continually been distressed, uh, impressed by her.* Not all such errors sound Freudian, however. We also observe errors like *The four blind, uh, deaf children* and *Look at the lady with the dachshund* (when what was intended was *Look at the lady with the Volkswagon*). Thus, while some word substitutions suggest a motivational explanation (*distressed* for *impressed* sounds like the unconscious slipping through), others do not (*blind* for *deaf* seems rather innocent). It may be that the sinister sounding errors are the result of the same processes that produce the innocent ones, that Freud and others have overinterpreted the data on the basis of a few outstanding and memorable examples.

In order to account for these semantic errors, we might make the following proposal. Assume that at some point during the production process the message is represented in a semantic code, perhaps including information similar to that represented by semantic features of the sort discussed earlier (see Chapter 5). One of the next stages in production involves the speaker recovering an entry from his mental lexicon that matches the intended item in the message. However, as the search of the mental dictionary proceeds, he may lose one or more of the semantic features or may accidently give it some new value. Thus, a positive concept like LOVE may lose its positive information, and a word that is similar, except that it is negative (e.g., *hate*), may be chosen instead of *love*. This error will result in the Freudian sounding *I really hate - I mean love to dance with you.*

Sometimes, too, the semantic specification may fit very well with two entries in the mental dictionary and both words may enter the later stages of the production process. This could help explain the speech errors called blends—combination words that are not in the language. Thus, a speaker may say *My data consists moinly . . .*, which is probably a blend of the two words *mainly* and *mostly*. A somewhat clearer example of this may be the speech error *He is an imposinator* (a blend of *imposter* and *impersonator*). A favorite example of a blend arose when someone tried to say *It's a lot of bother/trouble,* producing instead *It's a lot of brothel.*

We see, then, that certain forms of speech errors can arise from the semantic aspects of sentence planning. These errors, we suggest, have somewhat different sources than do spoonerisms or errors in stress assignment. Since not all speech errors have the same source, we are trying to use them to help us sort out

Malapropisms

One fairly obvious aspect of the semantic errors that we have just described is that the error word is not very similar phonologically to the intended word. There are other word substitution errors which have the opposite character—they are phonologically similar to the intended word, but not similar in meaning. This latter type of error is often called a *malapropism,* named after Sheridan's comic character Mrs. Malaprop, who produced many such errors. The malapropism is a standard comic device. A TV character may say *We need a few laughs to break up the monogamy.* Examples of spontaneously occurring malapropisms are the substitution of *equivocal* for *equivalent* in the utterance *If these two vectors are equivocal, then . . .* , and the utterance *He is a good magician* when what was intended was *musician.* Fay and Cutler (1977) have documented the similarities between malapropism errors and their intended words. The vast majority (93%) of the errors contain the same number of syllables as the intended word. Likewise, in 98% of the cases, the stress falls on the same syllable in both the intended and the produced word. Fay and Cutler also documented the degree to which the error word is similar in sound to the intended word: they are highly similar.

In order to account for malapropisms, Fay and Cutler proposed that words which are similar in syllable structure, stress, and sound pattern are stored "near" one another in the mental lexicon. That is, they suggested that phonological similarity is one of the important organizing principles in the mental lexicon. If an error occurs quite late during the process of looking for a word corresponding to the intended concept, then an item that is "next door" to the intended word might be picked instead. This will result in a word that is similar in sound, but not in meaning, to the intended word. According to this proposal, there are two sources of errors that can occur in lexical search. One is an early error in which an aspect of the semantic representation of the word is changed—this will result in a semantic (*love-hate*) substitution. The second is a late error in which a word that is "near" to the intended word is inadvertently picked out. This will result in a malapropism (*magician-musician*) substitution.

Sources of Shifting Errors

So far we have seen that some speech errors involve entire words shifting positions and that others involve only pieces of the words shifting. Garrett (1975) has noted that when entire words shift they most often do so between two separate noun phrases or other phrasal units. In his data, only 20% of the word transpositions occurred among words in the same NP. More typical were word shifts across larger units (e.g., *Every time I put one of these buttons off, another one comes on*). The facts are quite different when sounds exchange (e.g., *nife lite*). In this case 71% of the shifts occurred between words in the same NP. This suggested to Garrett that these two types of errors are controlled by different production mechanisms. His idea is supported by some other evidence, too. When whole words shifted, 87% of them were from the same part of speech (*off* and *on* in the above example). When sounds exchanged, only 19% of the errors occurred between words that were members of the same part of speech.

In order to account for the above pattern of errors, Garrett hypothesized that there are two distinct sources for the word exchanges and the sound exchanges. At an early point in the representation of the sentence the grammatical and functional relations are represented "simultaneously." That is, concepts that will serve similar syntactic or semantic roles in the intended utterance exist together in a storage mechanism. At this point syntactic or semantic features may be lost or may switch with each other. Later in the production sequence lexical items are inserted into the structure. When they are, they reflect the earlier error in syntax (e.g., direct and indirect objects exchanging: *She donated a library to the book*) or semantics (e.g., *love-hate*).

Still later in the production of the message the items are arranged into their serial (left-to-right) order. The positions of the words in the utterance will then have been chosen. It is at this point that items relatively near to each other in the surface representation can interact (they exist "simultaneously" in a storage mechanism). Errors among items that do not belong to the same form class can now occur. The probability of such an error occurring is a function of the degree of phonological similarity of the two words and their contexts.

In summary, then, Garrett believes that word exchanges and phonological exchanges have different origins. During an early stage of production, the functional relations exist together in one storage mechanism. At a later stage, the serially-ordered elements exist together in a different storage mechanism. Interactions in the first storage device lead to word or phrase exchanges; interactions in the second storage device lead to phonological exchanges.

A Model of Sentence Production

We have now seen that speech error data are a rich source of evidence both for the planning units that exist in sentence production and for ideas about the processing stages that occur during production. Let us try to use the speech error data to put together a very rough model of the sentence production process.

Our crude model is presented in Table 6.2. In building this model we have borrowed from those proposed by Fromkin (1971), Garrett (1975), and MacNeilage and MacNeilage (1973). In Table 6.2 we have specified not only the stages of production, but also the types of errors that are likely to arise at each stage. The order in which the events occur in this model is tentative at best. During the first stage of sentence production, the message is formulated in a non-linguistic code. At this point, the basic relations of the utterance under construction are chosen. It is possible for a concept to be incorrectly marked at this stage so that it ends up playing a different role (subject rather than object, indirect rather than direct object) in the underlying structure of the produced sentence.

Table 6.2

A Model of Sentence Production

Production Stages	Characteristic Actions or Properties	Typical Errors
1. Message formulation or plan	Basic functional relations are expressed in a nonlinguistic code. The unit is larger than the single clause.	Functional transpositions across phrases or clauses, e.g., direct and indirect objects are transposed.
2. Message formulation (continued)	Topic or focus chosen.	
3. Syntactic Structure	Grammatical items such as tense markers, question elements, etc., are inserted.	Markers may be inserted at the wrong locations, e.g., *I disregard this as precise.*
3A. Surface Syntactic Structure Assigned	(Questionable stage)	
4. Sentence Stress Assigned	This is a function of the syntax as well as the items to be focused upon.	
5. Lexical Look-up	Search made on the basis of semantic information from Stage 2.	Early error: Semantic feature switch, e.g., *hate* for *love.*
	Lexical items that are "near" each other are arranged by their sound structure	Two items are chosen resulting in a blend, e.g., *imposinator.*
	Syllable and featural information is transferred.	Late error: Malapropism, e.g., *magician* for *musician.*
6. Storage	Serially-ordered storage.	Sound exchange errors of many types, e.g., anticipations, perseverations, transpositions.
7. Adjustments to Morphemes	Late rules which adjust [*indef art*], etc.	Certain errors may be "repaired" (see text).
8. Motor Control Center		

Next, in Stage 2, other aspects of the message are chosen, such as the concepts that are to serve as the topic or focus of the sentence. This choice is made by considering the discourse structure up to that point as well as other, nonlinguistic facts, such as what one happens to be pointing at when speaking.

In Stage 3 a syntactic structure is assigned to the sentence. The ease with which this occurs depends upon how completely the message has been formulated. There are many uncertainties about Stage 3. It is not clear, for example, which syntactic structure, underlying or surface, the speaker first constructs. If it is the former, then Stage 3A occurs, as the direct incorporation model proposes. If it is the latter, then there is no need for Stage 3A. In either case, a question of some magnitude is how the syntactic structure is chosen. However, when the syntactic structure is assigned, it is possible that some syntactic markers might be inserted at incorrect locations relative to the semantic elements of the sentence. This could lead to the wrong items being negated, as when someone intends to say, *I said he couldn't go* but instead says, *I didn't say he could go.*

At Stage 4, stress is assigned to the sentence. Stress assignment is a function both of the items to be focused upon and of the syntactic structure of the sentence.

The next stage in our model, Stage 5, is that of lexical look-up. It is here that the morphemes are accessed and assigned their positions in the structure. Many different types of errors can occur at Stage 5. Early in lexical look-up some semantic information may be dropped. This, too, (like Stage 1 errors) can lead to Freudian-sounding utterances, as when *hate* is substituted for *love.* It is also at this point that two lexical items for the same concept may be retrieved, resulting in blend errors, as when *clarinet* and *viola* blend into *clarinola,* or when *instantaneous* and *momentary* blend into *momentaneous.* At a somewhat later stage of lexical access an error may occur if an item "next to" the target item in the mental lexicon is chosen. This leads to malapropisms of the *magician* for *musician* type.

In order to account for many of the other errors, we must make the reasonable assumption that the information in the mental lexicon is arranged according to syllable structure and phonological features. In Stage 6 the syllabically-structured lexical items are stored in a memory while further adjustments to them are made. This memory probably has a capacity limited to roughly the size of a phrase. Note that we are now talking about a different memory than the one we discussed for Stage 1. Both memories operate continuously during production. At Stage 1, information considerably beyond the single phrase can be represented simultaneously in memory, while the memory capacity at Stage 6 is more limited. The earlier memory did not have information in a serial order, but the later one does. This may be one reason for their different storage capacities. Interactions within phrases are likely to occur while information is in the serially-ordered storage at Stage 6. These interactions are determined by the syllable structure of the items within the memory. That is, first elements of syllables interact with first elements, last with last, etc. We do not have a good explanation for why this should be so.

One reason we must assume that items are held in a serially-ordered memory at Stage 6 is so that the rules which adjust morphemes according to their "surrounding" phonemes can apply at Stage 7. In order for the rules to take into account the surrounding phonemes, serial information must be represented. The rules in question are those which adjust the indefinite article to *a* or *an,* plus numerous others of the same general type. These late rules can "repair" an error, as when a speaker intends to say *there's a small restaurant on the island* but instead says *there's an island on the small restaurant.* In this case the "repair" consists of changing *a* to *an.* If the repair had not been made, then the speaker would have said *there's a island* . . . , a double error.

At Stage 8, the information is forwarded to the motor control center of the brain where it is assembled into instructions to the speech musculature. This in itself is a highly interesting process and one that we will discuss in some detail in the next chapter.

We would again like to underscore the fact that this model of production is highly tentative and subject to change. It is possible to build a somewhat more precise model than we have done here by trying to expand upon each of the stages. This is beyond our present scope. Even if we tried to be as detailed as we could, there would still be a large number of holes when we were done. Although we are still a long way from having an adequate model of sentence production, the speech error data have given us some insight into the units and processes of this everyday procedure.

Summary

Producing an utterance requires making a large number of decisions, both about what to say and about how to say it. Very little is known about the determinants of what an individual says. There are, however, certain rules of conversation (conversational maxims) that seem to guide speakers when they decide upon the level of detail to include in their utterances. Such maxims also help the listener to determine when the speaker is being ironic or witty. A few determinants of sentence structure (as opposed to content) have been studied. There is some evidence that explanatory speech requires more difficult sentence planning than does descriptive speech.

Considerably more is known about the structural units involved in sentence production. The main source of evidence about structural decisions comes from disfluencies, such as hesitations, and errors in sentence production. A simple left-to-right serial model of production was shown to be inadequate, primarily on the basis of hesitation data. A top-to-bottom model of production received somewhat more support from the hesitation data. The present chapter also described a production model that is directly related to a transformational grammar—the direct incorporation model. While there are some data consistent with this model, there are other data that give it trouble.

Evidence from speech errors supports the hypothesis that such linguistic units as phonetic features, segments, syllables, morphemes, and phrases are all psychologically real planning units. Also, speech error data were used to support various hypotheses about the organization of the mental lexicon and about the "editing" processes that occur during production. Furthermore, these data supported the idea that sentence planning had both functional and serial phrases. Table 6.2 summarizes a model of production that was constructed on the basis of the error data.

SUGGESTED READINGS

The work of Grice (1975) is the basic reference for conversational maxims. This work is briefly and clearly introduced by Katz (1972). Our discussion of planning units relied heavily on speech errors. The collection of readings edited by Fromkin (1973) is the single best source on this topic. The later paper by Garrett (1975) is also important.

7

Producing Speech
After It Is Planned

The preceding chapter ended with a diagram of some of the stages of processing involved in the production of language, the last being labeled simply *To Motor Control Center*. Our task in this chapter is to consider the rest of the process of production, to look at what happens between the point when an utterance is specified in its linguistic form and the point when it issues forth as sound. If we were simply to continue developing Chapter 6's diagram in terms of successive stages of processing, we would begin by considering both the mechanisms that control the speech motor system and the kind of representation which the motor control process might involve. However, before we can understand the kind of neurological control necessary for producing speech, we need to learn a bit about the kinds of physical structures being controlled and about how they operate.

Speech Production Mechanisms

In describing the mechanisms involved in the production of speech sounds it is convenient to divide them into three kinds: *respiratory, laryngeal,* and *articulatory*. Together they provide the power for and shape the character of the speech sounds. We will discuss them in this order and in increasing detail.

Respiratory Mechanisms

The role of the respiratory mechanisms can be stated relatively simply: the air pushed out of the lungs provides the power for nearly all speech sounds. A number of muscles are used to produce this air pressure, the most important being those which pull the rib cage downward, decreasing its size and forcing air from the lungs. Normally, the air pressure created by this action is roughly constant when speech is being produced. However, considerable moment-to-moment variation in air pressure is introduced by the laryngeal mechanisms (see below). The air pressure is related both to the intensity of the resulting sound and to the fundamental frequency (F_0) of the speaker's voice.

Laryngeal Mechanisms

While the respiratory mechanisms are involved in all speech sounds, they do not contribute much to the differences among the various sounds. A far more important role in the production of different speech sounds is played by the laryngeal mechanisms. The larynx (see Figure 7.1) is the location of the vocal folds (or cords), small muscular folds that can be set into vibration by the air flow from the lungs. In those sounds characterized as voiced, the sound itself is produced by this vibration. In forming such sounds, the vocal folds are adjusted so that they are almost touching, leaving only a narrow slit between them for air to pass through. When air passes through this constriction, it creates a suction, drawing the vocal folds together and stopping the air flow. As soon as the flow stops, the suction no longer exists, and the folds come apart again, releasing the pressure that has built up. Once they are apart, the suction begins again, and the whole cycle of closing and opening is repeated. Since this opening and closing occurs at a relatively steady rate, the resulting sound is a regular or periodic vibration of the sort heard in vowels and other voiced sounds.

In addition to voiced sounds, all languages use voiceless sounds, such as the consonants in *sue, fee,* or *pie*. Whereas in voiced sounds the vocal folds are brought close enough together that they can close completely, in voiceless sounds they are held so far apart that they cannot be set into vibration by the flow of air between them. The result is, for voiceless sounds, a "noisy" or aperiodic sound of the sort heard in the beginning of *hie*. There are several muscles and cartilages involved in these different laryngeal actions, and how their actions are controlled and coordinated is complex and still not fully understood.

Characterizing sounds as voiced or voiceless refers to the *manner* of laryngeal action which gives rise to them. But in addition to providing the source of most speech sounds, laryngeal actions produce other effects as well. Probably the most notable one is the influence of the larynx on the fundamental frequency (i.e., rate of vibration) of voiced sounds. This is an effect produced primarily by varying the length and tension of the vocal folds. Shorter folds

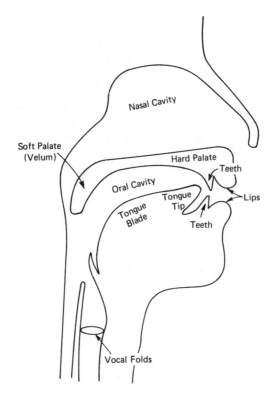

Figure 7.1. The human vocal tract showing most of the articulatory structures important in the production of speech.

produce higher pitches, and increasing the tension of the folds also raises pitch. Pitch varies considerably between speakers. The fundamental frequencies of adult male voices generally vary between 80 and 200 Hz (i.e., 80-200 cycles per second). The range for adult female voices is higher, up to 400 Hz; and for young children, the fundamental may be as high as 500-600 Hz. The fundamental frequency also varies considerably for any one speaker. Consider, for example, the range produced by an opera singer. In this instance the length and tension changes of the vocal folds interact with variations in air pressure to produce pitch changes.

When uttering a normal declarative sentence the voice tends to drop in pitch at the end. In a Yes-No question, on the other hand, the pitch tends to rise at the end. This rise appears to result primarily from an increase in laryngeal tension, for it occurs at a time when the air pressure is actually falling. The cause of the pitch drop in declarative sentences—whether it is primarily a pressure change or a tension change—remains a subject of debate (see, e.g., Lieberman, 1967; Ohala, 1970). In any event, it is clear that coordinating the actions of the laryngeal mechanisms with those of the respiratory mechanisms involves highly complex and subtle motor control of a diverse set of structures.

To summarize briefly, the respiratory mechanisms provide the power for most speech sounds. The laryngeal mechanisms translate this power, air pressure, into sounds. Thus, they are the basic sound source involved in speech, producing sounds that are either periodic or aperiodic in nature. However, before the sound emerges it undergoes a great deal of shaping, shaping that results in the distinctive qualities of different speech sounds. This is the function served by the portions of the vocal tract beyond the larynx—the articulatory mechanisms.

Articulatory Mechanisms

The vocal tract is divided into two portions: the oral tract, including the mouth; and the nasal tract, within the nose. Many speech sounds involve only the oral tract, the nasal passages being closed off so that no sound is transmitted through them. Other sounds involve both the nasal and oral tracts in their production. Within the oral tract the articulators can be divided into two groups: the lower articulators, including the tongue and lower lip; and the upper articulators, including the upper lip and teeth, and the palate. Many speech sounds are characterized by movements of the lower articulators toward the upper articulators. Figure 7.1 illustrates the referents of most of the terms used in describing the articulator movements of speech.

The *upper lip* and *teeth* are so familiar as to require no comment. The *alveolar ridge* is the small projection behind the upper teeth which can easily be felt with the tip of the tongue. Most of the roof of the mouth is formed by the *hard palate* in the front and, at the back, by the *soft palate* (*velum*). The velum is a muscular flap that can be raised to prevent air from passing through the nasal tract. When raised, it presses against the back wall of the *pharynx*.

The tongue is divided into several parts, the *tip* and *blade* being the most mobile. The remainder of the tongue, the *body,* is generally divided into the *front,* which is immediately behind the blade and lies under the forward part of the hard palate; the *center,* which lies beneath the rear of the hard palate and the soft palate; and the *root,* lying opposite the pharynx.

We saw in Chapters 2 and 3 that speech sounds can be distinguished from each other in terms of a set of distinctive features of the sort used by linguists in characterizing the phonological structure and rules of a language. There is a fairly close correspondence between these features and a characterization of the articulator positions involved in producing speech sounds, though the correspondence is less than perfect. Thus we can make use of the distinctive features in characterizing speech production.

Let us start by describing the manner in which the vowels are produced by the articulators. Vowels are typically characterized in terms of the positions of the lips and by the part of the tongue that is higher than any other part during the vowel's articulation. The tongue's highest point, produced with the tip or the blade, is in the front of the mouth for the vowels in *heed, hid, head,* and *had,* and these are classified accordingly as *front* vowels. The highest point of the tongue is produced with one or another part of the tongue's body for the vowels in *hod, hawed, hood,* and *who'd,* and these are referred to as *back* vowels. (If you try pronouncing these vowels you should be able to feel the different tongue positions.) Overall, the tongue is highest for the vowels in *heed* and *who'd* (*high* vowels), and lowest for the vowels in *had* and *hod* (*low* vowels). The height of the tongue is between these extremes for the others (*mid* vowels). The lips may be either *rounded,* as in the vowel in *who'd,* or *unrounded,* as in *heed.* Distinctions like high-low and rounded-unrounded are among the phonological distinctive feature distinctions used to characterize these vowels.

All of the vowels are, of course, produced with *voicing,* that is, with periodic vibration of the vocal folds. The voicing results in sounds which have, in addition to their fundamental frequencies, a series of higher frequencies, or harmonics. As the articulators change positions to make the various vowels, the shape of the vocal tract changes. As a result, some of these harmonics are reinforced and others are weakened or eliminated. An analogy may help in understanding this effect. When you blow into a bottle, the frequency of the sound you hear depends primarily on the amount of liquid in the bottle. Changing the amount of liquid (more accurately, changing the height of the column of air) in the bottle results in a different frequency being reinforced and, thus, changes the frequency of the sound produced. In this analogy, changing the amount of liquid in the bottle corresponds to changing the positions of the articulators and, hence, changing the size and shape of the vocal tract. As the articulators change positions, different sounds are produced even though the vocal folds are vibrating at a constant rate. That is, different patterns of harmonics are reinforced and eliminated as the vocal tract changes shape. Thus the function served by the different articulator positions is to create different patterns of reinforced (audible) frequencies. The frequencies that are reinforced are called the *formants* of the speech sounds (see Chapter 3).

Production of consonantal sounds involves obstruction of the air flow through the vocal tract, the consonants being differentiated from each other by the manner and place of the obstruction. Some of these differences were discussed briefly in Chapter 3, and we will expand upon that discussion here. One class of consonants—the *stops*—are, as their name implies, produced by completely closing the articulators and stopping the air flow. For the *oral* stops, /b, d, g, p, t, k/, there is complete blockage of both the oral and the nasal passages. When the closure is released and the articulators move toward the vocal tract shape for the following sound, the onset of sound has an explosive quality that characterizes these stops. In addition, because the articulators are moving toward another configuration, the formant frequencies for stops tend to change. That is, the stops generally involve formant transitions. For the nasal stops,

/m, n, ŋ/ (the last being the final sound in *sing*), the velum is lowered so that air continues to pass through the nasal passages during the closure of the oral passage.

The stop consonants differ among themselves in their *place of articulation,* that is, in the point at which the vocal tract is closed. For /b, p, m/, the closure is produced by bringing the lips together, a *bilabial* closure. /d, t, n/ have a closure produced by touching the tongue tip to the alveolar ridge behind the upper teeth, hence their characterization as *alveolar* stops. /g, k, ŋ/ involve touching the body of the tongue to the velum, and are called *velar* stops.

For other kinds of consonants the obstruction of the vocal tract is less than complete. *Fricatives* like the consonants in *shy, sigh, fie,* and *thigh* are produced by bringing two articulators, an upper and a lower, close together without actually touching. This produces a turbulence in the air flow, resulting in a "noisy" sound. Like the stops, fricatives differ in the articulators which are used to produce the constriction; thus, they too differ in place of articulation.

Still other consonants involve even less obstruction than the fricatives, too little to produce turbulence. These are often referred to as *approximants* or *semivowels* or *glides.* The consonants in *we* and *you* are of this sort. Some consonants, such as those in the word *lull,* are produced by obstructing the airflow through the middle of the vocal tract, while air continues to flow past both sides of the obstruction. These are called *laterals.*

Consonantal sounds can also be produced in a number of other ways, though the ones we have mentioned nearly exhaust the variety found in most dialects of American English. For example, a *trill* occurs when one articulator is held close to another, loosely, so that the air flow sets it vibrating. Trills with the tongue tip occur in some forms of Scottish English in words like *rye,* and trills produced with the lips occur in a few African languages.

We noted earlier that all vowels are characterized by voicing, a periodic vibration of the vocal folds. Consonants differ in this respect, for some are voiced while others are voiceless. The difference between a voiced stop and a voiceless one, for example, is a difference in the timing relationship between the release of closure and the onset of voice fold vibration or voicing. In *voiced stops* (/b, d, g/) these two events occur nearly simultaneously, while in *voiceless stops* (/p, t, k/) the onset of voicing lags behind the release by as much as 50–100 msec. Some languages other than English use stops in which voicing onset occurs before, or leads, the release, producing *prevoiced* stops. (In fact, some speakers of English often prevoice their voiced stops.) Similar differences in *voice onset time* distinguish among the fricatives. For example, the consonant in *vie* is voiced, while the one in *fie* is voiceless.

Up to this point we have been describing speech sounds in terms of their places of articulation and their manners of articulation (i.e., whether or not the tract is obstructed, and if so, how). We might think of these descriptions as being specifications of *target* articulatory configurations, articulatory states which represent the ideal forms of the phonemes. This is essentially a *static* characterization. But, clearly, producing speech is a *dynamic* process. Only rarely is a single phoneme produced in isolation; some, in fact, can never be produced in isolation (e.g., the oral stops). Consequently, in order to understand how speech is produced, we need to consider the effects of producing sequences of phonemes in rapid succession, the effects of articulatory dynamics.

Articulatory Dynamics

One of the basic facts about speech production is that, with rare exceptions, at least some of the articulators are always in motion during speech. One consequence of this continual motion is the great variability in the way even the same speaker will produce the "same" phoneme on different occasions.[1] The variability or lack in constancy in production is the source of the lack of invariance we saw in Chapter 3. In this section we will discuss some of the sources of this variability and some of the problems it poses for the production mechanisms.

Coarticulation Effects

One source of variability in production arises from *coarticulation effects.* Such an effect exists when the articulatory configuration (and the resulting sound) for one phoneme is affected by the phonemes which precede and follow it. One example of coarticulation was described in Chapter 3, where it was pointed out that the formant transitions characteristic of a particular stop consonant differ depending upon which vowel follows it. The lack of invariance in the sounds of stop consonants reflects a lack of invariance in the articulatory configurations and articulator movements that give rise to them. Consider, for example, how /k/ is produced when followed by a high front vowel, as in *key,* and when followed by a low back vowel, as in *caw.* The point in the vocal tract at which the closure for /k/ occurs is much farther forward in the first case than in the second, a difference you can feel if you pronounce the two words distinctly.

Coarticulation effects can occur in both directions. The preceding example involved an *anticipatory* coarticulation, an effect on the articulation of one phoneme by a phoneme which followed it. Though rarer, *perseverative* coarticulations also occur, in which characteristics of the articulation of one phoneme are carried through the phonemes that follow.

Such coarticulation effects are not limited to phonemes that are adjacent, but may carry across several segments. For example, the vowel in *coo* is pro-

---

[1] This variation is one source of what linguists refer to as *allophonic* variation, i.e., variations among sound patterns all of which are identified as being the same phoneme. These variations, of course, do not signal variations in the meanings conveyed by the sounds.

duced with considerable rounding of the lips. The rounding is detectable as early as the time when the closure for the /k/ is released. Some lip rounding (though less) also occurs when the /k/ and /u/ are separated by another sound, as in *clue.* (You can feel the effect if you pronounce *clue* and *clay.*) And there is even some lip rounding during the articulation of /k/ when /k/ and /u/ are separated by a word boundary as well as by other intervening phonemes, as in the phrase *tackle Lou* (Ladefoged, 1975). Such "long distance" effects are less frequent and are smaller in magnitude than effects between adjacent phonemes.

The existence of coarticulation effects indicates that we cannot think of speech as consisting of a sequence of invariant articulatory patterns strung together like beads. Rather, the form in which a particular phoneme occurs depends upon its context. The existence of long distance coarticulation effects indicates the substantial amount of context that must be considered in the planning of the articulator movements for a phoneme. The context must be more than just the word in which the phoneme occurs.

We suggested earlier that descriptions of the place and manner of articulating phonemes might be thought of as targets toward which the articulators "aim" as they move from one phoneme to another. What is indicated by the existence of coarticulation effects is that the amount of such movement, and even its direction, are determined both by where the movement starts and by where it is going to go afterwards. In some cases these effects are so great that an articulatory target is missed completely. For vowels occurring between consonants, we can observe cases where the articulators start moving from the target of the preceding consonant toward the vowel target but, before reaching it, change direction to move toward the target for the following consonant. Anticipatory coarticulation of the following consonant has begun before the target position for the vowel has been reached, producing an "undershooting" of the target. Undershooting of this sort appears to be limited primarily to vowels.

Producing speech is, then, not a matter of moving articulators in a slow, deliberate manner to achieve the target for one phoneme, and then moving to another fixed target for the next phoneme. Rather, there is considerable variability in the movements as a function of the context in which they occur, and even some variation in how close such movements bring the articulators to their target positions.

Rate and Stress Effects

The nature of articulator movements is also affected by such variables as the rate of speaking. Intuitively, it would seem reasonable to suppose that as one increased one's rate of speaking, the rate of movement of all the articulators would increase equally. However, this is not what happens, and for good reason. Instead, the speech segments whose durations are most affected by changes in speaking rate are the vowels. The period over which a vowel's target position is approached or maintained decreases as speech rate increases. One consequence of this is, of course, that the amount of target undershooting increases as rate increases.

The reason why speech rate should affect vowels more than consonants is not hard to find. Listeners distinguish some consonants from others primarily by differences in the rates of their formant transitions (see Chapter 3). For example, semivowels are characterized by slower articulatory movements than stop consonants and, hence, by lower rates of formant transitions. If speech rate affected the speed of articulator movements for these phonemes, the listener's task would be complicated enormously. A semivowel spoken at a fast speech rate (e.g., /w/) would sound like a stop consonant spoken at a slow rate (e.g., /b/). For the listener to determine whether he had heard a semivowel or a stop, he would have to take into account the rate at which the speaker was speaking. To the extent that phonemes like these are affected by changes in speech rate, the effects are upon the durations of the articulator movements rather than on the rates of those movements.[2]

There are, in addition, other variables that influence the durations of speech segments and introduce additional complexities into the control of the articulator movements. In English, for example, stressing a syllable generally increases the duration of its vowel and sometimes also produces small increases in the surrounding consonants (Fry, 1955). The longer duration of stressed syllables is accompanied by more movement of the articulators toward their target positions. The position of a syllable within an utterance also affects its duration. For example, there is a small though fairly consistent increase in the vowel duration of the last syllable when a word occurs as the final word in a phrase, and an even greater increase when the word occurs in the final position in an utterance (Oller, 1973).

It is sometimes suggested that speakers make many of their adjustments in articulation for the benefit of hearers. One might suppose that the reason for final syllable lengthening effects is to signal to the hearer that he is coming to the end of a major syntactic unit. On the other hand, it may be that the articulatory changes are just consequences of the characteristics of the articulatory system itself and of the manner in which it is controlled. Klatt and Cooper (1975) have shown that listeners are able to detect duration changes of the size involved in final syllable lengthening. It is not yet clear whether they make use of this information to guide their comprehension processing, but it does seem likely that some of the articulatory changes (e.g., duration changes with stress) are used by hearers, whether or not they were produced for that reason.

The discussion up to this point has focused upon the physical structures of the speech production mechanism and upon the nature of its movements when

[2]In fact, Chistovich et al. (1965) have reported an effect that seems almost paradoxical: the rate of articulator movements for consonantal phonemes tends to be *slower* at fast speech rates than at slow speech rates.

in use. In general, we have seen that producing a sequence of speech sounds involves controlled movements of several articulators in varying combinations that achieve approximations of a series of articulatory target positions. Furthermore, the direction, extent, and timing of such movements is highly variable even for a given target, depending upon such things as the preceding and following targets as well as the stress pattern, rate of speech, and syntactic position within the overall structure of the utterance. For the articulatory gestures that produce fluent speech, variability is the rule rather than the exception.

Synchronization of Movements

It goes almost without saying that the problems of controlling and coordinating the various structures of this speech mechanism are enormous. Each articulator in the vocal tract is controlled by several muscles, to say nothing of the many which control the respiratory and laryngeal mechanisms. And each movement of the mechanism involves a complex pattern of muscle contractions and relaxations. These movements must, of course, be coordinated, or synchronized. It would do little good, for example, for the tip of the tongue and the jaw to assume the appropriate positions for beginning a particular fricative if, at the same time, the vocal folds were out of position and the respiratory system was not providing the right air pressure.

The problem of synchronization is not simply one of simultaneously starting the contraction or relaxation of the necessary muscles. The amount of contraction needed is different for different muscles and for different speech movements, and their rates of contraction also vary. The synchronization must apply to the *results* of the movements, not their initiations. Getting all the parts of the mechanism into the right positions or states at the same time requires beginning the activation of different parts of the mechanism at different times. Clearly, this is a control problem of enormous complexity. Yet it is one which a speaker is able to handle rapidly, usually successfully, and without any conscious attention. At a normal speaking rate, phonemic segments (i.e., target positions) succeed each other at a rate of about one every 70 msec. And although speech errors do occur more often than is noticed, most such errors appear to arise during the planning of an utterance rather than in the execution of the motor movements themselves. Rarely do we find ourselves literally tongue-tied.

The Control of the Speech Motor System

The output of the speech production system is, as we have seen, both variable and continuous. The articulatory gestures used to produce a single phoneme differ considerably in different contexts. An examination of both the sound which results and of the articulatory gestures themselves fails to reveal segments that correspond to linguistic units like the phoneme, syllable, word, etc. We cannot point to a time interval and say that the articulatory gestures during that interval are a phoneme, and that the gestures during the next interval are the next phoneme, etc. Rather, successive phonemes overlap and merge to yield a continuity of both movement and sound.

The input to the system, on the other hand, is a sequence of discrete units, corresponding to something like phonemes or distinctive feature specifications. In addition, the input involves a relatively small number of invariant units: there is only one or, at most, a small number of units for each phoneme, perhaps something like 30–50 units in all.

Thus, the task for the speech production system is one of translating a discrete input of invariant units into a continuous and highly variable output. It is a translation from a highly abstract "mental" representation of a linguistic message into a continually varying pattern of muscle movements which, in turn, produces the vocal tract configurations that make the speech sounds to convey that message. If we assume that the decisions about which phonemes are to occur in what order have already been made by the language production system, then the main question about the speech production system is how this translation is made. How, that is, does one get from invariant phonemes to variable sounds?

Mental to Motor Translation: The Motor Command Hypothesis

Several hypotheses have been suggested to explain the nature of this translation. One that has stimulated a considerable amount of research on speech motor control is the *motor command hypothesis* (see, e.g., Liberman, Cooper, Shankweiler & Studdert-Kennedy, 1967). This hypothesis maintains that the phonemic input to the motor system consists of sequences of subphonemic units (perhaps corresponding to distinctive features). Thus, each phoneme in the input contains a number of lower-level units. These, in turn, correspond to invariant motor commands, neurological signals to particular articulators to perform specific movements.

According to this hypothesis, then, there is a one-to-one correspondence between the set of subphonemic units making up a phoneme and the corresponding set of neurological commands to the articulatory muscles involved in producing that phoneme. Thus, the invariance and discreteness of the input phonemes is preserved at least as far in the translation process as the muscle contractions associated with that phoneme.

It is not until the next stage of the translation—the conversion of muscle movements into vocal tract shapes—that the one-to-one correspondence is lost, and we get the kind of restructuring that is reflected in the continuous and variable vocal tract shapes themselves. There are three factors which may account for this transformation from discrete invariant motor commands and muscle contractions to continuous and variable vocal tract shapes. First, the articulators possess some inertia that makes them incapable of performing as rapidly as they are called upon to do, contributing some sluggishness to the system. Secondly, there are also some limitations on the speed of response of the neuromuscular system itself. That is, the movement times of the various muscles vary during execution of the neural command. And thirdly, the time intervals between successive commands are sometimes too short for the actions one of them calls for to be completed before the next arrives.

The essential feature of the motor command hypothesis, then, is that the discreteness and invariance of the input are preserved until very near the end of the production process, being lost only in the translation from muscle movements to vocal tract shapes. According to this hypothesis, we ought to find an invariant pattern of muscle activity accompanying the production of a particular phoneme, regardless of the context in which it occurs.

The motor command hypothesis has stimulated a number of investigations of the muscle activity occurring during speech. Many of these studies have involved implanting electrodes in various speech muscles. The electrodes are used to record the patterns of muscle contractions accompanying a phoneme when it is in different contexts. Although these studies have provided a great deal of information about muscle activity during speech, they seem in general to show that the predicted invariance of muscle activity does not occur (see MacNeilage, 1970, for a review and discussion of this research). Thus, the variability observed in vocal tract shapes is also characteristic of the muscle activity which produces those shapes. Variability appears to be introduced earlier in the speech production process than the motor command hypothesis allows. The hypothesis, then, is not correct. The reason for this is that the extent and nature of the vocal tract's movements are determined by where it is moving from (i.e., by the preceding phoneme) and where it is moving to, as well as by such things as stress and rate of speech.

Mental to Motor Translation: The Vocal Tract Target Hypothesis

The description we gave earlier of articulatory dynamics suggests an alternative to the motor command hypothesis. In discussing coarticulation effects we suggested that when the articulators produce a given phoneme, they tend to move toward a relatively invariant vocal tract shape or target. Several researchers (e.g., Lindblom, 1963; Stevens & House, 1963) have, in fact, suggested that the fundamental concept in speech production is the *vocal tract target* and not the motor command. According to the vocal tract target hypothesis, the phonemic input to the speech production system is translated into a motor representation of the vocal tract configuration that will produce that phoneme (this is the vocal tract target). The target hypothesis says that the particular movements that get made are the means; the vocal tract targets are the ends they serve. The movements are "calculated" by the production system so that they will reach the specified targets from wherever the articulators are at the moment the movements are initiated.

The vocal tract targets are, therefore, represented in the brain of the speaker. In order for the targets to be represented, the speaker must have an internal representation of the vocal tract itself. Putting this another way, the vocal tract target is a spatial pattern defined in terms of the spatial characteristics of the vocal tract. This implies that a speaker has an internal representation of the spatial properties of his vocal tract.

There has for some time been evidence suggesting that internalized targets and spatial representations exist for visual-motor coordination (see MacNeilage, 1970, for a review). And MacNeilage and MacNeilage (1973) point out that there is direct evidence that such a representational system exists for the control of the speech musculature. As they note, people are able to move their tongues to various positions in their mouths (or out of them) on verbal command. (Try, for example, touching the tip of your tongue to your *left* upper front tooth without also touching the right.) Such movements generally are not made by the process of trial-and-error: it seems that people know how to move their tongues to reach a particular target without ever having done so intentionally before. In addition, if one speaks with one's teeth clenched together or around a pipestem or other small object, the speech sounds virtually normal, even though it requires a considerably different organization of movements. For example, the lower jaw is usually involved in normal speech movements, but it is essentially immobilized when the teeth are clenched. Its functions are taken over by other muscles controlling other articulators. Lindblom and Sundberg (1971) have shown that the necessary adjustments do not require practice.

It seems a good possibility, therefore, that the representations used by the speech production system to guide the movements of the articulators is a representation of the spatial targets the articulators need to reach (or, at least, approach) in order to produce a particular phoneme. The first translation involved in speech production is a translation from a specification of phonemes into a specification of vocal tract targets. It is here that something close to a one-to-one correspondence of discrete units exists. The next stage involves translating target representations into motor commands to the articulators for producing the appropriate muscle movements for reaching the targets. It is at this second stage that continuity and variability are introduced.

Motor Control: Open-loop vs. Closed-loop

One question which remains unresolved is how this latter translation is controlled, i.e., how to account for coarticulation effects. One possibility here is that the control is *open-loop*. Under this kind of control, the particular movements to be executed are planned in advance. Suppose, for example, that we know both the first and second phonemes we wish to produce. Knowing the target for the first specifies the positions the articulators should be in at the time the first phoneme is produced. And, knowing those positions, we could use that knowledge in determining what movements are necessary to get from that target to the target for the second phoneme.

What this procedure requires is that the motor control system can consider, and plan for producing, more than one phoneme at a time. As we saw in the last chapter, it appears that long sequences of phonemes are in fact represented simultaneously in the speaker's memory system when he is planning an utterance. So it seems reasonable to suppose that the speaker can consider the target representations of several successive phonemes simultaneously, and that he can use the resulting information about the sequence to plan the articulatory movements necessary for getting from one target to the next.

In fact, no one questions whether this kind of open-loop or "planning" control of speech movements occurs. Clearly, it does. The unresolved question concerns whether or not this is the *only* kind of control over speech movements that the speaker has, for there are also several other possibilities, all involving one or another sort of *closed-loop,* or feedback, control.[3]

One might suppose, for example, that the speaker monitors the sounds he is producing, using the auditory feedback to assist in the planning of further speech movements. One sort of evidence that suggests this might be the case comes from studies of *delayed auditory feedback.* If the speaker hears his own speech, not as he utters it, but instead after a short delay, his speech tends to be disrupted and to lose fluency. The maximum disruption occurs with a delay of about 200 msec, about the time taken for the speaker to produce one syllable. If delayed feedback disrupts speech, then perhaps normal feedback is used in keeping it fluent—or so the argument runs.

Some theorists have argued that the effects of delayed auditory feedback do not indicate that the speaker is using such feedback when it occurs normally (see, e.g., MacNeilage & MacNeilage, 1973). Rather, they suggest, the effect occurs because delayed auditory feedback introduces a distracting, extraneous source of stimulation. In support of this, they point out that even normal auditory feedback is too slow, in that it arrives too long after the programming of the articulator movements to be useful in controlling speech. In addition, Huggins (1968) has shown that the amount of delay which produces maximum disruption remains unchanged whether the speaker is producing long or short syllables. This suggests that the effects of the delayed feedback are not directly related to the production of speech itself.

On the other hand, supporters of the view that auditory feedback assists in guiding the production of speech can point to evidence that supports their position. It is generally found, for example, that hearing another speaker's voice after a delay does not have as much disruptive effect as hearing one's own voice. And Webster and his colleagues (Webster & Lubker, 1968; Webster, Schumacher & Lubker, 1970) have found evidence suggesting that auditory feedback affects the *timing* control of articulatory gestures even if it does not affect what those gestures are. They have shown that for stutterers delaying auditory feedback

---

[3] In a closed-loop or feedback system, what happens at moment two depends both upon the prior plan *and* upon the results of the actions taken at moment one. Information about what just happened is *fed back* to the planner and can affect the next action.

actually decreases the amount of stuttering, an effect exactly the opposite of that found with non-stuttering normal speakers. In accounting for this, Webster suggested that a part of the problem for stutterers is that their speech perception mechanisms are defective. For them, normal feedback has the same kind of disruptive effect that delayed feedback has on normal speakers. If this is the case, it implies that auditory feedback is used by normal speakers, perhaps in maintaining the rhythmic fluency of their speech.

At present, the question of whether auditory feedback supplements the control provided by open-loop planning remains unresolved. Evidence can be found both for and against its influence on the control of speech production. It does seem likely, however, that speakers do monitor the auditory feedback from their own speech, using this as a means of detecting the occurrence of the kinds of speech errors described in Chapter 6. That this error-detecting mechanism is less than perfect is indicated by the fact that speakers are frequently unaware that they have produced errors.

There is, in addition, another kind of closed-loop mechanism that could be involved in the control of speech production: *somatic sensory feedback.* There are sensory nerve endings embedded in the speech musculature itself that provide information about the states and movements of the muscles. Such feedback does seem to be an almost universal feature of the control of motor behavior in animals. And some of the sensory feedback loops from articulators do seem to be sufficiently fast to provide information about articulator positions in time to be useful in guiding further movements.

But the evidence on the effects of this sort of control is very unclear (see MacNeilage & Ladefoged, 1976). Much of the research on somatic sensory control of motor behavior has involved either non-speech muscles or behaviors very unlike the spontaneous motor movements characteristic of speech. Such evidence is not very directly relevant to speech. Research on the somatic sensory control of speech has generally involved attempts to block feedback and observe the effects produced on the subject's speech. But while several interesting effects are often observed, it is not certain that the particular effects are related to the particular blocks induced. A part of the problem is that it is difficult to block feedback from a particular muscle without affecting the muscle's activity in other ways at the same time.

It does seem likely that the initiation of speech is under closed-loop control of this sort (see MacNeilage, Krones & Hanson, 1969). The initial articulatory gestures must start from preliminary, pre-speech positions, and these positions are not specified by the speech production mechanism itself. In addition, it seems likely that the kinds of adjustments made in articulator movements when speaking with clenched teeth must also be influenced by sensory feedback. But whether such somatic sensory feedback is *generally* used to supplement open-loop control is not yet clear. Basically the question is: if the open-loop planning system provides information about where the articulators ought to be, does it also help us to know where they actually are?

Temporal Patterning (Rhythm) in Production

We saw earlier that as the rate of speaking varies so does the extent to which the articulators approach their targets. In this section we will consider some additional issues and problems that arise from the fundamental fact that speech sounds are produced across time. Language is structured, and beyond that speech is temporally structured. By now we know that an utterance is not planned on a word-by-word, left-to-right basis alone. The speaker has in mind a structure for the utterance, but that structure must be assembled and eventually produced one word and even one phoneme at a time.

Lenneberg (1967, p. 219) likens the "composition of discourse to the assembly of a train, where the individual coaches have to be attached while the locomotive keeps moving forward. There is an overall plan that determines the order of the cars; they are held in readiness, but at a specific time they must be released and hitched onto the moving train." The train, of course, is moving quite rapidly. As we noted, someone speaking fluently produces a phoneme about every 70 msec, a rate of about 14 phonemes or six syllables a second. Lenneberg (1967, p. 107) estimated that, "Within one minute of discourse as many as 10 to 15 thousand neuromuscular events occur."

Since speech events occur in time, they have a rhythmic character. We can associate a hierarchical organization with the relative timing or rhythm of any sequence of acoustic events, and of course this includes speech. We can see this by examining Figure 7.2. This figure is meant to represent a sequence of eight brief "taps" occurring across time. You can produce this sequence by tapping eight times with the spacing between taps as given in the figure. The tree diagram shown above the taps shows the relationships among the individual taps in the sequence. Just as in a tree diagram for a sentence, those taps which occur beneath the same node are closely related to each other. As Martin (1972, p. 488) has noted, "sequences of sounds, speech or otherwise, that are rhythmic will

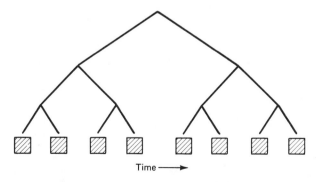

Time ⟶

Figure 7.2. A hierarchical representation of eight "taps" which occur across time (see text).

217

possess hierarchical organization, that is, a coherent internal structure, at the *sound* level."

The role of an individual tap in a rhythmic sequence depends upon its relative position in the sequence. Relative timing is what is important. As Martin (1972, p. 488) has also noted, "*relative timing* . . . means that the locus of each (sound) element along the time dimension is determined relative to the locus of *all* other elements in the sequence, adjacent *and* nonadjacent." Martin, among others, has tried to relate facts about the relative timing, or rhythm, of speech sounds to the planning and coordination of the speech sound sequence.

Natural Rhythmic Patterns

Let us add another variable to the rhythmic pattern of Figure 7.2. Such patterns can have some events (elements) which are louder than others. These are the "accented" elements in the rhythmic pattern. Some accent patterns are more "natural" than others. To see this, try tapping out the eight-element sequence of Figure 7.2 rapidly and repeatedly, putting the accent on the first and fifth taps. Then try to tap the sequence repeatedly with the accent on the first and sixth taps. It is much more difficult to tap out the second pattern than the first. This kind of difference led Martin (1972) to try to specify a set of rules characterizing natural rhythmic patterns which would distinguish them from unnatural patterns. He suggested that the natural rhythmic patterns play an important role in speech production, furnishing the temporal patterns into which the phonemes are fitted.

When the accent falls on a particular syllable during speech production, this often influences the durations of other syllables in the utterance. (These effects may extend over as many as seven syllables preceding or following the accented syllable.) Consider, for example, sentences (1) and (2), both of which are intended to have the primary sentence stress or accent fall on the last word.

(1) John saw Mary.

(2) John saw Marie.

Secondary stress falls on the first word in both sentences. In (1) the primary stress will fall upon the first syllable of *Mary*, while in (2) the primary stress will fall upon the second syllable of *Marie*. According to Martin, the time between the secondary stress (on *John*) and the primary stress will be the same in these two sentences. In order for this to happen, the duration of the word *saw* must be adjusted. In (1) the word *saw* will have a longer duration than it will have in (2). In the latter case, *saw* will be shorter because there is an additional syllable between the secondary and primary stresses—the first syllable of *Marie*. Here is a case, then, in which an adjustment of word duration must be planned in advance in order to accommodate the overall rhythmic pattern of the sentence.

According to Martin, the assignment of primary stress to an utterance is one of the factors which determine the relative durations of the syllables. Martin claims that since the "accented elements dominate the temporal organization of an utterance, they must in some sense be planned first" (1972, p. 499). This means that the durations of words and their phonemes cannot simply be listed in the mental lexicon, for the durations are context-dependent. The durations must be computed by the speaker during production on the basis of the utterance in which the phonemes occur; they are not simply stored and retrieved.

Martin goes on to suggest that ". . . one might think of accented syllables as the main targets in the organization of the articulatory program." We need not examine in detail Martin's hypotheses about the way in which stress is assigned to an utterance's phonemes. For our present purposes it is sufficient to note that the speech motor system apparently has some rhythmic patterns which it finds natural, and that speech planning is determined, in part, by these patterns. The temporal patterns themselves are, as we have suggested, rule-governed. So the rules for assigning relative durations of speech segments are part of those governing the translation from a linguistic representation of an utterance into a sequence of timed and coordinated gestures of the articulatory mechanisms.

In Chapter 4 we noted that stress and intonational cues to sentence structure are often unreliable guides for the listener attempting to comprehend utterances. If the speaker is producing his utterances according to a natural rhythmic structure, however, then it is reasonable to suppose that the listener can use the early portions of the sequence to "lock onto" the rhythm and to use that rhythm to predict where the points of high stress are going to occur. Since these usually occur in the words that convey the most important information in the sentence, focusing one's attention on such words during comprehension would appear to be advantageous. In fact, as we saw in Chapter 3, there is some evidence that listeners are affected by the rhythmic structure of utterances—they appear to be trying to predict where the high-stressed items are going to occur.

The Importance of Rhythm for Speech Production

The evidence we have reviewed so far points to the central role that timing plays in speech production. The relative durations and stress of the segments of an utterance are determined by an overall rhythmic pattern. Since such patterns provide important information to the listener, it is clear that disrupting them would have disastrous consequences for the intelligibility of speech. We have also seen that coordinated timing of the contractions and relaxations of the various muscles that move the articulators toward their target configurations for particular phonemes is essential to the production of those phonemes. It is thus apparent that rhythm and timing are extremely important aspects of the production of fluent, comprehensible speech.

In Chapter 12 we will consider some of the neurological mechanisms that underlie language and some of the pathologies that result if these mechanisms are damaged. We should point out here, however, that pathology will almost surely result if the timing of speech production breaks down. As Lenneberg (1967, p. 222) pointed out, "Most of the symptomatology [of language breakdown] may be seen as disorder of temporal integration, of 'lack of availability at the right time.'"

To summarize, we have shown that timing is one of speech production's most important aspects. We know that a speaker often has the linguistic form of an entire clause or phrase planned before he begins to speak; sequencing and timing the segments of the output is a necessary requirement for fluent speech. We have suggested that there are certain natural rhythmic patterns that guide this sequencing and timing process. Stress is assigned to important elements of the utterance as a function of both the words focused upon and the syntactic structure of the sentence. When stress is assigned, numerous adjustments of the elements in the utterance must be made. We have concentrated here on the timing and relative durational characteristics of such adjustments. But adjustments also occur in the pitch of the speaker's voice and the relative loudness of the elements (see Chapter 3). A theory of speech production must take such rhythmic factors into account. A beginning has been made in dealing with this problem (e.g., Martin, 1972), but a fully developed theory of this important aspect of speech production remains a goal for the future.

The Development of the Speech Production System

The speech production system is, as we have seen, an extremely complex one. The translation from a linguistically-encoded message into a sequence of speech sounds involves fine-grained control over a continually changing vocal tract and over the respiratory and laryngeal systems. Given this complexity, it is no small accomplishment for the adult speaker to be able to produce speech rapidly, fluently, and with little or no conscious attention to what he is doing. It is also not in the least surprising that the development of the ability to do this requires a considerable period of time. The failure of babies to produce speech is not merely because they have nothing to say.

Prelinguistic Development

The development of speech production in the child occurs only very gradually, with a number of prelinguistic stages leading up to the kinds of abilities we have been describing for adults. Throughout this growth there is a striking contrast between children's ability to perceive speech and their ability to produce it. Many of the speech perception capabilities of the sorts we described in Chapter 3 appear to be present in infants within the first few months of life, as early as it is possible to test for their presence (see Eimas, 1974, 1975; Morse, 1974). But this is not so with speech production capabilities.

The general course of development of speech production is reasonably clear, though a theory of this development is far more difficult and uncertain.

Vocalization during the first month of life is quite limited in variety, there being little but crying. The basic crying pattern involves an inspiration, a rest, a cry, and another rest, the entire pattern repeating itself rhythmically (Wolff, 1966). Gradually, crying becomes more differentiated. An "anger" cry emerges which maintains the same sequence and rhythm of the basic cry, but is much louder and less clearly defined in its formant structure. A "pain" cry also emerges, marked by a longer cry relative to the rest of the cycle.

In addition, other, non-cry vocalizations emerge, such as cooing and gurgling as infants gradually increase the variety of movements of their vocal tracts. At about 4 or 5 months, infants begin to *babble,* producing sounds that resemble speech sounds. During the next few months, a great variety of sounds are produced, some speech-like and others not. The variety is so great that some writers have summarized the babbling stage by suggesting that during it children produce every sound found in any human language and also many that are not. This picture is overdrawn, for it appears unlikely that any one infant produces quite that great a variety of sounds.

The infant's babbling often seems to have the stress and intonational characteristics of simple sentences, leading some (e.g., Lewis, 1951; Kaplan & Kaplan, 1971) to suggest that these are the first properties of speech production to be mastered by the infant. There is little doubt that one can hear such characteristics in infants' babbling. But it is far less clear that they reflect the operation of the same kinds of control processes which, for adults, determine the stress and intonational properties of speech. As we saw earlier in this chapter, the stress and intonational properties of an adult's utterances are determined by their structure. It seems unlikely that this is the case for the young infant. However, to the extent that the rhythmic patterns observed in adult speech are general patterns (i.e., not specific to speech), it is possible that the same patterns are involved in the infant's babbling.

Finally, somewhere between the ages of 9 and 12 months, there occurs the beginning of what can be identified as true, patterned speech, marking the end of the "prelinguistic" period of speech sound development. There has been considerable controversy over whether babbling leads directly into true speech production or whether there is a discontinuity between the two.

The Transition Period

The data collected by many investigators do not appear to show any strong evidence of qualitative or quantitative changes in sound production between babbling and later speech production (e.g., Irwin, 1957; Murai, 1963; Nakazima, 1966). On the other hand, there are several reasons for believing that there is a discontinuity, and that during babbling infants are doing something different with their articulatory mechanisms from what they do later in producing speech.

As many investigators (e.g., Jakobson, 1968) have noted, toward the end of the first year many children display a decrease in both the quantity and variety of sounds produced. It appears that some children fall virtually silent for a time during this period. But, more importantly, there are some sounds which occur frequently during babbling, (e.g., the laterals /l/ and /r/) and which, after babbling has ended, are not produced again until considerably later, often as late as 4 or 5 years of age. In addition, it is often noted that deaf children babble fairly normally; but after babbling diminishes toward the end of the first year, it is not replaced with anything else.

What all this appears to indicate is that there is a genuine discontinuity between what children are doing with their articulatory apparatus when they are babbling and when they are producing speech. For most children, on the other hand, there is not a sharp *temporal* discontinuity such that babbling ends and then speech production begins. Rather, the two kinds of sound production overlap; babbling gradually decreases in frequency, and speech gradually increases in frequency.

Part of the difficulty of observing the discontinuity arises because the infant's sound production is often transcribed directly in a phonetic representation rather than examined spectrographically. It is easy in many cases for an adult to "hear" an infant's sound as being a particular speech sound when in fact, if the sound were examined objectively, it would be found to differ substantially from speech.

What is perhaps the clearest evidence of a discontinuity comes from a study by Port and Preston (1972). They recorded the sound productions of infants and picked out all the occurrences of sounds that might have been the stop consonants /d/ and /t/. They then made spectrograms of these utterances and measured the voice-onset time (VOT) of each. At one year, nearly all such sounds had VOTs close to zero, similar in this respect to the voiced stops produced by adults. However, in the one younger child (34 weeks) whom they studied, the VOTs were scattered over a much broader range, including many VOT values that do not occur in English. Thus, the VOT distribution during babbling appears to be quite different from both the adult's and from that produced by the child at one year. Observing this same child over a period of months, Port and Preston found that the VOTs of her stop consonants became gradually less random, so that at 64 weeks nearly all were in the short-lag range characteristic of voiced stops for adult English speakers.

The general picture that emerges is that the stop-like sounds which appear during babbling are randomly distributed with respect to VOT. Gradually, as babbling gives way to "real" speech production, the distribution becomes more restricted to the range characteristic of voiced stops. This suggests that there is an increase in the child's control over the timing of the articulatory gestures of stop consonants. But at one year nearly all the stop-like sounds are voiced, there being few with the VOTs characteristic of voiceless stops. It is only gradually that children begin to produce voiceless stops that are different from voiced stops, a development that appears not to be complete until at least four or five years of age.

The sequence observed by Port and Preston seems to be fairly typical of children's development during the period when they are mastering speech sound production. Early in this period, production of one class of sounds predominates (in this case, voiced stops), a second, contrasting class being only gradually differentiated from it.

The Development of Contrasts

The rates at which different classes are differentiated and controlled vary considerably, but the order in which they are controlled appears to be fairly uniform among all children (Ervin-Tripp, 1966; Jakobson, 1968). Generally, the first contrast controlled is between a vowel (/a/) and a stop consonant (/b/). This is followed by a vowel-vowel contrast (/a/ vs. /i/) and by a contrast between stops and continuant consonants such as fricatives (/b/ vs. /f/). Stops are generally differentiated in terms of place of articulation (/b/ vs. /d/) before they are differentiated in terms of voicing (/b/ vs. /p/).

Other general features of speech production development include the fact that consonant contrasts are generally controlled in word-initial position before they are controlled in medial or final position, and the fact that consonant clusters tend to be controlled later than the consonants entering into those clusters. It also appears that the sounds substituted for ones not yet mastered tend to be quite regular (Eilers & Oller, 1976). For example, /r/ tends to be mastered rather late, having been produced earlier as something very close to /w/. The /tr/ cluster, on the other hand, tends to be produced as /f/.

The contrasts which children master, of course, are the ones utilized by the particular language they are acquiring. This is not characteristic of the sounds produced during babbling. Sounds frequently occur there that do not occur in the language the children hear. In fact, adult listeners apparently cannot hear differences between the babbling of prelinguistic infants from different linguistic communities (Atkinson, MacWhinney & Stoel, 1970). However, the sequence of linguistic development is markedly similar in all languages. Also, the contrasts children are likely to master early are the ones found in the greatest number of different languages. The rarer contrasts are likely to be mastered late. And it is these same rare, late contrasts that are most likely to cause the problems for which children are referred to speech clinics as having articulatory disorders. The relationships between generality, ease of mastery by normal children, and articulation disorders suggest that, in general, different contrasts differ in the complexity of the articulatory gestures necessary to produce them and in the complexity of the neurological control over these gestures.

Development of the Mechanisms Underlying Speech Production

We can point to two kinds of mechanisms whose development is necessary for producing speech sounds: the physical structures and muscles of the articulatory system itself, and the neurological structures of the speech motor control system in the cortex.

Concerning the first of these, we know that the newborn infants' articulatory mechanisms are structured quite differently from those of an adult. One major difference is that the infant's larynx is much higher and closer to the level of the oral cavity. As a result, even if there were no other differences, the infant could not produce the full range of vowels characteristic of all human languages (see, e.g., Lieberman & Crelin, 1971). In addition, analysis of the cries of newborn infants suggest that they have, at best, only very limited capabilities for such things as changing vocal fold tension and vocal tract shape during sound production (Lieberman, Harris, Wolff, & Russell, 1971).

Although there are many other differences between the physical structures of the newborn's and the adult's articulatory mechanisms, one should serve to indicate why considerable changes from the newborn's state are necessary before speech becomes possible. The infant's tongue is fairly close to its adult proportions; yet his oral cavity is far smaller. As a result, the infant's tongue nearly fills his entire mouth (Brodie, 1949). Imagine the difficulty you would have producing articulatory target configurations if your mouth were filled by your tongue!

The fact that a variety of speech-like sounds occurs during babbling after the age of four to five months suggests that during the first year of life the physical structures of the infant's articulatory mechanisms have developed considerably. It will, however, be several years before they fully reach their adult status. But if the physical structures are sufficiently mature during the second half of the first year to allow babbling, why does speech production not begin until later?

A part of the answer concerns the peripheral structures and muscles themselves. That is, it is a far different (and simpler) problem to produce a particular sound in a fairly sustained invariant manner than it is to produce the same sound in the context of a sequence of preceding and following phonemes. The latter requires that the articulatory system be able to change states in a rapid and controlled manner, and this demands considerably more of the articulators than that they just be able to assume the appropriate configuration.

The remainder of the answer most likely concerns the development of the cortical mechanisms which control the articulatory ones. The nature of those control mechanisms, even in the mature adult, is not yet fully understood. So it is difficult to describe the development of specific cortical control mechanisms. Nonetheless, there are several kinds of cortical development occurring during the first several years of life which are undoubtedly relevant to the production of speech.

Essentially all the neural cells that will ever be available are present at birth. But the first few years witness a great development of the neural processes (axons and dendrites) growing out of cell bodies and providing interconnections between cells. Figure 7.3 on pages 226-227 (from Conel, 1939-1959) illustrates this kind of development between birth and two years in Broca's area, an area of the cerebral cortex involved in the production of speech sounds.

Among other maturational developments relevant to the control of speech production is the *myelination* of the motor nerve pathways over which control is transmitted to the muscles involved in speech production. Myelin is a protein sheath which serves to insulate nerve tracts, preventing an impulse being transmitted along one tract from "short-circuiting" to adjacent ones. Such insulation is essential for the kind of fine-grained, synchronized control necessary for speech sound production. At birth, many of the relevant nerve tracts have not yet become myelinated sufficiently to be functional. Many will not be completely myelinated until adulthood, if ever. It is still unclear just how far myelination must proceed for effective control to be exerted. But it does seem likely that myelination provides part of an account of why controlled speech sound production begins only well after the relevant articulator structures have themselves matured, and of why some kinds of control (e.g., those involved in the production of late-development sounds) do not develop until even considerably later. Lecours (1975), for example, suggests that it is for this reason that babbling must be controlled by subcortical rather than cortical mechanisms.

In general, then, it appears that the development of the articulatory mechanisms and of the cortical mechanisms that control them is a long, slow maturational process. In light of the complexity of the mechanisms and the length of time over which they mature, it is hardly surprising that true speech production does not start earlier than it does or that it is a matter of several years before the child becomes capable of producing speech in an adult-like manner.

Summary

The production of speech involves translating an utterance from an abstract phonological representation into a sequence of synchronized movements of the physical mechanisms of the speech production system. These mechanisms can be divided into three sub-systems. First, the respiratory system is responsible for providing the controlled flow of air necessary for sound production. Second, the laryngeal mechanisms—the vocal folds and the mechanisms which control the states of the folds—are primarily responsible for translating air flow into sound. They impart to the voice its distinctive pitch, or fundamental frequency, and also provide the source for other, non-voiced sounds. Third, the articulatory system—a complex set of mechanisms including tongue, velum, jaw, etc.— is responsible for shaping the sound and imparting to it the qualities of the different speech sounds.

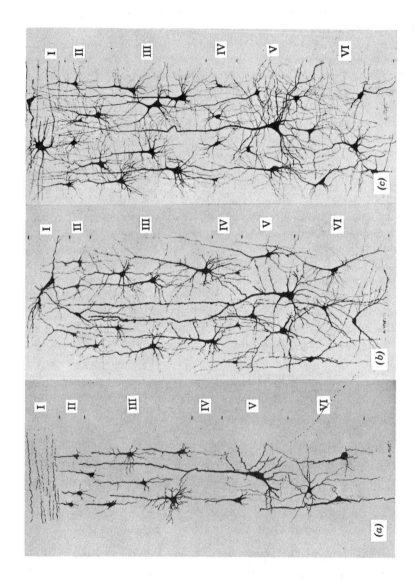

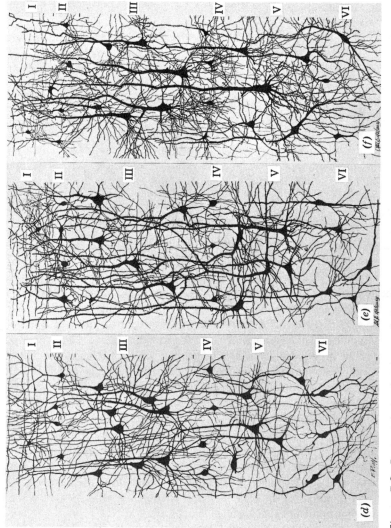

Figure 7.3. Postnatal development of the human cerebral cortex around Broca's Area (a language-related area; see Chapter 12). (*a*) newborn; (*b*) 1 month; (*c*) 3 months; (*d*) 6 months; (*e*) 15 months; (*f*) 24 months. (From Conel, J. LeRoy. The postnatal development of the human cerebral cortex, Vol 1–6. Harvard University Press: Cambridge, Mass., 1939–1959. Copyright by Harvard University Press. Used by permission.)

During speech these production systems are constantly in motion. The articulatory system in particular changes rapidly from the articulatory target configuration for one phoneme to that for a subsequent phoneme. There is considerable variability in the nature of these movements. The movements for attaining one target configuration are affected by both preceding and following targets (coarticulation effects) and by the rate of speech and the stress pattern of the utterance.

Since the production of any phoneme involves several articulators (as well as actions of the respiratory and laryngeal systems), a major problem in speech production is the synchronization of the various parts of the production system. We considered two theories concerning the nature of the control of these movements, the motor command hypothesis and the vocal tract target hypothesis. The first of these maintains that the translation from the phonological representation to a set of articulator movements involves a set of invariant motor commands for each phoneme. The commands instruct the articulators how to move to yield the appropriate sound. The evidence we reviewed suggested that there is too much variability in the articulator movements for this theory to be true.

We suggested that the more plausible theory is the vocal tract target hypothesis. This hypothesis maintains that control of the articulators involves a set of abstract representations of the target states toward which the articulators should move to produce particular sounds. The actual movements involved are determined by the sequence of target configurations to be produced. That is, how the articulators are to move to approach a particular target is determined by where they are moving from and where they will be moving to later.

It appears that the major form of control exerted over the speech motor system is open-loop, or planning, control. We noted, however, that this kind of control may be supplemented by one or more kinds of closed-loop control involving feedback from the speech musculature (or from the speech sounds themselves) that provides information about the moment-to-moment locations of the articulators. Whether the closed-loop control plays an important role in guiding the speech motor system is still an unanswered question.

We saw also that speech has a rhythmical quality imposed upon it by the stress and intonational properties of the utterance. These properties provide a structure for the timing of speech segments and exert an important influence on the planning of speech sound production. It appears that there may be some "natural" rhythmical patterns for speech production and that these may provide important information for listeners.

We also touched briefly on the development of the speech production system in the child, noting that speech production does not really begin until the age of nine to 12 months and that control over the speech production system continues to develop for several years. One reason for this slow development is the necessity for maturation of the physical structures of the speech motor system. The newborn infant's vocal tract is very different from the adult's. A second reason is that the kind of neurological control which is required for implementing the synchronized activity of the many physical structures involved in speech production appears to develop even more slowly than the structures themselves.

SUGGESTED READINGS

Ladefoged (1975) provides an excellent introduction to articulatory phonetics. (See also Abercrombie, 1966, and Denes & Pinson, 1973.) More advanced discussions of speech production and of the mechanisms involved may be found in MacNeilage (1972) and MacNeilage and Ladefoged (1976). Mac-Neilage (1970) is an important paper on the nature of the theory necessary to account for speech production. And Martin (1972) discusses the nature of the rhythmical structure of speech.

IV
Language Development

INTRODUCTION

In earlier sections we focused on the processes involved in understanding and producing language. We saw that these processes, as executed by adults, are enormously complex, and furthermore that there are no simple relationships between the processes involved in comprehension and those involved in production.

Both comprehension processes and production processes reflect a common theme, however. They both involve translations between the external, phonological forms of language and its internal, semantic forms. The differences lie, in part, in the direction of the translation. We have seen also that the semantic representations of language are essentially representations in a general cognitive code that is not unique to language.

It is time now that we turn our attention to another aspect of language processing—the question of how children acquire the ability to comprehend and produce language. Language development has intrigued researchers for a very long time, for the changes in children's language that occur in a relatively short period of time are truly enormous. But with the emergence of the transformational generative approach to grammar in the 1950's and 1960's, there was a blossoming of interest in and research on language development. The new views on the nature of language brought with them the view that language was somehow special and unique in the nature and complexity of its structure. And the focus of language development research during this period was primarily upon the structure of language, its syntax, and the ways in which the syntax of children's utterances moved toward that of the adult language.

This focus upon syntax and upon the uniqueness of language resulted in a tendency to study language development in isolation, to try to deal with it as a special problem, separate from the rest of the child's cognitive development. This approach had a strong influence on both the kinds of data that language development researchers collected and the explanations which they offered for those data.

It was perhaps inevitable that for a time language development should be treated as separate and different from other kinds of human development. Until a great deal is known about both language development and cognitive development it is difficult to see how the two might be related. This isolation of language development studies is the same kind of phenomenon that occurred with language comprehension and production, which were also treated as being separate and different from other aspects of cognition. But such isolationism is no more warranted when considering language development that it is when considering comprehension and production in the adult.

We have already seen the intimate link which the semantic code furnishes between language and cognition. Given this link, it is not surprising that there are also close relationships between the child's developing linguistic abilities and his developing cognitive abilities. Since our main concern here is with language and language development, we will not dwell at great length on the nature of cognitive development. (See Flavell, 1977, for an introduction to this fascinating and complicated topic.) But the relationships between language development and other aspects of cognitive development are too striking and too important to ignore. In many cases, the explanation for a phenomenon observed in language development is to be found in the developments in cognitive processes that occur at the same time.

We saw in Chapter 7 that it is probably not until the last quarter of the first year of life that children begin to produce sounds that can reasonably be regarded as speech. (There is, of course, considerable evidence that infants are perceptually sensitive to speech sounds far earlier than this.) The main question with which we will deal in this Section is how children get from this beginning to the variety of language abilities they exhibit as mature and linguistically sophisticated adults. There is good reason to believe that the processes involved in comprehending and producing language are different; and there is also good reason to believe that the developments of these processes are also different. For this reason, we will deal with them somewhat separately.

Chapter 8 will focus primarily upon children's emerging language production abilities. Chapter 9 will consider some of the variables that appear to be important in language development and will also consider the nature of children's developing abilities to understand the utterances they hear. Chapter 10 will focus upon the development of other kinds of linguistic abilities. We noted earlier that adults are capable not only of producing and understanding language but also of reflecting upon it. These reflective or "metalinguistic" capabilities are the ones that underlie such things as linguistic intuitions about ambiguity, grammaticality, and the like. Chapter 10 will demonstrate that these metalinguistic abilities tend to develop somewhat separately from and later than the abilities involved in comprehension and production. They appear to be related to cognitive development in a way different from comprehension and production abilities.

8

Language Development in the Child: I. Learning to Produce Utterances

The child's production of language begins during the last quarter of his first year of life. At about 8 to 10 months the infant's production of speech-like sounds begins to shift from babbling to true speech production. Within the next few months the child produces an ever-increasing number of sound patterns that are recognizable as utterances. That is, on the basis of the contexts in which speech sounds occur it is possible to infer that the child is now using sound in a regular and systematic way—he is attempting to communicate something rather than just producing sounds.

Determining just when language production begins—when, for example, a child says his first word—probably makes little difference (except, of course, to the child's parents). We saw in Chapter 3 that the infant is responsive to the speech sounds he hears long before he begins to produce speech (see also Condon & Sander, 1974). But there appears to be a change in the child's perception of speech occurring at about the same time he begins to produce speech (Shvachkin, 1973; Garnica, 1973). The fact that there are simultaneous changes in both perception and production suggests that shortly before his first birthday the child discovers something about language and begins to regard speech differently.

The nature of this discovery is something of a mystery. But it seems likely that it is related to the child's emerging ability to conceptualize objects—the development of what many researchers have characterized as "object permanence" (Bower, 1974; Flavell, 1977). Only when the child has developed the concept that an object is an enduring, identifiable part of the world can he begin to notice that the sounds he hears and is beginning to be able to produce are systematically related to objects and events in his environment. That is, the beginnings of language production probably result from the emergence of the notion that the sounds of language can refer to objects and events.

Over the next few months the frequency of babbling diminishes markedly and the number and variety of recognizable utterances increases equally markedly. These utterances are generally short and most often correspond in their surface form to the words of the adult language, though often in abbreviated form. Thus, *giraffe* is likely to come out as *'raffe,* and *elephant* may be *e'phan.*

There are many questions that can be asked about these early utterances, both about their nature and about what they reflect about the child's knowledge of language. In the following section we will consider some of these questions.

One Word At A Time

The most frequent kind of word in the child's early utterances is what would be classified as a noun if used by an adult. Not surprisingly, children quickly develop "names" for things they encounter frequently and things that are interesting to them—things to eat and drink, animals, clothes, toys, people, etc. (see Nelson, 1973). Nelson notes that the child's early nouns most often refer to things with which the child can interact: objects that are not fixed, unmovable parts of his environment. One is unlikely to find words for objects like tables, bookcases, and windows.

Generally the child's early vocabulary also includes a few words related to actions. Some of these seem to be used to describe actions that are either ongoing or have just been completed; others are used to express demands (e.g., *up* used to indicate that the child wants to be lifted up). For the adult, the words used to characterize actions are generally verbs; for the child they need not be. The child often uses words such as *bye-bye, up,* and *out,* which are not verbs, to describe or request actions.

There are also likely to be some words that refer to attributes of objects, states, or locations, such as *pretty, big, allgone, hot, outside,* and a few "social" words like *yes, no, please,* and *ouch.* There are, however, several kinds of words that are notable because of their almost complete absence. Many of these are the sort characterized as "function words": prepositions, articles, auxiliary verbs, interrogative words, etc.

The particular words used, and even the kinds of words, vary greatly from child to child (Nelson, 1973, 1975). Some children have relatively more names for objects than others; and those who have relatively few object names seem to have more social words. These differences may reflect differences in children's approaches to language and may be related to differences in the child-rearing styles of their parents.

Most studies of early vocabulary growth suggest that new words are added very slowly at first, with the rate of vocabulary growth increasing greatly as the vocabulary becomes larger. But vocabulary development may be more complicated than this, for words not only enter the child's vocabulary but also leave it (Bloom, 1973). For example, one child whom Bloom studied used the word *dog* at age 12-13 months, after which it no longer occurred. At 19 months, the child began using *bowwow* in situations where earlier *dog* had occurred.

The Nature of Early Utterances

We have spoken of the child's earliest utterances as words. Is this an appropriate way to characterize them? Certainly there is a correspondence between such utterances and the words of the adult language. But are the child's words the same kinds of linguistic units as the adult's words? Do they serve the same functions for children that they do for adults?

In part this is a question about what and how much the child knows about language when he is producing only a single word at a time. To make the question clearer, consider an example. Suppose we are standing in some friends' kitchen when their 15-month-old looks at the stove and says something that sounds like *hot*. What are we to make of this?

It seems likely that the child has been told that stoves are hot, and perhaps he has confirmed this through direct, and uncomfortable, experience. Should we infer that the child is saying what an adult would say with a full sentence, namely, *The stove is hot?* This is just the kind of inference parents are likely to make about their children's utterances. But is the inference justified? The problem is one of trying to find a way of deciding whether the child is compressing the meaning of a full sentence into a single word. As we will see, there is no way of being certain.

Inferring that a single word expresses the meaning of a full sentence requires at least two assumptions. First, it assumes that the child has conceptualized a relationship between an object—the stove—and a property of that object—its hotness. Second, it assumes that the child is unable to produce a full sentence to express the relationship. A possible reason for such an inability is that the child does not yet know all the words for the full sentence. Another possible reason is that there is some kind of limit on his language production ability such that in the process of encoding the relationship into the utterance every word but one is lost.

One-Word Utterances as Sentences. The hypothesis that early one-word utterances stand for entire propositions has been proposed by a number of investigators (e.g., De Laguna, 1927; McNeill, 1970). This sort of hypothesis has given rise to labeling such utterances "holophrases" (from the Greek *holos*, meaning "whole") and to viewing them as being simultaneously words and sentences. McNeill has expressed this view quite explicitly, suggesting that the child's early words can be treated as serving the same syntactic functions they have for adults, so that *hot* would be an adjective referring to a particular property of an object.

At the same time, one-word utterances would convey the same meanings as (simple) adult sentences. That is, the interpretations which adults place on such utterances can be taken as the meanings which the child, rather imperfectly, is trying to express.

In McNeill's view the young child already knows a great deal about the grammatical relations which simple sentences convey. The part of a sentence most likely to be expressed in a one-word utterance is its predicate. The remainder remains unexpressed because of the child's limited ability to plan utterances for production and to execute the plans. As the child's production planning and execution capacities increase, less and less of the content of his sentences is lost during production, and more and more is overtly expressed in his utterances. Thus, this hypothesis attributes to the young child a considerable knowledge of language and its grammatical categories and syntactic relationships, and attributes the fragmentary character of his utterances to his limited ability to express what he knows.

More recently, Greenfield and Smith (1976) have proposed a modification of this hypothesis about early utterances. They note that adults typically use the situational contexts in which children's utterances occur as a guide to interpreting them. They suggest that the context can be viewed as providing the rest of the child's utterance, the parts that are not expressed linguistically. That is, the utterance itself is only a part of what the child is expressing. It is the relationship between the utterance and its context that provides what, for adults, is provided by the relationships between the parts of an utterance.

On the basis of an extensive study of two children's utterances during the one-word stage of development, Greenfield and Smith argue that the child does not yet know very much about language *per se,* that is, about the syntax by which the language expresses relationships. Rather, the child's knowledge is better characterized as semantic or conceptual. The relationships between the children's one-word utterances and the situations in which they occurred led Greenfield and Smith to propose that 14 different semantic relationships occur. For example, they suggest that the utterance *mommy,* said when the child heard someone coming, expresses the relationship of an agent to the action in which the agent is involved. Similarly, they suggest that *down,* said after the child has gotten down from a table, expresses the relationship of an action or state to the agent of that action. Not all of the relationships are present from the beginnings of one-word speech. Rather, Greenfield and Smith argue, the relationships emerge in a regular sequence up to the time the children begin to combine words to form longer utterances.

If Greenfield and Smith are correct, children in the one-word stage do not yet know very much about language *per se.* Specifically, they do not know how the syntax of a language encodes semantic relationships. They do know some words and something about the meanings or concepts associated with them; and they know something about the kinds of relationships that can hold among the concepts themselves. Thus, children's one-word utterances, taken in context, are expressing the kinds of semantic relationships that underlie simple sentences. But at this early stage of development there is a more direct relationship between utterances and concepts than will be the case later. In this sense, the children's cognitive development is in advance of their linguistic development—their utterances are primitive expressions of the conceptual relationships they have discovered.

Greenfield and Smith's view is rather more attractive than the hypothesis that one-word utterances already reflect a knowledge of *linguistic* relationships. There is some independent evidence that the appropriate kinds of conceptual relationships are developing during this period (see Greenfield & Smith, 1976, Chapter 4; Bower, 1974). But there is little or no evidence to justify the existence of syntactic relationships like subject and predicate of a sentence, direct object of a verb, etc. (Bloom, 1973).

Yet many investigators are reluctant to accept even the hypothesis that one-word utterances express a variety of semantic relationships (e.g., Brown, 1973; Bloom, 1973). The basis for concern is, in part, the fact that a "rich interpretation" of utterances and their relations to situations is required. For example, Greenfield and Smith assume that the meanings which children associate with their words are similar to those of adults, i.e., that *mommy* is understood by the child to be the sort of thing that can be the agent of actions, while *spoon* can be the object of an action but not its agent. In addition, they assume that the interpretations which adults place on children's one-word utterances are correct, i.e., that the child means the same thing by saying *hot* while looking at a stove than an adult would mean by *The stove is hot*. But the more conservative view of one-word utterances is that they are only loosely associated with situations and do not yet represent parts of sentences or of differentiated semantic relationships. That is, *hot* may indicate nothing more than that there is some relationship between the word, stoves, their hotness, and the child's experience with such things. If so, then we are not justified in characterizing one-word utterances either as words or as parts of sentences or propositions (i.e., semantic relations).

It is difficult to decide just how much we can legitimately infer from one-word utterances at a time when that is the only kind that occurs. The problem is, in part, that the utterances themselves furnish so few clues as to what the child intends when he utters them. We will soon see that this problem remains, though it is somewhat diminished, when the child's utterances are longer and a little more complete. But at present we can only note that the question of how much the child knows at the stage when his utterances are no longer than a single word remains unresolved. It seems unlikely that he knows very much about the syntax of language, but whether his utterances reflect a differentiated set of semantic relationships or should even be considered words remains unclear.

The Phenomenon of Overgeneralization

Children often use the words of their one-word utterances in ways that adults find appropriate. It is this that allows adults to make inferences about the meanings of the utterances. But children also use words in situations in which adults would not. Children often use *doggie,* for example, to refer not only to dogs but also to cats and other animals. And *ball* may be used for things as diverse as coins, the rounded heads of screws on the child's highchair tray, and the moon.

With few exceptions, however, the child's use of words does not seem to be random or haphazard. There is generally a sensible relationship between the things a child refers to by a word and the word's appropriate referents. For this reason, the child's extended usage of words can be characterized as *overgeneralization.* That is, the child is generalizing the use of a word from the situations in which he has heard it to other, similar situations. Some generalizations are appropriate, as when a child generalizes *doggie* from the particular dogs he has heard called that to other dogs, pictures of dogs, and stuffed toy dogs. But other generalizations are inappropriate, as when the child generalizes *doggie* to cats, pictures of cows, etc. In these cases, the child is overgeneralizing.

E. Clark (1973a) has reviewed the evidence on children's early overgeneralizations and has concluded that most of them occur for referents that look like the words' appropriate referents; in other words, overgeneralization has a perceptual basis. Thus, *ball* tends to be used to refer to other things that have rounded shapes. Clark hypothesized that children overgeneralize because they first associate with the word only a few of the semantic features which specify the adult's meaning. Thus, the first meaning that children are likely to associate with *dog* may be something like "four-legged animal," and it is only gradually that they learn the additional features that distinguish the meaning of *dog* from that of *cat, cow, horse,* etc.

Clark's "partial meaning" hypothesis is an appealing account of the manner in which children learn meanings for words, suggesting that learning involves adding a semantic feature at a time until the child's meaning corresponds to the adult's. This does seem to be consistent with the existence and nature of early overgeneralizations. It also has some interesting implications, which we will explore in Chapter 9, for semantic development in later language acquisition.

However, the facts about children's overgeneralizations seem to be more complicated than the partial meaning hypothesis would suggest. Since the child's meaning places fewer restrictions than the adult's on the class of things the word can be used to refer to, the hypothesis predicts overgeneralization. But it does not predict that children will also *undergeneralize.* There should not be dogs which the child fails to refer to as *doggie.* Undergeneralizations are impossible to detect in the child's spontaneous speech. If he sees a dog and does not say *doggie,* we cannot tell whether this is because he does not know the word is appropriate (undergeneralization) or because, for example, he simply chooses not to comment upon the presence of a dog. For this reason, it is difficult to determine whether undergeneralizations occur early in language acquisition. However, Anglin (1977) has presented data from somewhat older children which suggest that undergeneralizations are at least as frequent as overgeneralizations. Anglin obtained these data by creating a situation in which children could be expected to use a word if they knew that the word applied. That is, he asked children to provide names for pictured objects. The undergeneralizations were the cases where, for example, children failed to name a picture of a dog as being a *dog.* Thus, Anglin's data indicate that this kind of error occurred at least as often as errors involving children naming non-dogs as *dog.*

In addition, the partial meaning hypothesis predicts that children should make the same kinds of overgeneralization errors in comprehension that they make in production. That is, if a child calls a cat *dog,* he should also be as likely to pick a picture of a cat as to pick one of a dog when he is shown several pictures and asked to pick out the *dog.* Huttenlocher (1974) and Thomson and Chapman (1975) have presented evidence suggesting that such errors are rare.

A final difficulty for the partial meaning hypothesis is that children's concepts during this period of development seem to be *functional* concepts. That is, objects seem to be conceptualized primarily in terms of what they do, what the child can do with them, etc. Yet, as Clark correctly notes, the overgeneralizations are mostly based on perceptual characteristics of objects. How could it be that the children's concepts of objects are functional but their meanings for the words associated with those objects are in terms of perceptual features?

Nelson (1973, 1974) has suggested an answer to this question which implies that overgeneralizations occur for a different reason. She has found that whether children overgeneralize on a perceptual basis depends upon the amount of experience the children have had with the objects. Initially, they generalize on a perceptual basis as Clark suggested. But with increased experience with particular objects they tend to shift to generalizing on a functional basis. Nelson suggests that overgeneralizations occur because children do not know, without experience, whether an object that looks like a ball is an object that they can use like a ball rather than because they know only a part of *ball's* meaning. That is, the concept "ball" is defined for the child in terms of the kinds of actions that can be performed with balls. When the child encounters a new round object, he initially infers that because it looks like a ball he can perform the appropriate actions with it. He only discovers whether or not it really does have the right functional properties by playing or experimenting with it.

Thus, it appears that the meanings (concepts) that young children associate with words are different from those of adults. But the difference is not simply that the child's meaning is a part of the adult's meaning; the relationship is more complex. Overgeneralizations reflect what the child knows about the objects themselves as well as what he knows about words. Overgeneralizations (and undergeneralizations) seem to imply that the relationships between words and objects are vague and not yet well-formulated.

Many studies of early language development suggest that the child's tendency to overgeneralize decreases markedly at the time he begins producing utterances longer than one word. Both of these changes also coincide with the beginnings of a change in the child's cognitive processes. The cognitive change is a complex one, but it appears to be a change from dealing with objects and events as global, undifferentiated wholes to dealing with them as collections of properties. That is, the child is beginning to analyze objects, actions, etc. into the properties of which they are composed, and to be able to attend to individual properties. This is the change referred to by many cognitive development theorists as the transition from the sensory-motor stage of development to the preoperational stage (see Flavell, 1977).

The fact that all these changes occur simultaneously suggests that the transition from one-word to longer utterances reflects a change in the child's view of the relationships between words and the things to which they refer. Utterances are no longer related to situations in global, undifferentiated ways. The child is beginning to be able to analyze these relationships and also the relationships between words. Words are now parts of utterances rather than being the same as utterances. This transition is an important one, for once it has begun the child's language progresses from one-word utterances to a nearly adult-like mastery of language production within a period of only 2-1/2 to 3-1/2 years. Let us now describe this rapid development.

The Acquisition of Structured Utterances

Utterances longer than a single word occasionally occur quite early in the development of language production. But during the last half of the child's second year they begin to occur in substantial numbers. The next 2-1/2 to 3-1/2 years witness a remarkable increase in the length, variety, and complexity of the child's utterances. The increase is so striking that many investigators have claimed that by the age of 4 or 5 years the child has mastered all of the essentials of his language (e.g., McNeill, 1970; Slobin, 1971). We will see later that this claim requires many qualifications. But it is close enough to the truth to indicate that the period from roughly 18 months to 5 years is an extremely important one for language development.

One problem in describing this development is that the age at which a particular linguistic development occurs is variable from child to child. As a result, it is difficult to describe language development in terms of the ages at which particular kinds of development characteristically occur. What would be useful is an index of language development that would allow us to compare children of different ages who are engaged in the same kind of development.

Ages and Stages

One measure which has proven to be a useful index of language develop-ment is the *mean length of utterance* (MLU). Determining a child's MLU involves counting the number of distinct meaningful units (morphemes) per utterance in a sample of the child's spontaneous speech. (See Brown, 1973, pp. 53–55, for a description of the procedures.) MLU is useful in that children of the same MLU have made roughly the same amount of progress in language development, even though their ages may be quite different.

Figure 8.1 shows the relationship between MLU and age for three children studied longitudinally by Brown and his colleagues. These data give some sug-gestion of the variation in the ages at which different language developments occur among children. The three children were all within the normal limits (i.e., niether extremely precocious nor retarded), yet the age at which Eve attained a given MLU was consistently several months younger than was the case for either Adam or Sarah.

Figure 8.1 is marked off in a series of stages, each characterized by a par-ticular MLU value. These stages are convenient reference points for describing the general characteristics of children's language at different points in its devel-opment. But the stages are just reference points on the course of a continuous development. The fact that Stage II occurs at MLU = 2.25 does not mean that at that MLU some striking new language development occurs.

Stage I

By the time a child reaches Stage I he has already been producing utter-ances longer than single words for some time. One-word utterances still make up a large proportion of his total speech, and they have many of the same character-istics that they had earlier. But it is the increasing proportion of the child's speech consisting of utterances longer than single words that is most important, for it is these that allow us to gain some insight into the nature of the child's utterances and the language abilities which they reflect.

Table 8.1 presents a small sample of spontaneous speech from a child whose MLU was between Stages I and II, and gives some indication of the variety of utterances likely to be found. Many of the utterances are difficult to interpret, for the table presents only the utterances and omits nearly all information about the situation in which they occurred.

The immediate question is: how should we characterize the child's Stage I utterances? We would like a characterization that sheds some light on what the Stage I child knows about the syntax and semantics of his language, and on the processes involved in his producing utterances.

Units in Stage I Utterances. Let us begin by considering the units that occur in these utterances. The child clearly has a larger vocabulary than he had earlier. More importantly, there is a basis here for claiming that the child's words

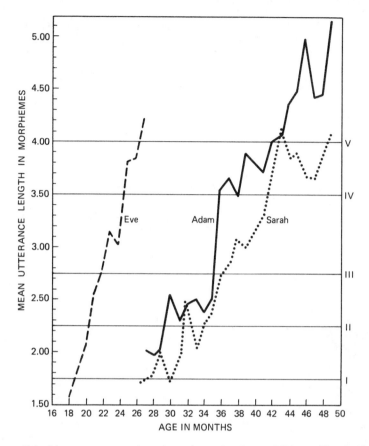

Figure 8.1. Mean utterance length and age in three children. The horizontal lines I–V indicate stages used in characterizing language development. (From Brown, R., Cazden, C., & Bellugi-Klima, U. The child's grammar from I to III. In J. P. Hill (Ed.), *Minnesota symposium on child psychology, Vol. 2.* Minneapolis: University of Minnesota Press, 1969, pp. 28–73. © Copyright 1969 by the University of Minnesota Press, Minneapolis. Used by Permission.)

are really words. For example, in the dialogue presented in Table 8.1, *chair* occurs in three different utterances: *I sit chair, Daddy chair,* and *No, Daddy chair home soon.* Thus, *chair* is a unit within longer utterances rather than an entire utterance. There now appears to be a distinction between words and utterances. Does this really indicate that the child is putting together units of one kind (words) to form units of another kind (utterances)? Might it not be that the child has simply learned several utterances as such, each of which happens to include what adults would consider to be the word *chair*?

The nature of many of the utterances themselves suggests that the Stage I child is capable of constructing utterances and, hence, that there is now a

Table 8.1

A Fragment of a Child-Adult Conversation

Child	Adult
	Would you like some soup?
No	
Mott apple juice	
	What kind of soup?
Candy	
I sit chair	
Daddy Chair	
No, no (said to a third person)	
	Well, you told her to sit there.
No, Daddy chair home soon	
No, no	Do you want to bring over the high stool
	for me to sit on?
Sit water?	
	That's the stool I use when I wash dishes.
	Minestrone.
Minestrone	
I sleepy tired	
My tea	
	What's that?
Daddy tea	
Mommy tea	
	Mommy's tea?
Mommy tea, yeah	
More tea, Mommy	
	What are you doing, Adam?
Tea	
My tea	
	What do you want a napkin for?
Wipe hand	
Dirty my hand	
My chair	
No, no, my chair	
Sleepy tired	

(From Roger Brown, unpublished data. Used by permission)

distinction in his speech between utterances and the units of which they are composed. It is extremely unlikely that the child whose speech is presented in Table 8.1 has ever heard utterances like *I sit chair* or *Daddy chair*. He would more likely have heard utterances like *I am sitting in Daddy's chair* and *That's Daddy's chair*. Thus, the Stage I child's utterances selectively omit some elements that would be present in an adult's utterances. To say that the omission is selective is to say that some *units* have been omitted, and this indicates that the utterances are composed of units.

The "omissions" from children's utterances are not only selective; they are also quite consistent. The types of words omitted are just those that were missing entirely from the vocabulary of earlier one-word utterances—articles, auxiliary verbs, etc. Also missing are parts of words like verb tense endings and possessive inflections. It is this selective omission that gives Stage I speech the appearance of "telegraphic speech" (Brown & Bellugi, 1964)—the things omitted are those that an adult would omit if composing a telegram. One would not send a telegram reading, *My schedule has changed. I'm sorry, but I won't be able to join you in London next weekend.* More likely it would read, *Schedule changed; no London weekend; sorry.* The function words omitted are ones that would contribute to the grammaticality of the telegram, but convey much less of the meaning than the words that remain. This is also characteristic of Stage I utterances.

Even stronger evidence that the Stage I child is constructing utterances out of word-like units comes from the "mistakes" he makes. Such children frequently say things like *allgone cookie, allgone milk* and even *allgone outside,* consistently putting *allgone* at the beginning of utterances. Yet they have rarely, if ever, heard this word order. The fact that children consistently produce such utterances suggests that they are not true mistakes. Their consistency suggests, rather, that they are products of the child's knowledge of the language and the rules he has for constructing utterances. For him, they are grammatical utterances; but his grammar is different from an adult's.

Thus, the best evidence that the Stage I child is constructing many of the utterances he produces is the fact that the utterances are novel—they are combinations of words for which there are no models in the utterances he hears. The fact that the Stage I child can construct utterances does not mean that all of his utterances are constructed. Most children have some utterances that have been memorized as such. These tend to be repeated in exactly the same form and to exhibit grammatical structures and vocabulary different from the child's other utterances. It seems likely that the phrase *Mott apple juice* in Table 8.1 is of this sort, and the nursery rhymes which young children often recite have this fixed-form character. But there is not a complete separation between fixed forms and utterances that are constructed as they are produced. R. Clark (1974) suggests that many early multiple-word utterances are actually combinations involving a fixed form to which something has been added.

From this evidence, then, it appears that at Stage I children have distinguished between words and utterances and that many of their utterances are constructed as they are produced; that is, they are novel utterances. Words are now clearly units within utterances, whereas there was little evidence for this at the earlier stage when utterances were no longer than a single word at a time. But are the Stage I child's words the same sorts of units as the adult's words? That is, do they play the same roles (e.g., as nouns, verbs, etc.) in the child's utterances that they will later? This is basically a question about how much the Stage I child knows about language. Let us consider how we might bring the evidence of the child's utterances to bear on this question.

The Method of Rich Interpretation. Earlier, in discussing children's early one-word utterances, we considered the possibility of treating them as representing only part of what children were trying to convey, the remainder being conveyed by the situations in which the utterances occurred. This method of interpreting children's utterances has been called the *method of rich interpretation;* it is certainly the method used by parents in trying to understand what their children say. The major problem in using the situational context to interpret one-word utterances is that the utterances themselves have so little content that their interpretation is highly uncertain. At Stage I, however, many utterances are longer than a single word. The method of rich interpretation allows us to use the situational context as a guide to interpreting the relationships between the words in an utterance. Since the utterances themselves have more overt content than the earlier one-word utterances, there is less risk of misinterpreting or over-interpreting the utterances.

To understand how the method of rich interpretation can be applied to Stage I utterances, consider an example. Kathryn, one of the children studied by Bloom (1970), produced the utterance *Mommy sock* on two different occasions. On one of these occasions, Bloom reports, Kathryn's mother was putting Kathryn's socks and shoes on her. From this Bloom inferred that the utterance meant something like *Mommy (is putting on my) sock.* Thus, the relationship between *Mommy* and *sock* is the relationship between the actor performing an action and the action's object.

On the other occasion on which *Mommy sock* occurred, Kathryn's mother was loading laundry into the washing machine. Kathryn picked up a sock (one of her mother's, not hers) from the floor and handed it to her. From this Bloom inferred that the utterance meant something like *(Here is) Mommy('s) sock.* Thus, the utterance here is expressing a relationship between a possessor and a possession.

Proceeding in this way, it is possible to provide interpretations for the relationships between the words in the short and fragmentary utterances of Stage I children. The method is, of course, not infallible. It might be, for example, that in the first occurrence of *Mommy sock* Kathryn was using *sock* to express an action meaning something like "to dress" and was commenting upon the fact that her mother was dressing her rather than expressing an actor-object relationship. Insurance against this kind of ambiguity is provided by other utterances that the child produces (and does not produce). Thus, if Kathryn produced other utterances that could be interpreted as actor-object relationships, but never used *sock* in situations where its interpretation would have to be an action rather than an object, we could be reasonably certain that Bloom's interpretation was correct. So, although errors of interpretation undoubtedly do occur, the method works well enough to provide a valuable supplement to the information provided by the utterances themselves.

Regularities in Stage I Utterances. A regularity that aids considerably in interpreting children's early multiple-word utterances is the nearly unvarying order of the words in their utterances (see Braine, 1976). That is, all utterances that express a given relationship have the same word order, not only within one child's speech but for children in general. In utterances expressing an actor-object relationship, for example, almost without exception the word referring to the actor precedes the word referring to the object. This regularity of word order extends even to children learning languages in which, for adults, word order is quite variable. The major exception to the regularity of word order appears to occur when the child is first beginning to produce multiple-word utterances. Braine (1976) calls these early variable-order utterances "groping patterns," suggesting that they occur before the child has discovered an order for expressing a particular relationship.

The general use of fixed word orders allows us to infer that Stage I children are expressing relationships in systematic ways, and not haphazardly stringing together words that comment upon different aspects of a situation. What is less clear is how these relationships should be characterized. There is considerable agreement among different investigators that Stage I utterances express a limited set of semantic, or conceptual, relationships, and that these tend to be the same relationships for different children. There is much less agreement about whether Stage I utterances express consistent syntactic relationships. That is, do Stage I children know very much yet about the syntax of the language they are acquiring, or is there a more direct relationship between meanings and utterances for the children than is the case for adults? In attempting to answer this question, let us first consider the kinds of conceptual relationships that are expressed by Stage I children's utterances and then consider what these utterances imply about the children's knowledge of language structure.

Semantic Relationships in Stage I Utterances. Table 8.2 presents the kinds of two-word utterances most often found during Stage I. The examples have been drawn from a number of different children but do not exhaust the possible types of Stage I children's utterances. Other kinds of two-word utterances occur occasionally. In addition, many of the children's utterances are still only single words, and some are longer than two words. Similar listings can be found in a variety of sources (e.g., Bloom, 1970; Braine, 1976; Brown, 1973; Schlesinger, 1971). The lists presented by different authors vary, as do the characterizations of the semantic and syntactic relationships which the utterances express.

Many authors (e.g., Macnamara, 1972; Sinclair de Zwart, 1971) have suggested that the conceptual relationships expressed in these utterances are the ones also represented in children's thought early in the preoperational stage of cognitive development. This stage is contemporaneous with Stage I of language development. The suggestion is, essentially, that children's utterances are expressions of the conceptual relationships the children also express in other ways. That is, the child's language development is a reflection of his general cognitive development and is not, as some have suggested (e.g., McNeill, 1966, 1970), a separate, unique development.

Table 8.2
Types of Utterances Commonly Found During Stage I

Semantic Characterization	Syntactic Characterization	Forms	Examples
1. Nomination (i.e., naming, noticing)	Existential	$\left.\begin{array}{l}\text{here} \quad \text{it} \\ \text{there} \quad \text{'s} \\ \text{this} \quad \text{see} \\ \text{that} \quad \text{hi}\end{array}\right\}$ + Noun	there book that car see doggie hi spoon
2. Possession	Noun Phrase	$\left.\begin{array}{l}\text{Noun} \\ \text{Pronoun}\end{array}\right\}$ + Noun	my stool baby book Mommy sock
3. Attribution	Noun Phrase	Adjective + Noun	pretty boat party hat big step
	or		
	Predicate Adjective	$\left.\begin{array}{l}\text{Noun} \\ \text{Pronoun}\end{array}\right\}$ + Adjective	carriage broken that dirty Mommy tired
4. Plurality	Noun Phrase	Quantifier + Noun	two cup all cars
5. Actor-Action	a. Subject + Predicate	Noun + Verb	Bambi go Mommy push (Kathryn) airplane by
	b. Subject + Predicate	Noun + Noun	Mommy (wash) jacket Lois (play) baby record
	c. Predicate	Verb + Noun	pick glove pull hat helping Mommy

248

Category	Structure	Pattern	Examples
6. Location			
a. object location	Subject + Prepositional Phrase	Noun + Prep P	sweater chair lady home baby room
b. action toward location	Verb + Prepositional Phrase	Verb + Prep P	sat wall walk street
7. Requests & Imperatives			
a. Verb + Object	Verb + Object	Verb + Noun	want milk gimme ball
b. Quantifier + Object	Quantifier + Object	{ more / 'nother } + Noun	more nut 'nother milk
8. Negation			
a. non-existence	Neg + Sentence	Neg + { Noun / Verb / Adjective }	allgone milk no hot nomore light any more play
b. rejection	Neg + Sentence	Neg + { Verb / Noun }	no dirty soap no meat no go outside
c. denial	Neg + Sentence	Neg + { Noun / Verb / Adjective }	no morning (it was afternoon) no Daddy hungry no truck
9. Questions			
a. requests & imperatives	Yes/No Question	Same word order as statements and imperatives; signaled only by rising intonation	
b. Information requests	Wh- Question	Fixed forms with Wh-	What dat? What (NP) do? Where (NP) go?

(Drawn from Bloom, Bowerman, Braine, Brown, and others)

The suggestion is a reasonable one. But it is difficult to specify in more detail the parallels between a child's utterances and his cognitive developmental status. Unfortunately, the age period of greatest interest to language development researchers (i.e., from roughly 18 months to 4 years) is a period that until very recently has not attracted much attention from cognitive development researchers. We will further discuss the relationship between language development and cognitive development in the next chapter, when we consider the development of children's abilities to understand utterances.

The characterizations of the conceptual relationships expressed by the kinds of utterances in Table 8.2 are fairly straightforward. It is worth noting, however, that they do not correspond very closely to the kinds of semantic concepts and relationships proposed by any linguistic theory. For example, many researchers have attempted to characterize Stage I utterances in terms of the case grammar theory proposed originally by Fillmore (1968, 1971). (See Bowerman, 1973; Brown, 1973, for discussions of this approach.) In Fillmore's theory the central concept underlying a sentence is that expressed by the sentence's verb. The noun phrases in the sentence are systematically related to the verb in a variety of ways, different kinds of noun phrases standing in different kinds of semantic, or conceptual, relationships to the verb. One semantic role which Fillmore defines is that of *Agent,* the entity which causes the action expressed by the verb. The role of Agent seems similar to that of Actor, which occurs as Type 5 in Table 8.2. But the variety of nouns that serve as Actors in the children's utterances is much smaller than the variety that occur as Agents in adult's utterances. Thus, the two do not really correspond very closely (see Braine, 1976).

This lack of correspondence between the semantic concepts and relations found in Stage I utterances and those in adult language points to an important characteristic of the children's utterances. The concepts and relationships expressed by the children's utterances are among those expressed by adult utterances. But the variety of concepts and relationships is far more restricted for the children than for adults.

This point is nicely illustrated by the children's negative utterances. As Table 8.2 suggests, the method of rich interpretation allows identifying three functions which children's early negative utterances serve: (1) commenting upon the non-existence of an object; (2) rejection of some action or object which someone else has proposed; and (3) denial of the truth of what someone else has said (Bloom, 1970). But when the child comments upon the non-existence of an object, it is generally an object that has just recently disappeared or one (e.g., a favorite toy) that is not in its expected place. Stage I children do not produce non-existence negatives comparable to *There are no black spiders on the table* when there are none and they have no particular reason to expect there might be. That is, the negatives are confined to quite concrete and immediate situations and do not include negations of possibilities. This reflects the inability of young children to deal with possible states of affairs, a general limitation on their cognitive capabilities (Flavell, 1977).

Bloom (1970) suggests that the three kinds of negative utterances do not develop together. Rather, at a time when non-existence is generally expressed by utterances of two words or longer, rejection and denial tend to be still limited to one-word utterances. Rejection, in turn, develops before denial. The reason, Bloom suggests, is that some kinds of negation are more difficult to conceptualize than others. For example, denying the truth of what someone else has said requires considering the utterance they produced and its relationship to the existing situation. This is clearly more complex for the child than commenting upon the fact that he has just finished eating his cookie. Thus, there appears to be a relationship between the complexity of what the child wants to say and the complexity of the utterance—the more complex the concept, the less complex the utterance. The implication is that the child has only a limited amount of processing capability available when producing an utterance, and the more of the capability that is needed for conceptualizing the thought to be expressed, the less there is available for constructing the utterance to express it. We will consider this limited capacity notion more fully later.

Not all of the kinds of utterances listed in Table 8.2 occur with equal frequency during Stage I, and there appears to be considerable variation from child to child in the frequencies of the different kinds. In addition, not all of the kinds of utterances listed in Table 8.2 emerge as multiple-word utterances at the same time. Instead, the variety of types of two-word (and longer) utterances increases throughout Stage I. Braine (1976) suggests that the order in which different kinds of utterances emerge varies among children (see also Nelson, 1975). On the other hand, Bloom, Lightbrown and Hood (1975) argue that for the four children they studied the order of emergence of the different kinds of utterances in this stage was quite similar. As this disagreement shows, it is not yet clear whether or not there is a regular, universal sequence in which the different kinds of semantic relationships come to be expressed in multiple-word utterances.

What is clear is that Stage I utterances represent a considerable advance over the child's earlier one-word utterances. The variety of semantic concepts and relationships expressed suggests that the child's ability to analyze situations and to respond to specific aspects of situations has increased considerably, along with his ability to encode those more complex cognitions into utterances. But this raises the question of whether the increased complexity of the child's utterances reflects an increase in his knowledge of language. Should we attribute the increased length and complexity of the child's utterances entirely to the increased complexity of his conceptual, semantic structures? Or does it also reflect an increase in his knowledge of the syntactic structures by which the language encodes semantic concepts and relationships?

Syntactic Relationships in Stage I Utterances. The fact that Stage I children use different, but invariant, word orders to express different semantic relationships suggests that they already know something about the syntactic structure of language. That is, the correlation between semantic functions (relationships) and utterance forms suggests that they know something about the word orders which the language allows for expressing those semantic functions. The question is, do Stage I children know much more about syntax than just word orders for expressing semantic relationships?

This is a question that has been vigorously debated by language development researchers for a number of years, without any clear resolution. To understand what the question involves, we must first consider the relationships between semantic concepts and syntactic categories and between semantic relationships and syntactic structures. The utterances characterized in Table 8.2 as expressing Actor-Action relationships bear a superficial resemblance to fragmentary sentences with a Subject-Predicate syntactic structure. But the syntactic category Subject is a very general and highly abstract one, defined only as a noun phrase immediately dominated in a sentence's phrase structure by the category Sentence. The Subject category is abstract in the sense that there is a great variety of semantic concepts that can assume the role of a sentence's subject—actors, objects, possessive constructions, attributive constructions, etc. To claim that the Stage I child knows the syntactic relationship Subject-Predicate requires claiming that he knows that all of these semantic concepts are equivalent—that they are all constructions of the same kind (noun phrases) and that these are the sorts of constructions that can occur as sentence subjects.

The syntactic category Predicate is abstract in much the same way. A predicate can consist of only a verb (i.e., an intransitive verb); it can also consist of a verb and a noun phrase object, expressing a variety of semantic relationships; and there are numerous other possibilities. Thus, claiming that the child knows the syntactic Subject-Predicate relationship requires claiming that he knows that these relationships are equivalent. Further, it requires claiming that he knows that the kinds of constructions that can serve as sentence subjects can also serve as the direct objects of certain kinds of verbs, that is, as parts of predicates.

McNeill (1970) has strongly argued the position that there is a close relationship between utterance types of the sorts listed in Table 8.2 and syntactic structures. For example, he suggests that possessives, attributives, locatives, and several other utterance types are predicates in the syntactic structure of sentences. The utterances expressing these semantic relations do not, however, have overt subjects. Similarly, the Actor-Action utterances consisting of an Actor and the Object of the action represent a sentence subject and a part of a sentence predicate, the remainder of the predicate—the verb—not being expressed overtly. Bloom (1970) has suggested a similar syntactic interpretation for such utterances.

One difficulty with this claim is that it suggests that the child knows a great deal more about syntactic categories and structures than is expressed in any one utterance. For example, in utterances describing actions, many of the actions involve relations among three terms—an actor, the action, and the object of the action. Syntactically, these would be characterized as involving a subject and a predicate, the latter including a verb and a direct object. Yet rarely are all three terms expressed in a single utterance. On some occasions the "subject" is omitted, on others the "verb," and on still others the "direct object." The problem for a syntactic account of Stage I utterances is to explain why these omissions occur. Put differently, what basis is there for believing that the child conceptualizes the set of syntactic relations underlying such utterances when the relationships are not overtly present in the utterances themselves?

The intuitively plausible answer is that there is a limit on the child's production capabilities such that in his attempt to encode the set of syntactic relationships into an actual utterance something "gets lost." Bloom (1970) and Bowerman (1973a) have attempted to formulate this view explicitly by hypothesizing that the child's knowledge of syntax includes not only the syntactic categories and relationships of simple sentences but, in addition, some "reduction rules" that eliminate items as utterances are being formulated. These rules are essentially transformations of the sort involved in a grammar for the language of adults.

These reduction rule proposals have been sharply criticized on a number of grounds (see, e.g., Braine, 1974, 1976; Brown, 1973). One problem with such rules is that the term reduced (i.e., omitted) is different in different utterances. To account for this either the reduction rule must be optional and must apply to different terms on different occasions, or else there must be different reduction rules that apply on different occasions. If the reduction rules are optional, we would expect that there would be some utterances in which none of the optional reductions occurred. But such complete utterances do not occur at Stage I.

The proposal that there are different reduction rules that apply under different circumstances is empty unless it is possible to specify the conditions under which different reduction transformations apply. This appears to be extremely difficult to do, though Bloom, Miller, and Hood (1975) have recently suggested some possible conditions.

Another kind of problem with reduction rules is that they have no parallels in adult language. Thus, children have no models of utterances involving the kinds of reductions which occur in their own utterances, making it difficult to understand on what basis they might formulate such rules. In addition, using reduction rules to account for the fragmentary character of Stage I utterances means implying that such rules are used less and less as the children's utterances become progressively more complete after Stage I. Since no other cases have ever been suggested in which a rule is used less and less as development progresses, this seems somewhat implausible. Finally, there is no evidence that children's utterances involve any other sort of transformational rules until later than Stage I. If reduction rules exist at all, they must be quite unique kinds of transformations.

The problem of characterizing children's fragmentary Stage I utterances remains unresolved. One reason for this is that we are not yet able to describe with any certainty the processes involved in producing utterances, either in adults or in children (see Chapter 6). Consequently it remains unclear how constraints on the child's production capabilities might be characterized. The reduction rule formulation implies that such constraints are a part of the child's knowledge of language (i.e., his linguistic competence). Thus, accounting for Stage I utterances in terms of a reduction rule operating on a syntactically structured representation implies that the child's knowledge of syntax is directly involved in the process of utterance production. This is essentially the direct incorporation model of production described in Chapter 6.

We noted earlier that the claim that children's Stage I utterances reflect a knowledge of syntactic categories and structures requires assuming that children know that words which serve different semantic roles belong to the same syntactic category. Bloom, Lightbrown and Hood (1975) have presented evidence which, they suggest, supports this assumption. They point out, for example, that children use pronouns and nouns in different utterances to fill the same semantic roles. Similarly, they use *there* and words like *floor* to express the same kinds of locative functions. This does suggest that the children recognize that these different kinds of terms serve the same syntactic functions. But while Bloom et al.'s data *suggest* that Stage I children know something about syntactic categories, they do not *require* that interpretation (see Bowerman, 1975, for further discussion of these data).

To summarize briefly, there is considerable agreement among language development researchers about the general kinds of semantic roles and relationships that are expressed by children's early structured utterances. There is considerably less agreement about the amount of knowledge of language structure that is reflected in these utterances. The conservative view is that Stage I utterances do not reflect much more knowledge of syntax than is involved in the word orders used to express semantic relationships (e.g., Bowerman, 1973; Braine, 1976). The more liberal view is that the Stage I child already knows a considerable amount about the syntax of simple sentences but that there are limitations on his ability to express this knowledge in his utterances (e.g., Bloom, Miller & Hood, 1975). Where the truth lies remains unclear.

What is clear, however, is that language development after Stage I presents abundant evidence of the child's increasing knowledge of syntactic structure. The simple sentences which, at Stage I, are reflected in fragmentary two- and three-word utterances rapidly become more complete. Complex utterances also develop rapidly. There is, in addition, a considerable increase in the variety and complexity of semantic concepts and relationships expressed in utterances after Stage I. Let us turn now to considering some of the ways in which children's utterances develop in later stages.

Beyond Stage I

During the three years following Stage I the child's utterances show a development of structure that is truly extraordinary in both its extent and its complexity. It is, however, a development that is likely to go largely unnoticed unless one deliberately sets out to study the development of syntactic structure. Normally, when listening to a child speaking, one is listening more to *what* the child is saying than to *how* he is saying it. Thus, it often appears that the major development between 2 and 5 years (and beyond) is a development in the variety and complexity of the semantic content of the child's utterances.

There is no denying that a great deal of semantic development does occur during this period. Whereas at Stage I the child talks mainly of the here-and-now, there is subsequently a gradual expansion of his frame of reference, allowing him to talk about things that happened in the remote past and about things that might happen in the future, to consider things that he has not directly experienced, and to talk about the temporal and spatial relationships between objects and events. And the vocabulary which the child uses to describe such things expands greatly, both in the number of words he uses and in the amount he knows about the meanings and uses of words.

But there is also a remarkable expansion of the child's ability to express himself fully and explicitly. Utterances become more complete, coming to include an increasing number of the obligatory syntactic features of the adult language—tense markers, articles, possessive markers, etc. Brown (1973) has documented the emergence of many of these syntactic features, showing that their development occurs in a regular order. More important, the manner in which such syntactic features emerge indicates quite clearly that the child is not simply learning to produce particular forms but, rather, is learning the rules governing each kind of syntactic feature. For example, locative prepositions (e.g., *in* and *on*) all appear within a short period of time and appear simultaneously in a wide variety of utterances. Since the children have had no models for many of the utterances in which they use them, the implication is that they have acquired a general rule for the syntactic structure of prepositional phrases. Thus, we have in later language development clear evidence that the child is discovering and learning to use the syntactic structure of the language, evidence that is difficult to obtain from Stage I utterances.

Utterances also become longer and more complex, expressing a larger amount of content within a single utterance. Complex modifiers emerge, as do several kinds of subordinate clause structures.

Rather than attempt to describe all the kinds of development that occur beyond Stage I, we will focus on the development of two related kinds of structures in simple sentences—first utterances containing negation, then questions. We will then briefly discuss the development of complex utterances, ones which express more than one proposition.

How Children Say "No." The most common sentence form containing a negative is sentence negation, a form in which the proposition asserted by the sentence is negated. For example, in *John did not go to the store,* it is the proposition that John went to the store that is negated. Typically, the word order for sentence negation is

$$NP - Aux+Neg - V \ldots ,$$

with the negative attached to the first-occurring auxiliary verb (e.g., *John could not have gone to the store*). If the sentence would not otherwise have an auxiliary, the auxiliary *do* is added. Thus, the negation of *John went to the store* is *John did not go to the store*.

Children's earliest negatives occur as one-word utterances—*no, allgone*, etc.—which express the semantic functions of nonexistence, rejection, and denial that were described earlier. During Stage I multiple-word negative sentences emerge, generally with the negative at the beginning of the utterance (see Table 8.2) (Bellugi, 1967).

From 3 to 7 months later, when the MLU is between 2.5 and 3.0 (between Stages II and III), the form of negative utterances has changed, with the negative now generally occurring between the subject and the verb, e.g.,

> No, that not circus train.
> I not going to be banker.
> He not little, he big.
> Cromer not writing with the pencil. (Bellugi, 1967)

These utterances are clearly more complete than those at Stage I, as they contain more of the elements of full sentences. But the major change is that the negative is now occurring within the utterance rather than at the beginning.

In addition, some utterances at this stage appear to contain auxiliary verbs, e.g.,

> I don't 'member.
> I don't want some soup.
> She can't stand up, huh? (Bellugi, 1967)

However, auxiliary verbs occur *only* in negative sentences. They do not occur in affirmative sentences or in questions. (The auxiliary verb *be* is an exception to this, as we will see shortly.) That is, *don't* occurs, but *does* does not; *can't* occurs, but *can* does not. *Don't* and *can't* frequently occur in inappropriate contexts. For example, *I don't eat my lunch* seems close to something an adult might say, indicating that he habitually skips lunch. But the child who produced this utterance appears to have meant *I am not eating my lunch*.

Bellugi (1967) suggests that children at this stage are not yet really using auxiliary verbs. That is, *don't* is not constructed from Aux + Neg. Rather, *don't* and *can't* appear to be alternative ways the child has learned for saying *not*, ways that are used with particular main verbs. Consistent with the conclusion that children are not yet using auxiliary verbs is the way in which they use forms of *be*. These occur in utterances like

> He's dancing.
> He's going.
> They are going sleep. (Bellugi, 1967)

Be occurs only when the sentence subject is a pronoun, never when it is a noun or noun phrase. This suggests that forms like *he's* are alternative forms of subject pronouns. The child has not yet discovered that *he's* is a form of *he is,* but treats it as a form of *he.*

So, children have not yet discovered the nature and function of auxiliary verbs at the time when they are beginning to produce negative utterances with the negative inside the utterance. The fact that auxiliaries seem to occur is misleading, for they are not yet true auxiliary verbs. The negative sentences with *don't* and *can't* are not yet as close to adult forms as they appear to be.

The development of true auxiliary verbs is not delayed for long, however. It occurs within a few months of the stage we have just described, at a point at which the child's MLU is about 3.5 (Stage IV). The difference is that auxiliary verbs now occur in a greater variety of forms and in both negative and affirmative utterances. For example,

I don't like Boston.
You didn't get some water in there.
This doesn't work.
I'm not a turtle.
But he isn't here.
A lady wasn't coming with Fraser.
I won't ruin her hair.
I can't call the baby.
You can sit down by me.
That will make me happy.   (Bellugi, 1967)

(Notice that these utterances are far more complete than those we have seen earlier, sounding for the most part like utterances one might hear from an adult.)

The major development in Stage IV is, then, a development of the auxiliary verb system. The fact that a great variety of auxiliary verb forms begins to appear within a very short time period, and to appear correctly in a variety of syntactic structures, indicates that this is a general development involving a major part of the syntactic system. Again, the development is not piecemeal, only one form at a time.

It is the development of the auxiliary verb system that gives children's negative utterances a different appearance than they had earlier. The negative element is correctly positioned between the auxiliary and main verbs, and *do* is provided where it is appropriate. The basic development of sentence negation is largely complete. This is not to say that the Stage IV children have learned all there is to know about negation or that they never make mistakes. For example, the relationship between negation and indefinite terms will not be correctly dealt with for some time to come. Stage IV children produce utterances like *You didn't get some water in there* rather than *You didn't get any water in there.* But the negation of simple sentences is reasonably well-mastered.

One interesting development that is just beginning at Stage IV is what Bellugi (1967) has called the "thick layer of negation"—the use of several negatives in a single utterance. For example,

> He never won't scare me. I'm not frightened of nothing.
> No one's not going to do what I'm doing.
> Now, it's not no big job, look.

These are not errors. Rather, they are indicative of what children at Stage IV and beyond believe to be the correct forms. This is shown by examples like,

> No one know . . . don't know, except Mr. G knows.

in which the child started to produce the accepted adult form and then made a "correction" to produce a multiple negative.

The tendency to produce multiple negatives lasts quite a long time, as most grade-school teachers can testify. It appears that children often use multiple negatives to emphasize the negative character of what they are saying. It is interesting that the majority of the world's languages regard this use of multiple negation for emphasis as perfectly acceptable, even though English does not.

How Children Ask Questions. We have already described the general form and rules involved in Yes/No and Wh- questions in Chapter 2. Since both kinds of questions involve operations on an utterance's auxiliary verb—inverting the subject and auxiliary, inserting *do,* etc.—we might expect that the development of questions in children would closely parallel that of negatives. And in fact this is the case, though with some interesting exceptions.

Both Yes/No and Wh- questions occur during Stage I, but are relatively primitive and restricted in variety (see Table 8.2). Yes/No questions are indicated only by rising intonation, having the same word order as statements. And there is so little variety among Wh- questions, both in form and in content, that they are best regarded as being fixed forms rather than productive constructions. For example,

> What dat?
> Where doggie go?
> Why not?

Between Stages II and III, when apparent (but not real) auxiliary verbs are beginning to appear in their negative utterances, children's questions are little changed in form from Stage I. They are asked about a greater variety of things. *Don't* and *can't* appear in some negative questions, for example,

> You can't fix it?
> Why not . . . me can't dance?   (Bellugi, 1965)

But, as in negative statements, these are not true auxiliaries, In addition, they do not invert with the utterances' subjects. So there is little real progress in forming questions.

At Stage IV, when the major development of their negative utterance forms occurs, there is also a striking development in the forms of children's questions. The same variety of auxiliaries that has begun occurring in negative utterances also appears in Yes/No questions. And almost without exception the auxiliary verb is correctly inverted with the subject. This is shown in Table 8.3 for one child. Auxiliary verbs began appearing in Yes/No questions in Samples 25–34. There were 198 affirmative Yes/No questions in these samples in which the auxiliary verb was correctly inverted, and only seven in which it was not. There were only three negative Yes/No questions with inverted auxiliaries; but there were none in which the auxiliary was not inverted. By and large, children's Yes/ No questions now have the same form as those of adults.

Wh- questions, however, present rather a different picture. Auxiliary verbs are often missing; and when they are present, they are generally not inverted with the utterances' subjects, e.g.,

What he can ride in?
Where I should put it when I make it up?
What we saw?
Why you caught it?

For the child whose data are presented in Table 8.3, the same samples (25–34) in which the auxiliary is nearly always inverted in Yes/No questions yield only eight inverted auxiliaries in Wh- questions, and 31 that are not inverted. Thus, Stage IV Wh- questions are further from the adult form than is the case for either Yes/No questions or negative statements. At first glance, the difference would seem to suggest that the development of the auxiliary verb system and of the rules governing it is less general than we have suggested.

There is, however, a better explanation for the difference. The formation of Wh- questions is a more complex process than that of Yes/No questions. Both question forms require auxiliary inversion and, sometimes, *do*-insertion. But Wh- questions also require providing the appropriate Wh- word and placing it at the front, in advance of the inverted auxiliary. If we were to assume that the steps taken in producing an utterance correspond to the rules of the grammar, then we could explain the difference between Yes/No and Wh- questions in terms of the same kind of production complexity argument suggested by Bloom and others as an account of the fragmentary character of Stage I utterances. (This is essentially the direct incorporation model of sentence production discussed in Chapter 6.) That is, the additional complexity of forming Wh- questions places an additional burden on the child's limited production capabilities. The result is that the auxiliary inversion (and insertion) processes which are executed correctly for the simpler Yes/No questions are omitted for the more complex Wh- questions.

Table 8.3

Occurrence of Auxiliary Verbs in Questions in Successive Language Samples

Samples	Yes/No				Wh-			
	Affirmative		Negative		Affirmative		Negative	
	Non-Inverted	Inverted	Non-Inverted	Inverted	Non-Inverted	Inverted	Non-Inverted	Inverted
1–16	0	0	0	0	0	0	0	0
17–24	1	0	0	0	3	0	2	0
25–34 (Stage IV)	7	198	0	3	22	8	9	0
35–42	*	*	*	*	5	33	5	0
45–51	*	*	*	*	4	27	0	5

(Data are for one child.)

*Data not reported; performance essentially perfect (i.e., auxiliaries always inverted).

(Adapted from Bellugi, U. Simplification in children's language. In R. Huxley & E. Ingram (Eds.), *Language acquisition; models and methods.* Academic Press, London, New York, San Francisco, 1971. Copyright 1971 by Academic Press, Inc. Used by permission.)

Bellugi (1971) has suggested this possibility and provided some further evidence for it. Negation is another kind of complexity which should place a burden on the child's limited production capabilities. Thus, the form of negative questions should be more primitive than that of affirmative questions. This appears to be the case, as is apparent in Table 8.3. Just as auxiliary inversion appears later in affirmative Wh- questions (Samples 35–42) than it does in Yes/No questions (Samples 25–34), it also occurs later in negative Wh- questions (samples 45–51) than it does in affirmative Wh- questions. That is, adding the complexity of inserting a negative tends to force out the complexity of auxiliary inversion. At the same time that affirmative Wh- questions with correct auxiliary inversion are beginning to occur, negative Wh- questions have their auxiliary verbs in incorrect, uninverted positions, e.g.,

Old Lady, what will you do now?
Old Lady, why you can't sit down? (Bellugi, 1971)

These data provide some support for the direct incorporation model of sentence production. They also lend support to the claim that the child's developing utterance production abilities involve an increase in the amount of processing that can be performed in producing an utterance. The limitation on the complexity of the utterances the child produces is a limitation on his production capabilities rather than a limitation on his knowledge of syntax. The child clearly knows about the syntax of auxiliary verbs, including auxiliary inversion, at the time when auxiliaries are produced appropriately in Yes/No questions consistently. The fact that auxiliary inversion occurs only later in Wh- questions, and later still in negative Wh- questions, indicates that there is a limit on the number of processing operations the child can perform and that this limit is raised as language development progresses. We will consider other evidence bearing on the notion of an increasing processing capability in the following chapter.

We have seen that the development of the child's negative utterances and questions involves an interrelated set of developments. Basic among these is an increase in the child's knowledge of auxiliary verbs and the syntactic rules involving them. That this is a single development is indicated by the fact that the development of auxiliary verb structures are parallel and simultaneous in both negative utterances and questions. Thus, one cause of the child's developing ability to produce adult-like utterances is an increase in his knowledge of the syntax of his language. But there is, in addition, an increase in his ability to perform the production processing operations necessary for producing complete, adult-like utterances. Less obvious in the development of negatives and questions is the maturing of the child's cognitive capabilities, allowing him to formulate increasingly complex meanings to be expressed in his utterances. This is more easily seen through the development of complex utterances—utterances that express more than a single proposition.

The Development of Complex Utterances. During Stage I children rarely produce utterances that contain complex modifiers. Modification of a noun is limited to a single attributive adjective, possessive, or quantifier (see Table 8.2). Even more rare are utterances containing complement constructions, i.e., utterances with embedded sentence-like structures serving as the subject or object of a verb (e.g., *Bill to go to the store* in *John wants Bill to go to the store*). Nor do we find utterances with relative clauses, conjoined clauses, or subordinate clauses.

Shortly after Stage I a few such complex constructions begin appearing. The first complement constructions generally involve main verbs like *want* (*to*) (produced as *wanna*), *gonna,* and *hafta,* and occur in utterances in which the complement verb has the same subject as the main verb (Limber, 1973). Such utterances (e.g., *I wanna go*) are probably conceptually simpler than ones involving different subjects (e.g., *I want him to play*), and the latter do not appear until later.

Within a few months utterances containing simple relative clauses have begun to appear (e.g., *I show you what I got, I don't know who it is*). These appear at about the same time as well-formed Wh- questions. Like complement constructions, relative clauses involve a relationship between two propositions. The child's ability to produce utterances that are complex in this way represents a major advance over the one-proposition utterances of Stage I and reflects an increased capacity to conceptualize such relationships. An interesting feature of this development is that all of the kinds of complexities we have mentioned—complex modifiers, complement constructions, and relative clauses—appear first in the predicates of children's utterances and only later in utterance subjects. Thus, we find utterances like *I saw the dog that scared the kitty* occurring earlier than ones like *The dog that scared the kitty chased me*. Limber (1976) suggests that a similar asymmetry exists in the frequency of subject and predicate complexities in adults' utterances. He argues that it stems from the fact that it is the predicates that are most likely (for both adults and children) to contain the new information in utterances. It is the new information, rather than the old information occurring in the utterances' subjects, that is likely to require the kind of elaboration and modification that appears in relative clauses, complements, and other complex modifiers.

A similar kind of development is seen in utterances involving coordinate or subordinate clauses. Initially, utterances on the same topic appear simply as successive utterances, not joined together in any way. Somewhat later, such utterances begin to appear as single utterances conjoined by *and,* and still later they are joined by a variety of coordinating and subordinating conjunctions—*so, because, when,* etc. (Limber, 1973). The development is in the direction of the child's becoming able to formulate and express a greater variety of relationships between propositions.

Clark (1970) has found a similar sequence of development in utterances describing the temporal relationships between events. Initially these occur as separate utterances, with the order in which the events are mentioned corresponding to the order in which they occurred (e.g., *I eat lunch. I go play.*). Later the utterances may be joined by *and* or *and then* (e.g., *I ate lunch and then I went to play*). Still later, children explicitly describe simultaneous events with utterances involving *when* (e.g., *He cried when I hit him*). And finally, the subordinate conjunctions *before* and *after* are used to indicate the sequence of events in utterances (e.g., *I ate lunch before I went to play*). But it is only after all of these forms have appeared that children are able to produce utterances describing temporal relations in which the events are mentioned in an order that does not correspond to their order of occurrence (e.g., *I went to play after I ate lunch*).

Thus, the general course of development is from fragmentary, simple utterances which express only a single semantic relationship to ones that are both more complete syntactically and also express a greater variety and complexity of semantic concepts and relationships. The sequence of steps in this development appears to be quite consistent for different children. And, as we suggested earlier, the development appears to involve three kinds of changes: increases in the ability to conceptualize relationships; increases in knowledge of how these relationships are expressed linguistically; and increases in the capacity for producing utterances that express them in an adult-like manner.

The rate of this development is quite rapid. Generally, only 2-1/2 to 3 years separates the stage when the child is first producing structured, two-word utterances from the stage when he is producing utterances like

I think it means it might stick on me.
May I keep everything that she has?
I wanna really show you how to draw one.
Now let me fix those bombs so that I can beat anyone who comes near me.

(Bellugi, 1967)

Clearly, 4- and 5-year-old children are not yet talking like adults. But the structure of their utterances is remarkably adult-like.

Up to this point, we have focused on the utterances that children produce and the ways in which such utterances change as children develop. Having seen some of the characteristics of this development, we are now in a position to ask about the factors which underlie this rapid and complex development. Certainly, we can assume that children learn a great deal about language by listening to other people's utterances. How do they do this? Is there anything more involved than just hearing well-formed adult utterances? We will consider these and other, related questions in the following chapter.

Summary

Children begin producing recognizable utterances shortly before the end of their first year. These earliest utterances appear to correspond to the words of adult utterances; they include names for objects, some words that describe actions and properties of objects, and a few other kinds of words. There is considerable uncertainty about how these earliest utterances should be characterized. Some theorists have argued that they are both words and sentences and that they reflect considerable knowledge on the part of young children about the semantic and syntactic properties of language. A more conservative view is that children's earliest utterances stand in vague and undifferentiated relationships to the situations in which they occur, and that the children do not yet know very much about language.

During the stage of one-word utterances children tend to overgeneralize the use of words. They use words to refer to referents that are similar to, but different from, the words' appropriate referents. These overgeneralizations have often been taken as indicating that children know only a few of the semantic features that define a word's meaning for adults. But other evidence on children's word usage suggests that the relationship between a child's meaning for a word and an adult's is more complex.

Between 12 and 18 months the frequency and variety of one-word utterances increases greatly, and at about 18 months children begin to produce utterances longer than a single word. Other changes that occur at the same time suggest that the beginnings of longer, structured utterances reflect a general change in the child's cognition, the beginning of a new stage of cognitive development.

These early structured utterances indicate that the child is already able to express a variety of semantic concepts and relationships. It is clear that by this stage of language development children know a good deal about word order, for their utterances show invariant word orders associated with particular semantic relationships. But it is much less certain whether two- and three-word utterances reflect very much knowledge about the syntactic structure of language. This question continues to be debated.

Within a few months of beginning to produce structured utterances, children's utterances develop considerably, becoming progressively more complete and adult-like. It appears that this development is relatively systematic; essentially the same order for adding syntactic features occurs in all children. The nature of the changes that occur indicates that the children are acquiring general syntactic rules rather than learning particular utterance forms. When a particular syntactic feature begins to appear, it tends to appear simultaneously in a wide variety of utterances.

Several kinds of evidence suggest that the development of children's utterances involves three kinds of changes. First, there is an increase in the number, variety, and complexity of semantic concepts expressed in utterances. Second, there is an increase in children's knowledge of the syntactic structures and rules involved in producing utterances. And third, there is an increase in the capacity for performing the production processing required for producing complete well-formed utterances.

Progress in all of these areas is rapid enough that by the age of 4 or 5 years children are producing utterances that are very similar to those of adults.

SUGGESTED READINGS

Flavell (1977) provides an excellent and useful introduction to cognitive development in young children; and MacNamara (1972) and Sinclair (1971) discuss the relationships between cognitive development and early language development. For discussions of children's earliest utterances, see Bloom (1973), Greenfield and Smith (1976), and Nelson (1973). Brown (1973) contains an extensive discussion of structured utterances and their development; for a different point of view, see McNeill (1970). Collections of readings on a broad range of language development topics may be found in Ferguson and Slobin (1973) and Rogers (1975).

9

Language Development in the Child: II. Acquisition Processes and Learning to Understand Utterances

In the preceding chapter we saw that children begin producing recognizable utterances about the time they are 1 year old. By the time they are 4 or 5 years old their utterances are nearly like those of adults. What is being acquired between these ages is a very extensive and very complex knowledge of language. The rapidity of this development and the fact that it occurs relatively effortlessly pose a major problem for anyone trying to understand how this development occurs. Indeed, there is still much about it that we do not understand very completely. Nonetheless, we do know a great deal about some of the processes involved.

In considering the nature of language development, it is important to keep in mind what it is that the child is acquiring. The processes by which adults comprehend utterances are quite different from those by which they produce utterances. Thus, it is not surprising that the acquisition of comprehension abilities is different from the acquisition of production abilities. We saw some evidence of this in Chapter 8, in that children make overgeneralizations in the early one-word utterances they produce that are different from, and more frequent than, their overgeneralizations in comprehension at the same stage of language development (see also Bloom, 1974; Goldin-Meadow, Seligman & Gelman, 1976).

In spite of these differences, there is a close relationship between the acquisition of comprehension abilities and that of production abilities. In general, the sequence in which features of sentence structure appear is much the same for both, but the development of comprehension tends to precede that of production. That is, children generally give evidence of understanding a particular syntactic feature before that same feature appears in their own spontaneously produced utterances (Fraser, Bellugi, & Brown, 1963; Kuczaj & Maratsos, 1973). This is an important fact to remember. As we will see, many of the processes that psychologists and parents alike have thought to be important in language acquisition are specifically concerned with the development of production abilities. But since comprehension generally precedes production, any account that concerns itself only with production is, at best, incomplete.

Processes Involved in Language Acquisition

Certainly a child must be exposed to a language in order to acquire it. How else could we account for such obvious facts as that children who are exposed to Chinese but not English learn Chinese and not English? But beyond the mere fact of exposure to a language, is there anything about how children interact with adult language users that is important for their acquiring the adults' language?

Most parents believe that there is, and if asked are likely to say that they taught their children to talk. Several processes are frequently mentioned in this context—reinforcement, imitation, and expansion being prominent among them. Let us briefly consider each of these and see what effect, if any, each has on children's language acquisition. Then we will consider the influence on acquisition of the kinds of utterance models the child hears.

Reinforcement

The general notion about how reinforcement works is that adults respond positively to some of the utterances children produce but not to others. By encouraging the children, agreeing with what they say, showing interest, etc., they reinforce these utterances, making the children more likely to use them in the future. If reinforcement is selective, and only the most adult-like utterances are reinforced, it is these that are strengthened. The other utterances, the ones that are unreinforced because they are less adult-like, come to occur less frequently. Thus, over a period of time, the child's utterances become more and more like those of adults (see, e.g., Skinner, 1957).

Such a proposal has an appealing simplicity; it sounds like something that might happen in interactions between adults and children. Unfortunately, the proposal's apparent plausibility is highly misleading, because this account of language development is wrong. Reinforcement is not a central part of language development.

The question about reinforcement is not whether the sorts of reinforcing interchanges we have mentioned actually occur. They do. The question is whether reinforcement has the kind of effect on language acquisition that the proposal suggests. That is, what does the child learn about language by having certain utterances reinforced?

The reinforcement proposal suggests that language acquisition is a process of strengthening and shaping particular behaviors, in this case utterances. In order for a child's utterance to be strengthened or shaped, he must first produce it. Hence, reinforcement cannot easily account for the initial occurrence of utterances. And, as we have already said, utterances are understood before they are produced. Thus, there are many aspects of language acquisition about which the reinforcement proposal has nothing to say.

In addition, after an utterance has occurred and been reinforced, its strengthening is a gradual, cumulative process involving many occurrences and many reinforcements. This implies that there should not be sudden changes in children's utterances. But as we noted in Chapter 8, the development of auxiliary verbs is a very rapid one, extending across a great variety of utterances. Auxiliary verbs do not appear first in one utterance, then in a few, only gradually spreading throughout the range of children's utterances, as the reinforcement theory would predict.

An even more striking example of an incorrect prediction following from the reinforcement proposal is found in the way past tense forms develop in hildrens' utterances. For most verbs, the past tense is formed by adding -*ed* t the verb stem. However, English has many irregular verbs that are exceptions to this rule—the past tense of *see* is not *seed*, but *saw*; and the past tense of *go* is not *goed*, but *went.*

Ervin (1964) and others have observed that when children start producing past tense forms, the first ones they use are the past tenses of irregular verbs. (This is not very surprising—some of these verbs are among the most frequently used in the language, e.g., *go, put, eat,* etc.). Furthermore, children generally produce the correct irregular past tenses for such verbs. However, when they later begin producing the past tenses of regular verbs, they tend to use the regular past tense ending even on the irregular verbs for which they were earlier using the correct irregular forms. Thus, after correctly producing *went,* a child is likely to shift to *goed* or sometimes *wented.* In fact, the regular past tense ending may begin to appear on irregular verbs even before it appears on regular verbs.

It is difficult, and most likely impossible, to reconcile this developmental sequence with the proposal that reinforcement shapes children's immature utterances into correct adult forms. The correct irregular past tense forms occur early and frequently. Since they are correct, they are likely candidates for reinforcement. But despite this, they disappear and are replaced by incorrect forms, forms for which the child has no models and for which he is unlikely to be reinforced.

What is wrong is that the reinforcement proposal cannot account for what children are acquiring in learning to produce utterances. It is utterances that are being reinforced but it is not utterances *per se* that children are acquiring. Instead, they are acquiring rules for the formation of utterances. At the time children are producing correct irregular past tense forms, they have acquired only a few particular verb forms. The change from correct to incorrect forms occurs because they have discovered that there is a general rule for forming the past tense, a rule that they apply to all verbs. What they must still acquire is the fact that there are exceptions to the general rule—particular verbs to which it does not apply.

Brown and Hanlon (1970) have shown the inadequacy of a reinforcement account of language acquisition in another way. They examined the data for three children whose spontaneous utterances were recorded over a long period of time, seeking to determine the kinds of utterances that were and were not reinforced by adults. If reinforcement were a factor in the child's utterances becoming more and more like those of an adult, then one would expect it to be the better-formed, more adult-like utterances that were reinforced. But this is not what happened. The data showed that whether or not an utterance was reinforced had little to do with whether it was well-formed. Instead, adults reinforced the children's utterances when what was said was true.

Thus, we find interchanges like,

Child: Draw a boot paper.
Adult: That's right, Draw a boot on paper.
Child: Mama isn't boy, he a girl.
Adult: That's right.
Child: Her curl my hair.
Adult: Um Hmm.

where the child's utterance is not well-formed but is reinforced because what it states is true. On the other hand, we find interchanges like,

Child: And Walt Disney comes on Tuesday.
Adult: No, he does not.
Child: There's the animal farmhouse.
Adult: No, that's a lighthouse.

where the child's utterance is at least as well-formed as most utterances he is producing but is not reinforced because what it states is wrong. Brown, Cazden, and Bellugi (1969) summed up the evidence as follows:

> It seems, then, to be truth value rather than syntactic well-formedness that chiefly governs explicit verbal reinforcement by parents—which renders mildly paradoxical the fact that the usual product of such a training schedule is an adult whose speech is highly grammatical but not notably truthful. (p. 71)

There seems to be no way to escape the conclusion that reinforcement does not account for language development. Still, it seems unlikely that reinforcement has no effect at all on children's language development. Although there is no very convincing evidence, it seems likely that reinforcement has some effect on children's general inclination to talk, and this, in turn, may have some indirect effect on their language development. Children continually discouraged from talking probably talk less than ones continually encouraged to do so. But encouraging children to talk is not the same as teaching them *how* to talk.

Imitation

Young children often reproduce portions of utterances they have recently heard, though such reproductions, or imitations, are generally not exact copies of those utterances. It is often suggested that imitation serves to increase the child's language abilities, that is, that he learns about language through imitating it (see, e.g., Sherman, 1971). The question of interest here is not whether children imitate utterances they hear. Clearly, they do. The question is, rather, whether imitation has an effect upon language development.

There is clear evidence that imitating utterances is not a *necessary* condition for language development. Occasionally children are born who, because of disorders of the speech production mechanisms, are unable to produce the sounds of human speech. But such children show essentially normal development of the ability to understand language (Lenneberg, 1962; Mac-Neilage, Rootes, & Chase, 1967). Thus, being able to produce speech (and hence being able to imitate) is not essential for progress in other aspects of language development.

The question, then, is whether or not imitating utterances facilitates language development in children who do imitate. In thinking about this, it is important to be clear about the nature of the issues involved. Imitation involves a kind of social interaction in which someone, usually an adult, says something to a child. The child, either immediately or after a short delay, says something which reproduces at least a part of the adult's utterance. The adult's utterance, whether the child imitates it or not, provides a *model* of the adult form for a particular utterance, but the effects of such models are separate from the effects of imitation. The effects of imitation are only the additional effects on the child's later linguistic performance of his producing an imitative utterance. Does imitating have any effects beyond those of merely hearing a model utterance?

Ervin-Tripp (1964) and Kemp and Dale (1973) have compared the grammatical features which appeared in young children's spontaneous imitations with those in their other, non-imitative utterances. If children are learning by imitating, then their imitations should be more adult-like than their other utterances. Both Ervin-Tripp and Kemp and Dale found that the imitations were not more advanced than the children's other utterances, suggesting that imitation does not play a role in language development.

Bloom, Hood, and Lightbrown (1974) have conducted a similar study and have reached the opposite conclusion. In this study particular words and syntactic structures tended to appear in children's imitative utterances before they appeared in their nonimitative utterances. Their data suggest that imitation could facilitate language development, though they do not demonstrate that it actually does so.

Are children actually profiting from the experience they get from imitating? Perhaps when a child has a model for an utterance which he is not yet producing spontaneously he can reproduce some of the features of the model on the spot. But whether or not he learns anything from such imitation is a question about its influence on the child's *future* utterances. Do they incorporate the vocabulary and syntactic structures which he first used in imitated utterances? This is difficult to answer, for children's utterances will become more adult-like in syntax and vocabulary anyway. So the question about imitation is whether or not language development is faster with it than it is without it.

There are as yet no data which provide a definitive answer. But Bloom et al. do note that among the six children they studied the amount of imitation varied considerably. In one child's speech at least 27% of the utterances in each sample were imitations. Another child never produced more than 6% imitations. The data which Bloom et al. present do not suggest that the children who imitated more developed their language skills more rapidly.

At present, then, there is no evidence on the effects of imitation that is very conclusive. This in itself is somewhat surprising in view of the importance that many theorists have attributed to imitation. If it is an important factor in language development, it should be relatively easy to find evidence of its importance. We are forced to conclude that imitation, like reinforcement, does not contribute importantly to language development.

Both reinforcement and imitation are variables that involve the child's production of utterances. Since, in general, the syntactic features which appear in a child's productions are ones that he already comprehends, variables involving production should not be important for the acquisition of those features. There is, however, one possible exception. There is one variable involving the child's production—expansion—which might reasonably be expected to affect language development.

Expansion

Children imitate adults' utterances, but adults also "imitate" children. But while a child's imitations of an adult are likely to be reductions of the adult's utterances, the adult's imitations of the child are likely to be expansions, taking the child's incomplete utterances and expanding them into appropriate full sentences. For example,

Child: Baby room.
Adult: Yes, the baby is in his room.

Sometimes, as in this example, the adult's utterance confirms what the child has said. More often, though, expansion occurs for a different reason. It is frequently unclear what the child's fragmentary utterances mean. Expanding such fragmentary utterances is one way an adult has of finding out whether the child's meaning has been understood correctly. That is, expansions are often a way of asking, *Is this what you meant to say?* But regardless of the adult's intention, expansions provide the child with models of the correct, adult way of saying what the child may have expressed in incomplete form.

The model provided by an expansion is of a special sort, for it occurs when the child is actually trying to produce an utterance expressing the meaning more perfectly expressed by the expansion. In this sense, expansions are *contingent* models—the form and content of the adult's utterance are contingent upon what the child is trying to say. Because of this special contingent relationship, expansions might provide the child with a particularly useful kind of model, a model that shows him the relationship between the meaning he is trying to express and the correct form for expressing it. The reaction of the child might well be, *Ah ha! That's how you say what I was trying to say.*

Since expansion is something over which adults, rather than children, have control, its effects can be studied through experiments which systematically expand children's utterances. Cazden (1965) performed just such an experiment, using 3-year-olds as subjects. Children in one group (Expansion) were seen individually for 40 minutes a day, three days a week, for 12 weeks. During each session the experimenter expanded as many of the child's utterances as she could (the actual rate being about 80%). Children in a second group (Modeling) spent just as much time with the experimenter, but the experimenter avoided expanding the children's utterances. Instead, she offered comments on the child's utterances and tried to provide the child with a rich sampling of adult utterance models. Children in the third group (Control) were not involved in the training program, but were tested at its beginning and end to determine the amount of progress that could be expected without any special treatment.

Cazden's results, based on several measures of language development, showed that the greatest gains were made by the children in the Modeling group. The children in the Expansion group gained only slightly more than those in the Control group. On the surface, these results suggest that expansion is not an important influence in language development. However, several criticisms can be made of Cazden's study (see, e.g., McNeill, 1970). There were only four children in each group, a very small number on which to base a conclusion. More importantly, the children were black and were probably learning a dialect of English different from that of the white experimenters (see Chapter 13). This dialect difference might have caused the expansion treatment to interfere with language development rather than facilitate it. In addition, the rate of expansion was much greater than occurs under natural conditions—80% vs. no more than 30%. This could cause two problems. By expanding such a large proportion of the children's utterances, the experimenters were probably expanding many whose meanings were not clear. That is, they may have guessed incorrectly about what the child was trying to say, and consequently produced inappropriate and misleading expansions. Also, with an 80% rate of expansion, nearly everything said by the experimenters was determined by the children's utterances. Since the variety of utterance structures used by the children was fairly limited, the models provided by the expansions were probably a less rich and varied sample of adult utterance forms than was the case in the modeling condition.

A more recent study by Nelson, Carskaddon and Bonvillian (1973) avoided some of the problems of Cazden's study. Their subjects were 27 white, middle-class nursery school children whose dialect was similar to that of the experimenters. The children were also somewhat older and linguistically more advanced, and this contributed to one of the differences in the treatment the children received. Since many of the children's utterances were full sentences which could not be expanded, the expansion treatment was replaced by a Recast Sentence treatment, in which incomplete sentences were expanded, but complete sentences were answered by ones which also presented new syntactic information. This Recast Sentence treatment worked more like a combination of expansion and modeling, but it avoided some of the problems inherent in Cazden's expansion method. The second experimental condition was a New Sentence condition, corresponding fairly closely to Cazden's modeling condition, and the third condition was a Control condition. Children in the Recast Sentence and New Sentence conditions were seen for two 20-minute sessions a week for 11 weeks.

The general trend of Nelson et al.'s results indicated that the children in the Recast Sentence condition made the greatest gains, with those in the New Sentence condition gaining only slightly more than those in the Control condition. Thus, the results suggest that expansion may play a facilitating role in language development. The kind of contingent models provided by expansion do appear to have a greater effect than does either reinforcement or imitation. But it seems likely that this is only a facilitating role; expansion does not appear to be one of the major causes of language development. Contingent models appear to have an effect greater than that of noncontingent models. But we have yet to consider what effects the latter kind of model has.

Models and Modeling

We saw in Chapter 8 that children do not acquire their language utterance by utterance. This implies that they do not need models for all the utterances they will eventually be able to produce. At the other extreme, it seems unlikely that children who never heard any utterances containing a particular syntactic structure (e.g., relative clauses) would ever produce utterances containing that structure themselves. The question, then, is what kinds of models and how much exposure to those models children require in order to develop language.

We should consider first the nature of the utterance models children are likely to hear. Linguists have often suggested, for example, that much of the speech which adults address to other adults is ungrammatical. If this is so, and if the same holds for adults' speech to children, then children should have considerable difficulty discovering the appropriate linguistic forms.

The speech which adults typically address to young infants is rather different from that addressed to older children who are already talking. Adults speak to infants in much the same way they speak to other adults, though with the addition of diminutives (e.g., *doggie* rather than *dog*), raised pitch, exaggerated intonation, and other features of "baby talk." It is as if the adults expect that infants will not understand no matter what is said to them.

But when children themselves begin talking, the adult speech directed to them changes. A number of studies have examined the ways in which adults (typically mothers) talk to children at the one-word stage and at Stage I (e.g., Nelson, 1973; Sachs, Brown & Salerno, 1973; Snow, 1972a). In general these studies indicate that the speech which adults address to such children is both generally grammatical and structurally simple. When utterances that are syntactically complex do occur, they generally occur in situations where they are "conversationally" simple, that is, where the child has much conversational and situational information available to assist in understanding what the utterance means (see e.g., Newport, 1977). There is also a good deal of repetition and alteration, as when adults say the same thing in several different ways:

Pick up the red one. Find the red one. Not the green one. I want the red one. Can you find the red one? (Snow, 1972a, p. 563).

Thus, adults tend to speak to young children on a level of complexity that permits them to understand much of what is being said. As the children's own language develops, adults make corresponding changes toward greater syntactic, lexical, and semantic complexity (see, e.g., Moerk, 1975).

Obviously, the utterances that adults direct to children do not display all the richness and complexity of the adult language. However, data of the sort we have described should be interpreted with caution, for they deal only with speech that is addressed directly to children. Children undoubtedly hear other speech as well by overhearing adults talking to other adults, by listening to television, etc. It is not clear what effects such overheard speech has on children. But there are some indications that children listen selectively, "filtering out" utterances that are too far beyond their comprehension capabilities (see, e.g., Shipley, Smith & Gleitman, 1969; Snow, 1972b). That is, children seem to attend more to the relatively simple utterances directed at them than to more complex, overheard utterances. Thus, it is likely that the part of what children hear which has the greatest impact on their language development is that which is only slightly more complex than what they themselves are capable of producing.

Frequency of Models. Even if the young children's model is less rich and varied than the language allows, it is clear that they hear some kinds of utterances far more frequently than others. On first consideration it would appear that there is a straightforward relationship between how often children hear a particular kind of utterance and how early they learn to understand and produce it. For example, active sentences occur far more frequently than passives, and children understand and produce actives far earlier than they do passives (Bates, 1969; Bever, 1970). Similarly, sentences with relative clauses modifying their direct objects occur more often than ones with relative clauses modifying subjects, and children first use relative clauses in their sentences to modify direct objects. Examples of this sort could easily be multiplied, and they all seem to suggest that the more frequently children hear a particular syntactic structure, the earlier they acquire it.

But the real relationship between frequency of occurrence and acquisition is far more complicated than this. The problem is that structures which occur only rarely in adults' speech, such as passives, also occur only rarely in children's speech even after they know how to produce them. Consequently, it is difficult to determine whether we do not observe young children producing rare structures because they do not know them or because they simply do not use them. There are, however, a few syntactic features for which there are obligatory contexts. That is, the situation requires that an utterance must have a particular syntactic feature in order to be grammatical. If, for example, the child is talking about an event that occurred in the past, then the utterance's main verb should have a past tense marker. Thus, it is possible to determine when such obligatory-context features begin to occur in children's utterances as compared to how often they hear them.

Brown (1973) was able to identify obligatory contexts for 14 such syntactic features. He analyzed the speech samples of three children to determine the order in which these 14 features emerged, and found that the order of acquisition was much the same for all three children. But the correlation between the order of acquisition and the frequencies of occurrence of the 14 features in the speech of the children's mothers was low and non-significant. De Villiers and de Villiers (1973) have performed a similar analysis of data from a larger sample of children with much the same outcome: the order in which syntactic features are acquired is not related to the frequency with which they are modeled in the speech that children hear. Some minimal frequency of models for a particular syntactic construction or feature is undoubtedly necessary for acquisition, but greater frequency does not necessarily result in earlier acquisition.

To summarize, we have now considered several variables involving the interactions between children and adult language users that have often been deemed important factors in language acquisition: reinforcement, imitation, expansion, and frequency of modeling. From the data that are available, it appears that none of these variables has a very important influence on what children acquire or on how early they acquire it. Beyond providing children with some correct models for their utterances and encouraging them to talk, there may be little more that adults need to do (or can do) to facilitate language development. The prescription for parents seems to be: talk to your children a lot, and encourage them to talk. Beyond that, don't worry.

One implication of the research we have been discussing is that children themselves are the primary contributors to language development—acquiring a language is something children do, not something that is done to them. But this leaves two questions: (1) How do children do it? and (2) Why is it that some aspects of language are acquired earlier and more easily than others? We will consider the second question first. An answer to that question is a part of the answer to the first question.

The Role of Language Itself in Language Acquisition

If variables in the child's environment do not account for language development and for the differences in how easily and how early various aspects of language are acquired, then the answers must lie elsewhere. Two variables possibly affecting development lie in the language itself: the complexity of the concepts expressed by different syntactic structures and features, and the complexity of the syntactic structures and features themselves. We will refer to these as semantic and syntactic complexities, respectively.

As a background for thinking about how semantic complexity might affect language development, consider the development of children's concept of time. At Stage I children are primarily focused on the present, on what is happening now. They do not reflect much upon the past, nor do they distinguish at all well between events that happened recently and ones that happened in the more remote past (see, e.g., Piaget, 1969). To do these things they must be able to *decenter* attention from their own immediate (i.e., present) situation. That is, distinguishing between "then" and "now" requires being able to focus on the relationship between what happened earlier and the present. The ability to engage in this kind of decentering develops only slowly, over a period of years. An even more difficult task for children is dealing with the relationship of two events when neither is in the present.

Until children have developed some ability to conceptualize events in the past, it seems unlikely that they would use the past tense marker when they are talking about something that actually happened in the past. And without a concept of the past, it is also unlikely that they would understand the difference between utterances in the present tense and those in the past tense. Since the relationship between two past events is conceptually more complex than that between a past event and the present, we would also expect that children would not correctly use linguistic constructions describing such two-event relationships (e.g., *The horse jumped over the fence before it ran through the meadow.*) until after they learn to use the simple past tense. (This expectation is borne out by the available data, e.g., Clark, 1970.) Thus, it seems likely that the semantic, or conceptual, complexity expressed by different linguistic forms will affect the order in which the forms are acquired.

In addition, we might expect that even if children knew *what* they wanted to say, the linguistic form for expressing one kind of meaning might be more complex than that for expressing another kind of meaning. Thus, differences in syntactic complexity might also account for the order in which different linguistic forms are acquired. The acquisition of the syntactic forms for negation and for Yes/No and Wh- questions, which we described in the preceding chapter, provides some evidence that this is the case.

The difficulty in evaluating these suggestions is to find ways to determine which semantic concepts and syntactic forms should be considered complex and which simple. Brown (1973) approached the problem of syntactic complexity by assuming that the amount of processing necessary to produce a given syntactic form is reflected in the number of transformational rules a grammar needs to derive that particular surface structure. That is, he assumed that the direct incorporation model of sentence production (see Chapter 6) is correct. But since different transformations probably do not contribute equally to syntactic complexity, Brown used a concept of cumulative complexity. That is, he considered one structure to be more complex than another only if the first involved all the transformations of the second plus some additional ones. He developed a similar cumulative measure for semantic complexity based on the concepts (e.g., past time, singular vs. plural) expressed by the structures.

Brown evaluated the cumulative syntactic and semantic complexity of the 14 grammatical features whose order of emergence he had charted. He found that both syntactic and semantic complexity predicted the order in which the syntactic features appeared in the children's utterances.

De Villiers and de Villiers (1973) have also examined the relationship of syntactic and semantic complexity to order of acquisition in a study of 27 children's spontaneous speech. They used Brown's measures of cumulative complexity and examined the same 14 grammatical features. They found that the age of acquisition correlated well with both measures of complexity. Thus, it appears that syntactic and semantic complexity are much more closely related to the age of acquisition of syntactic features than is the frequency with which children hear the features in speech. The major determinant of age of acquisition is the complexity of what children must learn in order to produce a correct, adult-like utterance.

However, from the data concerning cumulative complexity we cannot determine whether it is semantic complexity or syntactic complexity that is the more important. For the 14 grammatical features that have been studied the two measures are very closely related to each other. That is, where one particular feature is more complex than another according to one measure, the same usually holds true for the other measure. Syntactic and semantic complexity go hand in hand.

Slobin (1973) has presented a very different kind of data which suggests that syntactic complexity may play a role above and beyond that of semantic complexity. The data, collected by Mikès (1967), concern bilingual children learning to express the same concept in their two languages. Slobin notes that the concept was expressed earlier in the language in which it had a simpler syntactic form than in the language in which its syntactic form was more complex.

At this point, the best guess is that both the complexity of the semantic concept underlying a linguistic form and the complexity of the form itself are major determinants of how easily and how early children begin producing that form. And we can infer that this conclusion probably also holds for the development of children's ability to comprehend different utterance structures. Most likely, the development of the semantic concept precedes that of the syntactic form. That is, children probably discover a semantic concept in ways other than by listening to utterances that express it. Only then do they discover and begin to understand the syntactic form used to express that concept. It seems quite unlikely, for example, that children discover the conceptual distinction between present and past time by noticing the difference in verb forms between the present and past tense utterances that they hear, and only then seek to discover what semantic difference is associated with the syntactic one. This is suggested by the evidence on children's selective listening. They tend to ignore parts of utterances they do not yet understand. Hence, until they understand the difference between present and past time, they probably do not attend to the syntactic difference between present and past tense verb forms (see Macnamara, 1972; Nelson, 1974).

But, overall, it appears to be the character of the language itself and of the semantic concepts it expresses that determine the course of language development. Other factors, such as those involving the character and quality of children's interactions with adult language users, seem to play far smaller roles.[1] Having discovered the kinds of variables that determine the course of acquisition, it is time we turned to considering how these variables exert their influence. How, that is, do children go about the task of acquiring language?

A Theory of Language Acquisition: The Child as Linguist

The evidence we have considered so far suggests that acquiring a language is something which children themselves accomplish. It is not something imposed on them by the language users around them. The evidence also suggests that

---

[1]This is probably true only within the normal limits of adult-child interactions. Hearing no models of utterances at all would certainly not be conducive to a child's developing a language. And it seems highly likely that a child who was consistently punished and never reinforced for producing utterances would show a pattern of language development that was quite abnormal.

children are acquiring, among other things, a set of rules. This is implied by the fact that the utterances children produce are systematic, as are many of the "errors" they make. In addition, the nature of the changes in children's utterances as language development progresses suggests the development of rules.

Consider, for example, the developmental changes in the ways children form the past tense, a development we described briefly earlier in this chapter. When children first begin using past tense forms, they seem not to have a rule for forming past tenses. Rather, they learn a few specific (usually irregular) past tense forms for particular verbs. Soon, however, a past tense rule emerges, indicated by the fact that the correct, regular past tense ending occurs on a great variety of verbs and is even overgeneralized to irregular verbs.

Although children appear to be acquiring rules, they are never explicitly told what those rules are. This has been taken by many theorists as suggesting that children learn language in much the same way in which linguists discover the rules of the grammar of a language, that the child is functioning as a "little linguist" (Chomsky, 1965; McNeill, 1966, 1970).

Essentially, this account of language development proposes that children begin by noticing how a semantic concept or relationship is expressed in the utterances they hear. On the basis of this evidence, they formulate an hypothesis about the syntactic structures and rules for that concept or relationship. The set of hypotheses they develop for different concepts and relationships is their grammar. They use this grammar both as a basis for formulating their own utterances and as a basis for understanding the utterances they hear from others.

Since the children's hypotheses are generally formed on the basis of only the few utterances they have heard, the hypotheses are often wrong. Consequently, their early utterances do not correspond very closely to those of adults. Their further language development consists of discovering the errors and correcting them by forming new hypotheses (rules) and by forming additional hypotheses for additional syntactic structures. Thus, the rules of the child's grammar gradually move toward those of the adult's grammar.

One problem with this account of language development is that since the children's hypotheses are formed on the basis of very limited data, there is a very large number of different hypotheses they could formulate that would be consistent with the data. And since the utterances different children hear are different, one would expect that different children would form different hypotheses. This should be reflected in their producing different kinds of utterances, and in their making different kinds of errors in the utterances they produce. Yet, as we have seen, the similarities in the utterances of different children are far more striking than the differences.

The advocates of the little linguist hypothesis deal with this problem by suggesting that there are restrictions on the kinds of hypotheses children can form. These restrictions are part of the biological endowment that children bring with them to the task of language acquisition, and are generally considered to be a set of innate linguistic universals. For example, children are assumed to know that sentences will have a basic subject-predicate structure, that the language they will be acquiring has transformational rules, etc. (see Chomsky, 1967). Consequently, the children's task is one of discovering how the subject-predicate structure is expressed in the particular language they are acquiring, what particular transformational rules there are, etc. Essentially, the reason that different children's utterances are similar and that different children show much the same pattern of linguistic development is that, because of the restrictions imposed by the innate linguistic universals, all children form essentially the same hypotheses.

In general, then, the hypothesis that language acquisition is a process of formulating a set of hypotheses (a grammar) and then revising and adding to the hypotheses fits rather well with many of the data on language development. But the little linguist theory also encounters a number of problems.

The theory suggests that children change their hypotheses (rules) when they discover that they are not correct. The evidence to prompt such a change could be of several kinds, such as cases in which their interpretations of utterances according to their rules are not consistent with what they see. But one source of evidence which ought to influence children to change their hypotheses is *correction*. If a child says something in a particular way—the way determined by his current rules—and an adult corrects him, this is quite direct evidence that he is not saying it properly. But children are not very responsive to this sort of evidence. Correction seems to have little effect on their future utterances. It is commonly observed, for example, that once children have begun using the regular past tense ending on irregular verbs, it is a matter of several years and a great deal of correction before they substitute the correct irregular past tense forms. And an example presented by McNeill (1966) makes the point about the ineffectiveness of correction quite clearly:

Child: Nobody don't like me.
Mother: No, say 'nobody likes me.'
Child: Nobody don't like me.
    (Eight repetitions of this interchange)
Mother: No, now listen carefully; say 'nobody likes me.'
Child: Oh! Nobody don't likes me.

A second, more serious problem with the little linguist theory is that it does not provide a very convincing account of how children might modify the rules of their grammar once they have discovered that those rules are wrong. The problem is that the evidence which should indicate to them that their rules were wrong does not indicate how the rules should be changed. How, then, do children arrive at the correct rules? (See Fodor, Bever & Garrett, 1974, for a discussion of this and of other problems with the little linguist theory.)

A final important problem is that the theory provides, at most, an account of how children acquire the rules of their language. There is, as we have seen, some reason to think that such rules might be involved in a fairly direct way in the production of utterances. But the evidence we reviewed in Chapter 4 strongly suggests that such rules are not directly involved in comprehending utterances, and the little linguist theory has nothing to say about how children develop the ability to comprehend.

There is an alternative theory of language development that focuses on the development of comprehension. Let us turn to the alternative and see how it proposes to account for language development.

An Alternative Theory: Strategy Development

In this and the preceding chapter we have seen that children's cognitive development is in advance of their linguistic development. That is, children understand the semantic concept or relationship which can be expressed by a particular syntactic form before they understand the syntactic form itself. This suggests that the children's task in acquiring a language is to discover the syntactic forms to express their meanings.

In doing this, children have more information available to them than just the utterances they hear. Many of these utterances are about events that take place in their immediate environment and involve familiar objects. Thus, they generally have non-linguistic data available that could suggest what the utterances might mean. This gives them pairings of utterances and situations that may help them to figure out the relationships between the actual forms of utterances and their meanings.

For example, suppose that a child is out walking with his mother and their dog, Sebastian. The dog races off, barking, and the child's mother comments, *Look, Sebastian is chasing a cat.* If the child looks quickly enough and in the right direction, he is likely to see Sebastian in hot pursuit of a cat. Thus, from the visual data, he has some indication of what the utterance might mean. And from the pairing of the utterance with the visual information, he has evidence which suggests, among other things, that *a* is the article to be used when a referent (*cat*) is first introduced into the conversation and that *is (verb)ing* is an appropriate verb form to use when the action is in progress at the time the sentence is spoken.

The usefulness of this kind of contextual information derives in part from the fact that adults talking to children generally follow the kinds of conversational rules we described in Chapter 6. That is, their utterances are generally informative and also take into account what children are capable of understanding. Thus, utterances directed to children are far more likely to concern the present and immediate situation than anything else. And it is these utterances that have the greatest contextual support for their interpretations.

This suggests that a reasonable strategy for children, in trying to discover the relationships between utterances and their meanings, is to attend to the relationships between features of the utterances themselves and features of the situations in which they occur. But this provides only a part of the answer to the question of how children acquire language, for this general attentional strategy says nothing about how they discover which features of the utterances are involved in these relationships. Slobin (1973), on the basis of an extensive examination of data from children acquiring several different languages, has proposed an additional set of strategies that children appear to use in solving this problem.

Strategies for Acquiring Language

Slobin has noted that there are several ways in which the expression of particular semantic concepts and relationships vary among languages. His approach to finding children's strategies for discovering how semantic concepts are expressed in their language is to compare language development between children learning different languages. The comparisons are between languages in which the same concept is expressed in different ways. For example, suppose that children learning Language A, in which the syntax expresses that concept one way, learn to express the concept earlier than children learning Language B, which expresses it in a different way. The difference suggests that children find it easier to attend to and utilize the syntactic form used in Language A. This, in turn, suggests something about the kinds of features children attend to in the utterances they hear and about the kinds of strategies that govern this attention.

For example, Slobin notes that in some languages, concepts like the accusative (direct object) or dative (indirect object) functions of nouns are expressed as inflectional suffixes attached to the ends of those nouns. In other languages, the same concepts are expressed as prenominal articles. Children learning the first kind of language use the suffixes in their own utterances considerably earlier than children learning the second kind of language use the pre-nominal articles. This, Slobin suggests, indicates that children find it easier to attend to information that occurs at the ends of content words than they do to attend to information that precedes content words. Thus, the strategy that children are using appears to be: "Pay attention to the ends of words" (Slobin, 1973, p. 191).

A second, very general strategy is one for which we saw considerable evidence in the preceding chapter: "Pay attention to the order of words and morphemes" (Slobin, 1973, p. 197). This appears to be one of the earliest and most pervasive strategies children use. As we have seen, from the time of the earliest multiple-word utterances, the word order in children's utterances is the same as the order which occurs most frequently in the adult language. This suggests that very early in the course of language development children know that word order is important and that different word orders signal different semantic relationships.

But attention to word order is affected by another general strategy. Having discovered the dominant word order for their language, children use that order even in cases where it is not correct. That is, they overgeneralize the use of the dominant order. For example, when children learning English first use auxiliary verbs, the verbs occur in the same position in questions as in statements. Subject-auxiliary verb inversion in questions does not occur until some time later than the time at which auxiliary verbs first appear. Slobin phrases this strategy as, "Avoid interruption or rearrangement of linguistic units" (1973, p. 199). Put a different way, children appear to be trying to keep things as simple as possible, avoiding exceptions to general rules. We have seen some evidence of this in the tendency of children to use regular past tense endings for irregular verbs, and we will see additional evidence of this kind of overgeneralization of general rules later.

Slobin suggested a number of other strategies that children seem to be following in discovering how their language expresses different semantic concepts and relationships. In general, his suggestion is that children attend selectively to particular features of the utterances they hear, approaching language with some pre-determined strategies for extracting information from those utterances. The fact that children learning different languages appear to apply the same strategies suggests that the strategies themselves do not develop as a result of being exposed to utterances in a particular language. That is, they seem to be universal strategies rather than language-specific ones. In this sense, they are linguistic universals, but they are universals involving the ways in which children process utterances.

We can gain a clearer view of the nature of these strategies and of how they are involved in language development by examining how some of the strategies are reflected in the changes that occur as language develops. Since, as we noted earlier, the development of comprehension generally precedes that of production, we can obtain the clearest evidence of language-processing strategies by examining the development of comprehension.

Strategies for Comprehension

We have already seen considerable evidence to suggest that young children attend to word order. Thus, we might expect that word order would play an important early role in their comprehension of utterances. In every language there is one word order that occurs in the surface form of sentences more often than any other. For English, this is the word order of simple active sentences, in which the first noun is the subject of the underlying sentence. The subject precedes the sentence's main verb which, in turn, precedes the direct object (if there is one). Thus, English may be characterized as an SVO (subject-verb-object) language. The import of this is that more often than not, if a child hears a Noun-Verb-Noun sequence in an utterance, he can correctly infer that that sequence corresponds to an SVO structure.

The word order of SVO structures, sometimes called the *canonical order,* concerns the content words—nouns and verbs—of utterances. Since content words appear far more frequently in young children's own speech than such function words as prepositions, auxiliary verbs, and articles, we may expect that these children are also more likely to notice the content words of utterances they hear than the function words. Hence, we might expect that an early strategy for understanding utterances would involve attending to and noticing the order of the utterance's content words and interpreting a Noun-Verb-Noun order as reflecting an underlying SVO structure. Such a word-order strategy would involve not only attending to the order in which content words occur but, in addition, interpreting the word order as directly reflecting the utterance's grammatical relations.

Evidence for the Word-Order Strategy. A strategy of this sort would result in children's arriving at correct interpretations for the majority of utterances they hear. But since some utterances involve other word orders than the canonical one, using this strategy should lead them to systematically *mis*understand such utterances. The misunderstood utterances should be ones in which the relationship between the word order and the underlying grammatical relations is something other than the canonical NVN = SVO relationship. Thus, if the canonical order strategy were the first to emerge, we should find a stage early in language development during which children correctly understand utterances that are consistent with the canonical order relationship, but misunderstand utterances that are not.

A number of experiments suggest that this is the case. Bever (1970), for example, asked young children to act out with dolls reversible active and passive sentences like (1) and (2), using the correctness of their acting-out as a measure of their comprehension of the sentences.[2]

(1) The alligator chases the tiger.

(2) The tiger is chased by the alligator.

The results showed that children between the ages of 2 and 2-1/2 years old performed only slightly better than chance (50% correct) on either active or passive sentences, suggesting that they were not yet using word order as a basis for inferring underlying sentence structures. Children older than 2-1/2 years showed improving performance on the active sentences with increasing age. Performance on the passives, however, did not improve. Rather, with increasing age, performance grew worse, reaching its lowest point at about 3-1/2 years,

---

[2]Reversible sentences are ones in which either of the two noun phrases could be the subject (i.e., either the alligator or the tiger could chase the other). Such sentences are used in experiments on children's use of word order since sentences which are not reversible (e.g., *The horse kicked the barn*) provide cues other than word order to their underlying structure and meaning—one could infer who kicked what just from knowing the meaning of the two nouns and the verb, even without understanding the word order.

when it was significantly worse than chance. This combination of better than chance performance on active sentences and worse than chance performance on passives indicates that the children are interpreting the NVN order as SVO. They are not yet attending to the other cues in passive sentences which signal that the canonical relationship between order and structure does not hold. Only after the age of 3-1/2 years did performance on the passives begin to improve.

Similar results for active and passive sentences have been obtained by de Villiers and de Villiers (1973) and Maratsos (1974). And Bever (1970) has found parallel results for children's performance with sentences like (3) and (4). These differ in the same way as actives and passives in that the NNV order in (4) corresponds to OSV, a non-canonical relationship.

(3) It's the cow that kisses the horse.

(4) It's the horse that the cow kisses.

The children's performance on sentences like (3) paralleled that on actives. Their performance on sentences like (4) paralleled that on passives, changing from chance to worse than chance performance, and only later improving to better than chance.

These results indicate that during Stage I, when children's own utterances reflect the dominant SVO order, they still do not know how to use word order information in interpreting the utterances they hear. As the canonical order strategy emerges over the next few months, their performance improves on utterances that are consistent with the strategy, but becomes worse on utterances that are not consistent with it. The children's later improvement in comprehending exceptional sentence structures like passives does not indicate that they are abandoning the canonical order strategy. Rather, the children have begun to notice the cues in exceptional sentences which signal the fact that they are exceptions, and are adding additional strategies for understanding the exceptions.

Thus, after the age of 3-1/2 years, the canonical order strategy comes to be applied only if the utterance contains no indication that it is an exception. Put differently, children are, after 3-1/2, coming to notice and appreciate the significance of such surface cues as the auxiliary verb and the preposition *by* that signal the passive. In effect, they are learning that there are exceptions to the NVN = SVO relationship, and are also learning to recognize and interpret the cues that signal the presence of the exceptions. We can think of language development as being, in part, the development of more and more strategies for interpreting a wider and wider range of relationships between the forms of utterances and their meanings. The end point of this development is, of course, the set of comprehension strategies used by adults (see Chapter 4). Adults do not comprehend utterances in ways different from those developing in young children. Rather, adults comprehend better, in that they have a more complete set of interpretive strategies.

The Earliest Strategy: Semantic Relations. If, as the data we have reviewed suggest, children do not begin interpreting word order in terms of underlying syntactic relations until about the age of 2-1/2 years, how do they comprehend utterances prior to that age? We saw in Chapter 8 that very young children (those in the one-word stage) understand something about the meanings of some of the words they hear. By the time they have reached Stage I, their own utterances suggest that they know something about the semantic relations expressed by combinations of words. This implies that in attempting to understand what they hear, children at Stage I and earlier are responding primarily to the meanings of the words in utterances, and ignoring their structures.

This, in fact, is what the available comprehension data suggest: Stage I children appear to rely mainly on the meanings of individual words in the utterances they hear, interpreting the utterances by fitting the meanings of the words together in any way in which they seem to make sense. For example, Bever (1970) collected comprehension data on "probable" and "improbable" active sentences like (5) and (6), respectively.

(5) The mother pats the dog.

(6) The dog pats the mother.

Given the meanings of the content words of the sentences —*mother, dog,* and *pats*—and ignoring the order in which the words occur, the most reasonable interpretation of either sentence is that the mother is the one patting the dog.

Bever's results indicated that his youngest subjects were interpreting both sentences in this reasonable way. Children between the ages of 2 years and 2-1/2 years were more likely than chance to act out the probable sentences correctly. But they were less likely than chance to act out the improbable sentences correctly. That is, they tended to interpret both kinds of sentences in the same way, as meaning that the mother patted the dog. Apparently they were responding mainly to the semantic relationships among the words and ignoring the word order (see also Sinclair & Bronckart, 1972; Wetstone & Friedlander, 1973).

It appears, then, that children begin comprehending utterances in terms of the meanings of the words they contain. At the beginning, they are not sensitive to the syntactic structures of utterances. The first aspect of structure they learn to interpret is word order. But initially, word order is interpreted in a far more rigid and invariant way than is the case later. The children use only word meanings and word order, interpreting word order as directly reflecting the underlying grammatical relations. It is only later that they learn to deal with exceptions to the general word order—grammatical relations relationship and begin to notice and understand the significance of the cues that signal the existence and nature of those exceptions.

Thus, children are learning to apply an increasingly complex and sophisticated set of strategies to the utterances they hear. Two kinds of strategies are involved: strategies governing which aspects of the surface forms of utterances the children attend; and strategies governing the interpretations that children associate with those utterance cues. Use of both kinds of strategies allows children to interpret the utterances they hear in terms of semantic concepts and relationships that they have discovered in other ways. There is, in addition, some reason to believe that the general kinds of strategies children use to interpret and discover the structure of utterances are not unique to language. Instead, they appear to be the same kinds of strategies that children use to interpret non-linguistic inputs. To develop this idea here would take us far afield (but see Bever, 1971; Flavell, 1977; Mehler, 1971). We mention it only to suggest that the kinds of strategies applied to language may not be language-specific but may instead be instances of more general cognitive strategies. To the extent that this is the case, such universal language-processing strategies are better thought of as cognitive universals rather than as just linguistic universals.

There is still a great deal to be learned about the nature of such strategies and, particularly, about how they develop. Bever (1970), Slobin (1973), and others have discovered a considerable amount about the strategies used early in language development. But there is a considerable gap between the early strategies that depend upon word order and the semantic relations between words, and the far more sophisticated set of strategies that are used by adults. In general, it appears that the strategies which develop first are those that are most broadly applicable—the general rules rather than the rules for dealing with the exceptions. The latter may emerge only quite late in language development and, for some members of the linguistic community, may never develop.

Late-Developing Strategies. Carol Chomsky (1969) has reported some research that sheds a bit of light upon some of the late-developing strategies. In one experiment Chomsky studied the comprehension of some complex constructions by children between the ages of 5 and 10 years. In sentences like (7), the infinitive *to please* is derived from a full sentence in the underlying structure, one that has both a subject and a direct object.

(7) John is eager to please.

Thus, (7) means essentially that *John is eager for John to please someone.* That is, *John* is the one who is eager and who is to try to please someone else; *John* is the underlying subject of both *is eager* and *to please.* For most sentences with this surface form, the underlying subject of the infinitive is the same as the sentence's surface subject even though the subject of the infinitive does not actually appear in the sentence's surface form.

There are, however, a few sentences which appear to be like (7), but whose underlying grammatical relations are different. For example, in (8), *John* is the direct object of *to please* rather than its subject.

(8) John is easy to please.

That is, (8) means essentially that *It is easy for someone to please John,* a meaning quite different from that of (7).

Since there are relatively few of these exceptional sentences, we might expect that children would acquire a strategy for interpreting the more frequent sentences (i.e., the *eager*-type sentences), and overgeneralize that strategy to the rarer *easy*-type sentences. Only later would they discover the exceptions and learn the cues and interpretations associated with them. (The cue to the exceptions is the adjective—adjectives like *easy, difficult,* and *impossible* signal the exceptional structure.) There is a parallel between what is being suggested for the adjective-infinitive sentences and what occurs with the past tenses of verbs. Children learn the general rule (i.e., the regular past tense ending) first and over-generalize it to cases that are exceptions (i.e., irregular verbs). Only later do they learn the exceptions.

To test this hypothesis, Chomsky presented children with a blindfolded doll lying on a table and asked, *Is the doll hard to see or easy to see?* Only 20% of her 5-year-old subjects answered the question correctly. The majority interpreted *doll* as the subject rather than the direct object of *see,* answering that the doll was hard to see because it was blindfolded (i.e., that the doll had difficult seeing). Only children older than 7 years answered the question correctly more often than not, saying that the doll was easy to see because they could see it easily. Thus, the data indicate that the strategy for interpreting the rarer, exceptional case emerges later than that for interpreting the more common case. Cromer (1970) and Kessel (1970) have found similar results using other, structurally similar sentences and different tasks.

Chomsky also tested the same children for their comprehension of sentences with the verbs *ask* and *tell.* For most sentences with structures like that of **(9)**, the noun phrase closest to the infinitive is the subject of the infinitive.

(9) John told Bill to leave.

Thus, in **(9)**, it is Bill who is to leave, not John. This rule of interpretation is called the *minimum distance principle* (MDP) (Rosenbaum, 1967). Sentences with *ask* as the main verb do not, however, always follow the MDP. *Ask* has two senses, one involving a request, the other involving asking a question. In the request sense, *ask* is interpreted like *tell,* according to the MDP. So, in **(10)**, it is the noun closest to the infinitive (*Bill*) that is its subject—it is *Bill* who is to leave.

(10) John asked Bill to leave.

In the question sense, however, the MDP does not hold for sentences with *ask.* Thus, in **(11)**, it is *John* rather than *Bill* who is the subject of *to do.*

(11) John asked Bill what to do.

That is, John is asking Bill what John should do, not what Bill should do.

Thus, sentences with *ask* sometimes involve an exception to a general rule about the relationship between a sentence's surface form and its underlying structure. But, though similar, this kind of exception is more complicated than the kind involving *easy*-type adjectives. There, the exception was consistent; for *ask* it is not. Whether or not an *ask* sentence is an exception to the MDP depends on which sense of *ask* is involved.

Chomsky collected data on children's comprehension of *ask* and *tell* sentences and found that the *tell* sentences were generally comprehended earlier than the *ask* sentences. In addition, the difficulty of the *ask* sentences depended on which sense of *ask* was involved. Some 9- and 10-year-old children still did not correctly understand sentences with the exceptional *ask* structure (e.g., **(11)**) (see also Kessel, 1970). More recently, Kramer, Koff, and Luria (1972) have found that even some teenagers and adults do not understand the exceptional *ask* sentences correctly.

It is interesting to note that the late-developing strategies for correctly interpreting sentences like the *easy*-type adjective sentences and the *ask* sentences are strategies for which the surface cues to the exceptional structures are individual words or small classes of words. That such strategies are associated with the meanings of words is particularly clearly indicated by the *ask* case—one strategy applies for one of the word's meanings, and a different strategy applies for the other meaning. In fact, this association of comprehension strategies with word meanings is a more general one. As we saw earlier, even before children begin interpreting word order information, their procedure for understanding utterances involves considering the meanings of the utterances' content words and the ways in which those meanings can be combined.

Given this close association of comprehension strategies and word meanings, it seems likely that children adopt the same general approach to learning to understand the meanings of words themselves. And given that children use the relationships between utterances and the contexts in which they occur to assist them in discovering the meanings of the utterances, it seems likely that they also use such contextual information to help them discover the meanings of the words in those utterances. Let us look a bit more closely at the development of word meanings. We will see the same kinds of patterns of systematic errors that we saw in the development of comprehension strategies for utterances.

The Development of Word Meanings

Donaldson and Balfour (1968), in a study of children's understanding of the words *more* and *less,* reported a rather surprising finding. The study involved a number of comprehension tasks, including one in which children were shown two cardboard apple trees with hooks on which cardboard apples could be placed. After placing equal numbers of apples on the two trees, the experimenter asked the children to *Make it so that there are more apples on this tree than on this one.* Later, the children were presented with a similar situation and asked to make it so that there were *less* apples on one tree than on the other.

Children between the ages of 3-1/2 and 4 years generally performed quite well with the *more* instructions. They usually added apples to the tree that the experimenter had indicated. But their performance with the *less* instructions was considerably poorer. Instead of taking apples off the tree, they usually added apples, just as they had done for the *more* instructions. Thus, it appears that the children understood *more* but *mis*understood *less,* behaving as if it meant the same as *more* rather than the opposite. If they had simply not yet learned the meaning of *less,* it seems reasonable that their performance would be random—sometimes adding apples, sometimes taking them off, and sometimes failing to respond. But their performance with *less* was not random—they consistently did the wrong thing.

This pattern of results for *more* and *less* has since been found in a number of similar experiments using a variety of materials and procedures (e.g., Holland & Palermo, 1975; Palermo, 1973; Weiner, 1974). And similar results have been obtained with other pairs of words whose meanings are opposites—*longest-shortest, fattest-thinnest,* etc. (Donaldson & Wales, 1970; Wales & Campbell, 1970). It appears that children understand the meaning of one of the terms in such pairs before they understand the meaning of the other. Furthermore, before correctly understanding the meaning of the second term, they appear to systematically misunderstand it, treating it as though it meant the same as, rather than the opposite of, the first term.

Results like these have generated an immense amount of research into children's understanding of word meanings, and also a number of attempts to account for the systematic, but strange, pattern of the results. The most prominent theory that has been advanced to account for children's developing knowledge of word meanings is an account in terms of semantic features (see E. Clark, 1973a).

A Semantic Feature Theory of Word Meaning Development

Clark proposed that children learn the meanings of words one feature at a time. Thus, for example, while learning the meaning of *tall,* there is a point at which children know that *tall*'s meaning involves "bigness," but they do not yet know that it is bigness in the vertical dimension that defines *tall* and distinguishes its meaning from that of *big, long, wide,* etc. She further proposed that terms like *tall* and *short* differ in that, while they both refer to the same dimension, *tall* refers to the extended end of the dimension and *short* to the non-extended end. She argued (see also H. Clark, 1970) that the meanings of the words for the non-extended ends of dimension are more complex than those for the extended ends. Essentially, they have an additional semantic feature—something like "non-extended"—as part of their meanings. Thus, until children add this additional feature to the meanings of terms like *little, short,* etc., they will have the same meanings for them as for *big, tall,* etc. Clark accounted for the data on *more* and *less, long* and *short,* etc. by arguing that this additional "non-extended" feature is the last to be added to the meanings of words.

There is considerable merit in the theory that words' meanings are composed of elements combined in complex ways (see Chapter 5). And it seems likely that children do not acquire all the components of a word's meaning at the same time. But although Clark's semantic feature hypothesis is consistent with many of the data on children's comprehension of word meanings, there are other data which suggest that the hypothesis is not the correct account of the children's apparent misunderstandings of words.

A Strategy Account of Word Meaning Development

Some of the relevant data come from an experiment by E. Clark (1972) herself in which she attempted to elicit antonyms from 4-year-olds. That is, she presented words like *little, wide, short,* etc., and asked the children to tell her their opposites. If the children understood a word like *short* as meaning the same as *tall,* then they should have given words like *little* as opposites. But they did not. They were as likely to give correct opposites for terms referring to the non-extended ends of dimensions as to give correct opposites for the terms for the dimensions' extended ends. And when they made errors, the errors indicated that they knew whether the term referred to the extended or non-extended end of a dimension, but did not know which dimension was involved. The common errors were of the sort that made *tall* the opposite of *thin.* These data are not consistent with the hypothesis that the last aspect of the meanings of dimensional terms that children learn is extended vs. non-extended.

But if extended vs. non-extended is not learned later than other features of a word's meaning, how are we to account for the data on word pairs like *more-less, long-short,* etc.? The answer is suggested by the data from another of E. Clark's experiments (1973b), this time dealing with the prepositions *in, on,* and *under.* The children were given instructions to place a small toy *in* (or *on* or *under*) some object. The youngest children (1-1/2 to 2 years old) performed consistently correctly with *in,* nearly at chance (61% correct) with *on,* and nearly always incorrectly with *under.*

At first glance, these data would seem to suggest that the children understood the meaning of *in,* did not know the meaning of *on,* and *mis*understood the meaning of *under.* Thus, the results appear to be very much like those with *more* and *less.* But there is another way of interpreting the children's performance. Suppose that the children did not know the full meaning of *in* or *on* or *under,* knowing only that they all referred to spatial relations but not knowing to which relationship each referred. When asked to place an object *on* or *under,* say, a toy bed, what would such children do? It seems unlikely that they would perform randomly, putting the object sometimes on the bed and sometimes under it. Even if they did not know the meanings of the words, they would know something about beds. Beds are the sort of objects things are generally put on, not under. So, most likely, they would put toys on the bed, regardless of whether they were asked to put them *on* or to put them *under*. This would make it appear that they understood *on* but that they thought *under* meant *on*. In reality, they would not know the meaning of either.

Clark analyzed the patterns of children's performances with *in, on,* and *under,* and the results suggest that the children did not yet know which spatial relationship the words referred to. The nature of the objects determined whether a toy was placed in, on, or under them. Wilcox and Palermo (1974) have obtained similar results. The children's performance in the comprehension task is determined both by what they know about the words' meanings and by what they know about the kinds of objects and situations used in the task. If children do not yet know enough about a word's meaning to use it as a guide to what they should do, they will do what they would do in that situation even if no word were involved. It is the children's strategies for dealing with non-linguistic situations that give the appearance that they misunderstand words.

The same explanation accounts for children's apparent misunderstanding of *less* in the experiments on *more* and *less*. The most convincing evidence comes from an experiment by Carey (1976). She used a glass partly filled with water and a pitcher of water. In addition to asking the children to *make it so that there is more water in the glass* and to *make it so that there is less,* she also asked them to *make it so that there is tiv*. Since *tiv* is a nonsense syllable, it has no meaning associated with it, and children could neither understand nor misunderstand it. So, if children respond to instructions with *tiv* the same way they do to instructions with *less,* we must conclude that they do not understand *less*. This is exactly what Carey found. Children who added water when asked to make it *less* also added water when asked to make it *tiv*. Children who were correct for *less* asked *What's tiv mean*? Thus, for children who do not yet know the meaning of *less,* the response of pouring water into the glass rather than out of it is the preferred one. The children's strategy appears to be: if you don't know what the words mean, do what you would do anyway.[3]

Thus, it appears that children's strategies for dealing with words whose full meanings they do not yet know incorporate their strategies for dealing with the situations in which they hear the words used. We may suspect that this is one source of information the children use in trying to discover the meanings of words. For example, if there is a general tendency to add rather than subtract, this may result in the children's learning the meaning of *more* before they learn the meaning of *less—more* would be consistent with their non-linguistic strategies while *less* would be inconsistent. But as yet we do not know whether the development of word meanings proceeds in this manner or not. The experiments to date shed light on how children deal with situations before they fully understand the word meanings, but they do not say much about how meanings are acquired.

---

[3] A further implication of these results is that we cannot tell whether the children understand *more* before they understand *less*. Because they tend to add regardless of the words involved, the fact that they add when instructed to make it *more* cannot be taken to indicate that they understand *more*. They would probably add anyway.

Summary

Common sense views of language acquisition generally stress the importance of certain characteristics of the interactions between children and adults. Frequently named as important variables in child-adult interactions are reinforcement, imitation, expansion, and providing the child with models of correct adult utterances.

The evidence concerning the effects of reinforcement suggests that it could not be an important influence on what children learn about their language. Among the evidence for this conclusion is the fact that adults do not reinforce children's utterances on the basis of whether or not they contain adult-like syntactic structures. Therefore, children could not be learning adult syntax through reinforcement.

The evidence concerning the effects of children's imitation of adult utterances is less clearcut. Some studies find that children's imitations are no more advanced than their other utterances, but one study suggests that they are more advanced. However, there is no evidence that children who imitate more develop linguistically any faster than those who imitate less. It seems likely that imitation is quite unimportant for the development of language.

Expansion, defined as an adult expanding a child's fragmentary utterance into a complete, correct one, is probably not an important influence on language development either. There is some evidence suggesting that children whose utterances are frequently expanded show slightly greater progress than ones whose utterances are not expanded. But the effects appear to be small.

There is no doubt that children need models of utterances in order to learn a language. But the available evidence suggests that the frequency with which a particular kind of utterance is modeled does not affect how easily or how early a child begins producing that kind of utterance.

It appears that the nature of the language itself and the semantic concepts and relationships which the language expresses are far more important determinants of language development than any of the characteristics of child-adult verbal interactions. The semantic complexity expressed by a syntactic structure is an important determinant of how easily and how early children begin using the structure. Similarly, the complexity of the structure itself also affects the point at which it begins being used. It appears also that the concepts expressed in children's utterances are ones that they have acquired in ways other than by hearing them expressed in adult utterances. Children's language development is a reflection of their cognitive development.

Many theorists have argued that children learn language by forming hypotheses about the structures and meanings underlying the utterances they hear. The children then test and revise their hypotheses on the basis of hearing and producing more utterances, with the result that children's hypotheses (i.e., their grammar) gradually become more like those of adults. This "little linguist" theory of language acquisition accounts for many of the data on language development, but cannot account for all of them.

An alternative theory of language development proposes that children attend selectively to certain characteristics of the utterances they hear. That is, they possess attentional strategies for noticing particular attributes of the surface forms of utterances. In addition, they develop strategies for associating underlying structures with patterns of surface cues. Initially, children attend primarily to the meanings of an utterance's words and the relations between them. Only gradually do they develop a sensitivity to the order in which the words occur. At first they associate the most common word order (NVN) directly with an underlying subject-verb-object structure. Once they have adopted this word order strategy, they correctly understand utterances whose word orders are consistent with it, but systematically misunderstand other utterances. Throughout the remainder of language development, children learn the surface cues that signal exceptions to the general word order—underlying structure relationship and also learn additional strategies for interpreting the exceptions.

It appears that similar kinds of interpretive strategies are involved in children's learning the meanings for words. Their word-interpretation strategies involve both the utterances in which the words occur and the situations in which the utterances occur. Their development of word meaning strategies is marked by the same kinds of systematic misinterpretations as their development of the understanding of utterance structures.

In general, the theory that language development is a process of acquiring strategies for interpreting words and utterances seems to account for the available language acquisition data better than the little linguist theory. But the strategy development theory is far from completely worked out. Much remains to be learned about how children acquire language.

SUGGESTED READINGS

Brown (1973) presents an excellent discussion of the variables affecting language development. Papers on adult-child interactions and the speech that children hear may be found in Lewis and Rosenblum (1977), Schaffer (1977), and Snow and Ferguson (1977). Bever (1970) and Slobin (1973) present important discussions of language development strategies. Useful collections of papers can be found in Bloom (1977), Ferguson and Slobin (1973), and Moore (1973).

10

Language Development in the Child: III. Becoming Linguistically Competent

During the first few years of life children develop a great deal of knowledge about and facility with their language. In fact, children's progress in learning to understand and produce utterances is so great that by the age of 5 years their comprehension and production abilities are approaching those of an adult.

There are, to be sure, many loose ends for them still to tie up. For one, the development of vocabulary—both in terms of learning more words and in terms of learning more about the meanings of words—continues throughout the rest of their lives. For another, there are still some syntactic structures which 5-year-olds do not yet understand correctly. And in production, 5-year-olds' utterances, while they contain almost the full range of complex syntactic structures found in the adult language, are unlikely to include as many complexities within a single utterance as adults' often do. But in general, the things that remain for older children to accomplish in rounding out their comprehension and production abilities all seem to involve developing further along the same lines established in their earlier language development. It does not seem to be the case that the adult's comprehension and production processes are different in kind from those of the young child.

We saw in Chapter 9 that it is not until well after the age of 5 years that children are likely to understand correctly sentences with *easy*-type adjectives or complement constructions with *ask*. But, as we noted there, learning to understand such constructions involves learning to deal with an exception to a general comprehension strategy: learning first that there is an exception; learning the surface cues that signal the presence of the exception; and learning the correct underlying structure and meaning to associate with the exception. These are the same things which characterize the way that children learn, much earlier, to deal with other exceptions to general comprehension strategies, such as passives. Thus, there appears to be considerable continuity between what younger children are doing and what older children are doing.

We have also seen that there are strong parallels between children's language development and other aspects of their cognitive development. The existence of these parallels suggests that there should be some major developmental changes in children's language during middle childhood (i.e., between 5 years and adolescence), for this is a period in which there are major changes occurring in cognitive development. Among these changes is the one which Piaget characterized as the transition from preoperational thought to concrete operational thought (see Flavell, 1977). Yet there appear to be no corresponding changes in children's comprehension and production abilities.

There are, of course, many aspects of language development which we have not yet considered. Up to this point, we have focused primarily on children's developing abilities to understand spoken utterances and to produce utterances. But clearly, the adult's linguistic capabilities involve more than just production and comprehension. We pointed out in Chapter 2 that adults typically are capable of making a variety of kinds of judgments about utterances, for example, whether utterances are ambiguous, whether they are grammatical, whether different utterances are synonymous, etc. Linguists often refer to such judgments as linguistic intuitions. Might it be that the abilities that are reflected in such intuitions about language are ones that do not develop until middle childhood? That is, might the emergence of such intuitions be the linguistic reflection of the changes in cognitive processes during middle childhood?

We will focus in this chapter on some of these additional aspects of linguistic development, the ones that round out children's linguistic skills, supplementing their abilities to understand and produce spoken language. Let us begin by considering a kind of development of language which has often been seen as occurring primarily in middle childhood: the development of children's skill as effective communicators.

The Development of Communication Skills

Children obviously do not acquire language simply to amuse themselves or because they have nothing better to do. One of the major functions that children's language serves for them is communicating—communicating information about what they know (and, in asking questions, about what they do not know), about how they feel, what they need, and so forth. Even young children communicate about such things, sometimes verbally, sometimes non-verbally, and often in both ways simultaneously.

But communicating *effectively* requires more than just knowing a language and having something to communicate. It requires, in addition, being able to take into account the characteristics of the audience to which the communication is directed—what they already know, what they might be interested in knowing, etc. In discussing sentence production in adults (Chapter 6), we discussed some of the considerations that come into play in an effective communication, considerations that we referred to as "conversational maxims." But in addition to such general conversational principles, adults usually know a good deal about appropriate ways of varying what they say as a function of the audience they are addressing.

If, for example, the audience already knows quite a bit about the topic, the speaker does not need to be highly explicit or to present a great deal of detail. Communicating in these circumstances consists mainly of indicating how the new information fits in with what the listeners already know, and filling in the bits and pieces which they did not know previously. Presenting material on a novel topic, on the other hand, requires far more explicitness and elaboration, and perhaps also more checking to be certain that the audience is following what is being said.

One situation in which adults display their communication knowledge and flexibility occurs when they are talking to young children. We saw in Chapter 8 that adults talk with young children considerably differently than they talk with other adults, taking into account the children's limited knowledge and ability to understand utterances. But the adult's flexibility in communicating is not limited to communicating differently with young children than with adults. Most professors speak very differently when they are lecturing than when they are talking in a small, informal seminar. And most adults talk differently to close friends than to casual acquaintances or strangers. Note that the differences here are not just differences in *what* is said (i.e., in the content communicated); there are also differences in style.

The question to consider here is when and how this kind of communicative flexibility develops. How effective are young children as communicators? And how do children develop the ability to vary their utterances to meet the needs of different audiences? We should note that these really are different questions. Children at Stage I, and even earlier, often do communicate effectively. Adults are usually able to discover reasonable interpretations for the children's very fragmentary utterances. But the effectiveness of young children's communications is, to a very large extent, attributable to their limited range of subjects and to the fact that there is generally much contextual information that assists their listeners in interpreting the utterances. As the content of children's utterances becomes more varied, such contextual cues will become less useful. The point here, however, is that whether children can be understood is a different question from whether they can control their utterances in order to make them understandable. The latter question is the one involving the ability to vary the content and form of utterances as a function of the audience, and this is the real test of communication skills.

Research on the development of communication skills has a long history which includes some of the earliest research performed by Piaget (1926). In observing 5- and 6-year-old children as they played and worked together, Piaget noted that their utterances often seemed to have the character of monologues. Each child would talk about what he or she was doing or planning to do, but the children appeared not to be noticing what others were saying, nor to be concerned with whether or not others were listening. One child would address a question or remark to another, and, without waiting for an answer, continue talking, sometimes answering his own question. Several children might be doing this simultaneously—taking turns talking, but each carrying on his own monologue—a phenomenon which Piaget labeled *collective monologue.*

Piaget suggested that this phenomenon and others like it indicated that the children were not yet taking their listeners into account when speaking. He called this kind of speech *egocentric speech,* implying that the child had not yet realized that others see the world through their own eyes rather than through his, and that others might not know everything that he did. Because young children do not realize that differences in perspective and knowledge exist, they cannot effectively take such differences into account and adjust what and how they communicate to different audiences. By the same token, when they listen to others, they probably are not paying very close attention to what the speakers are saying. If, as Piaget suggests, young children believe that others know the same things they know, there is no need to listen carefully—they already understand what is being said before it is said. Hence, children are often ineffective in communicating. It is not that they are not *trying* to understand and be understood. Rather, they fail to realize that they might not be doing so effectively.

In Piaget's view, egocentric speech is a manifestation of a general characteristic of the thought of young children and reflects their inability to *decenter* their attention from a single aspect of a situation—a single point of view—to take relationships into account. In speech situations the difficulty appears as an inability to take into account the points of view of the listener and the speaker simultaneously. In a wide variety of other situations it also appears as an inability to consider multiple properties of a situation simultaneously. Piaget argued that this is a general characteristic of the thought of children during what he termed the *preoperational* stage of cognitive development, a period lasting until the age of about 6 or 7 years. Thus, in Piaget's view, the beginnings of socialized speech—speech which takes account of the listener's knowledge and point of view—occur when children move from the preoperational stage to the later *concrete operational stage* of cognitive development. And this does not occur until they are 6 or 7 years old. (See Flavell, 1977, for a discussion of these cognitive developmental stages and their characteristics.)

Since the time of Piaget's original observations, a great deal of research has been devoted to the question of when and how socialized speech develops. Piaget's argument was, of course, that it did not begin to develop until middle childhood, and numerous experimental studies also suggest that not until relatively late in the course of language development are children able to vary the form and content of their communications according to the knowledge and needs of their audiences.

Experimental Research on Children's Communication Skills

In addition to observing children's spontaneous verbal interactions, Piaget (1926) also observed these interactions in an experimental setting. He constructed situations in which, for example, an experimenter told a story to one child, and that child was then asked to retell the story to another. Thus, Piaget could observe the nature of the story as told by the child as well as the reaction of another child to that version of the story.

The stories told by the children were generally much shorter and less detailed than the ones they had heard. More important, information that was essential for understanding the stories was often missing. For example, it was often impossible to tell from the child's version the order in which the events occurred or how they were related to each other. In general, the children's stories were so vague and incomplete that an adult listener could not have understood the story without knowing it beforehand. But the children who told the stories believed that they were telling them quite well, and the children to whom they told the stories appeared to believe that they had understood them. These children, like the ones whose spontaneous speech Piaget characterized as egocentric, were 5- and 6-year-olds who, in Piaget's view, had not yet made the transition from preoperational to concrete operational thinking.

In a more controlled version of Piaget's experiment, Flavell, Botkin, Fry, Wright, and Jarvis (1968) taught children a board game they had invented. To be sure that the children did not learn to describe the game from the experimenter, the game was taught to the children by actually playing it with them, using pantomime rather than verbal descriptions to convey the rules. They played the game until the experimenter was certain that each child understood it.[1] Then the child was asked to explain the game to one of two adults. One of these adults was blindfolded, a fact that was explicitly pointed out to the child.

Flavell et al. evaluated a number of characteristics of the children's explanations of the game to the sighted and blindfolded adults. These analyses indicated clearly that even children in the 2nd grade (7- to 8-year-olds) provided very fragmentary and incomplete explanations of the game to their listeners.

---

[1] This provided a control that was missing from Piaget's story-telling studies, where there was no check on how well a child understood the story before he was given the task of retelling it. The results Piaget obtained could have resulted from the story-teller not having understood the story rather than from an inability to retell it accurately.

More importantly, there were few differences between the explanations given to sighted and to blindfolded listeners—the children did not differentiate listeners according to whether or not they could see the game board and pieces and, hence, whether or not a description of these was necessary. At ages older than 7 or 8 years, there were gradual increases in both the completeness of the children's explanations and the amount of difference between the explanations given to sighted and to blindfolded listeners. Thus, Flavell et al.'s results appear to be consistent with Piaget's: it is not until middle childhood that children begin to be sensitive to the characteristics of the audiences to whom they are talking.

Much research on the development of children's communication skills has used a "communication accuracy" task in which the speaker and listener are visually separated. They are given identical sets of stimuli, and the speaker's task is to describe each stimulus so that the listener can pick it out from his set. Glucksberg, Krauss, and Weisberg (1966), for example, found that in this task 4- and 5-year-old subjects were unable to communicate adequately when the stimuli were novel line drawings, though they were able to communicate reasonably well when the stimuli were pictures of familiar objects. They suggested that the reason for the difference is that the children are, essentially, describing the objects for themselves rather than for their listeners. Because the familiar objects have common names, these "self-encodings" actually do communicate sufficient information for the listener to choose the correct objects. But the descriptions of the novel stimuli were so idiosyncratic that other children could not use them to select the correct stimuli. These descriptions included ones like *Daddy's shirt, Somebody running,* and *Mother's hat,* all given to abstract geometric patterns. Consistent with their interpretation of their results, Glucksberg et al. found that the children who had given such descriptions could themselves use them later to select stimuli correctly.

O'Brien (cited in Krauss & Glucksberg, 1977) attempted to train children from nursery school through the 5th grade in the communication accuracy task by giving them feedback on their mistakes after each trial. Over 16 trials, the nursery school and kindergarten subjects showed no improvement at all. First graders showed some improvement, but even the fifth graders did not reach adult levels of performance. These results are consistent with those we have described earlier, and with many more as well, in suggesting that younger children do not take their listener's characteristics and needs for information into account in attempting to communicate. In general, the results of several experiments seem to show that the ability to do this does not begin to emerge until the age of 6 or 7 years, and then develops only gradually over a long period of time. (See Glucksberg, Krauss & Higgins, 1975, for a review of this research.)

Something seems to be amiss, however. Observations of very young children and even infants suggest that they do make some differentiations between different audiences. It is commonly observed, for example, that 6-month-old infants differentiate between familiar and unfamiliar faces, tending to cry in the presence of strangers but not in the presence of their parents. Why is there such a discrepancy between the time when this sort of audience differentiation begins and the time when children perform effectively in communication tasks? We can perhaps obtain some clues from studies of young children's spontaneous utterances.

Observational Studies of Children's Communication Skills

Gleason (1972) and Shatz and Gelman (1973) have found that even 4-year-olds tend to speak differently when talking to children younger than themselves (2-year-olds) than they do when talking to their peers or to adults. Their speech to 2-year-olds has many of the characteristics of the speech of adults to young children: utterances tend to be short and structurally simple; there is a good deal of repetition and rephrasing; and many speech devices occur that are intended to get the younger child to attend to what is being said (e.g., *Watch, Perry . . . Watch this. . . . Look here, Perry. . . .*) (Shatz & Gelman, 1973). In short, 4-year-olds can use many of the utterance features that we would expect to hear in speech addressed by an adult to a listener who is likely to be inattentive and whose language comprehension abilities are limited.

Four-year-olds do not address 2-year-olds in exactly the same ways adults do. For example, in a structured task in which the speaker is required to talk to a 2-year-old about toys and to demonstrate them, mothers give hints, and 4-year-olds do not. Mothers make suggestions about how the 2-year-old might use a toy; the 4-year-olds tend to use direct imperatives (see Gelman & Shatz, 1977). But it is clear that the 4-year-olds are taking the limited linguistic capabilities of 2-year-olds into account in both what they say and in the ways in which they say it. Furthermore, this happens even with 4-year-olds who do not have younger siblings (Shatz & Gelman, 1973), suggesting that it is not simply a mimicking of the way children have heard their mothers talking to their younger siblings. In addition, it does not depend on the 4-year-old's receiving feedback from the 2-year-old (i.e., evidence that he is not attending or not understanding). Much the same kinds of utterances occur when 4-year-olds talk to baby dolls (Sachs & Devin, 1976).

Thus, no later than the age of 4 years, children show a considerable amount of skill in adapting their communication style, at least in some situations. The data on children's style of adjustments in spontaneous speech appear to conflict with those derived from experimental communication tasks. There are several probable reasons for this conflict. One very likely reason is a difference between what the two kinds of situations require of the children. In spontaneous speech situations, children generally talk about subjects they know a good deal about. In the experimental tasks, on the other hand, they are generally dealing with materials that are relatively novel and, in many cases, inherently difficult to describe.

We have seen earlier that for young children the complexity of the concept they are trying to express affects the complexity and completeness of the utterance they use to express it—the more complex the content, the less complex the utterance. We suggested then that there are limitations on young children's utterance production capabilities such that the greater the amount of this capability needed for formulating a thought, the less capability there is left for expressing it. We may suggest that the same kind of limitation affects children's ability to take the characteristics of their audience into account. The experimental tasks used to study the development of communication abilities place heavier demands on children's language production capabilities than are present in most spontaneous speech situations. Hence, children are not able to deal effectively with the demands of both the experimental tasks and an adjustment for their audience until later, when their overall production capabilities have increased.

It also seems likely that children's comprehension of the differences among audiences and of the kinds of speech adjustments made necessary by them increases throughout childhood and beyond (see, e.g., Ervin-Tripp, 1977; Flavell, 1977). But it appears that the development of children's communication skills actually begins quite early. The experimental studies which appear to suggest that such skills do not *begin* to develop until middle childhood are misleading, but there clearly are great gains in such skills during and even after that time. However, in other aspects of children's language development the contrast between the abilities displayed in early childhood and those displayed in middle childhood is more striking than in the case of communication skills. And we will now turn to considering some of these.

The Development of "Metalinguistic" Abilities

We have seen earlier that adults are able to do many things with language above and beyond being able to produce and understand it. Many of these additional abilities involve, in one way or another, being able to reflect upon language itself. These are the sorts of abilities that linguists refer to as linguistic intuitions; we will describe them here as "metalinguistic" abilities.

Adults' ability to reflect upon their language shows up in a variety of subtle ways. Included among these are the abilities to decide whether a sentence is acceptable[2], whether it is ambiguous, whether it is funny, and so forth. These all have in common the characteristic that they involve doing something more with language than just producing or understanding it.

It seems unlikely that children near the beginning of language development (e.g., at Stage I) have as yet any well developed metalinguistic abilities. They have, at that time, mastered very little of what is involved in comprehension and production. Perhaps for this reason few researchers have attempted to elicit

---

[2] Although linguists generally talk about grammaticality, the judgments adults make are typically judgments of acceptability (see Chomsky, 1965). That is, it is often difficult and sometimes impossible to determine whether a sentence that one finds odd is unacceptable because it is ungrammatical, because it is grammatically well-formed but meaningless, or for some other reason. Hence, we will speak here of sentences being "acceptable" or "unacceptable" rather than of their being "grammatical" or "ungrammatical."

metalinguistic judgments from young children. However, there have been a few attempts to elicit acceptability judgments from children at or near Stage I.

Early Acceptability Judgments

When Brown and Bellugi (1964) attempted to elicit judgments about acceptability from a child somewhat beyond Stage I, this was the result:

> Another week we noticed that Adam would sometimes pluralize nouns when they should have been pluralized and sometimes would not. We wondered if he could make grammatical judgments about the plural, . . . "Adam," we asked, "which is right, 'two shoes' or 'two shoe'?" His answer on that occasion, produced with explosive enthusiasm, was "Pop goes the weasel!"

Attempts of this sort have not always been quite this unilluminating. Gleitman, Gleitman, and Shipley (1972), working with three 2-1/2-year-olds, were able to engage them in a game in which they judged sentences to be "good" or "silly." Using simple imperatives (e.g., *Bring the ball*) and imperatives in which the word order has been reversed (e.g., *Horn the blow*), they found that the children were more likely to say that the reversed imperatives were "silly" than to say that the normal ones were. But even the reversed imperatives were more likely to be judged "good" than to be judged "silly." So it appears that even very young children are able to make some acceptability distinctions, but the distinctions are not sharply drawn.

These results give rise to the question of the basis on which such judgments are being made. A study by de Villiers and de Villiers (1972) suggests a possible answer. They studied acceptability judgments in children between the ages of 28 and 45 months, using normal and reversed-order imperatives. In addition, they obtained the children's judgments of "imperatives" that were semantically anomalous (e.g., *Apple the soap, Chew the push*). Nearly all the children judged the anomalous imperatives "wrong" more often than they did the well-formed imperatives. But only the older, more linguistically mature children judged the reversed imperatives "wrong" more often than the well-formed ones.

The pattern of results obtained by de Villiers and de Villiers suggests that young children judge acceptability on a different basis than adults do. Children the age of the de Villiers' younger subjects have not adopted the canonical word order strategy for comprehending utterances; that is, they are insensitive to the order of words in utterances (see Chapter 9). Consequently, they have no difficulty in "understanding" an imperative in which the word order has been reversed—there is a way for the words to be fitted together so that they make sense. There is, on the other hand, no way in which the words of an anomalous imperative can be fitted together to make sense.

Thus, the de Villiers' results suggest that young children judge acceptability in terms of whether or not they think they understand an utterance. The younger subjects accept the reversed imperatives since they are not yet sensitive to word order and so can make sense of them. They reject the anomalous sentences because they do not understand them. The older subjects have begun using the canonical word order strategy in comprehension and, for this reason, find both the reversed and anomalous sentences incomprehensible. Thus, it appears that young children's earliest metalinguistic judgments are tied very closely to their comprehension strategies: if their strategies allow them to understand an utterance, they will accept it; if not, they will reject it.

Adults, on the other hand, judge acceptability relatively independently of comprehensibility. There are many sentences which they will judge to be unacceptable but which they have little difficulty understanding (e.g., *There was four donuts on the plate*). The independence is not complete, for there are some sentences that are grammatically well-formed but which adults will judge to be unacceptable simply because they are difficult to understand (e.g., doubly self-embedded sentences like *The lion the tiger the gorilla chased killed was ferocious,* which is synonymous with *The gorilla chased the tiger that killed the lion that was ferocious*). Nonetheless, adults' judgments of acceptability are far less closely linked to comprehensibility than is the case for young children. This implies that sometime during the course of language acquisition, there is a change in the basis on which such judgments are made.

Developmental Changes in Acceptability Judgments

A study by Hakes, Evans, and Tunmer (1976) provides a suggestion about the nature of this change and about when it occurs. They collected acceptability judgments on a wide variety of grammatical and ungrammatical sentences from children between the ages of 4 and 8 years. The results indicated that the older children rejected as unacceptable a larger proportion of the ungrammatical sentences than did the younger children. This suggests that the older children knew more of the rules of English grammar than did the younger ones. In addition, the reasons the older children gave for judging sentences unacceptable were much like those given by adults. Even the 8-year-olds, however, tended to accept some sentences which violate subtle grammatical rules, such as *The boy didn't have some cookies in his lunch.*

Hakes et al. also found that 4- and 5-year-old children, in addition to rejecting some of the ungrammatical sentences, rejected some sentences that the older children and adults found perfectly acceptable. The reason for this peculiar behavior became apparent upon examining the explanations the children gave for their judgments of unacceptability. The 4- and 5-year-olds judged a sentence to be unacceptable when they did not believe that what the sentence said was true or when they felt what it said was bad. For example, many of them judged the sentence *The big rock was in the middle of the road* to be unacceptable, giving reasons like *A car might run over it and get a flat tire* or *It would make a car go 'bump' and wake the baby.*

The 4- and 5-year-olds tended to give similar kinds of explanations for rejecting sentences that were in fact ungrammatical. For example, many of them judged *The boy hit* to be unacceptable, but not for the same reasons given by the older children. The older children tended to say that it was incomplete (e.g., *He has to hit something*). The younger children, on the other hand, explained that hitting was a bad thing to do.

This suggests that the younger children were judging not the sentences themselves, but rather what the sentences said. That is, their judgments were based on sentence content—what was asserted—rather than whether the linguistic form used to make the assertion was acceptable. The tendency to judge on the basis of content rather than form had virtually disappeared in the 6-year-old children.

Thus, it appears that the basis on which children judge acceptability undergoes at least two changes before they reach the adult criterion. Initially, judgments are made in terms of whether or not a sentence is understood. As children grow older and learn more of the comprehension strategies and rules for their language, they tend to find more and more ungrammatical sentences unacceptable, for those sentences violate the rules that they know. But there is an intermediate stage during which judgments tend to be based on content rather than form. During this stage, children will reject some sentences, both grammatical and ungrammatical, which they understand but which say things they either do not believe or do not like. Not until the age of about 6 years do children become able to separate a sentence's form from its content and to judge on the basis of form.

Hakes et al.'s results indicate that it is not until middle childhood, a period when substantial changes are occurring in children's thinking processes, that children judge sentence acceptability on an adult-like basis. A number of studies suggest that there are other major changes in children's metalinguistic abilities during the same period.

Changes in Other Metalinguistic Abilities

Hakes et al. (1976), in addition to studying children's acceptability judgments, also studied their judgments about whether or not pairs of sentences were synonymous. Judgments were obtained for a large number of sentence pairs, some synonymous and some not, with a variety of syntactic structures. Overall, the results revealed that children do not correctly judge the synonymy of a pair of sentences until well after they are able to understand both sentences. Similar results have been obtained by Beilin and Spontak (1969) and Sack and Beilin (1971).

In addition, Hakes et al. found that children's judgments of sentence pairs that were synonymous were quite different from their judgments of ones that were not synonymous. Even the youngest subjects (4-year-olds) were correct more often than chance for the non-synonymous pairs. But on the synonymous pairs their performance was significantly worse than chance. Examination of the changes in performance with increasing age suggested a reason for the youngest subjects' performance—they judge on a basis different from that of older children and adults.

Hakes et al. argued that a correct synonymy judgment requires understanding both of the sentences in a pair, and then comparing their meanings and their superficial forms. The reason both of these comparisons are necessary is that synonymous sentences have essentially the same meaning but have different superficial forms (e.g., *The doctor called the nurse; The nurse was called by the doctor*). If two sentences have the same meaning and also have the same form, they are not synonymous but rather are two occurrences of the same sentence. The pattern of the children's synonymy judgments suggested that the younger children were judging solely on the basis of the sentences' forms, without considering their meanings. Hence, they were correct more often than chance for the non-synonymous pairs because such sentences differed in meaning and in form. But because they judged on form alone, they were usually wrong for the synonymous pairs, which differed in form but not in meaning.

Thus, what occurs in children's judgments of synonymy with increasing age is a change in the basis on which they judge. They change from considering only the sentences' forms to considering both their forms and their meanings. Synonymy judgments have therefore allowed us to identify one of the major changes in children's performance that occurs during middle childhood.

Several studies reveal changes in children's abilities to deal with the properties of spoken words that take place during this period. Papandropoulou and Sinclair (1974), for example, in exploring children's knowledge of words, asked some of them to name a long word. The responses from 4- and 5-year-olds tended to be words like *train,* a short word that names a long object. And when asked for a short word, the 4- and 5-year-olds gave words like *dandelion,* a relatively long word, but one that names a very small plant. It was only older children that were able to respond in terms of the properties of the words themselves rather than the properties of the things to which the words referred. This result is very similar to the results Hakes et al. obtained for children's acceptability judgments.

Rozin, Bressman, and Taft (1974) have also demonstrated the difficulty that young children have in dealing with the properties of spoken words. They presented children with pairs of written words, one long and one short, such as *motorcycle* and *mow.* One of the words was then spoken, and the children were asked to point to its written form. 4- and 5-year-olds performed little better than chance in picking out the long and short words they had heard, but they had little difficulty when they were shown the pairs of long and short printed words and simply asked to pick out the long or short one. That is, the difficulty seemed to occur in dealing with the spoken words, not in dealing with the written words.

Not all properties of the spoken language are equally difficult for children to deal with. For example, Liberman, Shankweiler, Fischer, and Carter (1974) studied whether or not children can learn to count the number of syllables in spoken words by tapping a number of times equal to the number of syllables (e.g., *but* = 1; *butter* = 2; *butterfly* = 3). They found that nearly half of the 4-year-olds they tested could master this syllabic segmentation task, as could nearly all the children older than 4 years.

Liberman et al. also studied children's ability to count the number of phonological segments in syllables in a task similar to the syllable segmentation task (e.g., /oo/ = 1; *boo* = 2; *boot* = 3). They found that it was not until children were 6 years old or older that a majority of them could master the phonemic segmentation task. It appears that the recognition of syllabic segments is easier and develops earlier than that of phonological segments. Consistent with the difficulty which 4- and 5-year-olds have in dealing with phonological segments, Knafle (1973, 1974) has found that it is not until later than this that children can accurately discriminate between pairs of words that rhyme and pairs that do not.

Kessel (1970) and Shultz and Pilon (1973) have found that it is not until 6 years of age or later that children begin to be able to detect ambiguities in sentences (e.g., *The boy found the bat in the attic.*). Younger children tend to know both of the possible meanings (see, e.g., Evans, 1976), so it appears that the difficulty lies in becoming aware of both meanings at the same time rather than in failing to understand one of the meanings.

The results on rhyming and ambiguity are consistent with research and with everyday observations, both of which suggest that it is not until the age of 6 or 7 that children begin to understand puns, riddles, and other sorts of linguistic jokes (see McGhee, 1974). These jokes depend for their humor on such properties of the spoken language as ambiguity and the phonological similarities involved in rhyming (e.g., puns). Children begin to understand such jokes at about the same time that they begin to be aware of those properties in their language.

There are, then, a number of kinds of evidence which suggest that children's ability to reflect upon their language (i.e., their metalinguistic abilities) develops rather later than their abilities to produce and understand language. Just as the earlier period in children's language development—from, roughly, 1-1/2 to 5 years of age—is marked by major developments in their comprehension and production abilities, the period of middle childhood—beginning sometime after the age of 5—is a period of major development in their metalinguistic abilities.

Metalinguistic Abilities and Cognition

Throughout this book we have emphasized the close relationships that exist between language processing and development on the one hand and other aspects of cognition and cognitive development on the other. We suggested earlier in this chapter that there are no close relationships between the development of children's comprehension/production abilities during middle childhood and other aspects of their cognitive development during the same period. It appears that it is the emergence of children's metalinguistic abilities that provides the parallel with cognitive development during this age period.

The kinds of abilities we have been describing—detecting ambiguities, judging acceptability and synonymy, rhyming, etc.—all seem to require treating language as an object of thought rather than merely using it. Only when children are able to focus attention on language and to reflect upon its properties do they become able to think about it, judge it, "play with it," and do all the other things that adults can do with language.

The metalinguistic abilities that emerge during middle childhood sound very much like the cognitive abilities that emerge during the same period. In general, those are also abilities that involve decentering—mentally standing back from a situation—and reflecting upon and integrating its properties (see Flavell, 1977). This similarity suggests that the linguistic developments and cognitive developments during this period may both reflect the same underlying changes in the child's cognitive abilities. The available evidence indicates that this is, in fact, the case.

Hakes et al., in the study mentioned earlier, examined children's judgments of acceptability and of synonymy. In addition, they collected data from the same children on the phonological segmentation task developed by Liberman et al., and on their performance in a series of tasks of the sort often used to assess cognitive developmental changes during middle childhood. The children's performances on all the tasks were highly correlated. This indicates that the linguistic and cognitive developments occurring during middle childhood are not isolated, individual developments that merely happen to all take place during the same age period. Rather, they are all parts of the same general cognitive developmental change.

To summarize briefly, the period of middle childhood is one in which there is a flowering of children's linguistic abilities. At the beginning of the period (4 to 5 years of age), children are already quite skilled at understanding and producing utterances and have begun to develop the kinds of control over language styles that will allow them to become effective and flexible communicators. During middle childhood, children develop a variety of additional linguistic abilities, ones which allow them to use their language for more than just communication. The result is an increase in the richness and variety of things children can do with their language.

Middle childhood is also the period during which most children learn to read. Having seen some of the other kinds of linguistic development that occur during this period, let us turn our attention to that development. Our main concern here is with the nature of the linguistic development involved in learning to read. Put differently, what does the child need to know about language in order to be able to learn to read?

Learning to Read

In thinking about learning to read it is reasonable to separate what beginning readers need to know about language (and what they are doing when they first begin dealing with the written language) from what skilled readers do as they rapidly and efficiently extract information from the printed page. There is probably no simple relationship between what beginning readers are doing and what skilled adult readers are doing. Consequently, we will focus here on the beginning reader. What the skilled reader is doing will be considered in Chapter 11.

A great deal about learning to read remains uncertain, but a few facts are reasonably clear. Relatively few 4-year-olds can truly read, though many can identify a number of written words. Most 8-year-olds can read, though many can do so only haltingly and with great effort and difficulty. This would suggest that the differences between the 4-year-old and the 8-year-old in reading might be related to the other linguistic and cognitive differences that we have considered in the preceding sections of this chapter.

In addition, it appears that learning to read is quite a different kind of problem from learning to produce and understand the spoken language. The latter kind of development begins very early and occurs so effortlessly and naturally for most children that it seems it would be next to impossible to keep them from learning to talk. Learning to read, on the other hand, requires a great deal of work, even for children who encounter no unusual difficulty. One has only to watch the faces of first graders struggling with a simple text to realize that learning to read is neither natural nor effortless.

The Difficulty of Learning to Read

A disturbing fact, which has had an immense impact on our conception of the reading process, is that there are large numbers of children who, at best, learn to read only marginally. These are children for whom reading never becomes an enjoyable or rewarding activity. Estimates of the number of such children vary widely (see Downing, 1973). But even if we omit children who have special problems which interfere with reading (e.g., severe mental retardation, general vision problems, etc.), between 10 and 20 per cent of school children are also "poor readers." Such children are often referred to as *dyslexic*, though the term does nothing more than describe the fact that they encounter unusual difficulty of one kind or another in learning to read.

Why is learning to read so difficult? Why do so many children have such extreme difficulty that they never effectively master reading? For nearly a century questions like these have prompted the search for more effective ways of giving children the reading skills they need. That the problems are not simple ones is suggested by the fact that their magnitude has not diminished markedly during that time. Recently, viewing the situation with alarm, the U.S. Office of Education has felt it necessary to mount a major attack on reading problems.

We cannot hope to solve these problems here. But we can at least try to learn something about what kinds of problems they might be. A reasonable place to start is by considering the kinds of abilities and knowledge that children bring with them to the task of learning to read. As we have seen, children approaching this task already know a great deal about language in its spoken form. They have mastered many, though not all, of the strategies necessary for extracting meanings from utterances. And they know a great deal about the meanings associated with the sound patterns of a great many words.

Given these facts, most reading researchers have concluded that the major problems in learning to read must involve the visual representations of language, that is, letters and written (printed) words. The two problems most often mentioned involve learning to recognize letters and printed words, and learning the correspondences between written forms and sound patterns.

With regard to the first of these, beginning readers have already had considerable experience in recognizing two- and three-dimensional forms. But identifying letters introduces them to a novel kind of pattern recognition problem. With most kinds of visual patterns, the orientation in which the pattern occurs is something to be ignored—a book is a book whether it is right side up, upside down, or sideways. But alphabetic patterns are different in that orientation does matter for many of them—a backwards *b* is not a *b* but a *d*, and upside down and backward it is a *p*. One might well expect children to encounter difficulties in learning to recognize and deal with these patterns.

The written language poses other problems as well. For children to be able to read aloud and make use of what they already know about the meanings associated with the spoken forms of words, they must establish some sort of correspondence between visual letters and sound patterns. This is referred to as the problem of developing *grapheme-phoneme correspondences.* Here there is a multitude of difficulties. The visual patterns, or graphemes, correspond roughly to phonological segments. But in English, at least, the unit-to-unit correspondences are by no means simple and straightforward. The problem is basically that how a given phonological segment is spelled, or how a given grapheme sounds, varies widely depending on context. Consider, for example, how the grapheme *e* sounds in *bet, her, the, she* and *love,* or how the phoneme /u/ is spelled in *rude, move, fruit, group, moon, rue, rheumatic, grew,* and *canoe.*[3] The task of learning the correct sound in each context for each grapheme is clearly a formidable one.

Grapheme-phoneme correspondences are not the only problems in establishing the relationship between the language's written and spoken forms. There are also larger units—words and sentences—to be dealt with. If children are to make use of what they already know about the relationships between the sound

---

[3]We noted in Chapter 2 that the notorious irregularity of English grapheme-phoneme correspondences may not be as great as is often suggested. The units at the level of underlying phonological representation correspond fairly closely to graphemes. Nonetheless, there is still a considerable problem (see C. Chomsky, 1972).

patterns of words and their meanings, they must be able to establish correspondences between the sequences of the graphemes of written words and the sequences of the sounds corresponding to those same words. This is often characterized as the problem of learning to *blend,* of learning to produce the sounds of individual graphemes fast enough to be able to "hear" the word.

In addition, if children are to understand what they read, they must be able to do more than just find the meaning of each word in the text. Meaning is conveyed not only by individual words, but also by the syntactic structures in which they are embedded. So children must also be able to read a sequence of words quickly enough to discover the sentence's structure. That is, they must be able to decode graphemes and words with sufficient speed that by the time they reach the end of a sentence they will not already have forgotten what was at the beginning.

These are some of the major problems which, according to reading researchers, face children who are beginning to learn how to read. Different researchers emphasize different problems, and often the problems are characterized differently than we have done here. But there has been considerable agreement for some time that the major problems are those involving the visual language code and the relationships between that code and what children already know about the spoken language. Most researchers have assumed that the spoken language does not contribute to reading problems—that children already know enough about the spoken language that it should not be a source of difficulty in learning to read. They already know how to associate sounds with meanings and how to discover the structures and meanings underlying spoken utterances. Therefore, whatever difficulties learning to read poses must lie in the language's visual forms and the relationships of those forms to what children already know.[4]

Approaches to Teaching Reading

Most of the commonly used approaches to teaching reading have grown from the kind of analysis of the learning problems we suggested in the preceding section.[5] Probably the two most widely accepted approaches fall under the general headings of *look-and-say* and *phonics.* These are two very different attempts at solving the problems of learning to read, but both start with the assumption that the problem of grapheme-phoneme correspondences is the central difficulty for the learner.

---

[4] Bear in mind that this is what reading researchers have generally *assumed.* We will see later that there is good reason to question this assumption.
[5] Notice that the problem of learning to read is also generally assumed to be a problem of *teaching* reading. This in itself suggests that learning to read is a very different process from learning to understand and produce the spoken language. In fact, as we suggested earlier, this assumption is quite a reasonable one.

Look-And-Say. In general, the look-and-say approach to reading instruction assumes that the problems created by the irregularity of grapheme-phoneme correspondences are too great for the beginning reader to manage. Consequently, this approach attempts to bypass, or at least postpone, the difficulty by ignoring graphemes and phonemes and focusing instead on visual-auditory correspondences at the level of words. For this reason, this approach is sometimes characterized as the "whole word" approach. Thus, for example, instead of teaching that the letter *c* is sometimes given a "hard" pronunciation (as in *cat*) and sometimes a "soft" pronunciation (as in *cent*), children are taught that the visual form CAT is pronounced *cat* and the visual form CENT is pronounced *cent*.

The rationale of this approach is to teach children a large enough vocabulary of recognizable visual forms that they can quickly progress to reading texts that use these words. That is, by postponing dealing with the problem of grapheme-phoneme correspondences, the hope is that children will be able to make faster progress in solving the other problems. Sometimes, in less than pure look-and-say approaches, there is also an effort made to teach the more simple and straightforward grapheme-phoneme correspondences. But the emphasis of this approach is always on words and the association of their visual and auditory patterns rather than on graphemes, phonemes, and their relationships.

There is something to be said for trying to avoid or postpone the grapheme-phoneme problem, for it would certainly appear to be a difficult one. But avoiding it introduces other problems, the main one being that it is difficult to provide beginning readers with a sufficiently large number of "sight" words for them to read any but the simplest (and, generally, most boring) texts. That is, children taught to read in this way are limited to reading the particular words they have been taught as whole-word visual patterns. They are given no way of dealing with words they have not yet been taught—they have no way to find out for themselves what sound pattern (and, hence, what meaning) corresponds to a novel visual word.[6]

The problems introduced by teaching children individual words as whole-word visual patterns are sizeable. There are 26 letters in the English alphabet and some 44 phonological segments in the English phonological system. But this small number of units can be combined to yield an extremely large set of words, numbering in the hundreds of thousands. Thus, while a small basic vocabulary can be taught word by word, there is an enormous number of additional words children must learn if they are to read more than the simplest texts or to avoid having to consult the nearest adult every time they encounter a word they have not yet been taught. This is why the problem of grapheme-phoneme correspondences can only be postponed, not avoided. Sooner or later, children must be

[6]It is often observed that some children who have been taught by a look-and-say method work out for themselves the nature of the grapheme-phoneme correspondences. This suggests that perhaps this correspondence is not as great a problem, or not the same kind of problem, as is commonly assumed. We will consider a bit later the implications of this and other related observations.

provided with a means for discovering on their own how to find the sound patterns that correspond to the novel words they see.

Phonics. The other major approach to teaching reading—phonics—attempts to face the grapheme-phoneme correspondence problem directly rather than to postpone it. This approach focused early reading instruction on teaching the correspondences, complex though they may be. Generally, the correspondences taught first are the simple, regular ones, with a sprinkling of the few complex, irregular ones children are likely to encounter in beginning texts. The rarer and more complex cases (e.g., the -OUGHT in *bought*) are left until later. In addition, the phonics approach stresses blending. Children are trained to sound out the successive sounds in a word rapidly so that they can hear the sound of the whole word.

The ideal products of this kind of training are children who can sound out words they have not previously learned to recognize. The goal, of course, is to produce readers who are able to read texts composed of words they have not been explicitly taught and in this way to avoid the problem of having to teach each new word individually. But this is a difficult goal to achieve. A major source of the difficulty is, of course, the large number of grapheme-phoneme correspondences that children must learn before they can actually use them to read. In addition, sounding out a new word is generally a slow process. Because it is slow, the problem of reading rapidly enough to understand sentences is magnified. So children must learn not just a great deal about grapheme-phoneme correspondences, but also how to sound out words rapidly before they can really begin to read books.

To summarize briefly, both of the major approaches to reading instruction start from a common set of assumptions about what children already know when they begin learning how to read, and about the nature of the problems involved in learning to deal with the written language. True, they adopt very different methods for dealing with these problems. But, as we have seen, both approaches generate their own difficulties, making them less than ideal. The consequence of using either approach is that a significant number of children never learn to read efficiently or effectively. (Regardless of the approach taken, however, most children do eventually reach at least a moderate level of reading competence.)

The history of reading instruction over the past several decades is a series of pendulum swings between one approach and the other. Initially, one approach is favored, but it gradually becomes evident that many children are having difficulty. So the pendulum swings toward the other approach, often yielding approaches that combine aspects of both, until once again it becomes apparent that the problems have not disappeared. And then the pendulum swings back. Actually, of course, a number of other approaches have been tried. The picture is not quite as simple as we have suggested. Let us briefly consider one alternative which takes a different approach to the basic problems.

An Alternative Approach: i.t.a. One approach to the complexity of the grapheme-phoneme correspondences involves attempting to simplify them. Generally, this requires creating a new alphabet, composed of more symbols than the standard one, whose symbols come closer to standing in one-to-one correspondences with phonological segments. One version of such an alphabet is the Initial Teaching Alphabet (i.t.a.) (Pitman & St. John, 1969). Not all the i.t.a. symbols correspond exactly to phonological segments, but they come much closer than those of the standard alphabet. For example, the phoneme /u/, which is spelled in several different ways in the standard alphabet, is always represented by the symbol ω in the i.t.a.

The rationale behind the i.t.a. is, of course, that children should begin reading in an alphabet that causes them less difficulty in sounding out the words they encounter in print. Only after they are reading reasonably well are they shifted from the i.t.a. to the standard alphabet. So, in a sense, the grapheme-phoneme correspondence problem of the standard alphabet is postponed until children are already reading.

But delaying the problem does not eliminate it, and the i.t.a. approach involves the additional problem of making the children switch from one alphabet to another. In addition, the use of a special alphabet restricts beginning readers to the texts that have been specially prepared in that alphabet.

Research on the i.t.a. and other simplified writing systems suggests that they are not really solutions to the problems of learning to read. Gillooly (1975), in reviewing the evidence, suggests that in the early stages of reading, the simplified writing systems have some advantage over the standard alphabet. Word-recognition and spelling are better, but comprehension is not. But by the fourth grade children who have been taught with the standard alphabet read better than those who have been taught with the simplified ones.

At this point we might reasonably conclude that learning to read is extremely difficult no matter how it is approached. But there is an alternative way of looking at the problem. As we have seen, regardless of the approach to reading instruction they advocate, reading researchers generally agree on the nature of the problems involved. Essentially, they assume that the problems do not directly involve children's knowledge of the spoken language. This assumption implies that learning to read is something different and separate from the rest of language development. Suppose we question this assumption? Is it really the case that learning to read is separate from other aspects of language development and that the child's knowledge of the spoken language is great enough at the time he begins learning to read that it does not present any problems?

The Beginning Reader's Knowledge of the Spoken Language

However we approach the problem of learning to read, there is no way of completely avoiding the problem of grapheme-phoneme correspondences. If children are ever to be able to read material they have not encountered before, they must have some way of bringing their knowledge of the spoken language to bear upon the written language. Most reading researchers believe that the difficulty of this problem arises from the fact that graphemes and phonemes do not stand in one-to-one correspondence.

But much of the research we discussed in the section on children's meta-linguistic intuitions suggests that the problem may be of a different sort. We saw there that most 5-year-olds and even many 6- and 7-year-olds are not able to deal explicitly with the phonological segments of the spoken language. They do not know how many phonological segments there are in spoken words, and they cannot rhyme.

If beginning readers are not aware of the phonological structure of spoken words, they cannot understand what the graphemes of the written language are supposed to correspond to. They may be able to learn individual grapheme-sound relationships. But without some awareness of how those sounds relate to the words and meanings they know, they cannot make effective use of this knowledge. Thus, a major reason many children have difficulty learning to read might be that at the time reading instruction begins they are not yet aware of the properties of the spoken language which are directly related to the written language.

If this is the case, then many beginning readers should have difficulty sounding out words as a means of getting from graphemic representations to phonological ones (and from there to meanings). In sounding out a word, beginning readers typically sound it out to themselves, checking on whether the pronunciation is acceptable (i.e., whether they recognize it as the sound of a word they know). If it is, they accept it. If it is not, they change the pronunciation of a single grapheme and try again. But, as Venezky (1976) pointed out, altering the sound of a single grapheme requires being able to attend to a single sound in the context of other sounds. And the evidence we have reviewed earlier suggests that many beginning readers cannot do this—they cannot consciously attend to the relevant properties of the speech sounds themselves.

Related to this is a difficulty pointed out by Liberman, Shankweiler, Liberman, Fowler, and Fischer (1977):

> Consider, for example, what is involved in reading a simple word like *bag*. Let us assume that the child can identify the three letters of the word, and further, that he knows the individual letter-to-sound correspondences—the sound of *b* is /b/, the sound of *a* is /ae/, and *g* is /g/. If this is all he knows, however, he will sound out the word as *buhaguh*, a nonsense trisyllable containing five phonetic segments, and not as *bag*, a meaningful mono-syllable with only three phonetic segments. If he is to map the printed, three-letter word *bag* onto the spoken word *bag*, which is already in his lexicon, he must know that the spoken syllable also has three segments.

The data on phonological segmentation (Liberman et al., 1974; Hakes et al.,

1976) indicate that many children do not have this kind of knowledge of spoken syllables and words at the time that reading instruction begins.

Savin (1972) has reported a number of observations concerning children who have not learned to read by the end of first grade that are consistent with this view of the problem. Such children are generally insensitive to rhymes and to such sound properties of words as that *cat* and *cow* begin with the same sound. They are also unable to learn Pig Latin, a secret language that requires moving a word's initial consonant or consonant cluster to the end and then adding an additional vowel. Yet these same children have little difficulty dealing with syllabic units in words, a fact consistent with Liberman et al.'s finding that children can deal with syllabic segments considerably earlier than they can deal with phonological segments (see also Gleitman & Rozin, 1973).

All of this suggests that a major part of the problem of learning to read English stems from the fact that the correspondences between the written and spoken forms of the language exist at a level of the spoken language that many children cannot deal with explicitly. To learn to read, children must be able to deal explicitly with phonological segments. Until they can do so, they do not know what it is that graphemes correspond to.

Thus, the view that the grapheme-phoneme correspondence problem is a central one is correct. But the reason many beginning readers have difficulty with the correspondences is that they do not yet have the necessary awareness of the phonemes themselves, not simply that the correspondences are complex. That the complexity of the correspondences in English is not the source of the problem is suggested by the fact that the frequency of reading problems is not much lower in other countries whose languages use alphabetic writing systems than it is in the United States. In many such languages (e.g., German), the grapheme-phoneme correspondences are far simpler and more regular, but children still have difficulty learning to read (Weinschenk, 1965).

To summarize briefly, children at the age when reading instruction usually begins do know a great deal about the spoken language. But the metalinguistic ability to reflect upon the phonological properties of words does not begin to emerge until about the same time that reading instruction begins. Consequently, many children trying to learn to read do not yet know enough about the properties of the spoken language that are central to the relationships between the written and spoken language forms. These children are likely to encounter difficulties in trying to learn to read. It appears that the emergence of metalinguistic abilities is a prerequisite for being able to learn to read.

The fact that awareness of phonological segments is central to learning to read does not mean that this is all that is involved. The problems we discussed earlier (e.g., with recognizing graphemes, decoding written words quickly, etc.) are very real and, for some children, very large problems. Nonetheless, the emergence of the ability to deal with the spoken language in the appropriate way is central. And this implies that there is a far closer relationship between being able to learn to read and the development of other linguistic abilities during middle childhood than has generally been supposed.

Summary

The period of middle childhood (roughly from 5 years to adolescence) involves two general kinds of linguistic developments. One is the continuation of developments that began much earlier; the other is the beginning of several new linguistic developments.

Children's comprehension and production abilities continue to grow throughout middle childhood, but these developments appear to be of the same kinds as those that occurred earlier. In addition, middle childhood sees major increases in children's ability to communicate effectively. Children become increasingly skilled at taking the characteristics of their audience into consideration in formulating their utterances. The children increase their ability to vary the content and form of their utterances as a function of whom they are addressing.

Experimental studies of children's communication skills appear to indicate that children do not begin to develop this communicative flexibility until middle childhood. But observations of children's spontaneous speech addressed to different audiences suggest that children are aware of audience differences quite early in life, and that by the age of 4 years they are beginning to be able to vary the form and content of their utterances when they address different audiences. The discrepancy between the experimental and observational studies probably arises because the experimental studies place heavier demands upon children's limited abilities. It appears, in general, that the development of communication skills begins very early in life and increases slowly and continuously at least throughout childhood.

A major change that occurs during middle childhood is the development of children's metalinguistic abilities, the abilities that involve reflecting upon language rather than just comprehending and producing it. These are the abilities involved in such things as evaluating whether utterances are acceptable, whether they are ambiguous, and whether different utterances are synonymous. In young children, judgments about the acceptability of an utterance are very closely linked to whether or not the children understand the utterance. By the age of 4 or 5 years, acceptability judgments have changed, but children still have difficulty judging the utterance rather than what the utterance asserts. It is only after the age of 6 years that children are able to focus upon and judge the utterance itself.

Similarly, it is only after the age of 6 years that children are able to judge the synonymy or ambiguity of utterances in an adult-like way. It is at about the same time that they begin to be aware of the phonological properties of the spoken language and so become able to count the number of segments in a word, to distinguish between long and short spoken words, to detect rhymes, and to enjoy and understand linguistic jokes. All of these metalinguistic abilities appear to be closely interrelated, and their emergence appears to be related to changes in children's thought which occur during the same period.

Finally, it is during middle childhood that most children learn to read. Learning to read is difficult for many children. It is generally supposed that the major source of this difficulty is the fact that the relationships between visual representations (graphemes) and sound representations (phonemes) are extremely complex. Different approaches to teaching reading attempt to deal with the grapheme-phoneme correspondence problem in very different ways. But no existing approach has been entirely successful in reducing the number of children who have difficulty learning to read.

Research on the emergence of metalinguistic abilities during middle childhood suggests that one major source of difficulty in learning to read is that many children have not developed the ability to deal explicitly with the phonological segments of the spoken language. If a child cannot analyze spoken words into phonemes at the time he begins trying to learn to read, he does not know what the graphemes of the written language are related to. This makes it extremely difficult for him to establish the relationships between written forms and spoken forms that are necessary for reading.

SUGGESTED READINGS

A recent review of experimental research on children's communication skills can be found in Glucksberg, Krauss, and Higgins (1975). Flavell (1977) discusses how children's emerging communication skills are related to other aspects of cognitive and social development. There are, as yet, no good reviews of research on children's communication skills in spontaneous speech situations (but see Gelman & Shatz, 1977). Hakes, Evans, and Tunmer (1976) review the available research on children's developing metalinguistic abilities. For discussions of learning to read and of the language abilities that are prerequisite for this, see Gibson and Levin (1975) and Venezky (1976). Several recent papers on the topic are contained in Reber and Scarborough (1977).

V

Applications and Relations

INTRODUCTION

Up to this point our attention has been focused primarily upon what many consider to be the core topics of psycholinguistics: comprehension, production, and acquisition. But, like any other field, psycholinguistics does not have sharply drawn boundaries that separate it neatly from other, related fields. Consequently, there are a great many topics which are, if not at the center of the field, at least on its periphery. To call such topics peripheral is not, of course, to imply that they are unimportant or uninteresting. For many researchers concerned with language, these topics are central and the others, including some of the ones we have discussed at length, are peripheral.

We have touched on many such topics in the course of our discussion. But to have discussed them more fully at the points where they were mentioned would have led us away from our own main concerns. It is now time to rectify some of our errors of omission and consider some of the "peripheral" topics more fully.

Deciding *which* to submit to further scrutiny is difficult, for different topics are interesting to different people. We have selected three general topics for inclusion in this Section, partly on the basis of their broad interest, and in spite of the fact that each leads away in quite a different direction from the central core of psycholinguistics.

The first topic, the subject of Chapter 11, is that of skilled reading. At the end of the previous chapter we touched on some aspects of learning to read. We noted then that skilled reading by adults might be very different from reading by beginners. It is obvious, for example, that beginning readers know a good deal more about the spoken language than about the written language. And for this reason, to draw upon this knowledge, beginning readers look up their stored information about such things as the meanings of written words by essentially translating from the graphemes of the written language into the phonemes of the spoken language, and then using the phonological code to retrieve the information. Do skilled readers continue to perform this translation during reading? Or do they develop a way of gaining access to the stored semantic information directly through the graphemic code? This question has dominated a great deal of thinking and research on adult reading. Chapter 11 will review the evidence on this question and will also touch upon related topics such as speed reading.

Chapter 12 will take up the topic of language and the brain. Most of the "mental work" that is performed when understanding or producing utterances involves many of the structures of the cerebral cortex. Interest in the neurological structures and processes underlying language is of long standing. One reason for this is the 19th Century discovery that certain kinds of brain injuries and accidents were responsible for *aphasia,* a loss of one or more language functions. The interest provoked by this discovery has continued to this day.

Further stimulating interest in the cerebral structures underlying language processes is the discovery of *cerebral dominance,* the fact that one of the cerebral hemispheres (usually the left) is far more intimately involved in language processes than is the other. Although this fact was evident even to the 19th Century aphasiologists, interest in dominance and its implications for linguistic and other kinds of higher mental processes was spurred by research, begun in the 1950's, involving patients who had had the connections between the two hemispheres of the cortex severed, producing a "split-brain" condition in which the two hemispheres function largely independently of each other.

Chapter 12 will consider these issues, and then discuss other, related topics. Among these latter is the question of the extent to which the peripheral auditory and articulatory aspects of language are necessary for language. This will lead us into a consideration of recent research on "language" in non-humans.

Finally, in Chapter 13, we will consider several questions concerning language differences and their implications for the language-thought relationship. Many of these questions concern an hypothesis put forth by Benjamin Whorf and several others, often referred to as the *linguistic determinism* hypothesis. Whorf hypothesized that differences between the languages spoken by different people reflected corresponding cognitive differences—that speakers of different languages perceived and thought about the world in different ways. Going further, Whorf hypothesized that such cognitive differences were *caused* by the linguistic differences, a bold hypothesis and one that has stimulated a great deal of controversy and research.

Modern-day linguists, on the other hand, have argued that the obvious differences between languages are mostly superficial ones and that upon closer examination the important properties of human language turn out to be those common to all different languages—*linguistic universals.* In Chapter 13 we will ponder the question of where the truth may lie. In the course of this discussion we will examine one linguistic system that is different from Standard English—namely, Black English—and see how the similarities and differences between the two dialects bear on questions about linguistic differences and linguistic universals.

11

Reading

At the end of the previous chapter we discussed some aspects of reading acquisition, concentrating on what the child needs to know about language in order to learn to read. As we noted, there may be a considerable difference between how the beginning reader approaches reading and how the skilled adult reads. The present chapter discusses the nature of the processes involved in skilled reading.

The study of the processes involved in reading is one of the oldest concerns of experimental psychology. Wilhelm Wundt, widely considered to be the father of experimental psychology, founded the first psychology laboratory in 1879. Shortly afterwards, Wundt's first American student, James McKeen Cattell, wrote his dissertation on the topic of reading. In 1908, Edmund Burke Huey wrote his influential book, *The psychology and pedagogy of reading* (reprinted 1968). In it, he said:

> And so to completely analyze what we do when we read would almost be the acme of a psychologist's achievements, for it would be to describe very many of the most intricate workings of the human mind, as well as to unravel the tangled story of the most remarkable specific performance that civilization has learned in all its history. (1968, p. 6)

Huey also said, "Problem enough, this, for a life's work, to learn how we read" (p. 5). Oddly enough, soon after writing this, Huey became interested in the problem of mental retardation and gave up the study of reading. So, too, did most experimental psychologists, leaving questions about reading to those directly concerned with the teaching of reading. For the forty years after 1920, questions about the processes engaged in by the skilled reader were largely ignored. More recently, reading has again become a very active area of concern, with many books and papers on the topic appearing each year. A recent survey has been written by Gibson and Levin (1975), and critically reviewed by Calfee, Arnold, and Drum (1976).

Reading fascinates psychologists for a number of reasons. There is, of course, the hope that learning about this process might lead to some practical applications in the schools. Also, the topic fits well with the current interest in cognitive psychology. Attempting to analyze the processes involved in reading is a tremendous intellectual challenge, as Huey noted. In addition, psychologists are intrigued by the fact that reading is both closely related to speech processing and yet distinct from it. This relationship raises the question of how reading and listening differ and how they are the same. As we will see, a good bit of energy has been devoted to this question.

As we noted in the previous chapter, reading is a derived skill. It builds upon language that is, with such exceptions as the profoundly deaf child, already well-developed when the task of learning to read begins. And yet the derivation is not a simple one. There are huge differences in the facility with which people learn to read. As we also noted earlier, almost every human naturally and without conscious effort learns to speak and comprehend. One has to institute drastic measures, such as isolating the child from the speech community, to keep him from learning to talk. In reading, however, the situation is vastly different. Literacy is by no means a universal human possession. Many individuals who spend years in school still fail to reach more than a marginal level of reading skill. Thus, while speaking and listening abilities are natural—they evolved in the history of the species—reading and writing are inventions, and debates rage about how best to teach these inventions to children. Some of the issues of these debates were previously discussed. Before we look more closely at the actual processes that are involved in skilled reading (and a bit more at some aspects of reading acquisition), let us briefly consider the nature of the invention.

Writing Systems

It is tempting to think of written material as simply a way of making spoken language visible and permanent. However, this view is too simple. For one thing, there are many written forms that do not correspond at all closely to the way that people talk. Consider, for example, the instructions on an income tax form, or those that come with a do-it-yourself electronics kit. No one, not even a government bureaucrat, talks like these written forms. Much descriptive writing also has a style quite unlike any spoken form (read any travel brochure for evidence of this). Since many things that we read are quite different in structure and style from what we hear, the view that writing is just speech made permanent simply cannot be correct. Writing is an abstract system which certainly bears an intimate relationship to the abstract system of spoken language, but that relationship is not generally one of simple and direct translation.

As we think about the way in which the reader translates the printed word into a meaningful message, our conception of this process must be shaped by the nature of the written code itself. Not all writing systems encode information in the same way. The inventions do not all have the same patent number. Early writing may have developed out of the use of symbols that represented animals and other images. These early symbols bore more-or-less direct relationships to the things they represented, as when a stylized picture of a horse was used to represent a horse. Around 15,000 B.C., some marks began to be used in more abstract ways, perhaps to represent lunar cycles (Marshack, 1972). This was an important step in the evolution of writing. However, we do not speak of symbolic notations as being writing until the symbols were used to represent elements of the spoken language (e.g., words, syllables, phonemes). Writing, then, did not appear until long after the early symbolic period.

Three major systems of writing have been invented, along with many that are combination forms. The three major ones are the *logographic*, the *syllabic*, and the *alphabetic*. The earliest writing of which we have records is Egyptian, and comes from the latter part of the fourth millennium B.C. The Egyptian system consisted of approximately five hundred symbols (hieroglyphs) which represented words for objects, actions, and abstractions (Lehmann, 1962). Since each symbol represented a word or concept, the system is called *logographic* (from the Greek *logos* or word). Later, the Egyptian system developed into one in which the hieroglyphs sometimes represented words and sometimes syllables. (When the written symbol represents a syllable, the writing system is, of course, *syllabic*.)

Some time before 1500 B.C. an important advance in writing systems was made by Semitic-speaking people. The Semitic system still used hieroglyphs, but it used only 24 such symbols, each of which stood for a consonant (Bloomfield, 1933). It was the Greeks who added written representations for the vowels and essentially made the writing system *alphabetic*. (In an alphabetic system the written symbol represents, approximately, a phoneme.) According to Lehmann (1962, p. 68), "This advance in writing systems has never been independently duplicated, nor have writing systems developed beyond it." The development of the alphabetic principle has stimulated scholars to rapturous admiration:

> The notion of representing a sound by a graphic symbol is itself so stupefying a leap of the imagination that what is remarkable is not so much that it happened relatively late in human history, but rather that it happened at all. (Goody & Watt, 1963)

Writing systems based upon all three principles still exist today. The

Chinese system is primarily logographic; the Japanese is a combination of logographic and syllabic; and, of course, English is primarily an alphabetic system. Not all symbols in English are alphabetic, however; the symbol "¢" is logographic, and a symbol like "4th" involves a combination of systems.

The processes involved in extracting information from a printed page no doubt depend heavily upon which kind of writing system is being read. Users of a logographic system are presented with a different set of problems than are users of an alphabetic system. Many psychologists have speculated that learning a logographic system like Chinese may be much more difficult than learning to read English. We will return to this issue below. First, however, let us look at some of the relations between listening and reading. We will begin with the most obvious difference—the fact that during reading information enters the eye rather than the ear.

Some Visual Aspects of Reading

What do your eyes do while you are reading this line of print? Somewhat surprisingly, it was only about 100 years ago that French ophthalmologist Juval noted that the eye movements during reading are not smooth and uniform. Although there are other types of movements of the eye, the two most important ones for reading are smooth tracking (or pursuit) movements and saccadic movements. If you slowly move a pencil in front of a person's eye and ask him to watch it, you will notice that the eye pursues its target with a smooth, nonjerky movement. But if you remove the pencil and ask him to duplicate the smooth motion, this time without the target to watch, you will note that it cannot be done. Now the eye moves in a rapid series of jerky movements, each called a *saccade.* Saccadic eye movements occur whenever the eyes move without a target to follow. In reading, of course, there is no moving target to follow; so reading involves saccadic eye movements.

After each saccadic movement the eye is relatively stationary, fixed at a single point. The movement itself takes only about 10 to 20 msec. The fixation consumes 200 to 250 msec. Thus, about 90% of the time during reading the eye is not moving at all (except for very small tremor-like movements), but is fixing itself on a given point on the line of print. So, contrary to what you might first think, when you read you do not sweep your eyes smoothly across the page, taking in all of the information in one movement. In fact, your eyes are not moving constantly; and, in addition, you see very little during the actual eye movements. All of the usable information is taken in during the pauses or fixations. It is also worth noting that the time between saccades (200 msec) is a physiological limit. You cannot make more than five saccadic eye movements per second no matter how hard you try.

Good readers make fewer fixations per line of print than do poorer readers. Also, the duration of the average fixation tends to be shorter for good readers than for poor readers (Tinker, 1965). More importantly, good readers also tend to have a nice, regular pattern of fixations—the eye moves step-wise from left to right across the line of print with few backward regressions. Poor readers make many regressions so that the eye movement pattern has something of a two-step-forward, one-step-back character. As you might expect, the eye movements of beginning readers are not as disciplined as are those of more advanced readers. Novices have more fixations and more regressions per line. By about the fourth grade, however, eye movement patterns have become stable. At one time it was thought that teaching poor readers how to make effective saccades would improve their reading. If one would only learn to make few fixations and not to regress, this would improve reading. This line of reasoning confuses symptom with cause, however. Erratic eye movements are a symptom of reading difficulty, not its source.

Information Available During a Fixation

During each fixation the reader takes in information on both sides of the point of fixation. However, the drop in clarity of the available information is very sharp as one moves away from the fixation point. In a moment, not yet, look at the circled X in Figure 11.1. Don't fix your vision on any other part of the line; when you look at the figure (not yet), go directly to the X in the middle. As you fix on the X, first try to take in as much of the information to the left of it as you can without moving your fixation point. Then try the same thing with the information to the right of the fixation point. Don't move your eyes. O.K., try it.

You have now demonstrated for yourself how fast visual acuity drops off past the fixation point. It is exceedingly difficult to make out any letters more than about ten letters and spaces away from the fixation point. You will also note that there is some information available in peripheral vision even though details cannot be seen. Thus, you may have been able to discern that the symbol at the far right stands alone, even though you probably could not tell that it is a question mark. Also, you can get some idea about the length of the words, even though the letters cannot be identified. And on the right side, the shape of the word (e.g., *away*) may have been visible since it is in lower case letters. Lower case permits identification of word shape because of the "ascending" letters (e.g., b, d, f, h, etc.) and the "descending" letters (e.g., g, j, p, etc.). The same is not true of the comparable word on the left, *SILK,* since upper case letters do not convey as much word shape information. Then, too, since the words on the right make sense, you may have been able to figure out a few more of the letters

ONE HOP SILK BUT EYE NOW (X)   How   far   away   can   you   see ?

Figure 11.1. Information available from peripheral vision.

on that side. In all, though, it is easy to believe that no more than about four words can be accurately taken in during any given fixation.

Some of the peripheral information may, however, be used in deciding where to put the next fixation. The factors that determine where the next fixation will occur have not yet been widely studied. Most of the information in a word occurs at its beginning, so there may be some advantage to placing saccades near beginnings of long words (just as there is an advantage to fixing your sight slightly to the right of the beginning of a line of print because the first few letters will be accurately readable even though they are not at the fixation point).

A "Maximum" Reading Rate

Given the facts about rate of saccades and the number of letters that are "clearly" available with each saccade, it is possible to compute a "maximum" reading rate. Such a rate assumes that each word must be clearly seen in order to be read (an assumption that some will dispute). Thus, with five saccades per second and four words available per saccade, a reading rate of 1200 words per minute is possible (5 × 4 × 60). This is an optimal rate, assuming no overlap in the information taken in with any two saccades. Most adult readers read considerably slower than this. A rate of 200 to 400 words per minute is the commonly accepted figure for reading newspaper material (Gibson & Levin, 1975). Of course, this figure can vary greatly depending upon the type of material being read (a point we will amplify below). Clearly, it is physiologically possible for most people to read faster than they do. Also the "maximum" rate of 1200 words per minute is slower than that attained by some skilled readers. It is not unusual to clock a good reader at 2000 words per minute. And everyone has heard about so-called speed readers who supposedly reach rates five times this figure. We will return to this matter later in the chapter. For now we will keep our attention on the reader whose performance is at the more common reading rates.

We can now answer the question with which we began this section, What do your eyes do while you are reading this line of print? As you read, you move your eyes in saccadic fashion, taking in about two to four words per fixation. Most of the time your eyes are not moving during the reading process; when they are moving, they are not taking in relevant information.

Visual or Iconic Memory

The eye differs from the ear in that the former accepts information in parallel while the latter is a serial device. By parallel we mean that much information—information concerning three or four words—is (potentially) available at one instant. By serial, we mean that the information is spread out over time. During our discussion of speech perception (Chapter 3) we saw that information necessary for the identification of phonological segments was spread over time. At any given instant of time there is not enough information available in the speech signal to permit the listener to identify the input phonemes. This limitation is not necessarily present for visual information. With each saccade the reader gets information concerning about ten to twenty letters. The visual information is coded in the nervous system in a representation that is called the *iconic memory*. The iconic representation of the visual stimulus is one that is quickly built up when visual information enters. Even if the source of the information quickly disappears (as when one looks through a shutter and gets only, say, a 10 msec look at the world), it is still represented in the iconic memory for a longer period of time. Iconic memory lasts up to about half a second after the source disappears, depending upon the character of light. Sperling (1960) showed that the entire contents of three rows of six letters are stored in this memory, but that the information there quickly decays.

Information in iconic memory is "raw" and uninterpreted. That is, the representation of the letters is in terms of the lines and angles that constitute the letters and not in terms of the letters themselves. At this stage the letters have not been identified. Thus, the iconic storage system is one way-station during the processing of written material; it is a stage at which there has been little loss of information (the spatial aspects of the input are preserved), and at which no linguistic analysis of the stimulus has yet occurred. We assume that information that is critical for the reading process (the letters or logograms) appears as a result of an analysis of the raw material that is stored in this iconic memory. (A further discussion of iconic memory can be obtained in Lindsay & Norman, 1977, or Turvey, 1973.)

What happens to the information that is stored in iconic memory? How is it treated or analyzed? The answer to this question is much debated. Some theorists think that the next stage results in identification of the entire word. Others say that letters are identified next. Within the latter group there are still further debates. Some say that the letters are identified serially, i.e., one at a time—even in a left-to-right order; others claim that the letters are identified in parallel, all being worked on at once. Still other theorists feel that the letters themselves are identified, but only after the features that constitute them are first identified. That is, these latter theorists claim that letters are built out of a set of features in the same way that phonological segments are constructed from features. Feature theorists argue, then, that the next step in reading is to analyze the contents of the icon for its features and then to build graphemes[1] or significant groups of graphemes out of these features.

We will not review all the arguments that bear on these matters; they are many and complex (see Gough, 1972; Gibson & Levin, 1975). For one thing, the perceptual unit in reading (for that is what the debate concerns) is unlikely to be a constant. The units that are perceived are likely to depend upon the particular reading task at hand. To take a simple example, at one point a reader may be

---

[1] A grapheme, you may recall from Chapter 10, is an abstract concept corresponding to a letter. Any printed or written letter is a surface manifestation of a grapheme. The analogy to the concept of the phoneme is clear.

searching in an English text for a passage that is written in the Chinese logographic system. It is clear that a very brief glance at the page of print will tell him if it contains Chinese characters. The same amount of information may not be sufficient to tell whether the page is about, say, the construction of dams. Actually, we cannot totally avoid the issue of the unit into which iconic information is translated. This issue will come up in other contexts as we explore in more detail the points of similarity and difference between listening and reading.

The Relation Between Listening and Reading

As we noted earlier, the reader is also a listener—the reading process is grafted onto the listening process. The two skills are not completely separate from one another. Having acquired a language and the ability to comprehend it is surely the most important factor in learning to read that language. This is shown by the enormous difficulty that children who are profoundly deaf from birth have in learning to read. Gough (1975) has made the point about the close relation between reading and listening in a persuasive way:

> Here I am, for example, with an intact brain, a sound memory, adequate visual and auditory perceptual systems; I can recognize letters, organize them into larger units, make the appropriate saccadic eye-movements and return sweeps. But I cannot read a word of Polish or Tagalog or Urdu or any other of the world's several thousand languages, save English. Of course I can learn to read one of those languages, but only, I would submit, by learning the language. (p. 15)

This observation leads to an important question for our understanding of the reading process, namely where does the process of reading intersect with or join the process of listening comprehension? Every theorist agrees that reading makes use of many of the same mechanisms as listening comprehension. It would be absurd to think that readers learn all over again the syntactic and semantic analyses that they apply in understanding speech. But which mechanisms are common to the two processes and which are distinct? Where do the two come together? Basic theoretical differences about the process of reading hinge on the answer that the theorist gives to this question.

There are three major hypotheses about the relationship between listening and reading. The first we will call the *Subvocalization* hypothesis. It expresses the view that reading involves talking to oneself, converting the print into subvocal speech. The second, which we will call the *Direct Access* hypothesis, says that printed words make contact with information stored in the mental lexicon without any speech process intervening. The third hypothesis, called *Phonological Recoding,* says that print is converted into an abstract representation which has a phonological character. This hypothesis is distinct from the Subvocalization hypothesis, as we will show. There are also hypotheses that combine aspects of the above three. We will discuss the three major views and one which combines the last two.

The Subvocalization Hypothesis

The Subvocalization hypothesis asserts that reading is equivalent to talking to oneself and listening to what one says. Roughly, the hypothesis asserts that the reader first converts the written form into subvocal speech. The signals that arise from subvocal speech are assumed to be similar to those that arise when listening to another person talk. Since readers are already skilled at translating speech into lexical representations, parsing them, etc., they do the same operations on the stimuli that arise from their own subvocal speech. The Subvocalization hypothesis asserts, then, that the process of reading intersects with the process of listening at a very early stage in listening comprehension. This viewpoint is schematically shown in Figure 11.2. Learning to read is learning to convert the printed form into (subvocal) speech.

One source of evidence which appears to support the subvocalization theory of reading comes from an experiment that measured the covert movements of readers' speech muscles (Hardyck & Petrinovich, 1970). The technique involved placing sensors on the skin surface near the larynx and on the lower lip of the subjects so that small amounts of muscle activity in these areas could be detected. In the experiment, a set of students from a freshman class in remedial English was used. Each subject read two passages, one that was conceptually difficult and one that was easy. The subjects were divided into three groups. One group simply read the material. A second group was given feedback about when the muscles near the larynx and lower lip were moving. This was done by converting the muscle movement activity into an audio signal and letting the readers hear this signal. These subjects were instructed to keep the signal from occurring. In effect, they were being given information about when they were subvocalizing and were being trained to inhibit this subvocal activity. The subjects could in fact learn to inhibit such activity. A third group was given feedback from muscles

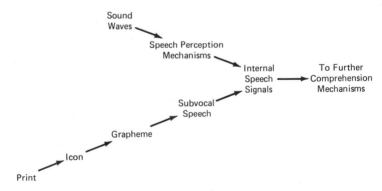

Figure 11.2. Reading and listening according to the Subvocalization hypothesis.

in the forearm and were told to keep activity in those muscles low. The latter group was used as a control for the distracting effects of having feedback.

Hardyck and Petrinovich found that reading comprehension for the conceptually hard material dropped for those subjects who were inhibiting their subvocal speech. The same drop did not occur for the other subjects. The authors interpreted this finding as support for the subvocal theory of reading. Normally, they argued, the subvocal activity is very, very covert. The gross muscle movements of speech are only represented by "unidentified neural analogues" (p. 651). However, when the task is difficult, as it was when the material to be read was conceptually difficult, the muscle activity may be reactivated to help the reader over the rough spots. If such activation does not occur, as in the subjects who learned to inhibit it, then comprehension will suffer. While perhaps plausible at first glance, this interpretation of the results has been questioned by a number of critics. For example, Gibson and Levin (1975) suggest that the subjects in the group that was suppressing their subvocalizations had to devote their attention to the act of suppression. This led to a drop in comprehension for the difficult material. Also, the subjects were not very practiced in suppressing subvocal activity. With practice, the group differences might disappear.

There are a number of sources of evidence which argue against the Subvocalization hypothesis. For one thing, the time it takes to initiate a vocal response seems to be longer than the time it takes to understand a word. This should not be so if understanding follows the subvocalization. If we put a word on a screen and ask you to read it aloud as fast as you can, the average time before you initiate a vocal response will be in the neighborhood of 525 msec for a three-letter word (Cosky, 1975). However, Rohrman and Gough (1967) and Sabol and DeRosa (1976) have shown that subjects can gain access to a word in the mental lexicon in under 200 msec (see our earlier discussion of this in Chapter 4). Therefore, readers cannot have waited to receive the subvocal information before they gained access to the word.

Another problem with the subvocalization theory, if taken at face value, is that it precludes reading rates of even an everyday sort. This view suggests that we should not be able to read any faster than we can talk. Even very rapid speech is not much faster than five syllables per second. This would limit the reading rate to 300 words per minute if all of the words were monosyllables, and to slower rates if some were longer. Of course, one can argue that subvocal speech can go faster than vocal speech, but there is little evidence to support this claim. Reflection suggests that fast silent talking is not much more rapid than fast overt talking; and Landauer (1962) has collected data which argue that people do not count to themselves any faster than they count aloud. So the rate of speaking vs. the rate of reading argues against the subvocalization theory.

Another bit of evidence against the subvocalization theory was provided by Kolers (1966). He tested a group of French-English bilinguals on some passages that were written in a mixture of French and English. For example, a passage might contain a sentence like (1).

(1) His horse, followed de deux bassets, faisait la terre résonner under its even tread.

The bilingual subjects were asked to read these passages aloud as rapidly and as accurately as they could. Kolers noted that the subjects made certain kinds of interesting errors in their readings. For one thing, they sometimes translated one section of the text into the other language. Thus, the reader might say *His horse, suivi by deux hounds.* The readers also sometimes corrected awkward syntax. A passage might actually have read, *in a cell dark,* but the readers would say, *in a dark cell.* If you observe yourself carefully while quickly reading aloud, you will discover that such corrections and changes are not rare. Both of these types of errors argue that readers are not converting the print into subvocal speech. If they were, why wouldn't they simply vocalize the subvocalization when requested to read the passage quickly? Kolers' observations are difficult for the subvocalization hypothesis to counter. The bulk of the evidence certainly argues that the subvocalization view is incorrect. It is unlikely that reading and listening come together this early in the process of comprehension. Let us turn, then, to the Direct Access hypothesis.

The Direct Access Hypothesis

The Direct Access hypothesis asserts that readers are able to go directly from the graphemic representation of the printed word to the lexical representation in their mental dictionary. According to this hypothesis, reading and listening have nothing in common at the phonological level. The two processes do not come together until the stage at which the meanings of words have been recovered. After that, reading and listening comprehension are carried out by the same mechanisms. The broad outlines of this theory are shown in Figure 11.3.

It seems likely that the human information processing system is capable of being organized in accordance with the Direct Access hypothesis. We say this

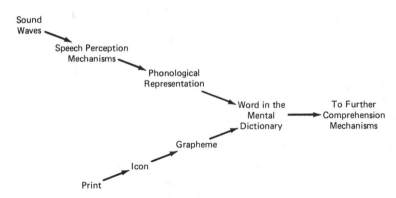

Figure 11.3. Reading and listening according to the Direct Access hypothesis.

because direct access is quite plausible for readers of Chinese and other logographic writing systems. In such systems the logograms do not specify the sounds of the words; it is unlikely that the reader "sounds out" the word in the way that readers of alphabetic writing systems often do. Even in English some symbols seem by introspection to make contact with their interpretations without going through a silent speech stage. For us, the symbol "$" appears to go directly to its interpretation; it does not seem to be mediated through its name. Of course such introspections cannot carry too much weight; they may be as misleading as many other self-analyses have been. But they correspond with the idea that readers of logographic writing systems probably have the ability to go from print to meaning without an intermediate speech-like stage.

The discussion of reading a logographic writing system does not, of course, bear very directly on the reading processes of the skilled readers of an alphabetic writing system. Readers of alphabetic systems may not go directly from print to meaning even though it is within their potential to do so. The principal argument usually raised against the direct access model is that it is enormously costly to readers when they acquire the reading skill. The direct access theory says, essentially, that each English word is a logogram. For each written word, readers must learn the lexical item with which it is paired. This task is the same as that put before persons learning to read Chinese; each word is a separate entity. Having learned 10,000 of them, there is no principled way in which the interpretation of the 10,001st can be deciphered.[2] Explicit training is required for each word. This means that there are two independent paths to the lexical item (as shown in Figure 11.3) and that two separate connections between the visual and auditory stimuli and each word must be established. As a consequence, readers will have to acquire 50,000 to 100,000 new connections if they are to be highly literate members of the society—a truly enormous task.

The alternative is to make use of the alphabetic principle. Although the relationship between letters and sounds is not a simple one (as we will document momentarily), the complexities are nowhere near as large as they are for the Direct Access hypothesis. In short, then, an economy argument says that readers make use of the information that is inherent in the alphabetic writing system. Not to do so will extract a very high cognitive payment. While the argument from cognitive economy certainly has some merit, it is not decisive. There are experimental data which bear on the question. And there are, too, some more sophisticated models of direct access. Before we review some of the experiments, though, let us look at the third hypothesis. We will be using the results of the experiments to judge these points of view.

---

[2]This is probably overstating the case because of the existence of a small set of "radicals"—written forms, not political ones—in the Chinese writing system. But the system is difficult enough that (a) in 1956 the authorities in the People's Republic of China simplified the written characters, and (b) the late chairman Mao wrote that China should adopt alphabetic writing systems.

The Phonological Recoding Hypothesis

The Phonological Recoding hypothesis is similar to, but distinct from, the Subvocalization hypothesis. It is similar because it asserts that readers convert the graphemic representation of the letters into a speech-related code, that the phonological system is involved in reading. The hypothesis is distinct because it does *not* say that the point where reading and speech comprehension meet is at the level of subvocal speech; it says they meet later in the system. The point at which reading and listening comprehension meet is at a level of representation called the "level of systematic phonemes." According to the Phonological Recoding hypothesis, one of the way-stations of speech perception is a stage where the input is represented in terms of underlying or systematic phonemes. The written input, too, is translated into this format. After that, listening and reading are the same. This viewpoint is outlined in Figure 11.4.

In order to understand the Phonological Recoding hypothesis, it is necessary to understand the code into which speech and print are said to be translated. The concept of the underlying or systematic phoneme was introduced in our discussion of the phonological system in Chapter 2. There we noted that, like syntax, the phonological system has both surface and underlying levels of representation. These levels are related by rules. We pointed out that the initial phonetic segment of *pan* is the aspirated [pʰ], while the second phonetic segment of *span* is the unaspirated [p]. These two segments are physically different at the surface (phonetic) level but are represented as the same underlying or systematic phoneme, /p/. Whether the underlying /p/ becomes the aspirated or unaspirated version depends upon the context in which it occurs. Thus, the rules relating the underlying systematic phoneme to the surface phonetic segment take the context into account when they operate.

Chomsky and Halle (1968) developed and extended the concept of the systematic phoneme in a way that is relevant to the question of letter-sound relationships. They argued, for example, that the pronunciation of the word *divinity* can be accounted for by a rule that combines *divine* and *-ity*. According to this view, then, there is a sense in which the second vowel in the word *divinity*

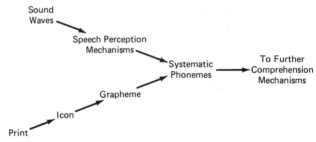

Figure 11.4. Reading and listening according to the Phonological Recoding hypothesis.

is a long i. Long i is the vowel in the underlying phonological representation of the word. At the level of systematic phonology, *divinity* is represented as *divIn +ity* (where I stands for long i). A phonological rule converts I to short i when *-ity* is added to the word.

To observe another example, say the words *telegraph* and *telegrapher* out loud and listen to the second vowel in each. They are quite different phonetically, i.e., they are pronounced differently. Chomsky and Halle argued that the underlying representation of these two words has the same second vowel. The pronunciation of *telegrapher* is also governed by rules which apply when *telegraph* is combined with *-er*, rules which Chomsky and Halle provided.

One more example. Rapidly speak aloud the words *illustration, consolation,* and *immigration* and again attend to the sound of the second vowel in each. In every case the second vowel sounds very similar; it is a "reduced" sound something like *eh*.[3] Since these words sound alike in the second vowel position, why not spell them with the same letter in that position? Is this just another case of the famed eccentricity of English spelling? Not so, say Chomsky and Halle. Although these three words are pronounced with the same second vowel, they do not have the same vowel in their underlying representation. *Consolation,* for example, is derived by rule from *console + ation.* The long o sound is clearly present in *console* and, according to the hypothesis, it is present in the underlying representation of *consolation* too. In this case the English spelling system is telling us something about the underlying form of *consolation,* namely that it is related to *console.* Spelling *consolation* "the way it sounds" would hide this fact from the reader. Chomsky (1970) has argued that the English spelling system is far from imperfect. In fact, he claimed that it is nearly ideal since it represents vast amounts of information about the underlying forms of words. We won't linger over this last point (see Francis, 1970, for some discussion). For now we hope that you have a feeling for the extended concept of the systematic phoneme.

According to the Phonological Recoding hypothesis of reading, at some point during the processing of *consolation* it is represented as *console + ation.* This point occurs before the semantic information associated with the word has been retrieved from the mental lexicon. The search of the mental lexicon occurs in terms of systematic phonemes. To reiterate, when one claims that the input is represented at the level of systematic phonology this is *not* equivalent to the claim that readers have spoken the word to themselves. Instead one is claiming that there is a translation process which converts the written input into this abstract phonological code. Phonological information is indeed represented at this stage, but it is not subvocal speech. Therefore the arguments used against the Subvocalization hypothesis cannot be used directly against the Phonological Recoding hypothesis.

---

[3] The degree to which the vowels are reduced to *eh* varies somewhat between dialects.

Evidence Concerning Phonological Recoding

We have been at some pains to sketch the concept of the Phonological Recoding hypothesis for two reasons. First, the Subvocalization theory is wrong. Second, there is a good deal of evidence that phonological information is often used during the decoding of written English. Since this evidence should not be used to try to rescue the Subvocalization theory—the latter has too many strikes against it to try to save it—an alternative theory involving a phonological stage but not subvocalization is an attractive candidate. We now turn to some of the evidence which bears on the hypothesis that phonological information is extracted during the course of translating the print into meaning. First, we will examine evidence in favor of this view.

Evidence for Phonological Recoding

There is a great deal of evidence that readers are affected by the phonological information signaled by the material they are reading. To the extent that this evidence is convincing, it argues against the Direct Access hypothesis and for the Phonological Recoding hypothesis.

One source of evidence to implicate a phonological stage in reading is some recent work on the detection of spelling errors. Corcoran (1967) and others have shown that spelling errors resulting in a letter string that is pronounced like a word go undetected more often than errors leading to letter strings that do not sound like words. For example, McCusker and Gough (cited in Gough & Cosky, 1977) asked subjects to read a text and to indicate spelling errors by circling them. Two types of errors were used; in one, the misspelled string preserved the pronunciation of the word (e.g., *werk* for *work*), while in the other, the pronunciation was not preserved (e.g., *wark* for *work*). The number of spelling errors detected was significantly greater when correct pronunciation was not preserved. This suggests that the reader has translated the word on the page into a phonological representation. If the latter corresponds to an entry in his mental lexicon, the error will go undetected.

MacKay (1972) demonstrated a similar phenomenon. His subjects briefly (120 msec) looked at a word or word-like item and were asked to spell exactly what they saw. The subjects knew that the item would sometimes be a misspelled word. When they were told in advance what the word was to be (e.g., *work*), they were more likely to detect a phonologically deviant misspelling (*wark*) than when they were not told what word to expect. This was not true for the phonologically regular misspellings (*werk*). The subjects were no more likely to detect such a "regular" error when they knew what word to expect than when they did not know what to expect. Again this suggests that the word is coded into a phonological representation even when the reader is attending to aspects of the spelling of the word. In both of these experiments it is to the subjects' advantage *not* to convert the written form into a phonological representation. Doing so leads to errors. Yet in both cases the subject apparently made such conversions. This suggests that phonological recoding may be mandatory.

Another set of experiments supporting the Phonological Recoding hypothesis was devised by Rubenstein, Lewis, and Rubenstein (1971). They presented letter strings to their subjects and simply asked them whether or not each letter string was an English word (this is called a "lexical decision" task). Some of the letter strings were words, others were not. The investigators measured the time from the onset of the stimulus to the subject's response. Let us focus on the letter strings that were not words. Rubenstein et al. used two different types of non-words. Some (like *melp*) were pronouncible letter strings that could be English words but happen not to be. Others (like *brane*) are also pronouncible non-words, but these items are homophonous with (sound like) real English words. Rubenstein et al. found a difference in the amount of time it took the subjects to reject these items as words. Items like *brane* took significantly longer to reject than did items like *melp*. (The authors also found that non-pronouncible items like *sagm* were rejected most rapidly.) They concluded from these results that the subjects had recoded the letter strings into a phonological representation. If that representation did not correspond to any item in the mental lexicon (as in the case of *melp*), then the decision that the item was not a word was rapid. If, however, the phonological representation did have a match in the lexicon (as in the case of *brane*), then the subjects had to double check to see if the spelling of the test word matched the spelling of the item found in the lexicon. This checking operation took additional time and led to the longer RTs for items like *brane*.

A third source of evidence in favor of the Phonological Recoding hypothesis is some work conducted by Meyer, Schvaneveldt and Ruddy (1974). These experimenters presented their subjects with pairs of letter strings and asked them to respond "yes" if both letter strings were words and "no" otherwise. This time, let us consider only the trials on which both letter strings were words and look at the response times for saying "yes." Among the word pairs that Meyer et al. used were some like those in (2) and some like (3).

(2) set—wet   candle—handle   bribe—tribe
(3) few—sew   lemon—demon   mint—pint

The pairs in (2) all follow the normal rules of English pronunciation, and the two members of each pair rhyme with one another. The examples in (3) include exceptions to the normal rules, and the members of the pairs do not rhyme. According to the Direct Access hypothesis, there should be no difference in response times between pairs like those in (2) and (3). The fact that the members of each pair in (2) follow the same recoding rules, and that they rhyme, is irrelevant to the Direct Access hypothesis. However, the Phonological Recoding hypothesis suggests that there should be a difference between (2) and (3) in response time. If the words are recorded into a phonological representation, nearly the same operations can be used for each member of the pairs in (2); this is not true for the pairs in (3). Thus, the total time for lexical access and response should be less for pairs like (2). That is what was found. Items like *set - wet* were responded to significantly faster than pairs like *few - sew*.

We will cite one final source of evidence that implicates a phonological stage in reading. G. C. Ellison (cited in Crowder, 1977) devised a modification of Rubenstein's task in which the subjects were shown a word and asked to decide quickly whether it had a specific meaning. Thus, the subjects might be asked to decide whether a letter string was the name of an animal. Sometimes the subjects would be given a word like *bare,* which is homophonic with an animal name. The time to say that *bare* is not an animal was longer than the time to say that *beat* was not an animal. As Crowder points out, this is an elegant demonstration of phonological recoding. The decision required is based on a semantic aspect of the word, so there is no reason for the subjects to code the input phonologically. Apparently they do so anyway.

In sum, there are a number of experiments using a variety of techniques which have obtained evidence that the phonological character of a word affects its visual processing. This evidence is consistent with a Phonological Recoding hypothesis.

Evidence Against Phonological Recoding

Not all experimenters are agreed that phonological recoding *must* occur before the item in the mental lexicon is accessed, and the doubters have some evidence which they can cite in their support. Baron (1973), for example, asked subjects to classify strings of words as sensible or not and then timed their decisions. Among the word strings which did not make sense were some like (4) and some like (5). The former includes a word which is homophonous with another word that would make the string sensible (e.g., *don't do it*). The latter is nonsense even if a homophonous word is substituted (e.g., *knew I can't*).

(4) don't dew it

(5) new I can't

If the words are recoded into a phonological representation, then the subjects should be tempted to say "yes" to *don't dew it.* Their time to reject it as sensible should be lengthened by this temptation. Baron found that the times to reject these two types of word strings as sensible did not differ. From this he concluded that a word string does not go through a stage of phonological recoding.

One difference between Baron's study and the others we have discussed is that it used sentence-like materials instead of single words or word pairs. Perhaps this is a crucial determiner of whether or not phonological recoding takes place. Baron argued that phonological coding can occur and sometimes does (no one denies this), but that it need not. However, we need not accept Baron's findings at face value. For one thing, the data which support the Direct Access hypothesis are those that depend upon finding no difference between conditions. This is always weak evidence since a finding of no difference can arise from many irrelevant sources. Also, the subjects made more errors in responding to strings like (4) than they did to strings like (5). If the error rates were equal, perhaps strings like (4) would have taken longer to reject.

Somewhat stronger evidence against phonological recoding was gathered by Cosky (1975). He showed words to subjects and asked them to say each word as quickly as possible. The time it took them to begin saying the word was measured. Cosky presented some words which contained three phonemes and others which contained four. In all other respects (e.g., word frequency, number of letters in the words) the words were very similar. If phonological recoding occurs, it seems reasonable to assume that it will take longer when there are more phonemes to recode. However, Cosky found no difference between the phonologically longer and shorter words. He did find that naming time was affected by the number of letters in a word, so his experiment was not just an insensitive one.

Perhaps the strongest evidence in favor of the Direct Access hypothesis comes from an experiment conducted by Kleiman (1975). He presented subjects with pairs of words and asked them to make judgments about the relationship between them. On some trials the judgment requested was whether the words were phonemically similar (e.g., whether they rhymed). The first pair in (6) is a positive instance while the second pair is a negative instance.

(6) blame–flame (= true)   rough–dough (= false)

Both positive and negative instances were identical after the first letter. The subjects pressed a button marked "true" if the words were phonemically similar and a button marked "false" if the words were not; these decisions were timed. On other trials, the requested judgment was based upon the graphemic similarity of the words. A "true" response was required when all of the letters after the first were the same in the two words. See (7).

(7) nasty–hasty (= true)   shadow–fallow (= false)

On still other trials a "true" response was to be made if the members of the pair were similar in meaning, a "false" response if they were not, as in (8).

(8) mourn–grieve (= true)   depart–couple (= false)

Kleiman added an additional variable to his experiment. On some trials the subjects heard a rapid seris of digits (92 per minute) and were required to "shadow" these digits (i.e., to say each digit aloud as soon as they heard it) while they were performing the decision task. On other trials, the subjects performed only the decision task.

Kleiman reasoned that the shadowing task requires use of the subjects' phonological processing facilities; that is, they have to use their speech perception capabilities to understand which digit has been presented. Making a judgment about the phonological similarity of two words, as in examples like (6), should also require use of the phonological processing facilities. Therefore, during shadowing trials the requirement to shadow will compete with the judgment of phonological similarity, and the time to make the judgment should increase dramatically. What about judgments of graphemic similarity? If subjects must recode the stimuli into a phonological form, then shadowing also ought to interfere with graphemic judgments as well. Once again, the judgment time ought to greatly increase on the shadowing trials. If such recoding is not necessary, however, then the shadowing task will not interfere with the graphemic similarity judgment since the latter will not be competing for use of the phonological processing facilities. (Shadowing might cause some increase in graphemic decision time just because it is distracting, but the increase should not be as great as in the case of the phonemic judgment task.) Similar reasoning applies to the judgment of meaning similarity. If phonemic recoding is not necessary, then the increase in judgment time on the shadowing trials ought to be minimal.

The results of Kleiman's experiment are shown in Table 11.1. Both the graphemic and the meaning judgments took somewhat longer on the shadowing trials. However, shadowing led to a much larger increase in the time required to make the phonemic similarity judgment. On the two tasks which did not explicitly require a phonological decision, the task interference due to shadowing was minimal. When a phonological decision was explicitly required, shadowing had a large interference effect. This is the pattern of results that is predicted by the Direct Access hypothesis, according to Kleiman. He concluded that phonological recoding is not necessary in order for lexical access to occur. This pattern of results was replicated in another of his experiments in which the words occurred in a sentence context.

As we noted earlier, Kleiman's results probably are the best evidence so far in favor of the Direct Access hypothesis. It is not clear how the Phonological Recoding hypothesis could account for these results. That is not to say that it can't be done. Two quick observations are relevant. First, in order to understand what is going on in Kleiman's experiment one would want to have a good understanding of exactly what is involved in shadowing and how shadowing interacts with other experimental tasks, such as graphemic decision making. So far, no

Table 11.1

Mean Reaction Times and Reaction Time Increases (msec) with Shadowing

Type of Decision	Example	RT Without Shadowing	Increase With Shadowing
Phonemic	Blame–Flame	1137	372
Graphemic	Nasty–Hasty	970	125
Semantic	Mourn–Grieve	1118	120

(Modification of Table 1 from Kleiman, G. M. Speech recoding in reading. *Journal of Verbal Learning and Verbal Behavior,* 1975, *14,* 323–339. Copyright 1975 by Academic Press, Inc. Used by permission.)

model of this interaction has been provided. When one is, perhaps the Phonological Recoding theorist will find an escape route. Second, Kleiman's experiment actually lacks a control group. The increase in time to make the graphemic decision when shadowing (125 msec) may be due in part to phonemic recoding and the interference of the shadowing task with this recoding. Kleiman argues that this increase is due to distraction, but there is no evidence that this is the only source of the increase. Perhaps if a totally non-linguistic decision were required (e.g., are the two words printed in the same color?), then the effect of shadowing would be even less (say, 50 msec). In that case, part of the 125 msec increase when shadowing in the graphemic decision task might be due to the subjects' phonologically recoding the stimulus. The large effect in the rhyme task might be explained on other grounds once we understand shadowing. So, Kleiman's results are an important bit of evidence in favor of direct access, but more work is needed if the debate between the Phonological Recoding and the Direct Access theorists is going to be decided.

Kleiman (1975) also argued that information from the lexicon is often converted into a phonological representation. Thus, while he said that phonological recoding need not occur before lexical access, he also stated that it often does occur after lexical access. After the word has been looked up the information associated with it (often including its phonological code) is stored in a memory while the parsing procedures operate on it and the words around it. It is at this point that the "silent talking" aspects of reading occur—after lexical access and not before. There is plenty of evidence that the phonological character of written information affects memory. Thus, Conrad (1972) and others have shown that confusions in memory often are made on the basis of the phonological properties of the words and not just on the basis of their meanings.

Both are Right: The Dual Access Hypothesis

More than one theorist (e.g., Kleiman, 1975; Meyer & Ruddy, 1973) has suggested that subjects can gain access to their mental lexicons via both a direct route and phonological recoding, and that therefore both hypotheses are correct. (There may, of course, be specific conditions in which one access route or the other is more likely to be used.) Let's call this the Dual Access hypothesis. In many ways it makes a good deal of sense. Many people are taught to read via a phonics based method (see Chapter 10). They are taught to sound out unfamiliar words, and they are given a set of more-or-less effective rules to aid them in this process. For these individuals a phonological recoding stage seems certain in some circumstances. However, some letter strings occur so often that they may acquire a direct route from the letter pattern to the lexicon much in the fashion of a reader of a logographic writing system. Thus, patterns like *the, and,* etc., may result in direct access. Also, when skimming for key terms, or in other styles of reading, the direct access route may be more likely than in reading poetry or difficult technical material.

One of the more explicit attempts to develop a Dual Access hypothesis appears in the work of LaBerge and Samuels (1974), who were concerned with the development of automaticity in reading. They first pointed out that reading is a skilled act. Then they noted that in learning a new skill, such as driving, certain components of the skills are at first effortful and require conscious attention. Later on, with practice, the components of the skill can be performed without any conscious attention. As LaBerge and Samuels noted, Huey (1908) anticipated their hypothesis. Huey said, ". . . repetition progressively frees the mind from attention to details, makes facile the total act, shortens the time, and reduces the extent to which consciousness must concern itself with the process" (p. 104). According to LaBerge and Samuels, some input words are automatically translated into a visual code of the entire word, which in turn automatically activates the meaning of the word in the mental lexicon. Still other words lead to an automatic activation of a phonological code, and from there activation of the meaning is also automatic. This does not exhaust the possibilities, however. For some words attention is required to activate a visual code for the word, while for others attention is required to activate the phonological code. Thus, according to their view, there are multiple routes into the lexicon, some requiring attention on the part of the reader and others not. LaBerge (1973) has presented some evidence for the automatic encoding hypothesis.

Although the Dual (or in the case of LaBerge and Samuels, Multiple) Access hypothesis makes a good deal of sense, there is one problem with it as presently formulated—it is difficult to see what data could possibly refute it. The hypothesis is consistent with most of the experimental studies since it says that both of the theories are correct. This is not altogether a good thing. A hypothesis that cannot be refuted by data is not much of a hypothesis at all. Only a detailed Dual Access hypothesis, one which makes specific predictions, can be evaluated. Theorists such as LaBerge are in fact trying to formulate more specific Dual Access hypotheses.

The question of how we get from print to our internal representation of the meaning of the word would seem to be a relatively simple one. Yet it has not been resolved. We see now that the answer is not going to be simple. It is true, though, that we know a lot more about aspects of the process than we did ten years ago.

Lexical Access: Context and Speed

In this section we will explore the effect of context on the process of lexical access. So far we have discussed studies of lexical access which typically did not make use of normal sentence contexts. The process of lexical access may, however, be greatly influenced by the surrounding context. That is, the words that have already been looked up and the sentence structure that has already been calculated by the reader may affect the access for the next word.

In most situations, context is probably an aid, but this need not always be the case. The idea that context affects lexical access is a reasonable one; we discussed a related issue in Chapter 4.

There is some evidence that written context can affect word identification time. For example, Tulving and Gold (1963) presented words at very brief display times (they started with 10 msec durations) and increased the display times by 10 msec every other trial until the subject could say what the word was. The subjects were given context words that were either relevant to the target word or else were misleading. Thus, in **(9)** the context is helpful for the target word *socialism,* but misleading for the target word *raspberry.*

(9) Far too many people today confuse communism with $\begin{Bmatrix} \text{socialism} \\ \text{raspberry} \end{Bmatrix}$

Tulving and Gold varied the amount of the context sentence that was presented. Sometimes the entire eight words were given; sometimes four, two, one or none of them were presented. They found that giving even two context words affected the amount of time that the target word had to be displayed before it was identified. When all eight words were given, the display time needed to recognize the target word was affected still further.

Tulving and Gold's results need to be interpreted with care since there is one aspect of their experiment that is unlike normal reading: the context words were available for many seconds before the target word occurred. When we are reading, however, the immediately preceding two to eight words are not available until the previous fixation or two. Thus, the immediate context is present only for about 200 to 500 msec before the word of interest. Cosky and Gough (1973) showed that giving a two- or four-word context for only 250 msec did not help in identifying a briefly displayed target word. There was no difference at all between the context and the no context conditions when the context was available for such a short time in advance of the target word. When the context was given 500 msec in advance of the target it somewhat facilitated target identification, but even then the increase was not dramatic. So context can affect lexical access, but a model of just how this happens in normal reading will have to take time factors into account.

Before we leave the topic of lexical access, there is one more point we would like to make. No matter how the lexical item is retrieved, it is clear that readers have to acquire the skill to do it quickly if they are going to comprehend the text. The words that constitute a phrase must all be in the reader's short-term memory at the same time for the parsing operations to work upon them. If looking up the successive words in a phrase takes so much time or requires so much cognitive effort that the first word is lost before the last word has been retrieved, then comprehension of higher-level units will fail even if each and every word in the phrase has been looked up. This is a problem that plagues beginning readers (Conrad, 1972). By the time they get to the end of a sentence they may no longer have the first part of it in memory to integrate with the last part. We can put you in the place of the beginning reader by asking you to read a transformed text à la Kolers (1968). In example **(10)** the text has been printed upside down and backwards. Read **(10)**, a sentence borrowed from Marshack (1972, p. 837), from beginning to end. Start at the #.

(10)   can be used and read by the maker by definition, writing is a notational
and by anyone familiar with the formal tradition. Formalized so that it

As you can see, laboriously slaving over each word takes time and is hard work. This is not conducive to easy comprehension of the message as a whole. Spending so much of one's time and cognitive resources on the lexical access task leaves little room for analyzing and reflecting on the content. Such demonstrations usually give people a bit more sympathy for the plight of the beginning reader for whom a lot of text is like **(10)**.

The argument is often made that word recognition drills should not be presented to beginning readers because word lists have no content and thus cannot be intrinsically interesting. New readers need interesting material, the argument runs, to keep up their motivation for working on this difficult task. There may be something to this argument. If all students ever saw were word lists, reading might soon lose whatever charm and attractiveness it holds. However, it is not so clear that drills on single words need to be boring. One of us watched a beginning reader work for ten or fifteen minutes happily decoding the odd names under a set of paint chips (e.g., sky blue, mood indigo, green green). And learning via drill to gain access quickly to some words may permit the child to carry out the parsing and other higher-level processes that will, in fact, make reading intrinsically enjoyable. The moral here is that proscriptions against word drills may not be well-founded if they are based only upon a motivational argument.

Reading Rates Again

Earlier in the chapter we computed an upper limit of 1200 words per minute to the reading rate, given the assumption that every word has to be seen in order for the text to be read. We must point out, however, that what experienced readers do (or should do) when reading depends upon their prior knowledge, their purposes in reading the material, and on the nature of the material itself. There is not a single reading rate for any of us. An experienced professor of psychology can skim an introductory text of 200,000 words in less than half an hour to see whether the book is a serious candidate as the text for the course. Does this mean that he or she is reading at a rate in excess of 6,000 words per minute? The answer to this question depends upon one's definition of reading. The professor could, no doubt, take a test over the content of the book and do very well on it, better than most freshman who had spent 15 to 20 hours reading the book. But of course the professor could probably do quite well on the comprehension test had no time whatever been spent reading it. Clearly, there is a large difference between reading material on a topic that is already well known and getting new information from the text. Also, if the comprehension test were to cover very detailed matters from the book, then everyone, prof included, would need to spend more time on the material.

The bottleneck in reading does not usually arise at the stages of visual input, lexical access, or parsing. Rather, the bottleneck comes from the requirement to add the information on the page to the structures that the reader has in memory, or from the requirement to build new structures. If there is no new information, there is no bottleneck. It is at the higher levels of comprehension processing that the primary limitations on reading rates arise for most normal readers.

Can we learn to read faster? For most people, the answer to this question is almost surely yes. But will our comprehension suffer if our reading rate goes up? The answer to this question is far from clear. Rankin (1962, cited in Gibson & Levin, 1975) reviewed numerous studies on the relationship between speed and comprehension. The correlations between the two varied enormously from study to study, ranging from -.47 to +.96. That is, in some experiments fast reading was associated with low comprehension, while in others fast reading and high comprehension went together. The true relationship between speed and comprehension is going to be complex. However, in attempting to increase reading speed, some of the advice that is given by teachers in the so-called speed reading courses strikes us as quite sound. Thus, the often heard advice to preview what one is going to read before oficially starting to "read" is good advice. Having in mind some of the major issues to be covered (often obtainable from summaries, the table of contents, and the preface) can activate relevant memory structures and perhaps ease some of the burden on the higher-level processing of the text. Also, previewing time can itself add relevant information to the memory structures, information that then need only be retrieved when one is doing the actual reading. In addition, speed reading teachers often tell their students to avoid distractions while they read, to attack the page as though it were a problem solving situation that demanded all of their attention. This, too, strikes us as sound advice from the perspective of cognitive psychology. Processing the input from a radio announcer may well compete with processing written material (the Phonological Recoding hypothesis in particular suggests that this is so).

Much of what we read contains redundancies. Some of the material is redundant with what we already know, and some is redundant with other material in the text. It is often possible, as with our professor friend above, to get the gist of what is being communicated without seeing every word or even every page. However, this does not mean that the most efficient way to take in information is to read only down the pages and not across them, as some courses in speed reading recommend. It is sometimes said that practice in reading down the page will develop something called "soft focus" which permits one to read every word on a line even though the eye only fixes itself on one place per line (or one place for every set of lines). There is absolutely no evidence that one can expand the area of high visual acuity with practice. Since the bounds of acuity are due to physiological limitations, there is no prospect that training could achieve this goal.

In sum, then, there is little doubt that most people can improve their reading skill. Previewing and devoting full attention to the task will alone increase reading speed. In addition, when readers recognize that they have different reading styles available to them—that they are flexible in the way that they can attack the material to be read—then they can use this knowledge to decide consciously what type of reading is called for in any particular situation. One of the common faults of adult readers is to approach every reading situation with the same plodding style of attack which is appropriate only for some material. For other types of material "skimming" will permit the reader to get just as much out of the text as will the word-by-word approach. Thus, it is not hard to become a speed reader. Speed readers skim. Sometimes this is perfectly appropriate, and sometimes it is not.

A Model of Reading

We will close this chapter with a rough outline of a model of reading (see Figure 11.5). This model incorporates many of the stages and processes that we have discussed. In this model, the circles are meant to represent operations or processing mechanisms, and the rectangles are meant to represent the products or output of these mechanisms.

Reading begins with a visual input. The first processing stage is sensory, converting the input stimulus into an iconic representation which, as we noted, is really a very-short-term memory. The visual decoding mechanism operates on the information in the iconic memory, converting it into a visually-based code of letters, syllables, or words. As we indicated, the units upon which the visual decoder operates and the units that it produces are matters of much debate. It would be easy to fill a chapter on this question alone. To continue straight down Figure 11.5 would be to follow the Phonological Decoding hypothesis. According to this hypothesis, a phonological decoding mechanism takes the visually-based letters or words and, by applying a set of rules, transforms them into a set of systematic phonemes. These are then used to search the mental lexicon to find a matching item. When such an item is found, the syntactic and semantic information that is associated with it is transferred into a short-term memory which, in turn, is the input to the parsing and other higher-level sentence processing mechanisms.

Had we detoured at the box labeled "Visual representation of the letter or word," then we would have followed a direct access route to the lexical search mechanism. This detour is really a short-cut around the phonological recoding mechanism and a representation of the input in terms of systematic phonemes. As we have noted, whether (or when) this detour is available to readers of English

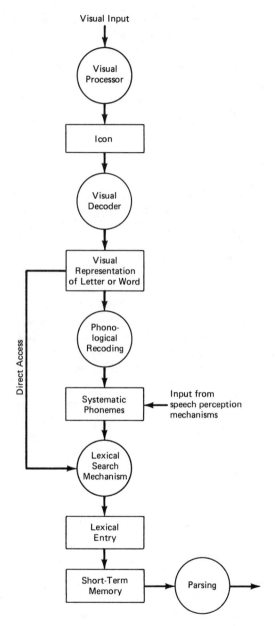

Figure 11.5. A model of reading.

is a matter of debate. The figure also shows where reading and listening comprehension might come together in the processing system. According to this view, everything from the stage of lexical search onward is common to both listening and reading.

The model presented in Figure 11.5 is, of course, greatly oversimplified. We will understand the cognitive processes involved in reading only when we know more exactly which sequence of operations and representations is actually used by the reader, and when we can look inside each of the circles and describe in full detail the processes that the circles only hint at. And there is one respect in which Figure 11.5 is so oversimplified as to be misleading. It suggests that the "flow of information" is in one direction only. That is, Figure 11.5 says that the only input to, say, the lexical search mechanism is the visual representation of the word or a set of systematic phonemes. However, it is possible (and even likely) that the results from higher-level processes "feed back" to affect the operation of the earlier stages. Thus, the lexical search mechanism may have as inputs the item that was just looked up in the lexicon and information about what part of speech it is. This information may greatly affect the process of searching for the next item. A truer picture of the reading process would probably be shot through with arrows going both forward (as in Figure 11.5) and backward—high-level decisions just reached affecting low-level decisions now being taken. There is evidence for such feedback in both the reading and the listening comprehension literature. Figure 11.5 is then, highly oversimplified. But even so, it suggests something of the complexity of the process that you are carrying out with relative ease right this instant.

Summary

The chapter began by noting that the processes involved in reading depend upon the kind of writing system that is being read. Three major writing systems, logographic, syllabic, and alphabetic, were described, and some of the implications of these writing systems for the reading process were pointed out. Next, some of the visual aspects of reading were discussed. The workings of the visual system introduce constraints on reading which apply to all readers, independent of the writing system with which they are dealing. While reading, the eyes move via a series of saccades, brief, jerky movements. The usable information enters the visual system only during the 200 msec or so when the eye is fixed on a point, and not during the 10 msec when the eyes are moving. Only a limited amount of useful information can enter the visual system during each fixation. From these considerations, a "maximum" reading rate of about 1200 words per minute was calculated.

The major aim of the chapter was to discuss the relationship between the reading and listening processes. It was suggested that reading is a derived process and that reading and listening "come together" at some point during the processing of the linguistic input. Hypotheses about reading differ on the point where this meeting might occur. Three major hypotheses concerning the relationship between reading and listening were reviewed. The first was the Subvocalization hypothesis, which states that we read by sounding out the words to ourselves and then listening to what we have produced. According to this view, reading and listening come together very early in the processing sequence. The available experimental evidence does not support this hypothesis.

The second and third views examined were the Direct Access and the Phonological Recoding hypotheses. The former says that the reader goes directly from print to meaning without involving the phonological system. The latter states that print gets translated into an underlying phonological representation (i.e., that the underlying or systematic phonemes are extracted during reading). Evidence both for and against the Phonological Recoding hypothesis was reviewed. There is a substantial amount of evidence suggesting that phonological recoding often occurs, and there is also some evidence suggesting that it need not always occur. A Dual Access hypothesis was then briefly discussed. It says that both the phonological recoding and direct access routes are available to the reader. But the Dual Access hypothesis must be made more specific before it is testable.

The process of lexical access must be carried out rapidly. If it is not, information from prior words is lost, and the parsing processes cannot operate effectively. Also, a word's ease of access is affected by its context and by the time at which the context is available. It was pointed out, however, that the main bottleneck in reading is typically due to cognitive limitations and not to visual or lexical access problems. Some advice on effective and efficient reading was dispensed.

Finally, a tentative model of the reading process was discussed along with one of its more important limitations.

SUGGESTED READINGS

The book by Gibson and Levin (1975) provides a recent survey of many of the topics in the area of reading. Smith's (1971) book provides an introduction to the topic from a perspective different from that taken in this chapter. The collections of papers in Kavanaugh and Mattingly (1972), Singer and Ruddell (1976), and in Reber and Scarborough (1977) are worth examining for more detailed statements of many issues in reading. Venezky (1977) provides historical perspective in a brief space. Huey (1968, originally published in 1908) is still worth perusing.

12

Language and the Brain

The existence of a relationship between the brain and language has been recognized for a very long time. The ancient Egyptians recorded reports of head injuries that resulted in the loss of speech, the phenomenon we now know as *aphasia*. Many of the phenomena we have discussed throughout this book point to the central role which the brain plays in linguistic competence and performance. We saw in Chapter 7, for example, that the development of speech production capabilities in children depends crucially upon the maturation of the cortical mechanisms that control the speech motor system. We have also seen that the brain must provide a temporal (timing) organization for the speech production system, and that this is one of the most important aspects of the brain's involvement in speech. Similarly, the speech perception and comprehension processes discussed earlier are to be accounted for mainly in terms of cortical mechanisms and functioning. In this chapter we will focus directly on the nature of the brain's involvement in language.

Three themes will guide our discussion. One concerns the possible relationships between specific brain structures and specific language functions. This topic is generally referred to as the *localization of language functions*. The second topic, closely related to the first, concerns the effects of brain damage upon language functions. The primary focus here will be on the kind of language deficit known as *aphasia*. The third topic concerns the extent to which language is unique to humans. We will be concerned here with whether or not the human brain is the only one possessing the structures and capabilities necessary for

350

language. This is the question of the *species specificity of language*. Throughout the discussion our guiding concern will be to discover what can be learned from a study of the brain-language relationship about the psychological processes involved in language.

The Study of the Brain-Language Relationship

Since the ancient Egyptians first discovered aphasia, we have learned a great deal about the brain and about language. But although we have acquired a great many facts, a coherent account of the relationships between these two areas of interest still eludes us. Almost every aspect of the brain's involvement in language still gives rise to heated arguments. We should not find this too surprising, for we have seen abundant evidence that the processes involved in such performances as understanding and producing utterances are enormously complex. And it is equally apparent that the human brain is unequalled in complexity by any other organ. Finding the relationships that hold between one set of complexities and another has to be very difficult.

However, it is not just their complexity that underlies our ignorance of the relationships between the brain and language. Rather, it is that much of what we know about the brain is the wrong sort of knowledge. The relevant things we know about language are largely about the processes involved in translating from a speech signal to a meaning and back again. In the case of the brain, we know a great deal about the anatomy and physiology of its many interrelated structures, but we are still all too ignorant of the functions those structures serve. That is, we know what kinds of things the brain must be doing when producing or understanding utterances, but we do not know very much about *how* it does those things.

One reason for this unhappy situation is the immense difficulty of obtaining relevant data about brain functions. To discover such data generally requires studying the brain *while it is functioning* (though a certain amount can be learned from anatomical data collected at autopsy). In the main, we are forced to work with two kinds of data: records of brain activity occurring during language-related activities (e.g., electrophysiological data), and data on the effects of pathological brain conditions on activities involving language.

There are, essentially, two relevant kinds of electrophysiological data concerning brain activity. One comes from stimulating brain structures electrically while those structures are exposed for surgery (see, e.g., Penfield & Roberts, 1959). Since patients are generally conscious during such surgery, it is possible to observe the effects that stimulating a particular area has on their speech performance. But brain surgery is not performed for the purpose of collecting such data. It is done to treat some pathological condition (e.g., to remove a tumor). Thus, such data are available only for brains that are not functioning normally, and it is difficult to interpret them in terms of language-related brain functions in the normal, nonpathological brain.

The second kind of electrophysiological data comes from recording the brain's surface electrical activity (electroencephalographic, or EEG, activity) while subjects are engaged in some language activity. This technique can, of course, be used with normal subjects, giving it an advantage over other techniques. The difficulty is that there are no simple relationships between such surface electrical activity and the underlying brain processes which give rise to it. The data are very "noisy." One of our colleagues has remarked about EEG studies of auditory perception that learning about audition from them is like trying to learn how baseball is played by analyzing recordings made with a microphone attached to the top of the Houston Astrodome. It is not that there is nothing to be learned this way. The problem is, rather, that unless you already know what you are looking for in the EEG data it is very difficult to find it amid all the other, irrelevant things that are also there. For this reason we will not be able to make much use of the EEG data available.

The other main source of evidence on the brain-language relationship is studies of language deficits produced by such pathological conditions of the brain as those resulting from cerebral hemorrhages, tumors, and injuries. A wealth of data concerning such effects has accumulated over the past century. As we will see shortly, there is considerable debate over both the usefulness and the interpretation of these data. For example, it is generally difficult to pinpoint the exact nature or extent of brain damage. Although techniques for obtaining such information have improved in the past few years, the relevant anatomical data are usually unavailable until an autopsy can be performed, often many years after the initial damage. During the interim, many brain changes can occur, clouding the picture of the damage which produced the language deficit in the first place.

But although there are major difficulties in interpreting the kinds of data available on the brain functions underlying language, they are all the data we have. We have little choice but to try to make as much sense of them as we can. Before considering these data on the relationships between brain structures and language functions, it will be useful to very briefly review some of the relevant structures.

Brain Structure and Language

In discussions of language and the brain, one often hears the statement that humans have large brains, relative to body weight, compared with other animals. This fact is sometimes used to "explain" why humans alone have language: only they have large enough brains to cope with linguistic complexities. It is true that the ratio of brain weight to body weight is relatively high in humans (Lenneberg, 1967). This ratio is about 1/47 (with a brain weight of 1.35 Kg) for an adult human, compared to about 1/104 (with a brain weight of .45 Kg) for an adult chimpanzee.

It appears, however, that neither the mass of the brain nor the brain/body weight ratio is the crucial determinant of language capabilities. Humans with remarkably small brains have acquired language. There is, for example, a rare condition known as nanocephalic dwarfism in which, unlike other dwarfs, the individuals preserve the body proportions of normal humans. Such individuals may be only 75 cm (2 1/2 feet) tall as adults. The adult brain weight of nano-cephalic dwarfs may be as little as .4 Kg, barely more than that of a normal newborn infant. Their brain/body weight ratio is about 1/34, about the same as a 3-year-old (i.e., still immature) chimpanzee, whose brain weight is also .4 Kg. Although these dwarfs are mentally retarded, with a mental age of 5 or 6 years, the majority master language skills at the 5-year-old level. We know from Chapters 6 and 7 that this is a substantial mastery of language.

The nanocephalic dwarf has a very small brain and almost masters language. Other creatures match these individuals in brain weight and in brain/body weight ratio and do not acquire language. This calls into doubt the argument that brain size is all-important to language. Lenneberg (1967) noted that the important fact about the nanocephalic dwarf's brain is that it is a *human* brain—it has the structural and organizational characteristics distinctive of the human species. It is not the brain's size that is important for language. Rather, it is the brain's structure and organization.

The human brain, viewed from the outside, looks rather like a wrinkled boxing glove (see Figure 12.1). Somewhat more accurately, it looks like two boxing gloves held tightly together with the thumbs along the outside edges. Like the rest of the body, the brain is roughly symmetrical around the midline— its left and right halves, or *hemispheres,* are nearly mirror-images of each other. Most concern about the brain's involvement in language has focused on the *cerebral cortex,* the thin layer of fissured and convoluted tissue which covers the surface of the brain and gives it its wrinkled appearance. The two hemispheres of the cortex are almost completely separated at the midline, being joined only by a sheet of nerve fibers known as the *corpus callosum.* All communication between the cortical areas of the two hemispheres occurs through the corpus callosum.

Two areas of the cerebral cortex that are generally accepted as being intimately involved in language functions are *Broca's area* and *Wernicke's area* (see Figure 12.1). The first of these is named for Paul Broca, who is generally regarded as being the first (1861) to point out a relationship between damage to a particular brain area and aphasia. Broca argued that the structures of this area are the ones primarily involved in the production of speech, a view still accepted by many, though not all, authorities.

Wernicke's area, named for another pioneering aphasiologist, is often regarded as being involved mainly in receptive aspects of language processing. A third cortical area regarded as important for language is the supplementary motor area. That these areas are involved in language functioning is indisputable. What is far more controversial, as we shall see, is *how* they are involved.

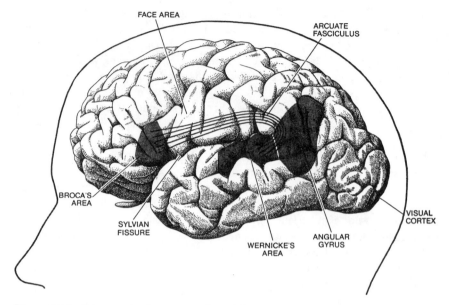

Figure 12.1. The cerebral cortex, viewed from the left side and showing the approximate locations of Broca's Area and Wernicke's Area. (Adapted from Geschwind, N. Language and the brain. *Scientific American,* 1972, *226,* No. 4 (April), 76–83. Used by permission of the author and publisher.)

There are, in addition, a number of subcortical structures involved in one way or another with language. But although the anatomy of such structures is generally well known, the nature of their involvement in language is still largely undetermined, and we will not discuss them further here (see Lenneberg, 1967, pp. 62–65).

One fact on which there is considerable agreement is that the brain's left hemisphere is more intimately involved in language than the right hemisphere. Since the time of Broca, for example, it has been apparent that damage to the left hemisphere is far more likely to result in aphasia than is corresponding damage to the right hemisphere. This lateral difference, sometimes referred to as *cerebral dominance,* appears to be related in a complex way to handedness. For nearly all right-handed adults, it is the left hemisphere that is dominant for language. The correlation is more complex for individuals who are left-handed. The majority of these (60–70%) are also left-hemisphere dominant for language, while the remainder are right-hemisphere dominant. There is little doubt that the two hemispheres of the cortex serve somewhat different functions and that these differences are in some way involved with language. But, as we shall see later, the nature of the difference is highly complex and a matter of considerable controversy. In any event, Broca's observation that aphasia was associated with left hemisphere damage was the first indication that language functions might be localized in particular areas of the brain. We will turn now to the topic of aphasia, since the study of this disorder has led to much of the evidence—and the debate—about localization.

Aphasia and the Localization of Language Functions

Aphasia is the general term used to refer to a variety of language deficits resulting from brain damage. The damage can come from internal sources such as a cerebral hemorrhage or a tumor, or from external sources such as head wounds. Aphasic symptoms are quite diverse and vary considerably from patient to patient, both in their pattern and in their severity.

Asphasia: Symptoms and Sources

It is common to label some symptoms as *expressive,* in that they appear in various aspects of language production. Many aphasic patients produce little speech, showing considerable difficulty in describing or discussing things which, on the basis of other evidence, they know well. Their speech is often lacking in fluency, being produced slowly, with many pauses and with considerable effort. They make frequent articulatory errors, substituting inappropriate sounds for appropriate ones, often without apparent pattern. They often omit function words or morphological inflections entirely.

Such symptoms often appear when there is no evidence that the speech musculature or speech motor control system is affected (Darley, Aronson & Brown, 1969). Patients who generally show extreme difficulty in producing speech may still, if provoked sufficiently, curse with considerable fluency; and some may be able to sing a melody with little evidence of difficulty (Geschwind, 1972). Frequently, however, such symptoms are accompanied by partial or complete paralysis of the side of the body opposite the site of the damage (i.e., generally the right side of the body).

Other aphasics show, not a disfluency in speech, but rather a superfluency. They produce speech rapidly and, unless listened to closely, may sound quite normal. Geschwind (1972) notes that such speech tends to be lacking in content, as when a patient says, "Before I was in this one here, I was over in the other one. My sister had the department in the other one" (p. 78).

Many aphasics also encounter considerable difficulty in "finding" words, a difficulty not unlike—though far more severe than—the occasional difficulty we have when a word is on "the tip of the tongue." Sometimes a word associated with the appropriate word is substituted for it (e.g., *fork* for *knife*). Other times the difficulty results in patients using elaborate circumlocutions to indicate that they know what they want to say but cannot find the proper words. For example, a patient asked to say what one pounds with replied, "You pound with—we know that thing—what it is. We have him back down there—we go down there—the pound bench." (Jenkins, Jiménez-Pabón, Shaw & Sefer, 1975). Notice that this patient was not only having difficulty finding the word *hammer* but also having difficulty sequencing his message and selecting the appropriate pronouns.

Although expressive symptoms are probably the most easily noticed manifestations of aphasia, there can also be a variety of *receptive* symptoms. Patients often have difficulty in understanding heard speech, sometimes to the point of being unable to repeat or otherwise indicate that they have understood single words spoken to them. Since they often use the same words spontaneously in other situations, it seems clear that the difficulty lies in the kinds of perceptual and comprehension processing discussed earlier. Occasionally, the receptive deficit is so great that a patient is diagnosed as being deaf, even though non-linguistic auditory testing may reveal no hearing deficits. As in the case of expressive symptoms, it is sometimes noted that the receptive deficits are more severe for auditory language than for visual language. That is, reading ability is less disturbed than speech perception *per se.*

In examining aphasic patients, or even in reading reports of such examinations, it quickly becomes apparent that the symptoms vary enormously from patient to patient. One patient may show very severe and general expressive symptoms but relatively mild and scattered receptive symptoms. For another, the pattern may be almost completely reversed. One may show only mild and occasional symptoms; for another, the symptoms may be so severe and general that there is virtually no language of any sort remaining. And often, the patient's reactions to his or her own symptoms produces other, secondary symptoms such as depression or an unwillingness to use the linguistic capabilities that remain.

Aphasia and the Brain

The kinds of brain damage that produce aphasic symptoms are likely to disturb other, non-linguistic functions as well. Although difficulty in articulating speech sounds is not necessarily accompanied by a general loss of control or weakness of the speech musculature, or by a reduction in feedback from that musculature, such non-specific deficits do often occur. Nature is proverbially an extremely sloppy experimenter, and it rarely produces the kinds of very circumscribed damage that would best illuminate the roles that particular brain mechanisms play in language functions. This is one reason why bringing aphasia data to bear on brain-language relationships is so difficult.

An additional problem was mentioned earlier: it is generally difficult to pinpoint the locus or extent of brain damage. But even if we knew exactly where the damage had occurred and what brain structures had been affected by it, we would still be hard put to relate that damage to the resulting language behavior symptoms. As Lenneberg (1975) has pointed out, the brain's structures are very complexly interrelated, with the result that damage to one structure is likely to produce changes in the functioning not only of that structure but of many others as well. A relevant, though extreme, analogy is the effect on the overall functioning of an automobile of damaging its carburetor.

It is, in part, for reasons like these that there has been so much and such long-standing debate about how aphasic symptoms reflect the brain's involvement in language. The most basic disagreement is between those who maintain that specific language functions are controlled by specific brain mechanisms—the *localists*—and those who maintain that there is a single, general language ability that can be disrupted—the *generalists*. Put differently, the disagreement is over whether there is one or more than one kind of aphasia. Is it possible for a particular, localized kind of brain damage to produce a deficit in selected language functions while leaving the others intact? The localists believe so. Or does any brain damage that affects language at all have an effect on all the language functions? The generalists hold this view.

Throughout the history of research on aphasia, one or another form of the localist view has been the most common. Broca (1861), for example, maintained that damage to the area named for him resulted in aphasias that were primarily expressive, marked by disfluency in speech production. Wernicke (1874) suggested that damage to quite a different area—Wernicke's area—resulted in aphasias whose major symptoms were receptive rather than expressive. And many other localists have argued that at least some of their patients have shown the kinds of restricted patterns of symptoms that would suggest that different language deficits result from damage to different brain mechanisms. For example, cases have been reported in which oral language production is severely disturbed, but writing and receptive functions remain unimpaired.

Over the years a set of descriptive labels for patterns of aphasic symptoms has developed that suggests the existence of several distinct kinds of aphasia (see, e.g., Jenkins et al., 1975, p. 155). Occasionally, extremely fine-grained classifications have been suggested. For example, Kleist (cited in Lenneberg, 1967) proposed that receptive aphasias could be classified as phonemic deafness, word deafness, name deafness, and sentence deafness; and that each was associated with damage to a specific anatomical site. But while such extreme forms of localization are generally not accepted, some form of localization and specificity is probably the most common current view (see, e.g., Geschwind, 1972, 1974).

What poses a problem for the localists is the fact that aphasic patients rarely (if ever) show "clean" patterns of symptoms, that is, patterns in which a few language functions are severely affected while others are unaffected. Some aphasiologists claim never to have seen such cases. The localists' reply is, of course, that the underlying damage is rarely so circumscribed as to affect only a single function.

The generalists argue that pure cases of one or another kind of aphasia simply do not exist. They claim that reports of "pure" cases of expressive aphasia, for example, are the result of inadequate testing of other language functions. It does seem to be true that patients who are reported to be pure cases have (relatively) mild symptoms; more severe cases generally show a broader range of symptoms. This raises the possibility that among the "pure" cases other symptoms existed that were sufficiently mild to escape detection.

Part of the disagreement about pure cases arises from the often informal testing procedures that have been used, leaving it likely that some relatively mild symptoms were simply missed.

Probably the strongest recent advocates of a general underlying language ability affected by brain damage are Schuell and Jenkins (1959; see also Jenkins et al., 1975). On the basis of extensive standardized testing with a large sample of aphasics, Schuell and Jenkins argued that there is a central language deficit that appears in all aphasics. The impairment is, they suggest, in the ability to formulate propositions in a symbolic (i.e., linguistic) mode. It is thus a general communication deficit, showing its effects in both the perceiving and the producing of language: "The observed communication deficit is not modality specific and exhibits a rather impressive regularity of symptomatic errors. This regularity is shown both in the kinds of errors that occur and in the level of impairment observed" (Jenkins et al., 1975, p. 101).

Schuell and Jenkins are not suggesting that aphasia is a disorder of thought. Rather, it is a disorder of the ability to translate into and out of a linguistic code, showing itself in a reduction of available vocabulary and in a reduction of the memory for verbal material. In sum, they are suggesting that there is a central core of language ability, and that impairment of that core of ability is common to all aphasics. What varies between aphasics is the severity of the impairment of this ability and also the extent to which other functions, not specifically linguistic, are impaired.

This is not the place to attempt a resolution of the debate between localists and generalists. (It may be apparent, though, that our sympathies lie with the generalist view that there is a single, central core of linguistic ability that underlies all language functioning.) It is extremely difficult to bring data on aphasia to bear on questions about the localization of brain functions when there is little agreement about the data themselves or about what they show. But the localist-generalist debate is not the only interesting question surrounding aphasia. Data on the effects caused by brain damage occurring at different ages and on recovery from those effects shed some interesting light on the relationship between the maturational state of the brain and language functioning.

Aphasia: Age of Onset and Prognosis

The kinds of brain damage that result in aphasia are not reversible: destroyed cerebral tissue does not regenerate. This fact would seem to suggest that the language deficits resulting from brain damage should also be irreversible. In fact, the picture is considerably more complicated.

One complicating factor is that aphasic symptoms are initially unstable. That is, there is generally a period of several months following the onset of symptoms during which the symptoms change, generally becoming less severe. The reason for this is that the kinds of cerebral accidents and injuries that result in aphasia usually involve not only the permanent destruction of tissue but also temporary changes, such as swelling and accumulation of fluid. Until these temporary changes have disappeared, and with them such things as the abnormal pressure on the involved brain structures, it is difficult to obtain an accurate assessment of the remaining symptoms. Thus, there is likely to be an initial period following damage during which there is considerable improvement, a period likely to last as long as six months or a year.

Following this period of initial improvement, however, there is likely to be relatively little further recovery. What further improvement there is seems attributable to the patient's learning to exploit his remaining linguistic capabilities rather than to a redevelopment of the damaged capabilities. But although the outlook for long-term improvement is rather bleak, this does not mean that it is useless to engage in therapy with aphasic patients. Therapy is difficult, and the prospects for dramatic improvement are slim once the symptoms have stabilized. But the available therapy procedures are far from useless (see Jenkins et al., 1975).

A second factor that complicates the picture of aphasia is that the prospects for recovery depend upon how old the person is when the aphasia-producing accident or injury occurs. In general, it appears that the nature and durability of aphasia can be characterized in terms of three general age periods (Lenneberg, 1967; Bay, 1975). If the damage occurs early enough, there is unlikely to be any substantial permanent language deficit. Instead, following the period of initial recovery, language development appears to continue from the point it had reached prior to the onset of damage. Lenneberg (1967) suggests that this period lasts until the age of about four years, though it appears that the earlier the damage occurs, the greater the likelihood of complete recovery.

During the second age period, lasting from roughly four years until puberty, there is much more residual effect. But here, too, it appears that the outlook for a redevelopment of language functions is quite good. That is, if the onset of aphasia occurs before puberty, there appears to be a loss, followed by a gradual reacquisition of language. The reacquisition may be less than complete, and it is not clear whether the course of reacquisition is the same as that of initial acquisition. Still, the prognosis for eventual recovery is reasonably promising.

After puberty, the picture changes again, this time to the one we described earlier—an initial recovery period of six months to a year, followed by relatively little further improvement.

The difference between childhood and adult aphasias has generally been supposed to be related to the fact we mentioned earlier, that it is damage to the left cerebral hemisphere that results in aphasia. The aphasia data suggest that early in life both cerebral hemispheres have the capabilities necessary for language, though perhaps not equally so. Thus, if the left hemisphere is damaged early, the right hemisphere continues developing its language capabilities, and there is little permanent effect.

The aphasia data suggest that by the age of four years the left hemisphere has begun to assert its dominance, suppressing further development of the right hemisphere's language processing capabilities. But although the right hemisphere's capabilities do not continue developing in the same way as those of the left, the capacity for further development is not lost. Hence, when the dominant left hemisphere is damaged, the right hemisphere assumes control and continues to develop from the point at which its initial development had ceased. It is for this reason that, following left hemisphere damage between four years and puberty, there is some reacquisition of language ability. The right hemisphere is, so to speak, picking up its language development where it had earlier left off.

The fact that people do not recover well from aphasias occurring after puberty is generally taken as a sign that by this time the right hemisphere has lost its capabilities. Thus, the language deficits of adult aphasics may be attributed to the inability of the adult right hemisphere to process language or to acquire the ability to do so.

We have seen how the aphasia data suggest that as the brain matures language functions become increasingly localized in the left hemisphere. This, of course, is quite different from the kind of localization proposed by many localist theories. The latter concern such things as whether, for example, language production capabilities involve brain structures separate and different from those involved in language comprehension. Left hemisphere localization of the kind we have discussed is generally referred to as *lateralization*, or sometimes *cerebral dominance*. There are many kinds of data other than those concerning aphasia which bear on the nature of this lateralization of language functions, and we will now consider some of those data and their implications.

Localization of Language Functions: Lateralization

There are numerous approaches to the study of lateralization. One which has been used to demonstrate left-hemisphere lateralization involves injecting sodium amytal into the major (carotid) artery supplying one or the other hemisphere. The sodium amytal effectively paralyzes the hemisphere on the side of the injection, leaving the functioning of the other hemisphere unaffected. The general effect of immobilizing the left hemisphere is the almost complete loss of the ability to produce speech. Immobilizing the right hemisphere has little effect on speech (Wada & Rasmussen, 1960).[1] But such techniques are difficult (and somewhat risky) to apply, and consequently are seldom used. Much more has been learned from behavioral measures of lateralization, measures that are easier to obtain from normal subjects.

---

[1] We noted earlier that there are some individuals for whom lateralization is reversed, the right hemisphere serving the functions that in most people are served by the left. Since it is the left hemisphere that is more likely to be "dominant" for language functions, we will continue to speak in terms of that hemisphere alone. The important question here is not which hemisphere is dominant, but rather the nature and extent of that dominance.

Evidence from Normal Subjects: The Right-Ear Advantage

Kimura (1961) was the first to demonstrate that behavioral techniques could be used to demonstrate lateral differences in language processing capabilities in normal individuals. Kimura presented subjects with three pairs of spoken digits, arranged so that the two digits of each pair were presented simultaneously, one to each ear. The presentation of different auditory signals to the left and right ears is referred to as *dichotic listening*. Her subjects were able to repeat more of the digits presented to the right ear than those presented to the left.

What is not immediately apparent, of course, is why a *right*-ear advantage (REA) should reflect a *left* hemisphere language dominance. The general account of this relationship rests on several facts about the auditory system. Each ear transmits signals to the auditory areas of both hemispheres. The crossed connections—right ear to left hemisphere and left ear to right hemisphere—are known as the *contralateral* connections. The connections between each ear and the hemisphere on the same side are known as the *ipsilateral* connections. These relationships are shown in Figure 12.2.

Research on lower animals indicates that when a signal is transmitted along a contralateral pathway it tends to inhibit a signal along the ipsilateral pathway

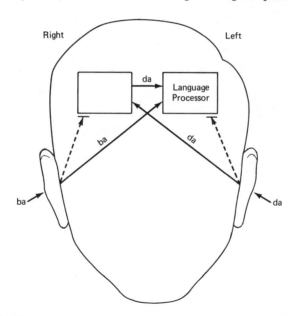

Figure 12.2. The neural connections between ears and cerebral hemispheres, showing that when sounds are presented to the two ears simultaneously (dichotically), the signal presented to each ear is transmitted to the hemisphere on the opposite side. The location of the hypothesized language processing center in the left hemisphere is also shown.

to the same hemisphere. Thus, with dichotic presentation, the right-ear signal travels along the contralateral pathway to the left hemisphere. But the left-ear signal, because the ipsilateral pathway is suppressed, is not transmitted to the left hemisphere and reaches only the right hemisphere via its contralateral pathway. If the language processing mechanisms are located only in the left hemisphere, a right-ear speech signal will reach them directly. But a left-ear speech signal, since it is transmitted only to the right hemisphere, must then be transmitted across the corpus callosum before it can reach the left-hemisphere language processor. Thus, because of the longer pathway a left-ear signal must follow, some information might be lost before the signal ever reaches the language processor. Hence, left-ear signals might be less likely to be identified correctly than right-ear signals because the latter have direct access to the left-hemisphere language processor (see Darwin, 1973).

Since Kimura's first demonstration of a REA in speech perception, there has been a truly extraordinary amount of research, using dichotic listening techniques, on the nature of the left hemisphere's special role in language processing (see Darwin, 1977; Studdert-Kennedy, 1976, for reviews). As often happens, the more we learn about a phenomenon, the more complex the phenomenon becomes. It now appears that the account we just suggested for the special relationship between right-ear speech signals and a left hemisphere language processor is far too simple.

Several recent studies have suggested, for example, that the initial stages of speech perception processing are performed in both hemispheres—that the phonetic features of a left-ear speech signal are processed by a set of feature detectors independent of those processing the right-ear signal (Ades, 1974; Warren & Ackroff, 1974). Thus, it is apparently not the case that all of the processing of linguistic stimuli is performed only in the left hemisphere. The available evidence does suggest, however, that many of the higher-level processes involved in comprehension and production are performed exclusively in the left hemisphere by normal adults.

Evidence from "Split-Brain" Subjects

Additional evidence on the nature and extent of hemispheric differences in language processing comes from studies of persons in whom the connections between the brain's two cerebral hemispheres have been surgically severed. These are the persons often referred to as having "split brains."

A number of years ago, in an attempt to control severe epilepsy in patients for whom other treatments were ineffective, Bogen and Vogel (1962) developed a surgical procedure that involved severing the fibers of the nerve tract connecting the two cerebral hemispheres. This sectioning of the corpus callosum and the anterior commisures did tend to reduce the patients' problems with epileptic seizures, but it also produced a condition in which the two cerebral hemispheres functioned independently of each other.

For obvious reasons, such drastic surgery has been performed only rarely. But several of the patients on whom it has been performed have been studied quite extensively. In general, it requires rather subtle testing procedures to discover the deficits resulting from hemispheric disconnection. Nonetheless, the pattern of these deficits makes an intriguing story, suggesting that the two hemispheres can function quite independently, though differently, and without one being aware of what the other is doing (Sperry, 1968).

Much of the testing of split-brain patients has involved presenting stimuli such that they are registered in only one hemisphere. For example, information about objects handled by the left hand (and not seen) is registered only in the right hemisphere. Similarly, visual stimuli presented to only the left half of either eye are registered only in the right hemisphere.

Among the findings of interest here is that split-brain patients cannot generally name pictures or say printed words shown only to the right hemisphere. In fact, they report them only as flashes of light, denying having seen anything at all (Sperry, 1968). Yet if the word they have been shown is the name of an object, they are able to pick that object out from among several others using the left hand (i.e., the one controlled by the same hemisphere as saw the visually presented word). They can also draw pictures of such objects with the left hand, but not with the right hand (Levy, Nebes & Sperry, 1971). The same stimuli, presented only to the left hemisphere, can readily be named.

In addition, if speech sounds are presented dichotically, the split-brain patients yield a much larger REA than normal subjects. The stimuli presented to the right ear are identified about as accurately as by normals, but those presented to the left ear yield extremely poor identification performance (see Gazzaniga, 1970, for a discussion of these and related findings).

Data like these from split-brain patients suggest, as do the data from aphasics and normals, that the language processing capabilities of the left hemisphere are greater than those of the right hemisphere. But they also suggest that the distinction between the two hemispheres' capabilities is not an absolute one. As we mentioned earlier, printed words shown only to the right hemisphere are often understood. The patient can pick out the correct object. What he cannot do is name it. In general, it appears that the right hemispheres of split-brain patients can recognize many nouns and some adjectives and can understand some kinds of simple utterances. For some reason, verbs appear to be much more poorly understood (see Levy et al., 1971). But the split-brain patients' right hemispheres cannot formulate and produce utterances; they are effectively mute. Thus, it appears that some linguistic functions may be more strongly lateralized than others.

Exactly why this pattern should exist is far from clear. One suggestion about the nature of the left hemisphere's dominance is that its functioning inhibits the functioning of the right hemisphere. That is, the right hemisphere has the potential for processing language far better than it actually does, but is prevented from using its potential by the dominant left hemisphere. If this is the case, then it is also necessary to account for the poorer performance of the right hemisphere in split-brain patients, for these individuals have no connections between the two hemispheres. One possibility is that the inhibition is mediated by subcortical connections that are unaffected by the severing of the direct interhemispheric connections. Alternatively, it might be that the right hemisphere's poor performance is an aftereffect of a long period of inhibition prior to the time the patients' hemispheres were disconnected. That is, many years of inhibition may have resulted in the right hemisphere's losing much of its language processing capability.

Consistent with this last possibility is evidence from individuals in whom the interhemispheric connections of the corpus callosum have never developed. Although the evidence is far from conclusive, it appears that language functions may be equally good in both hemispheres for such individuals (see Selnes, 1974). And this is what we would expect if one hemisphere had never been able to exert an inhibitory influence on the other.

It does seem fairly certain that the language processing capabilities of the left hemisphere are, in normal adults, greater than those of the right hemisphere, though the reasons remain unclear. All the kinds of evidence we have considered point to this conclusion; but at the same time, they indicate that the difference is a complex one and less than absolute.

The Nature of Left-Hemisphere Dominance

Up to this point we have been considering the differences between the two cerebral hemispheres in terms of their language processing capabilities. But several kinds of evidence suggest that the difference is not exactly a language processing difference.

Research on split-brain patients suggests, as we have seen, that the right hemisphere is inferior to the left in many kinds of processes that involve language. But such research also suggests that there are some processes in which the right hemisphere excels over the left. Among these are such things as the recognition of geometric forms and of faces (see Bogen, 1968a, 1968b; Bogen & Bogen, 1968).

Similarly, in normal subjects music and many other non-speech sounds are recognized more accurately when presented to the left ear than to the right in a dichotic listening task, a LEA, the reverse of the REA found with speech. All of this would seem to indicate that the right hemisphere is specialized for dealing with some kinds of non-linguistic stimuli while the left hemisphere is specialized for dealing with linguistic stimuli.

But a variety of recent experiments suggest that the distinction is a bit different from this. Haggard and Parkinson (1971) have found, for example, that in a dichotic presentation a subject's identification of the content of speech shows the customary REA, but his perception of the emotional tone of the same speech stimuli yields a LEA. And Bever and Chiarello (1974) have found that the recognition of melodies, which in most subjects demonstrates a LEA, yields a REA for subjects with a moderate amount of musical training.

These and a number of other findings suggest that the nature of the hemispheric difference lies not in the stimuli the subjects are processing, but in the kind of processing they are performing. The exact nature of the difference is still far from clear. But the evidence has led many theorists to conclude that it has something to do with whether one is attending to the global, "Gestalt-like" properties of a stimulus or whether one is attempting to analyze the stimulus. If one is doing the first of these, the right hemisphere tends to have the advantage; if the latter, it is the left hemisphere that has the greater capability.

For example, in the perception of melodies, most listeners who are not musically sophisticated appear to be attending to the flow of the musical pattern, basing recognition on the overall contour. Musically sophisticated listeners, on the other hand, appear to approach music more analytically, listening for the fine-grained detail of the chord structure and sequencing. Likewise, understanding the content of a spoken message requires, as we saw earlier, some highly sophisticated perceptual, syntactic, and semantic analyses, while recognizing its emotional tone does not.

The Development of Lateralization

Earlier, in discussing aphasia, we noted that the age at which the injury occurs makes a great deal of difference for the nature and likelihood of recovery. Taken quite literally, those data indicate that there are three general periods in the development of laterality—early childhood (birth to four years), middle childhood (four years to puberty), and adulthood. Other sorts of data concerning the development of lateralization lead to much the same picture and, in addition, suggest something about the nature of that development.

Both anatomical data (e.g., Witelson & Pallie, 1973) and behavioral data (e.g., Glanville, Best & Levenson, 1977) show that there is some lateralization observable very early in infancy. Quite possibly, this is a quantitative rather than a qualitative difference in the functioning of the two hemispheres (see Bever, 1975). That is, it may represent a difference in the efficiency with which the left and right hemispheres process speech stimuli.

Such an early quantitative difference in language processing may provide the basis for later, larger differences as more complex analytic (comprehension) and synthetic (production) processes develop. That is, the initially small quantitative advantage of the left hemisphere processors may become magnified as the child develops the kinds of sophisticated language processing capabilities that appear during childhood.

There is some reason to believe that during early childhood the language analyzing capabilities of the two hemispheres function independently. This is suggested by the fact that the corpus callosum, the bundle of fibers connecting the two hemispheres, develops only very gradually. In this sense, the young child may be effectively split-brained (Gazzaniga, 1970), with his brain's two hemispheres acquiring the same kinds of language abilities. Since the left hemisphere apparently has a slight initial advantage in the efficiency with which it performs, it might be expected to progress somewhat more rapidly in this acquisition. Such an independence of the two hemispheres early in childhood fits well with the aphasia data: damaging either hemisphere, if the damage occurs early enough, leaves the other capable of continuing the development of its language processing capabilities, with the result that there is no long-term language deficit.

The developmental aphasia data suggest that a change occurs at about four years of age, and there appears to be a corresponding change in normal children's speech perception performance. It is at about this time that a stable REA in dichotic listening emerges (Bever, 1970; Kimura, 1963). It may be that by this age the corpus callosum has matured sufficiently to have become functional (Bay, 1975). By this age also, the left hemisphere processor should be considerably advanced over its right hemisphere counterpart. Since the two hemispheres are now capable of interacting, the more developed left hemisphere can inhibit the functioning of the right hemisphere, preventing it from developing further.

This change would account for the developmental aphasia data. Since right-hemisphere processing has not continued to develop after age four, an injury to the left hemisphere during middle childhood leaves the right hemisphere, with its 4-year-old capabilities, to carry on. Hence, the child's language performance regresses from its pre-injury level to a 4-year-old level. But since the right-hemisphere mechanisms are still capable of performing and of further acquisition, there is a re-acquisition process. But if the left hemisphere has inhibited the language processing and development of the right hemisphere for several years before a left-hemisphere injury occurs, the right hemisphere will no longer be capable of developing its language processing capabilities. Hence, an aphasia-producing injury that occurs in adolescence or later results in a permanent loss of language processing capability.

It should be emphasized that this account of the development of laterality is rather speculative. It is only quite recently that the attention of researchers has focused on the topic. Performing the relevant kinds of research is extremely difficult, and there are still a great many gaps in our understanding of both laterality and its development. We can anticipate that our theories about these topics will change considerably as more becomes known.

Our discussions of laterality and its development, of localization, and of aphasia have not provided a firmly grounded theory of brain-language relationships. However, along with Lenneberg (1967, p. 216), "We intended nothing more ambitious than to furnish a few props to the imagination that may help to form an idea of the still incomprehensible complexity of the function of the brain and its relationship to behavior."

In the next section we turn to a different topic, but one that also has important implications for brain-language relationships. The question with which we will be concerned is whether the human brain is the only one that has the capabilities to acquire and use language. Put another way, is language a species-specific behavior, available only to humans?

Species Specificity: Language in the Chimpanzee

It may at first seem a bit odd to bring up the question of whether or not organisms other than humans have (or can have) language in a chapter devoted to language and the brain. But basically this is a question about the nature of the neurological structures and processes that underlie language. That is, asking whether any other species has enough of the appropriate neurological capabilities for language is one way of approaching the question of what the necessary capabilities are. This is essentially a *comparative* psychological approach to the nature of human language abilities.

In addition, the question of whether or not language is unique to humans has, in its own right, long been of interest to psychologists, linguists, philosophers, and laymen. Often, the interest has stemmed from attempts to demonstrate that humans are unique. Such attempts have tended to take the form of assuming that we are unique in our possession of language, and then seeking to prove the assumption by defining "language" so as to make it a foregone conclusion.

But, clearly, there are other reasons for finding the question interesting. Roger Brown (1970) suggested one when he wrote,

It is lonely being the only language-using species in the universe. We want a chimp to talk so that we can say: "Hello, out there? What's it like, being a chimpanzee?"

Naturally-Occurring Communication Systems

Many serious attempts to deal with this question have taken the approach of studying the naturally-occurring communication systems of other species, searching for similarities and differences between such systems and human languages. Work on the "language" of the bees is of this sort (see, e.g., Brown, 1958). Considering the relationships between such communication systems and human languages rapidly makes it apparent that we cannot think of "language" as a single, unified something that is either present or absent. Rather, we must conceive of it as a complexly interrelated set of abilities (see Chapter 1; see also Lenneberg, 1967, Chapter 6). In this respect, comparing other communication systems with language has helped to sharpen and clarify what is involved in human languages. But the results of such comparisons also suggest that naturally-occurring non-human communication systems lack too many of the characteristics of human languages to be considered comparable. For example, "talking" birds produce speech sounds in ways entirely different from those of humans. And the much acclaimed communicative abilities of dolphins appear to be mainly the flights of fancy of enthusiastic but naive researchers (see Sebeok, 1963).

Teaching Human Speech to Non-Humans

It seems reasonable to suppose that if there is any organism that shares our linguistic capabilities it would be a species close to us. Although the naturally-occurring communication systems of non-human primates seem far removed from human languages in a number of respects, this supposition has led many to approach the problem from a different direction: is it possible to teach a human language to a member of a closely related species?

A number of attempts have been made to answer this question. One of the more extensive studies of this kind was performed by Keith and Cathy Hayes (1951), who "adopted" an infant chimpanzee named Viki and attempted to raise her in their home as one would a human child. One difference was that the amount of effort devoted to trying to teach Viki to talk was far greater than generally occurs with children. But despite intensive effort, the results were quite disappointing. After more than three years of training, Viki was only able to produce three words, and these were only barely recognizable.

Viki's language comprehension was apparently somewhat better. Although it was often difficult to determine from her behavior, she appears to have learned to understand a number of English utterances. But even here, Viki gave little evidence of understanding novel combinations of familiar words.

For a number of years, this was where the problem stood. Even with intensive training, Viki and other chimpanzees made little progress in acquiring a human language. As a result, it was widely believed that our linguistic uniqueness remained unchallenged. In recent years, however, the question has been re-opened, albeit in a somewhat different form. Many researchers, reflecting upon the earlier attempts to teach chimpanzees to talk, have noted that much of the training was directed at the production of speech sounds. And while this is a part of language, it is not clear that it is an essential part (see, e.g., Brown, 1958, Chapter 5). Might it be that the chimpanzees' problem was more involved with low-level aspects of speech production than with language *per se*? A variety of kinds of recent research suggest that this might be the case.

Why Chimpanzees Cannot Talk. We saw earlier (Chapter 7) that human infants are incapable of producing many speech sounds, in part because of the immature shape of their vocal tracts, and in part because of an inability to make some of the kinds of controlled articulator movements necessary for speech sound production. Lieberman (1968; Lieberman, Klatt & Wilson, 1969) has found that many of the same limitations characterize the vocal tracts of mature nonhuman primates. From examinations of the vocal tract anatomy of primates he has concluded that the primates' vocal tracts are quite similar to those of human infants and, hence, quite different from those of adult humans. The consequence is that the primates can produce only a very limited range of vowel sounds. Analyses of the sounds produced spontaneously by primates also show that they do not vary the shape of the vocal tract very much during sound production. In particular, the kinds of tongue movements necessary for attaining the vocal tract configurations for many consonantal sounds do not occur. Given such limitations, it is not surprising that attempts to train chimpanzees to produce speech sounds have not been very successful.[2]

There have also been some recent attempts to determine whether non-human primates perceive speech sounds in ways similar to those of humans (Morse & Snowden, 1975; Sinnott, Beecher, Moody & Stebbins, 1976). It appears that the primates are not as sensitive to speech sound differences as are humans. The available data are quite unclear as to whether the primates show the kind of categorical perception effects characteristic of human speech perception (see Chapter 3). In any event, we cannot be at all sure yet that they do.

In sum, it appears that non-human primates are not particularly well-endowed for learning to communicate using speech. But, of course, speech itself is only a peripheral manifestation of language. And while it is an obvious one, it is not a centrally important one. Children who are unable to produce speech sounds appear to show quite normal language functioning in other respects, such as comprehension (Lenneberg, 1962; MacNeilage, Rootes & Chase, 1967). Might it be that non-human primates would do a better job of acquiring human language if a way were found for them to express themselves other than by using speech?

Chimpanzees and Sign Language and Other Means of Expression

Beatrice and Allan Gardner (1969) were among the first to undertake this approach to the problem of teaching human language to a non-human primate. Noting that primates are highly adept at using their hands, they decided to attempt teaching American Sign Language (ASL) to a chimpanzee. Their research with Washoe, a young female chimpanzee, is by now well known and has occasioned a great deal of excitement and controversy.

From the time the experiment started, Washoe was raised in a house trailer, interacting for long periods every day with a number of humans who never spoke in her presence but who signed to her extensively. The interaction was much like that between parent and child, the humans signing the names of objects and actions, signing requests and questions, and doing manually the kind

[2] Lieberman and Crelin (1972) have extended this kind of vocal tract analysis to prehistoric Neanderthal man, attempting to estimate Neanderthal's vowel production capabilities from a reconstruction of his vocal tract shape from fossil fragments. Their conclusion—that Neanderthal could not have produced enough variety of vowels to have had anything like human speech—is somewhat controversial. But their approach to the question of when human speech capabilities might have evolved is an interesting one.

of chattering typical of parent-child interactions. The humans also tried to induce Washoe to imitate signs and to condition her, using tickling as a reward, to use signs in appropriate situations.

Progress for the first several months was slow. After seven months, Washoe could use four signs fairly appropriately. The *more* sign, for example, was used to ask for repetition or continuation of a pleasurable activity, such as tickling, and also to ask for more food. Additional signs were added gradually, so that by the end of 22 months, Washoe's vocabulary included some 34 signs that she seemed to be able to use appropriately.

It is important to note that Washoe's signs, like children's first words, did not occur only in the situations in which she had seen others use them. Rather, Washoe used them in new situations as well, suggesting that she had some understanding of the appropriate meanings associated with the signs. And, like children's early words, Washoe's signs were also overgeneralized (see Chapter 8 above). The *flower* sign generalized not only to pictures of flowers but also to such things as a tobacco pouch and a smelly ointment.

But more impressive than Washoe's growing vocabulary is the fact that after several months of signing she began to combine signs to produce "utterances" longer than a single sign. Most of the recorded sequences were composed of two signs, though some longer ones occurred. For example, Washoe produced sign sequences that could be translated as *You drink, More tickle, Hurry open, Listen dog, Roger Washoe tickle, Hurry gimme toothbrush,* and *Key open food.* Such utterances were not imitations of ones she had recently seen signed, and many were ones she had never seen signed.

At first glance, Washoe's multi-sign utterances seem very much like the multi-word utterances produced by young children. And Brown (1970), in a thoughtful and sympathetic comparison of Washoe's sign sequences with children's early structured utterances, concluded that Washoe was expressing many, though not all, of the kinds of semantic relations found in children's Stage I speech.

Although Washoe's progress was slow, her achievements were highly impressive and far more than earlier studies attempting to teach chimpanzees to speak would have led us to think possible. Unfortunately, the Gardners were forced to end their research with Washoe before her linguistic education had progressed much further, leaving us with a great many unanswered questions.[3] For example, would Washoe's language have continued to develop in the directions in which it appeared to be going? Would she have encountered an upper limit on the semantic and/or syntactic complexity of the sequences she was capable of producing? And if so, where would the level have been?

Before Washoe's linguistic education ended there were already some indications that her development was not entirely parallel to that of children. For

[3]Washoe, since leaving the Gardners, has been under the care of Dr. Roger Fouts at the University of Oklahoma. Only informal reports of her behavior there are available, and it is unclear what further training she has received or what further progress she has made.

example, one of the sign sequences we noted above was *Roger Washoe tickle*, a sequence of signs whose order does not correspond to the word order likely to be used by a child. Sequences of this sort were fairly common and suggest that Washoe was operating with fewer constraints on order than are characteristic of children's early utterances.

What to make of this difference is, however, considerably less than clear. One reason for this difficulty is that as yet we know relatively little about sign language itself. Until recently, it was generally thought that a sign language like ASL was little more than a translation of English, with signs substituted (in most cases) for words. Recent investigations of ASL, prompted in part by interest in animal research like that involving Washoe, have revealed that this is not the case. Sign languages are instead distinctive languages with their own syntactic and semantic rules (see, e.g., Bellugi & Fischer, 1973).

Since work on the structure of ASL has not proceeded very far, it is difficult to determine what to make of the differences between Washoe's acquisition of ASL and children's acquisition of English. For example, is the fact that Washoe apparently did not order her signs very consistently a fact about Washoe? Or is it a fact about ASL? That is, does ASL itself differ from English in this respect? Answering such questions is further complicated by the fact that the people teaching Washoe were not themselves native "speakers" of ASL and were learning it while they were teaching Washoe. Consequently, some of the characteristics of Washoe's signing might be attributable to the kind of ASL she encountered rather than to characteristics of ASL *per se*. Such questions in no way detract from Washoe's impressive accomplishments. They do, however, leave unclear what to make of those accomplishments.

Other attempts to study chimpanzees' "linguistic" capabilities have proceeded along quite different lines. For example, Premack (1971, 1976; Premack & Premack, 1972) has worked extensively with a chimpanzee named Sarah. Sarah's medium of communication consisted of a set of distinctively colored and shaped pieces of plastic which could be stuck to a felt-covered board. An "utterance" consisted of a sequence of plastic pieces whose meanings had been taught to Sarah. Rather than trying to teach Sarah a translation of a human language, Premack focused on studying the kinds of relationships among symbols (the plastic pieces) that Sarah could learn to understand and produce. The details of Sarah's accomplishments would require several pages to describe and discuss. But although it is not clear that it was "language" that Sarah was acquiring, her intellectual accomplishments are the most impressive yet reported for a non-human.

The Gardner's success with Washoe and Premack's success with Sarah has, of course, attracted a great deal of attention. Their success has also led a number of other investigators to undertake similar projects. For example, Roger Fouts has been conducting systematic research on sign language acquisition with a number of chimpanzees (see Fouts, 1973). And Rumbaugh (1977) and his associates have been using an approach somewhat similar to Premack's.

As we might expect from Washoe's slow progress, such projects are long-term ventures. As yet they have not proceeded far enough for us to be able to say very much about what the eventual outcomes will be. One thing which seems quite clear already is that the cognitive capabilities of chimpanzees are considerably greater than most of us would have thought a few years ago. Beyond that, there is little that can be said with any certainty. We do not yet know nearly enough about the nature of the chimpanzees' accomplishments. And we also do not yet know nearly enough about language acquisition in children to be very confident about similarities and differences.

There do appear to be certain general differences that are worth pointing out. As we noted in considering language acquisition in children, nearly all children acquire language and do so with little direct effort, either on their part or on the part of the adults "teaching" them. In contrast, the linguistic achievements of chimpanzees have been gained only through extensive and intensive efforts by their teachers. With children, it seems next to impossible to keep them from acquiring language. But the data available to date suggest that this is hardly the case with chimpanzees. The impression one gets is rather that a great deal of extrinsic motivation, provided by reinforcements such as tickling, lettuce leaves, grapes, etc., is necessary to induce them to do what children do on the basis of largely intrinsic motivation. (See Flavell, 1977, for a discussion of this characteristic of children's development.)

A second difference, though one that is a good deal more difficult to pin down, lies in what children and chimpanzees use their languages for. Brown has noted that Washoe produced only some of the kinds of utterances characteristic of children whose utterances were otherwise on a level of complexity comparable to hers. Both produce utterances communicating what they want to do or want others to do. But the children also produce utterances describing what they are doing, and at least some of their utterances seem to serve primarily to furnish information to their audiences. Although the chimpanzees do this too, at least in the context of answering questions, it appears to us that there is a difference: the chimpanzees need to be induced to provide information, and children do not.

We think it is likely that when more prolonged studies of chimpanzee language development are performed, differences of this sort will become more readily apparent. Stage I children talk primarily about the here and now, and so do the chimpanzees. But children soon develop the linguistic (and cognitive) means for talking about events in the past and things that are only possible rather than actual. And it is less than clear that the chimpanzees will do likewise. (See Premack, 1976, for some interesting reflections on the chimpanzees' prospects.)

Beyond such general comments on similarities and differences, the available data allow little to be said. While there is a great deal that may be learned about language and language development from comparing and contrasting chimpanzees with children, most of this learning lies in the future. In the meantime, it is entertaining, if not productive, to wonder if we will ever be able to converse with chimpanzees about such things as the competence-performance distinction or about the relative merits of different theories of language acquisition.

Summary

This chapter explored some of the available data and theories about the nature of the brain structures and processes that underlie language capabilities. It also looked at how these capabilities may be similar to or different from those of non-humans.

Aphasia is the kind of language deficit produced by brain damage. The question of whether different language functions are localized in different parts of the brain was discussed in light of evidence from aphasics. Some areas of the cerebral cortex (e.g., Broca's and Wernicke's areas) play very important roles in language functions, but the nature of their roles is not entirely clear. Over 100 years of intensive study of aphasia has yielded a vast body of data about aphasic symptoms and about the relationship between age of onset and amount of recovery. But no fine-grained localization of language functions in the brain has yet been demonstrated, and evidence for the highly specific kinds of aphasia predicted by localist views of the brain-language relationship is weak. However, the facts about aphasia are extremely difficult to interpret and to bring to bear on the localist-generalist debate. The debate has not yet been resolved, and it seems likely that when it is resolved it will have a complex solution.

Data from aphasics, from normal subjects, and from "split-brain" patients were brought to bear on the kind of localization of language functions known as lateralization. There is abundant evidence that one of the brain's cerebral hemispheres is more involved in language processing than the other, at least for adults. However, the differences between the hemispheres are complicated ones with a complex developmental history. In all likelihood the belief that language is processed in one hemisphere, and other kinds of stimuli in the other, is too simple.

The linguistic and cognitive capabilities of chimpanzees are considerably greater than was thought possible only a few years ago. The fact that the vocal apparatus of chimpanzees is considerably different from that of humans—and that it is not well adapted to producing speech sounds—is sufficient to explain why chimpanzees cannot be taught to talk. When a different medium of communication such as sign language is adopted, chimpanzees do considerably better than they do with speech. But although chimpanzees' accomplishments are impressive, there are not enough data to allow anything more than the most general of comparisons between the language acquisition capabilities of chimpanzees and those of human children.

A great deal of the difficulty involved in studying these and other aspects of the relationship between the brain and language results from the immense problems encountered in obtaining relevant data. But part of the difficulty also lies in the complexity of the relationships themselves. The consequence is that, despite the enormous amount of research that has been devoted to the brain mechanisms involved in language processing, we know only a very small part of what we would like to know.

SUGGESTED READINGS

A useful general reference on the relationships between language and the brain is Lenneberg (1967). Many of the papers in the collection edited by Lenneberg and Lenneberg (1975) are also useful. For opposing viewpoints on the nature of aphasia and what aphasia reflects about brain-language relationships, see Geschwind (1972) and Schuell and Jenkins (1970) (see also Lenneberg, 1975). Harnad, Doty, Goldstein, Jaynes, and Krauthamer (1976) present several papers reviewing a variety of aspects of lateralization of the nervous system, including language. Darwin (1973, 1976) and Studdert-Kennedy (1976) discuss recent research on laterality in speech perception; and Bever (1975) and Kinsbourne (1975) discuss the development of laterality. For differing viewpoints on the significance of research on language in chimpanzees, see Bronowski and Bellugi (1970), Brown (1970), Gardner and Gardner (1975), and Premack (1976).

13

Language and Thought
in the Context
of Linguistic Diversity
and
Linguistic Universals

"On those occasions when language itself has come to your attention it has probably been in conjunction with some aspect of language diversity" (p. 4). In this chapter we again want to discuss some aspects of linguistic diversity and linguistic universals. Now, however, we have a good deal more background information to bring to bear on these topics. We will also use our discussion of diversity and universals as a springboard for an additional discussion of the relation between language and thought. Although we have already said something about this topic, in the present chapter we will discuss it from a more historical perspective, and we will also describe some new research which helps illuminate it. This research has had an important impact on how most psycholinguists view the relation between language and thought.

When discussing the relationship between two things, it is necessary to have a fairly good understanding of the "things" themselves. It would be difficult to discuss the relationship between, say, social structure and crime if one had no idea of the forms of social structure that exist. To some extent theorists who have discussed the relationship between language and thought have been in the position of not understanding the concepts they were trying to relate. In the past neither concept was well understood. Now we have at least some awareness of the structures that we acquire when we become competent in a language. And although our grasp on language is probably best thought of as a mere fingerhold, we will have to look closely to see whether we have even that much understanding of "thought."

A few years ago it was commonly believed that linguistic diversity naturally implied cognitive diversity. This argument ran roughly as follows. One's thought patterns are shaped to a considerable extent by the structure of the language that one speaks. Therefore, speakers of divergent languages will have divergent cognitive systems. Present opinion does not fully agree with the notion that cognitive diversity follows from linguistic diversity. In order to examine some of the issues that help shape these opinions, we will discuss a language that is different from Standard English. We will explore the ways in which this language differs from Standard English and then see whether the cognitive systems of its speakers are also different. However, instead of picking a vastly different and exotic language as the focus of our discussion, we have chosen instead to pick one much closer to home. We will look at what is often called Black English. Our reasons for doing so include the fact that many points can be made as readily with it as with a more remote language, and our belief that wider knowledge about this linguistic system is desirable.

Linguistic Diversity: Black English

We must begin with a caveat. The dialect that we are discussing here is not spoken by all black residents of the U.S. There are likely to be several varieties of Black English spoken within the same city and by the same individual at various times of his life. The version being discussed here is, however, a common one. According to Dillard (1972), this dialect is spoken by 80% of the black population of the United States. Sometimes this linguistic system is called the Black English vernacular, and sometimes it is called Negro non-standard English. In our discussion we will follow Dillard in calling it Black English (BE).

Sentence (1) is an example of a grammatical sentence in BE.

(1) You makin' sense but you don't be makin' sense.

On the surface, (1) is an odd sentence to the speaker of Standard English (SE). It appears to be self-contradictory and, thus, the product of a cognitive system that is quite different from that of a speaker of SE. However, before we discuss the structure of Black English and show how (1) is to be interpreted, we will make a brief detour to discuss the history of this dialect.

The History of Black English

In the context of our discussion in Chapter 1, BE is a valid language or dialect. That is, it would occupy a position in Figure 1B (p. 5). We should not think of BE as a sub-standard form of SE, but rather as a linguistic system with the full range of expression that any linguistic system provides its speakers.

The historical sources of BE are not yet clear. There is, however, one theory about its source to which no respectable linguist subscribes; it is essentially a racist theory. According to this view, BE is a degenerate form of SE. The former has its present form because of physical characteristics of the speakers (e.g., "thick lips") and because of their psychological deficiencies (e.g., "laziness"). Nothing in the world of scholarship can be found to support this view.

A much more interesting and plausible theory about the source of BE has been proposed by Stewart (1970) and others, and is summarized by Dillard (1972). According to this view, BE has some of the characteristics it does because of its historical connection with West African languages spoken by the people who were enslaved in the 16th, 17th, and 18th centuries. The tie is not, however, a very direct one. In order to make it, we must understand the concepts of a pidgin and a creole.

A *pidgin* is a language which has no native speakers. Such a language may develop when speakers of different languages engage in commerce and need to communicate with each other. Pidgins usually have a small vocabulary and very regular rule systems. For example, in Melanesian Pidgin English, verbs with a direct object must have the suffix *-m* (e.g., *Me dream kill'm onefella snake*). A pidgin combines lexical items and structure from the two or more languages whose speakers are interacting.

A pidgin based upon Portuguese developed along the west coast of Africa in the 15th and 16th centuries. This language probably provided a basis for communication not only between Africans and Portuguese, but also among native Africans who spoke a large number of mutually unintelligible languages. When the British began to trade in this area, a Pidgin English may have developed (linguists are not certain about this). Pidgin English was probably influenced by Pidgin Portuguese (for example, the word *pickaninny* is acknowledged to be Portuguese in origin). According to Stewart (1970, p. 359), "It is likely that at least some Africans already knew this Pidgin English when they came to the New World . . . " Slave traders made sure the slaves that they shipped spoke a mixture of different languages in order to decrease the possibility of effective planning and communication among them. Given that a variety of languages were mixed together, it may have been common for a Pidgin English to be spoken among the slaves. Later, on the plantations, the influence of English would of course be very great.

When a pidgin becomes the first language of a child, it is said to be a *creole*. Pidgin English became the native language of black children born on the plantations. Dillard uses the term "Plantation Creole" to refer to the language that developed in this fashion. By 1715, Daniel DeFoe (of *Robinson Crusoe* fame) could write a novel (*The Family Instructor*) in which influences of Pidgin English were unmistakable and, presumably, familiar to his readers. In the book, the creole speaker Toby says that he was born in the New World:

Toby: Me be born at Barbados.

Boy: Who lives there Toby?

Toby: There lives white mans, white womans, Negree mans, Negree womans, just so as live there (cited by Stewart, 1970, p. 357).

Creole English is spoken today in the West Indies. In the U.S. a creole English called *Gullah* is spoken on the sea islands off the coast of Charleston, S.C. This creole has been unmistakably influenced by African roots. Plantation creole has had a long time to develop and to be influenced by (and to influence) the vocabulary and patterns of SE.

To summarize, at least some scholars believe that BE has its origins in a creole which was spoken on plantations in the south. It has had a long time to develop and to be influenced by SE, especially as its speakers have come to have more contact with whites. According to this view, then, it is a mistake to view BE as a simple offshoot of SE, and a deficient one at that. Rather, BE has a separate historical basis.

The Structure of Black English

Some aspects of an unfamiliar dialect are relatively easy to pick up. Most northerners can give a moderately successful imitation of a southern drawl with only a little practice (this is not to say that they sound like natives). Likewise, certain slang expressions or other vocabulary items can easily be incorporated into one's dialect once the meanings of the terms are understood. The same is not true of structural differences—differences in syntax. These are not readily comprehended or produced without a good deal of practice with them. When a speaker of SE who is unfamiliar with BE hears a sentence like (1), his reaction may be one of confusion. It sounds strange and appears, to some extent, to be senseless. Let us look at a few examples of the grammatical differences between BE and SE. We will see that the expressions follow an organized set of rules and that simply knowing the rules does not make one fluent in the dialect.

One way in which BE differs from SE is that both tense and number are signaled somewhat differently in the two. Thus, if the context makes the tense of the verb clear, it is not necessary to have a past tense marker on the verb in BE. Sentence (2) is perfectly grammatical since the occurrence of the word *yesterday* tells us that the event happened in the past. The marker for past need not be so obvious; sometimes it can be quite subtle.

(2) He go yesterday.

Sometimes one verb will carry the tense marker *ed* while others will not, e.g., (3).

(3) The boy carried the dog dish to the house and put some dog food in it and put some water in and bring it out and called the dog (Dillard, 1972, p. 41).

To take an example from the number system of BE, the word *themself* is grammatical since the plural is already given by the term *them;* the redundant plural signal *selves* is therefore not required. In these two cases, then, the dialects differ in that SE redundantly marks tense and number while BE does not.

One of the most striking differences between BE and SE concerns the use of *be* in BE. Look at examples (4-7).

(4) He be workin' every night.

(5) He workin' right now.

(6) *He be workin' right now.

(7) *He workin' every night.

The first two examples are grammatical in BE, the second two are not. In BE verbs must be marked according to whether the action described is continuous, habitual, or regular on the one hand; or occasional or momentary on the other. The word *be* is the marker for continuous or habitual activity. Thus, *He be workin'* means that he usually works, that it is his habit to work. Likewise, *He be sick* means that he has been sick for some time, that he is sickly. Therefore, sentence (6) is ungrammatical since it combines the habitual *be* with the phrase *right now*. *He workin'* is a comment about some momentary state, not a habitual one. In SE the habitual vs. the momentary aspect of verb meaning is not explicitly marked.

We can now understand (1), *You makin' sense but you don't be makin' sense.* The speaker of (1) is saying that the previous speaker's remark was sensible even though as a general rule what the previous speaker says does not make sense. Dillard "translates" it as, "You've blundered into making an intelligent statement for once" (p. 46).

Among the other notable differences between BE and SE is the fact that the auxiliary verb *have* is replaced by *been, done,* and *is* in BE. Thus, (8) is grammatical in BE.

(8) Is they gone there?

Also, relative pronouns can be deleted more freely in BE than in SE. Example (9) is grammatical in BE.

(9) That's the chick I keep tellin' you about got all that money.

Some differences between BE and SE are found among young speakers of BE but then disappear as the children get older. This phenomenon, called age-grading, was discovered by Stewart (1965). For some young speakers, pronouns need not be marked for sex if the context makes the sex clear. Thus, (10) may be grammatical.

(10) He a nice little girl.

There are numerous other differences between the two dialects or languages (see Baratz, 1970, for a further list). Each of them is relatively superficial and easy for SE speakers to understand, though not necessarily for them to use. Taken together, however, they can result in sentences that sound very strange indeed to speakers of SE. Some BE sentences can readily be misunderstood by SE speakers.

Speakers of BE are no doubt at a disadvantage in a school system which values only SE. Considerable debate has taken place concerning the desirability of forbidding BE in the schools. Some want to get rid of it entirely. One main argument on this side is that only SE can get children into the mainstream of American society. It is only by possessing SE that economic doors are opened and the dominant cultural tradition of the country becomes available to the children. Proponents of BE point to the tremendous difficulty that comes with being schooled in a dialect other than one's own. Children have many failure experiences which are due not to their abilities or efforts but to their language. This may lead them to simply avoid going to school at every opportunity. It also gives them the message that their community is not a valued one. Baratz (1970, p. 17) cites a UNESCO report which stated that "It is axiomatic that the best medium for teaching a child is his mother tongue."

The debate about the role of BE in the schools is not by any means simple to resolve. To put it in stark terms, favoring the inclusion of BE in the schools can be looked at either as supporting the pride of a group of people or as favoring their subjugation (by keeping them from the mainstream of the economic and cultural life of the nation). One alternative to these stark options is to encourage BE to exist, to develop curricular materials in it, and also to teach SE as a second dialect. This approach is being taken by some students of the problem (e.g., Baratz, 1970). It will take some time before we can evaluate the success of this endeavor.

To summarize, we have seen that the rules for BE are somewhat different from those of SE. We have not made, nor can we make, any judgment about which set of rules is preferable since, from a linguistic or psycholinguistic perspective, neither is superior to the other. We have noted, however, that both upward mobility in the society at large and access to the dominant cultural heritage of the country may argue that speakers of BE should be taught SE as well. In principle this can be done without devaluing BE and its cultural heritage.

The "Logic" of Black English

Students who come to school speaking BE have sometimes been categorized as intellectually deficient or, more often, as culturally deprived. This "deficiency" theory has been challenged by a number of investigators, perhaps most notably by Labov (1970, 1972). Labov has argued that when in their own element children from so-called deprived backgrounds have as rich a logical system of cognition as do children from more "advantaged" backgrounds. Furthermore, Labov has pointed out that the tradition in Black communities is to value those who are linguistically skilled at certain street games such as "sounding." The upshot of Labov's claim is that differences in syntax do not necessarily lead to differences in logical abilities. This is a challenge to the hypothesis that linguistic diversity leads to cognitive diversity.

Let us look at one example, a fifteen-year-old speaker of BE. This individual, Larry, is characterized by Labov as one of the roughest and loudest members of a street group. He is being interviewed here about his beliefs in the afterlife (an interview that has something of the character of a verbal game). The remarks of the interviewer are in parentheses.

(What happens to your spirit [after you die]?)
Your spirit—soon as you die, your spirit leaves you. (And where does the spirit go?) Well, it all depends . . . (On what?) You know, like some people say if you're good an' shit, your spirit goin' t'heaven . . . 'n' if you bad, your spirit goin' to hell. Well, bullshit! Your spirit goin' to hell anyway, good or bad. (Why?) Why? I'll tell you why. 'Cause, you see, doesn' nobody really know that it's a God, y'know, 'cause I mean I have seen black gods, pink gods, white gods, all color gods, and don't nobody know it's really a God. An' when they be sayin' if you good, you goin' t'heaven, tha's bullshit, 'cause you ain't goin' to no heaven 'cause it ain't no heaven for you to go to (Labov, 1970, pp. 164-165).

Labov summarizes the logic of the argument as follows: "(1) Everyone has a different idea of what God is like. (2) Therefore nobody really knows that God exists. (3) If there is a heaven, it was made by God. (4) If God doesn't exist, he couldn't have made heaven. (5) Therefore heaven doesn't exist. (6) You can't go somewhere that doesn't exist. (7) Therefore you can't go to heaven" (p. 165). Labov notes that some of the steps in the argument are implicit. He concludes that the individual can and does carry on conversations (this one largely in fun) that some of the steps, e.g., to statement (5), are not really logically sound. However, the gaps here are typical of the reasoning of many 15-year-olds in any culture.

To repeat, Labov's conclusion is that differences in syntactic form do not necessarily lead to differences in underlying logical abilities. He cautions us against jumping to conclusions about cognitive skills from a superficial look at a speaker's dialect. This conclusion has implications that are quite wide ranging. For a long time many theorists have speculated that the cognitive system is shaped to a considerable extent by the form of the language that is spoken. Here we have a case of linguistic diversity that does not lead to obviously different logical abilities. The relationship between language and cognition has been touched upon at various points in earlier chapters (e.g., Chapter 6, Chapter 8). We will now take up this relationship more explicitly.

Linguistic Diversity and Cognitive Categories

Many volumes have been filled with speculations about the relationship that exists between language and thinking. There is a wide range of opinions about the general nature of the relationship. It is probably true to say that every logically possible relation between the two has been championed by some theorist or other.

Most classical theorists (e.g., Aristotle) argued that the categories of thought determine the categories of language. According to this view, words are symbols for mental experience. An opposite, and more radical, view about the relationship between thought and language was expressed by the behaviorist

John B. Watson (1930). According to Watson, thought *is* language. Watson believed that during development speech becomes sub-vocal (like a very quiet whisper to oneself) and then goes completely "underground." Thought was said to be identical with this sub-vocal speech. In its radical form, this position has no adherents today; the counter-arguments are simply too massive. (The philosopher Herbert Feigl once said in a lecture that Watson "made up his windpipe that he had no mind," an apt attack on Watson's position.)

A less radical view, but one that is also opposed to the classical theory, is that language determines thought. According to this view, thought is not to be identified with sub-vocal language, but the "categories" of thought are determined by linguistic categories. Theorists in this camp are divided between those who think that language completely determines cognitive categories and those who merely say that language strongly influences cognitive categories.

Before discussing these several viewpoints, we should note that the question of the relation between language and thought is not really a single one. Rather, it is a tangled skein of interrelated questions. For example, there are both developmental and processing questions involved. The developmental question is concerned with the course of acquisition of language and its relation to the acquisition of conceptual categories. To oversimplify, a "Language-Determines-Thought" theorist will say that linguistic categories are acquired first and determine what cognitive categories are acquired. A "Thought-Determines-Language" theorist will say that cognitive development comes earlier in the life of the child and that the cognitive categories he develops determine the linguistic categories that he will acquire. Of coure there are few "pure" theorists of either type.

The processing question is concerned with whether our thoughts are formed in advance of the words that we utter or whether our ideas are formed in terms of the words themselves. A "Language-Determines-Thought" theorist will say that our thoughts *consist of* mental representations of our words. A "Thought-Determines-Language" theorist will argue that our ideas are at least partially formed in a non-linguistic mental code before they are given a linguistic cloak. In our discussion of sentence production (Chapter 6) we clearly adopted the latter view, although we did not spend much time saying why. We will now examine these positions more carefully.

Language Determines Thought

Although the classical doctrine (thought determines language) held sway for a very long time, the opposite opinion has had a good deal of influence during this century. Many theorists were impressed both by the tremendous diversity of languages that are found around the world and by the diversity of the cultures in which these languages are spoken. In an attempt to account for the cultural diversity, some theorists claimed that the cultural patterns grew out of or depended upon the linguistic patterns. According to this view, people have great flexibility in how they organize their experience, and language has an important impact on how experience is interpreted.

The individual who did the most to popularize the "Language-Determines-Thought" position was Benjamin Lee Whorf (1897–1941). Whorf is an interesting figure in that he was trained as a chemical engineer and spent his life working as a fire prevention engineer for the Hartford Fire Insurance Co. He was a successful businessman who also devoted himself to the study of American Indian languages and culture. His life is described by Carroll in the volume of Whorf's papers that Carroll collected (Whorf, 1956).

According to Whorf, the child's cognitive system is very plastic; that is, the system is susceptible of being organized in many different ways. The primary determinant of how it is organized is the structure of the language that the child acquires. Since, according to Whorf, linguistic structures are highly dissimilar in different languages, the resulting cognitive systems are also dissimilar. Thus, Whorf's views have two parts. The first claim is usually called the hypothesis of *linguistic determinism.* It says that linguistic structure determines cognitive structure. The second claim is called the hypothesis of *linguistic relativity.* It says that the resulting cognitive systems are highly different in speakers of different languages.

Whorf argued that, "We cut nature up . . . as we do largely because we are partners in an agreement to organize it in this way—an agreement . . . that is codified in the patterns of our language" (1956, p. 213). This statement does not imply that the speakers of a language are aware of the "agreement" to organize the world in some particular way. Rather, the language imposes the organization upon each new speaker of the language. Hence, this is a theory of cognitive development. For example, Whorf noted that some languages have separate words for different types of snow. A child who grows up speaking such a language will develop more cognitive categories for snow than will an English-speaking child. When the former child looks out at a snowy environment he will, in some sense, see it differently from a child who has but the one word *snow.*

To take another example, Whorf claimed that the Hopi Indians have a different sense of time than do speakers of English, French, German, etc. (these languages being highly similar, from Whorf's perspective). The reason for the difference in time perception is that tense is not marked in the familiar way in Hopi: "The timeless Hopi verb does not distinguish between the present, past, and future of the event itself but must always indicate what type of validity the speaker intends the statement to have: (a) report of an event; (b) expectation of an event; (c) generalization or law about events" (Whorf, 1956, p. 217). According to Whorf's perspective, the very way in which we organize something as seemingly basic as the flow of time is linguistically derived.

Whorf claimed that the perceptual events that we experience can be very different from those experienced by a speaker of another language who is standing beside us. When you look at the rainbow, how many colors do you see? Most adult English speakers see red, orange, yellow, green, blue, and purple, and the intermediate shades. The colors just named are the basic ones. Whorf would say that the colors which we perceive as basic result from the color-naming practices that we acquired when we learned English. There is some evidence that appears to be consistent with his view. Some languages do not divide the colors into the same number of basic categories as does English. One language may not distinguish between green and blue, for example. Therefore, a speaker of that language will not describe the rainbow in the same way that we do. Whorf went a lot further, however; he said that the speaker will actually experience the rainbow differently.

Linguistic Determinism: The Strong Version. The view that our concepts are formed by the categories of our language has come to be called the "strong" version of the Whorfian hypothesis. It has been pointed out by many people, notably by Lenneberg (1953), that Whorf never provided any evidence for the strong version of his hypothesis. The only data that Whorf presented were observations about the linguistic practices of individuals. He did not provide any non-linguistic evidence about the cognitive states of the speakers. This resulted in circular reasoning. It goes like this: Language determines categories of thought. Categories of thought are different for speakers of divergent languages. How do we know? Well, look at all the different ways in which languages code the world, i.e., look at the different linguistic practices that exist. The hypothesis started with a set of observations about linguistic practices and ended with those same observations. For the theory to be properly supported, independent evidence about cognition must also be given.

There are some rather compelling reasons for doubting the strong version of the Whorfian hypothesis. A Minnesotan can recognize as many varieties of snow as can an Eskimo. The Minnesotan will express these differences by using phrases instead of the Eskimo's single words, but that is a relatively minor difference. Furthermore, if we test the abilities of individuals to discriminate colors, speakers from different language groups do not differ from one another. Their basic perceptual systems are highly similar. Also, Whorf's interpretations of sentences from, say, Hopi were based upon an analysis of the superficial structure of the sentences. He often interpreted the meaning of a sentence as the simple conjunction of the meanings of its parts. As we have seen earlier, that is a serious mistake. The meaning of a sentence depends upon its structure, and in particular upon its underlying structure. As Miller and McNeill (1969) point out, if one wants to understand the meaning of a sentence like *It is a dripping spring,* it will not do to look up the meaning of each word in a dictionary and then assume that the meaning of the sentence is simply that set of definitions strung together. The result would be nonsense. Whorf often made an analogous error when giving the meaning of a Hopi sentence. To this day there is no convincing evidence in favor of the strong version of the hypothesis.

Linguistic Determinism: The Weak Version. There is also a "weak" version of Whorf's hypothesis. According to this version of the hypothesis, the lexical items and linguistic structures that a language provides can have an important influence upon thought processes even though they do not determine all such processes. Brown (1976, p. 129) notes that "What is expressed easily, rapidly, briefly, uniformly, perhaps obligatorily in one language may be expressed in another only by lengthy constructions that vary from one person to another, take time to put together, and are certainly not obligatory." Those concepts which are easily or obligatorily expressed in the speaker's language (e.g., tense in Standard English) may be more available to his cognitive system than concepts which are not obligatorily expressed (e.g., whether the activity is habitual or momentary).

The weak version of the hypothesis is a good deal easier to accept on the face of it than is the strong version. Most of the negative evidence discussed above applies only to the strong version. There are a number of anecdotal observations which support the weak version. To cite just one, consider the influence that notation has on mathematical ability. The Arabic number system permits us to carry out such mental operations as addition, multiplication, etc. with considerably more ease than the Roman system does. What is XIV times XIII? To solve this you will probably translate the problem into the Arabic system, and for good reason. In the Arabic system the place that a digit holds plays a more important role in the calculation than it does in the Roman system. This fact, along with a few others, leads to easier mental manipulations of Arabic numbers. In his review of J. R. Newman's *The world of mathematics,* George Miller (1957) pointed out the importance of notation in the history of mathematics. As you may know, both Newton and Leibnitz independently devised calculus, and at about the same time. They chose different notations in which to represent the concepts, however. Unfortunately, the two became involved in a bitter dispute over who had first come up with the ideas. British mathematicians were loyal to Newton and adopted his notational system; continental mathematicians adopted Leibnitz's notational system. Liebnitz's system was more congenial to work within (it is basically the notation that is taught today). For over a century British mathematics lagged behind work on the continent, and it is tempting to suggest that this difference was due to the fact that Leibnitz's system was cognitively more economical. It took so much attention to keep Newton's notation clear that more substantial insights were missed. Although anecdotal, this is better evidence than anything offered for the strong version of Whorf's hypothesis.

Experimental Tests of Determinism: Question Answering. There are other, less anecdotal reasons for believing that the structure of language has a role in influencing thought. We cannot survey this whole area, but we will look at some examples of the existing work. First we will briefly examine an approach that tries to relate a theory of problem solving to certain aspects of linguistic theory.

Specifically, this approach claims that the linguistic information which is stored with lexical items has an impact upon the problem-solving process. Then we will look somewhat more comprehensively at a "classical" area of Whorfian research, the relationship between color names and the perception of and memory for colors.

Solving problems and answering questions of the sort shown in sentence (11) seem to require "thinking." How do we do it?

(11) If Lee isn't **as** bad as Joe, then who is best?

There are many theories about this process. We will here discuss one proposed by H. Clark (1969). Clark claims that the solution to problems like (11) involves a series of steps, some of which he has tried to specify. The first step is to code the sentence into an underlying representation, i.e., to recover the basic propositions. Clark does not say how this is done, but he does state that the underlying representation is propositional.

In the next step, the subject examines the statement and the question to see if the comparative terms are similar or "congruent." In order to clarify this, look at (12–13).

(12) If Lee is better than Joe, then who is best?

(13) If Joe is worse than Lee, then who is best?

In (12) the form of the comparative (*better*) in the statement is the same as the form of the question (*best*). They are both positive terms and are said to be congruent. In (13) the form of the comparative (*worse*) is not congruent with the form of the question. One is negative, the other positive. If (12) and (13) asked, "Who is worst?" then the latter sentence would be congruent. Clark argues that congruent questions are easier to process, that they are understood more rapidly than non-congruent questions.

There is one more step in the solution process, and for us it is the most important one. Clark notes that the word *better* does not necessarily imply that either individual is good. We can use (12) even if we are comparing, say, two big losers at poker. However, when we use the word *worse,* we are presupposing that both individuals are at the low end of the scale. We would not ask (13) if both were big winners at the card game. Words like *better, taller, smarter,* etc. can refer to dimensions and do not have to be used to refer to individuals who are at the upper end of the dimension. Thus, *Tom is smarter (taller) than Tim* can be said without presupposing that either individual is particularly smart or tall. According to Clark, the same is not true for *worse, shorter, dumber,* etc. *Tim is dumber (shorter) than Tom,* presupposes that both individuals are at the low end of the intelligence or height scales. Some linguists have said that the term which refers to both the dimension and also one end of it (e.g., *good*) is *unmarked.* The term which only names one end of a dimension (e.g., *bad*) is *marked.*

Now that we have the concept of lexical marking, it is easy to understand Clark's last step. He simply says that marked lexical items are more complex, that it takes longer to form the mental representations of marked comparatives. He calls this the "principle of lexical marking." It predicts that sentences using *bad* will take longer to comprehend than sentences using *good*. In general, sentences with positive adjectives will be easier than those with negatives. Clark (1974) has reviewed a body of evidence which supports this claim. We can now see why, according to Clark, even such a simple question as (11) may have stopped you momentarily. The question term (*best*) is not congruent with the comparative adjective (*bad*), and the comparative adjective is the marked form. Subjects do take a long time to answer questions like (11). In one of Clark's studies the mean response time was 1.73 seconds. In comparison, questions like (12) which are both congruent and unmarked took only .61 seconds to answer. This is quite a substantial difference in response time.

Not everyone agrees with Clark's theory (e.g., Huttenlocher & Higgins, 1971). However, if we accept it, then we are accepting the idea that aspects of linguistic structure (e.g., lexical marking, congruency, deep structure propositions) play an important role in some varieties of problem solving. This may be taken as evidence supporting a weak version of the "Language-Determines-Thought" position. It is important to note, however, that Clark himself (1973) believes that such "linguistic" properties as lexical marking originate in the ways in which our perceptual and cognitive systems are organized. Thus, for him, the basic determiner is cognitive, not lingusitic.

Experimental Tests of Determinism: Color. The number of basic color terms can differ widely between two languages. According to the linguistic determinism and linguistic relativity hypotheses, when two languages do differ in this respect, the speakers of these languages should experience the world of color differently. Color concepts, not just color names, are said to differ for the two sets of speakers. Earlier we criticized Whorf for relying solely on linguistic evidence to support this claim. In fact, a number of psychologists have tried to get independent evidence about the speaker's cognitive system for colors. We delayed discussing this work until now because some of the data has been interpreted as supporting the "weak" version of Whorf's hypothesis. We will see that the bulk of the evidence suggests quite a different conclusion.

Oddly enough, most of the tests of Whorf's hypotheses have used speakers of only a single language (usually English). This research tradition was begun by Brown and Lenneberg (1954), and much of it has been ably summarized by Brown (1976). These investigators reasoned approximately as follows. If some colors are more "nameable" than others, then those easily named colors ought to have a special status in the individual's conceptual system. In particular, if one is shown a color for which the language has a basic name, then that color should be more memorable. We can test the memorability of colors by first showing subjects a color and later asking them to find that color among a large array of various colors. They should be able to pick out the original color with greater accuracy if it is referred to by one of the basic color terms in the language. This is the test that Brown and Lenneberg carried out.

The first step that Brown and Lenneberg took was to find out which are the basic or best colors for English speakers. To do this they devised a scale called "codability." Colors that score high on this scale are those which have short names that subjects agree upon, and which are named quickly when shown. Brown and Lenneberg tested a set of colors and obtained a codability score for each. They then picked out the most codable colors from around the color wheel (the circle of hues that runs from red through orange, yellow, green, etc. back around to violet and purple). They also picked sixteen other colors that were at intermediate points around the color wheel. These latter colors had lower codability scores, and therefore were not considered to be basic. The investigators then briefly presented one (or more) of these colors to the subjects and, after a variable delay, asked them to pick out the color or colors they had seen from a larger array of 120 color chips.

The results of the experiment were interpreted as supporting a weak version of the Whorfian hypothesis. When the delay between presentation of the color and presentation of the 120-color test array was short, then codability did not matter much. However, when the delay was longer (seven minutes), and when the number of colors originally presented was relatively large (four), codability was important. The highly codable colors were picked out of the test array with significantly greater accuracy than the low-codability colors. In one case the correlation between recognition accuracy and codability was as high as .52, with highly codable colors being the most memorable. Here, then, is a correlation between the linguistic naming practices of a set of speakers and an important facet of their cognition, namely their memory for colors.

In some later studies (e.g., Lantz & Stefflre, 1964) it was found that the important predictor of color memorability was not Brown and Lenneberg's codability index. Rather, the "communication accuracy" scores for the colors predicted memorability. Communication accuracy is an index of how well one subject can describe a color so that a second subject can pick that color out of a larger array. The point remains, however, that the naming practices of the speakers did appear to predict the scores on another, cognitive task involving those colors.

In some related work, Brown (1958) argued that the names we give things affect the way that we structure certain parts of our conception of the world. In particular, Brown was concerned with the way in which parents name objects for children. In naming, say, a dime, we could call it *money, metal, a 1978 dime,* or many other things. Brown argued that parents name objects at a level of abstraction that has the most utility or everyday usefulness for the child. Some objects are called *dogs* because for many purposes the child is supposed to treat all such objects in the same way (be wary). During development the child will learn to be both more concrete (*poodles, collies,* etc.) and more abstract (*animals, pets,* etc.)

in his naming practices. Brown was suggesting, as he later (1976, p. 139) said, "that the names [for objects] given the child fixed the texture of his world in various parts . . . " (In other words, language determines thought.) By 1976, however, Brown went on to say ". . . but, of course, that need not be so. The language may largely reflect the given structure of reality." This latter remark is certainly a move away from the linguistic determinism that stimulated some of the earlier work. What happened in the intervening time to make linguistic determinism, and the Whorfian view in general, so much less attractive? To answer this question, let us return again to the work on color.

Thought Determines Language: Color Again

Much of the research involving color terms assumed that languages were free to divide up the color spectrum in any way their speakers chose. Thus, a boundary between color names could be put right in the middle of the color that English speakers would call a good blue. On the side toward green the blue would be called one thing, and on the side toward purple the good blue would be called something else. It turns out, however, that this assumption is not correct.

Probably the best evidence about the way in which speakers of different languages divide the color spectrum was provided by Berlin and Kay (1969). These investigators used an array of 329 colors which they presented to speakers of 20 diverse languages. Berlin and Kay first tried to ascertain the basic color terms in each language. For Berlin and Kay, the basic color terms could not be compounds such as *blue-green*; basic terms stand alone. Also, the authors were cautious about saying that a word which names an object (e.g., *lime*) is a basic color term. After they had the basic color terms for a language, Berlin and Kay then placed a piece of clear acetate over the 329 colors and asked the informant to draw lines around or to 'map' the colors that are named by each term. The informants were also asked to mark with an 'X' the best or most typical example of each color in their basic color vocabulary. This color is also referred to as the *focal color*.

There are a number of important results from the Berlin and Kay study. First, the basic color vocabularies of the 20 languages are restricted to a small set of terms. Some languages make do with two basic color terms, and no language has more than eleven. Second, the focal or best examples of color terms are the *same* across the 20 languages. That is, if language *A* has, say, four basic color terms and language *B* has six, the four focal colors chosen by speakers of *A* will closely correspond to four of the six focal colors chosen by speakers of *B*. True, the boundaries between the colors are highly variable across languages, but the focal or best examples of the colors are not variable. To return to the example at the start of this section, no language divides the color wheel in such a way that the English speaker's focal blue is divided in half.

Although not directly relevant to our concerns, it is worth noting that

Berlin and Kay also found evidence suggesting that there is a standard order in which basic color terms are added to languages. If a language has only two color terms, they refer to dark vs. light colors. If a third basic color term is added, it invariably refers to red. The next color terms to enter a language refer to yellow and green (or green and yellow; these two occur in either order). If there are six basic terms, the sixth one is always blue, etc.

For our purposes, the importance of the Berlin and Kay work is that it strongly argues against the hypothesis that languages are free to divide the world of experience in any convenient way. In the realm of color, at least, there appear to be some basic constraints that limit the way in which this aspect of our experience is coded in the language. This means that language is more a reflection than a cause of basic cognitive and perceptual categories. This conclusion is, of course, directly contrary to Whorf's hypotheses.

Further evidence damaging to Whorf's thesis was gathered by Heider and Olivier (1972). These authors also worked in the color domain, but their study had an important addition that was missing from previous experiments on color memory; it involved speakers from two quite different languages. Heider and Olivier studied both English speakers and speakers of Dani. The latter is spoken by a Stone Age agricultural people of Indonesian New Guinea. They have only two basic color terms: *mola* which refers to bright, warm colors; and *mili* which refers to dark, cool colors. Heider and Olivier obtained naming data and recognition accuracy (memory) data from both English and Dani speakers. First the speakers were shown an array of 160 color chips and asked to name them. The Dani used only the two terms *mola* and *mili* for the entire stimulus array. Then the subjects were shown a single color chip for five seconds. After waiting 30 seconds, they were shown a 40-chip array and asked to pick out the color chip they had just seen.

Two kinds of analyses were performed on the data. First the authors determined the "structure" of the Dani color system as revealed by their naming responses. That is, they determined exactly which colors were called *mola* and which were called *mili*. They did the same thing with the English color system, determining which colors were called *red*, which *green*, etc. Second, they determined the "structure" of the colors in memory. This structure was determined by seeing how often each color was confused with every other color in the memory task. If color i is often confused with color j, then the subject will be likely to pick j out of the color array after having seen i. In this case i and j are said to be psychologically close to one another. By looking at the entire set of confusions that are made in the memory task, it is possible to determine which colors are similar to which others. In this way, one maps the psychological structure of the color system. According to Whorf's hypothesis, the data from the naming part of the experiment (the naming structure) should correspond to the data from the memory experiment (the memory structure). The memory structure should resemble the naming structure.

The structures that were derived from the Dani and English naming data were not highly similar. For example, the Dani consistently named all bright colors *mola* and virtually ignored their distinct hues (that is, bright red and bright green were both called *mola*). Of course, bright colors of different hues were far apart in the naming structure for English speakers. In contrast, however, the structures that resulted from the memory data were very similar for the two groups. The Dani and the English speakers tended to confuse the same colors with each other in memory, and tended to keep apart the same colors. This is a case, then, in which the naming data do not predict the memory data. Heider and Olivier concluded that the nature of color memory is not much influenced by language.

Two other experiments carried out by Heider (1972; Rosch, 1973) cast further doubt on the importance of naming practices for the perception of colors. These studies also lend support to the suggestion that there is something universal about the focal colors of Berlin and Kay. First, Heider looked at the recognition accuracy for colors among Dani speakers, concentrating on colors that are either focal or not focal for English speakers. For example, she tested recognition accuracy for a focal red vs. a non-focal red. Recall that Dani does not have a word that refers only to red. She found that recognition accuracy was higher for the focal red than for the non-focal red. Here, then, is a case of the naming practices in language *A* (English) predicting the memory structure in language *B* (Dani). This can hardly be a case of linguistic determinism.

Second, Rosch (formerly Heider) carried out a learning experiment with the Dani, again making use of the focal vs. non-focal distinction. In this study she picked eight colors from positions around the color wheel. She also selected two additional colors to accompany each of the eight, one from either side of each (e.g., if the color was green, then one color was selected from the yellow side of green and one was chosen from the blue side). Thus, the stimulus set consisted of a total of 24 colors in eight groups of three colors each. Three different stimulus sets were chosen, though here we will discuss only two of them. In Set 1 the central color from each of the eight groups was a focal color. In Set 2 the central color of each group was a non-focal or intermediate color. Therefore, the Set 2 stimuli tended to violate natural color concepts. An English speaker looking at one of the groups from Set 2 might say that it contained both yellow and green.

The Dani subjects were presented the 24 stimuli from one or the other of the stimulus sets and were asked to learn a common Dani word for each of the three members of a color group. That is, they learned to give eight responses to the 24 stimuli; a common response was assigned to each of the three members of a color group. The prediction from Whorf's hypothesis is straightforward: there should be no difference in the time that it takes to learn the eight responses to the two sets of stimuli. Set 1 and Set 2 should be equally easy to learn. If, in contrast, the focal colors are somehow special, then Set 1 should be easier to learn than Set 2, which mixes colors from two focal areas in each of its eight stimulus groups. The subjects were given five trials per day (where a trial consisted of presenting all 24 colors) until they could go through the entire list of 24 without making an error.

Figure 13.1 shows the results of the experiment; it plots the number of errors made per day (24 possible). As can be seen, the subjects who learned the Set 1 stimuli made many fewer errors than did those who learned the Set 2 stimuli. Speakers of Dani found it easier to group colors around focal than around non-focal examples. This again supports the idea that there is something special about the focal colors. They are perceptually salient, not because English gives them basic color names but for physiological reasons (e.g., De Valois & Jacobs, 1968). It has even been shown that the basic color categories of four-month-old infants are similar to those of adults (Bornstein, Kessen & Weiskopf, 1976), a finding that cannot be due to linguistic similarities. Language, in this case, reflects the categories of perception; it does not form them.

To review, much of the early work that appeared to support a weak version of Whorf's hypothesis was carried out with colors as stimuli. There is now a considerable body of evidence that the linguistic system does not have the freedom to divide the color system in just any imaginable way. Even though the borders between focal color areas are flexible, the speakers of all languages agree on which colors are focal. The results of research involving color support the hypothesis that perceptual universals affect language. They do not support the hypotheses of linguistic relativity and linguistic determinism.

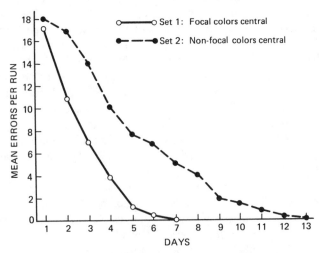

Figure 13.1. Average number of errors per day made by Dani speakers while learning a common response to stimuli centered on focal vs. non-focal colors. (Figure modified from Rosch, E. Natural categories. *Cognitive Psychology,* 1973, *4,* 328–350. Copyright 1973 by Academic Press, Inc. Used by permission.)

The work on color memorability and learning has had something of an ironic outcome. The work was begun when the idea of linguistic relativity was dominant, and the studies were devised to test that concept. Rather than supporting the hypothesis of linguistic relativity, however, the research has ended up supporting the opposite hypothesis. It appears now that there are perceptual universals which are represented in the languages of the world, although the way in which they are represented varies among the languages. Not every language has a term for each focal color, for example. But to the extent that color terms are in the language, they reflect the universals that we have stated. It is clear, therefore, that a strong version of the Whorfian hypothesis cannot be true. Our cognitive systems are not completely pliable and sensitive to whatever distinctions a language happens to make. Indeed, the languages of the world seem to reflect perceptual–cognitive universals.

Thought and Language

Although we have argued against a strong version of Whorf's hypotheses, there may be something to the weaker versions. The versions we have in mind, however, are probably so weak that Whorf would not recognize them. Learning a common term for a set of objects permits the set to be more readily manipulated in our cognitive systems. As a result, those objects in the culture that are referred to by a common linguistic term will tend to be manipulated together in the speaker's cognitive system. It is important to note, however, that the language does not have complete freedom to sort just any set of objects together. As we get further from perceptual objects such as shape and color, our flexibility in choosing what can be members of a common class may increase, but there probably are always cognitive constraints upon what conceptual (as well as perceptual) objects can go together as members of a useful cognitive category.

Let us return for a moment to the example of the verb *be* in Black English. We can ask whether speakers of BE are more aware of whether an event is momentary or ongoing than are speakers of SE. According to the weak version of Whorf's hypothesis, they should be. Since the language requires that this aspect of the event be coded in the verb system of BE, speakers must attend to it. Speakers of SE are not required to encode this aspect of events in their speech, and therefore they may not be as aware of the distinction.

We do not want to make the same mistake that Whorf made and stop here. The linguistic distinction is not in itself evidence about the cognitive state of the language user. We know of no direct evidence that bears on the point, so our comments must remain at the level of speculation for now. But there are plenty of reasons to be skeptical about the claim that speakers of BE are more aware of the ongoing or momentary nature of the events they describe than are speakers of SE. One reason for skepticism has to do with the notion of "awareness" that we have been using so loosely up to this point. When a language makes use of a distinction this fact alone does not imply that the language user is consciously aware of that distinction. The processing which makes use of the distinction may occur so automatically as to be outside of the speaker's conscious awareness.

For example, we are almost always *un*aware of whether the final phonological segment of singular nouns is voiced or unvoiced, but we consistently make use of the voicing information when we add plural markers. Words ending in voiceless consonants are made plural by adding /s/ while those ending in voiced consonants are pluralized by adding /z/. The operations that carry out this process occur outside of our awareness. Do we "pay attention" to the voicing feature when we form plurals? In one sense, we do. Our production mechanism takes voicing into account as it carries out its operations. In another sense, we don't. We are not consciously aware of the distinction and, in fact, probably were not aware of it even when we acquired it. A textbook can point out the distinction, but even then it does not become part of our conscious awareness as we are actually producing sentences and making use of it.

Analogously, it is not obvious that speakers of BE are consciously aware of the distinction between the ongoing or temporary state of an event even as they encode this information, by either using or not using *be,* in the sentences they produce. So, before we can answer the question of whether or not the cognitive state of the speaker of BE is different from that of the speaker of SE, we must clarify what is going to count as a difference in cognitive state.

In sum, then, whether or not one concludes that systematic linguistic differences lead to systematic cognitive differences depends on what one means by the latter phrase. If it is taken to mean, "differences in conscious awareness of aspects of the environment," then the answer to the question is not likely to be the same as when it means "differences in processing operations." In the latter case the weak version of Whorf's hypothesis is reduced to a truism. That is, if the linguistic code is different between two dialects (and it is, by definition) then the processing operations of the speakers who possess the two dialects must also be different. In the former case, however, more work has to be done before the hypothesis is shown to be true.

In order to make clear the relationship between language and thinking, we must first clarify our picture of each of these separately. We need to have a better theory of cognitive processes in general and of language processing in particular. In limited domains, such as solving the kinds of word problems that Clark put to his subjects, we have "mini-theories" of thought. In these cases some of the relationships between our theory of language and our theory of thinking have been spelled out. But Clark's theory and the other mini-theories that exist, even if correct, will not generalize to all aspects of question answering, let alone to all aspects of thinking.

Universals Again

We began with apparent diversity, and we end (at least in the color domain) with seeming universality. In Chapter 1 we also started by discussing diversity in languages and then presented a list of some universals which, we said, helped us to characterize our subject matter. In the light of what has transpired in the intervening chapters, it may be useful to examine the list again to see whether all of the universals have survived. We will also be able to say a bit more about the types of language universals that we discussed earlier.

Chapter 1 looked briefly at four universals. The first of these was *discreteness*; it had to do with the fact that linguistic messages are constructed from discrete elements. This universal still holds, and we now have some idea about both the nature of the discrete elements involved in language and the problem that they pose for speech perception. We have argued that there is a fixed set of features out of which all of the phonological segments in all of the languages are built. We also noted that morphemes and words are built out of a set of phonological segments, and we distinguished between surface and underlying phonology. The latter concept was even used in describing a model of reading. We saw that many speech errors during sentence production could be nicely accounted for by appealing to the concepts of feature and phonological segment (phoneme), and we looked at some evidence suggesting that infants perceive many of the same phonological contrasts as do adults. In sum, this universal has proved useful to us throughout the book, and we will certainly keep it on the list.

Two other universals introduced in Chapter 1 were *arbitrariness* and *duality of patterning*. The first says that there is no necessary connection between the sound of a word and its meaning. The second says that the language system can be divided into two large sub-systems, one having to do with sound and the other with meaning. These two universals are somewhat related. If the relationship between sounds and meaning were not arbitrary, then there would not be two sub-systems but only one.

We have no reason to doubt the universality of arbitrariness. Although we have not discussed the evidence for "phonetic symbolism" (the idea that the sound of a word gives some hint of its meaning), we believe that such symbolism plays an extremely minor role in language, if it plays any at all (see Taylor & Taylor, 1965, for a review).

We have seen that both the phonological and the semantic systems are rule-governed and that the rules for the former system are quite different in organization from those for the latter. Rules for the semantic system are far from completely worked out.

In the schema for a transformational grammar that we gave in Chapter 2, we divided the system into three sections, phonology, syntax, and semantics. Does this mean that we should have a trio of patterning rather than a duality of patterning? The answer to this question is controversial. Chomsky has often argued (e.g., 1975) that there are some universal syntactic operations which do not have any universal semantic interpretation. According to this idea, syntax is, at least in part, a separate and autonomous branch of the linguistic system. A trio of patterning is the result: phonology, syntax, and semantics. Other theorists disagree about the existence of a dividing line between syntax and semantics.

Psycholinguistic theories of performance or acquisition are not developed to the point where they can settle this issue, but most theorists would agree that there is at least duality of patterning.

In Chapter 1 we said that one of the most important universals was *openness,* the ability of language users to produce and comprehend an unlimited number of new sentences. The universal of openness posed one of the major theoretical problems for us. In order to solve this problem, we said that the language user possesses an internalized set of rules. The rules are finite in number, but permit an unlimited number of sentences to be produced and comprehended. In Chapter 2 we looked at some technical aspects of how a finite rule set can meet this goal. In the course of the book we discussed how such rules might be psychologically represented, but we were not able to come to a definitive decision about the way in which such information is coded. Thus, we have plenty of evidence that the language system is rule-governed and that openness characterizes every language, although we still do not know the mental code in which the rules are formulated.

Chomsky and other linguists have been concerned with finding universal regularities among languages. As Chomsky argues, such regularities will tell us a lot about the operation of the human cognitive system. His aim is to build a "universal grammar," one that specifies "the system of principles, conditions, nd rules that are elements or properties of all human languages not merely by a cident but by [biological] necessity . . . " (1975, p. 29). We would like to have a universal psycholinguistics as well. Such a science would specify the system of principles, conditions, and rules that are elements or properties of all human language processing. There's a puzzle worth solving!

Summary

The relationship between language and thought has been discussed since ancient time. Classical theorists believed that thought determines language while a number of more recent theorists have argued, in contrast, that language determines thought.

To help examine these issues, a dialect that is different from Standard English, namely Black English, was described. This dialect has a separate historical source from Standard English. It probably began as a pidgin and became a creole. There are a number of structural differences between Black English and Standard English. In particular, Black English verbs indicate whether the activity is continuous or momentary. Also, the rules for tense and number differ somewhat between the two dialects. The differences in syntactic form do not necessarily lead to differences in the underlying logical abilities of their respective speakers, however.

The view that language determines thought (linguistic determinism) was popularized by Whorf. There are both strong and weak versions of linguistic determinism. The strong version, which says that perceptions and concepts are formed out of the categories of language, has little evidence to support it. The weak version of the hypothesis states that language structures can influence cognitive processes and categories.

Tests of the weak version have been carried out using reasoning problems and, more commonly, memory for colors. Some early evidence suggested that colors which are highly codable in a language led to more correct answers on a recognition test than did low codability colors. More recently it has been shown that speakers of diverse languages do not react differently on color memory tests. Rather than language determining the color categories that are available to speakers, it appears that there is a universal system of color categories that are reflected in language. The basic or focal colors are determined by perceptual considerations, not linguistic ones.

The linguistic universals that were introduced in Chapter 1 were briefly reviewed here. We found that they had survived the intervening chapters and that they still pose deep and exciting questions about human nature.

SUGGESTED READINGS

Our discussion of Black English drew heavily from Dillard's (1972) book; it is worth consulting in the original. Whorf's writings are collected in a 1956 book. His ideas are carefully examined by Miller and McNeill (1969) and by Brown (1976). There are numerous interesting discussions concerning language universals in the volume edited by Hook (1969).

Bibliography

Abbs, J. H., & Sussman, H. M. Neurophysiological feature detectors and speech perception: A discussion of theoretical implications. *Journal of Speech and Hearing Research,* 1971, *14,* 23-36.

Abercrombie, D. *Elements of general phonetics.* Edinburgh: University of Edinburgh Press, 1966.

Abramson, A. S., & Lisker, L. Voice timing: Cross-language experiments in identification and discrimination. Paper presented at the meetings of the Acoustical Society of America, Ottawa, May, 1968.

Ades, A. E. Bilateral component in speech perception? *Journal of the Acoustical Society of America,* 1974, *56,* 610-616.

Akmajian, A., & Heny, F. *An introduction to the principles of transformational syntax.* Cambridge, Mass.: M.I.T. Press, 1975.

Ammon, P. R. The perception of grammatical relations in sentences: A methodological exploration. *Journal of Verbal Learning and Verbal Behavior,* 1968, *7,* 869-875.

Anderson, J. R. *Language, memory and thought.* Hillsdale, N.J.: Lawrence Erlbaum Associates, 1976.

Anderson, J. R., & Bower, G. H. *Human associative memory.* Washington, D.C.: V. H. Winston, 1973.

Anglin, J. M. *Word, object, and conceptual development.* New York: W. W. Norton, 1977.

Atkinson, K., MacWhinney, B., & Stoel, C. An experiment on the recognition of babbling. *Papers and Reports on Child Language Development* (Stanford University), 1970, *1*, 71–76.

Baars, B. J., Motley, M. T., & MacKay, D. G. Output editing for lexical status in artificially elicited slips of the tongue. *Journal of Verbal Learning and Verbal Behavior*, 1975, *14*, 382–391.

Baker, C. L. *Introduction to transformational generative syntax*. Englewood Cliffs, N.J.: Prentice-Hall, 1977.

Baratz, J. C. Teaching reading in an urban Negro school system. In F. Williams (Ed.), *Language and poverty: Perspectives on a theme*. Chicago: Markham Publishing Co., 1970.

Barclay, J. R. Noncategorical perception of a voiced stop: A replication. *Perception & Psychophysics*, 1972, *11*, 269–273.

Barclay, J. R. The role of comprehension in remembering sentences. *Cognitive Psychology*, 1973, *4*, 229–254.

Bar-Hillel, Y. Universal semantics and philosophy of language: Quandries and prospects. In J. Puhvel (Ed.), *Substance and structure of language*. Berkeley: University of California Press, 1969.

Bar-Hillel, Y. *Aspects of language*. Jerusalem: The Magnes Press, 1970.

Baron, J. Phonemic stage not necessary for reading. *Quarterly Journal of Experimental Psychology*, 1973, *25*, 241–246.

Bartlett, F. C. *Remembering: A study in experimental and social psychology*. Cambridge: Cambridge University Press, 1932.

Bates, R. R. A study in the acquisition of language. Unpublished Ph.D. dissertation, The University of Texas at Austin, 1969.

Bay, E. Ontogeny of stable speech areas in the human brain. In E. H. Lenneberg & E. Lenneberg (Eds.), *Foundations of language development, Vol. 2*. New York: Academic Press, 1975. pp. 21–30.

Beilin, H., & Spontak, G. Active-passive transformations and operational reversibility. Paper presented at the Biennial Meetings of the Society for Research in Child Development, Santa Monica, California, March, 1969.

Bellugi, U. The development of interrogative structures in children's speech. In K. Riegel (Ed.), *The development of language functions*. University of Michigan Language Development Program, Report No. 8, 1965, pp. 103–138.

Bellugi, U. The acquisition of negation. Unpublished Ed.D. dissertation, Harvard University, 1967.

Bellugi, U. Simplification in children's language. In R. Huxley & E. Ingram (Eds.), *Language acquisition: Models and methods*. New York: Academic Press, 1971, pp. 95–117. © 1971 by Academic Press. Used by permission.

Bellugi, U., & Fischer, S. A comparison of sign language and spoken language. *Cognition*, 1973, *1*, 173–200.

Berlin, B., & Kay, P. *Basic color terms: Their universality and evolution*. Berkeley: University of California Press, 1969.

Bever, T. G. The cognitive basis for linguistic structures. In J. R. Hayes (Ed.), *Cognition and the development of language.* New York: Wiley, 1970, pp. 279-362.

Bever, T. G. The influence of speech performance on linguistic structure. In G. B. Flores d'Arcais and W. J. M. Levelt (Eds.), *Advances in psycholinguistics.* Amsterdam: North Holland Publishing Co., 1970, pp. 4-30.

Bever, T. G. Cerebral asymmetries in humans are due to the differentiation of two incompatible processes: Holistic and analytic. In D. Aaronson & R. W. Rieber (Eds.), *Developmental psycholinguistics and communication disorders.* New York: New York Academy of Sciences, 1975, pp. 251-262.

Bever, T. G., & Chiarello, R. J. Cerebral dominance in musicians and non-musicians. *Science,* 1974, *185,* 537-539.

Bever, T. G., Lackner, J., & Kirk, R. The underlying structures of sentences are the primary units of immediate speech processing. *Perception & Psychophysics,* 1969, *5,* 225-234.

Bierwisch, M. Semantics. In J. Lyons (Ed.), *New horizons in linguistics.* Baltimore: Penguin Books, 1970, pp. 161-185.

Bloom, L. *Language development: Form and function in emerging grammars.* Cambridge, Mass.: M.I.T. Press, 1970.

Bloom, L. *One word at a time.* The Hague: Mouton, 1973.

Bloom, L. (Ed.), *Selected readings in language development.* New York: Wiley, 1977.

Bloom, L., Hood, L., & Lightbrown, P. Imitation in language development: If, when, and why. *Cognitive Psychology,* 1974, *6,* 380-420.

Bloom, L., Lightbrown, P., & Hood, L. Structure and variation in child language. *Monographs of the Society for Research in Child Development,* 1975, *40,* No. 2 (Whole No. 160).

Bloom, L., Miller, P., & Hood, L. Variation and reduction as aspects of competence in language development. In A. D. Pick (Ed.), *Minnesota Symposium on Child Psychology, Vol. 9.* Minneapolis: University of Minnesota Press, 1975, pp. 3-55.

Bloomfield, L. *Language.* New York: Holt, Rinehart, and Winston, 1933.

Bogen, J. E. The other side of the brain. I: Dysgraphia and dyscopia following cerebral commissurotomy. *Bulletin of the Los Angeles Neurological Society,* 1969, *34,* 73-105. (a)

Bogen, J. E. The other side of the brain. II: An appositional mind. *Bulletin of the Los Angeles Neurological Society,* 1969, *34,* 135-162. (b)

Bogen, J. E., & Bogen, G. M. The other side of the brain. III: The corpus callosum and creativity. *Bulletin of the Los Angeles Neurological Society,* 1969, *34,* 191-220.

Bogen, J. E., & Vogel, P. J. Cerebral commissurotomy in man. Preliminary case report. *Bulletin of the Los Angeles Neurological Society,* 1962, *27,* 169-172.

Boomer, D. S. Hesitation and grammatical encoding. *Language and Speech,* 1965, *8,* 148-158.

Boomer, D. S. Review of F. Goldman-Eisler, *Psycholinguistics: Experiments in spontaneous speech.* New York: Academic Press, 1968. *Lingua,* 1970, *25,* 152-164.

Boomer, D. S., & Laver, J. D. M. Slips of the tongue. *British Journal of Disorders of Communication,* 1968, *3,* 1-12.

Bornstein, M. H., Kessen, W., & Weiskopf, S. The categories of hue in infancy. *Science,* 1976, *191,* 201-202.

Bower, T. G. *Development in infancy.* San Francisco: W. H. Freeman, 1974.

Bowerman, M. *Early syntactic development: A cross-linguistic study with special reference to Finnish.* Cambridge: Cambridge University Press, 1973.

Bowerman, M. Commentary. In L. Bloom, P. Lightbrown, & L. Hood. Structure and variation in child language. *Monographs of the Society for Research in Child Development,* 1975, *40,* No. 2 (Serial No. 160), 80-90.

Braine, M. D. S. Length constraints, reduction rules, and holophrastic processes in children's word combinations. *Journal of Verbal Learning and Verbal Behavior,* 1974, *13,* 448-456.

Braine, M. D. S. Children's first word combinations. *Monographs of the Society for Research in Child Development,* 1976, *41,* No. 1 (Serial No. 164).

Bransford, J. D., Barclay, J. R., & Franks, J. J. Sentence memory: A constructive versus interpretive approach. *Cognitive Psychology,* 1972, *3,* 193-209.

Bransford, J. D., & Franks, J. J. The abstraction of linguistic ideas. *Cognitive Psychology,* 1971, *2,* 331-350.

Bransford, J. D., & Johnson, M. K. Contextual prerequisites for understanding: Some investigations of comprehension and recall. *Journal of Verbal Learning and Verbal Behavior,* 1972, *11,* 717-726.

Broca, P. Remarques sur le siège de la faculté du langage articulé, suives d'une observation d'aphémie. *Bulletin de la Société de Anatomie de Paris,* 1861, 330-357.

Brodie, A. G. On the growth pattern of the human head from three months to eight years of life. *American Journal of Anatomy.* 1949, *68,* 209-259.

Bronowski, J., & Bellugi, U. Language, name, and concept. *Science,* 1970, *168,* 669-673.

Brown, R. *Words and things.* Glencoe, Ill.: The Free Press, 1958.

Brown, R. How shall a thing be called? *Psychological Review,* 1958, *65,* 14-21.

Brown, R. The first sentences of child and chimpanzee. In R. Brown, *Psycholinguistics: Selected papers.* New York: The Free Press, 1970, pp. 208-234.

Brown, R. *A first language: The early stages.* Cambridge, Mass.: Harvard University Press, 1973.

Brown, R. Reference: In memorial tribute to Eric Lenneberg. *Cognition,* 1976, *4,* 125-153.

Brown, R., & Bellugi, U. Three processes in the child's acquisition of syntax.

Harvard Educational Review, 1964, *34*, 133-151. © 1964 by President and Fellows of Harvard College. Used by permission.

Brown, R., Cazden, C., & Bellugi-Klima, U. The child's grammar from I to III. In J. P. Hill (Ed.), *Minnesota symposium on child psychology, Vol. 2*. Minneapolis: University of Minnesota Press, 1969, pp. 28-73.

Brown, R., & Hanlon, C. Derivational complexity and order of acquisition in child speech. In J. R. Hayes (Ed.), *Cognition and the development of language*. New York: Wiley, 1970, pp. 11-53.

Brown, R., & Lenneberg, E. A study in language and cognition. *Journal of Abnormal and Social Psychology*, 1954, *49*, 454-462.

Brown, R., & McNeill, D. The "tip of the tongue" phenomenon. *Journal of Verbal Learning and Verbal Behavior*, 1966, *5*, 325-337.

Cairns, H. S., & Foss, D. J. Falsification of the hypothesis that word frequency is a unified variable in sentence processing. *Journal of Verbal Learning and Verbal Behavior*, 1971, *10*, 41-43.

Cairns, H. S., & Kamerman, J. Lexical information processing during sentence comprehension. *Journal of Verbal Learning and Verbal Behavior*, 1975, *14*, 170-179.

Calfee, R. C., Arnold, R., & Drum, P. Review of E. J. Gibson & H. Levin, *The psychology of reading*. Cambridge, Mass.: M.I.T. Press, 1975. *Proceedings of the National Academy of Education*, 1976, *3*, 1-80.

Caplan, D. Clause boundaries and recognition latencies for words in sentences. *Perception & Psychophysics*, 1972, *12*, 73-76.

Carey, S. "Less" never means more. Paper presented at the Psychology of Language Conference, University of Stirling, Stirling, Scotland, June, 1976.

Carney, A. E., & Widin, G. P. Acoustic discrimination within phonetic categories. Paper presented at the meetings of the Acoustical Society of America, Washington, D.C., April, 1976.

Cassirer, E. *Substance and function*. New York: Dover Publications, 1923.

Cazden, C. B. Environmental assistance to the child's acquisition of grammar. Unpublished Ed.D. dissertation, Harvard University, 1965.

Chapin, P. G., Smith, T. S., & Abrahamson, A. A. Two factors in perceptual segmentation of speech. *Journal of Verbal Learning and Verbal Behavior*, 1972, *11*, 164-173.

Chistovich, L. A., Kozhevnikov, V. A., Alyakrinskiy, V. A., Bondarko, L. V., Goluzina, A. G., Klass, Yu. A., Kuz'min, Yu. I., Lisenko, D. M., Lyublinskaya, V. V., Fedorova, N. A., Shuplyakov, V. S., & Shuplyakova, R. M. *Rech': Artikulyatisiya i vospriyatiya*, ed. by Kozhevnikov, V. A., & Chistovich, L. A. Moscow and Leningrad: Nauka. (Trans. as *Speech: Articulation and perception*. Washington: Clearinghouse for Federal Scientific and Technical Information, 1965. JPRS. 30, 543.)

Chomsky, C. S. *The acquisition of syntax in children from 5 to 10*. Cambridge: Mass.: M.I.T. Press, 1969.

Chomsky, C. Reading, writing, and phonology. *Harvard Educational Review,* 1970, *40,* 287–309.

Chomsky, N. *Syntactic structures.* The Hague: Mouton, 1957.

Chomsky, N. *Aspects of the theory of syntax.* Cambridge, Mass.: M.I.T. Press, 1965.

Chomsky, N. The formal nature of language. Appendix A to E. Lenneberg, *Biological foundations of language.* New York: Wiley, 1967.

Chomsky, N. Phonology and reading. In H. Levin & J. P. Williams (Eds.), *Basic studies on reading.* New York: Basic Books, 1970, pp. 1–18.

Chomsky, N. *Language and mind,* Enlarged edition. New York: Harcourt Brace Jovanovich, 1972.

Chomsky, N. *Reflections on language.* New York: Pantheon Books, 1975.

Chomsky, N., & Halle, M. *The sound pattern of English.* New York: Harper & Row, 1968.

Clark, E. V. How young children describe events in time. In G. B. Flores d'Arcais & W. J. M. Levelt (Eds.), *Advances in psycholinguistics.* Amsterdam: North-Holland Publishing, 1970, pp. 275–284.

Clark, E. V. On the child's acquisition of antonyms in two semantic fields. *Journal of Verbal Learning and Verbal Behavior,* 1972, *11,* 750–758.

Clark, E. V. What's in a word? On the child's acquisition of semantics in his first language. In T. E. Moore (Ed.), *Cognitive development and the acquisition of language.* New York: Academic Press, 1973, pp. 65–110. (a)

Clark, E. V. Non-linguistic strategies and the acquisition of word meanings. *Cognition,* 1973, *2,* 161–182. (b)

Clark, H. H. Linguistic processes in deductive reasoning. *Psychological Review,* 1969, *76,* 387–404.

Clark, H. H. Space, time, semantics, and the child. In T. E. Moore (Ed.), *Cognitive development and the acquisition of language.* New York: Academic Press, 1973, pp. 27–63.

Clark, H. H. Semantics and comprehension. In T. A. Sebeok (Ed.), *Current trends in linguistics, Vol. 12: Linguistics and adjacent arts and sciences.* The Hague: Mouton, 1974, pp. 1291–1498.

Clark, H. H., & Haviland, S. E. Psychological processes as linguistic explanation. In D. Cohen (Ed.), *Explaining linguistic phenomena.* Washington, D.C.: Hemisphere Publishing, 1974, pp. 91–124.

Clark, H. H., & Haviland, S. E. Comprehension and the given-new contract. In R. O. Freedle (Ed.), *Discourse production and comprehension.* Norwood, N. J.: Ablex Publishing Co., 1977, pp. 1–40.

Clark, R. Performing without competence. *Journal of Child Language,* 1974, *1,* 1–10.

Collins, A. M., & Loftus, E. F. A spreading-activation theory of semantic processing. *Psychological Review,* 1975, *82,* 407–428.

Collins, A. M., & Quillian, M. R. Retrieval time from semantic memory. *Journal of Verbal Learning and Verbal Behavior,* 1969, *8,* 240–247.

Condon, W. S., & Sander, L. W. Synchrony demonstrated between movements of the neonate and adult speech. *Child Development,* 1974, *45,* 456-462.

Conel, J. L. *The postnatal development of the human cerebral cortex. Vols. I through VI.* Cambridge: Harvard University Press, 1939-1959.

Conrad, R. Speech and reading. In J. F. Kavanagh & I. G. Mattingly (Eds.), *Language by ear and by eye.* Cambridge, Mass.: M.I.T. Press, 1972, pp. 205-240.

Cooper, W. E. Selective adaptation to speech. In F. Restle, R. M. Shiffrin, N. J. Castellan, H. Lindman, & D. B. Pisoni (Eds.), *Cognitive theory, Vol. 1.* Hillsdale, N.J.: Lawrence Erlbaum Associates, 1975, pp. 23-54.

Cooper, W. E., & Nager, R. M. Perceptuo-motor adaptation to speech: An analysis of bisyllabic utterances and a neural model. *Journal of the Acoustical Society of America,* 1975, *58,* 256-265.

Corcoran, D. W. Acoustic factors in proof reading. *Nature,* 1967, *214,* 851.

Cosky, M. J. Word length effects in word recognition. Unpublished Ph.D. dissertation, University of Texas at Austin, 1975.

Cosky, M., & Gough, P. B. The effect of context on word recognition. Paper read at the convention of the Midwestern Psychological Association, May 1973.

Cromer, R. F. "Children are nice to understand": Surface structure clues for the recovery of a deep structure. *British Journal of Psychology,* 1970, *61,* 397-408.

Crowder, R. G. Representation of speech sounds in precategorical acoustic storage. *Journal of Experimental Psychology,* 1973, *98,* 14-24.

Crowder, R. G. Language and memory. Presented at the conference "Implications of Basic Speech and Language Research for the School and Clinic", held at Belmont, Maryland, May, 1976.

Cutler, A. Sentence stress and sentence comprehension. Unpublished Ph.D. dissertation, The University of Texas at Austin, 1975.

Cutler, A. Beyond parsing and lexical look-up: An enriched description of auditory sentence comprehension. In R. J. Wales and E. Walker (Eds.), *New approaches to language mechanisms.* Amsterdam: North-Holland, 1976, pp. 133-149.

Cutting, J. E., & Rosner, B. S. Categories and boundaries in speech and music. *Perception & Psychophysics,* 1974, *16,* 564-570.

Darley, F. L., Aronson, A. E., & Brown, J. E. Differential diagnostic patterns of dysarthia. *Journal of Speech and Hearing Research,* 1969, *12,* 246-269.

Darwin, C. J. Ear differences and hemispheric specialization. In F. O. Schmitt & F. G. Worden (Eds.), *The Neurosciences, Third Study Program.* Cambridge, Mass.: M.I.T. Press, 1973, pp. 57-63.

Darwin, C. J. The perception of speech. In E. C. Carterette & M. P. Friedman (Eds.), *Handbook of perception, Vol. 7, Language and speech.* New York: Academic Press, 1976, pp. 175-226.

De Laguna, G. A. *Speech: Its function and development.* New Haven, Conn.: Yale University Press, 1927.

Denes, P. B., & Pinson, E. N. *The speech chain: The physics and biology of spoken language.* New York: Anchor Books, 1973.

DeValois, R. L., & Jacobs, G. H. Primate color vision. *Science,* 1968, *162,* 533-540.

de Villiers, J. G., & de Villiers, P. A. A cross-sectional study of the acquisition of grammatical morphemes. *Journal of Psycholinguistic Research,* 1973, *2,* 267-278. (a)

de Villiers, J. G., & de Villiers, P. A. Development of the use of word order in comprehension. *Journal of Psycholinguistic Research,* 1973, *2,* 331-341. (b)

de Villiers, P. A., & de Villiers, J. G. Early judgments of semantic and syntactic acceptability by children. *Journal of Psycholinguistic Research,* 1972, *1,* 299-310.

Dillard, J. L. *Black English: Its history and usage in the United States.* New York: Random House, 1972.

Donaldson, M., & Balfour, G. Less is more. A study of language comprehension in children. *British Journal of Psychology,* 1968, *59,* 461-471.

Donaldson, M., & Wales, R. J. On the acquisition of some relational terms. In J. R. Hayes (Ed.), *Cognition and the development of language.* New York: Wiley, 1970, pp. 235-268.

Dooling, D. J., & Lachman, R. Effects of comprehension on retention of prose. *Journal of Experimental Psychology,* 1971, *88,* 216-222.

Doty, D. Training ten- and eleven-year-olds to discriminate within phoneme boundaries along the voicing continuum. Unpublished paper, University of Minnesota, 1970.

Downing, J. *Comparative Reading.* New York: Macmillan, 1973.

Eilers, R. E., & Oller, D. K. The role of speech discrimination in developmental sound substitutions. *Journal of Child Language,* 1976, *3,* 319-330.

Eimas, P. D. Linguistic processing of speech by young infants. In R. L. Schiefelbusch & L. Lloyd (Eds.), *Language perspectives—acquisition, retardation, and intervention.* Baltimore: University Park Press, 1974, pp. 55-74.

Eimas, P. D. Speech perception in early infancy. In L. B. Cohen & P. Salapatek (Eds.), *Infant perception: From sensation to cognition. Volume II. Perception of space, speech, and sound.* New York: Academic Press, 1975, pp. 193-232.

Eimas, P. D., Cooper, W. E., & Corbit, J. D. Some properties of linguistic feature detectors. *Perception & Psychophysics,* 1973, *13,* 247-253.

Eimas, P. D., & Corbit, J. D. Selective adaptation of linguistic feature detectors. *Cognitive Psychology,* 1973, *4,* 99-109.

Eimas, P. D., Siqueland, E. R., Jusczyk, P., & Vigorito, J. Speech perception in infants. *Science,* 1971, *171,* 303-306.

Ervin, S. M. Imitation and structural change in children's language. In E. H. Lennenberg (Ed.), *New directions in the study of language.* Cambridge, Mass.: M.I.T. Press, 1964, pp. 163-189.

Ervin-Tripp, S. M. Language development. In M. Hoffman & L. Hoffman (Eds.),

Review of child development research, Vol. 22. Ann Arbor: University of Michigan Press, 1966.

Ervin-Tripp, S. Wait for me, roller-skate. In S. Ervin-Tripp & C. Mitchell-Kernan (Eds.), *Child discourse.* New York: Academic Press, 1977.

Evans, J. S. Children's comprehension and processing of ambiguous words in sentences. Unpublished Ph.D. dissertation, The University of Texas at Austin, 1976.

Fay, D., & Cutler, A. Malapropisms and the structure of the mental lexicon. *Linguistic Inquiry.* 1977, *8,* 505-520.

Ferguson, C. A., & Slobin, D. I. (Eds.), *Studies of child language development.* New York: Holt, Rinehart and Winston, 1973.

Fillmore, C. J. The case for case. In E. Bach & R. T. Harms (Eds.), *Universals in linguistic theory.* New York: Holt, Rinehart and Winston, 1968, pp. 1-90.

Fillmore, C. J. Toward a modern theory of case. In D. A. Reibel & S. A. Schane (Eds.), *Modern studies in English.* Englewood Cliffs, N.J.: Prentice-Hall, 1969, pp. 361-375.

Fillmore, C. J. Some problems for case grammar. In R. J. O'Brien (Ed.), *22nd annual round table meeting on linguistics and language studies.* Washington D.C.: Georgetown University Press, 1971, pp. 35-56.

Flavell, J. H. *Cognitive development.* Englewood Cliffs, N.J.: Prentice-Hall, 1977.

Flavell, J. H. (with Botkin, P. T., Fry, C. L., Jr., Wright J. W., & Jarvis, P. E.) *The development of role-taking and communication skills in children.* New York: Wiley, 1968.

Fodor, J. A. *Psychological explanation: An introduction to the philosophy of psychology.* New York: Random House, 1968.

Fodor, J. A. *The language of thought.* New York: T. Y. Crowell, 1975.

Fodor, J. A., & Bever, T. G. The psychological reality of linguistic segments. *Journal of Verbal Learning and Verbal Behavior,* 1965, *4,* 414-420.

Fodor, J. A., Bever, T. G., & Garrett, M. F. *The psychology of language: An introduction to psycholinguistics and generative grammar,* New York: McGraw-Hill, 1974.

Fodor, J., & Garrett, M. Some reflections on competence and performance. In J. Lyons & R. J. Wales (Eds.), *Psycholinguistics papers.* Chicago: Aldine Publishing Co., 1966, pp. 135-154.

Fodor, J. A., & Garrett, M. Some syntactic determinants of sentential complexity. *Perception & Psychophysics,* 1967, *2,* 289-296.

Fodor, J. A., Garrett, M., & Bever, T. G. Some syntactic determinants of sentential complexity, II: Verb structure. *Perception & Psychophysics,* 1968, *3,*453-461.

Forster, K. I. Accessing the mental lexicon. In R. J. Wales & E. Walker (Eds.), *New approaches to language mechanisms.* Amsterdam: North-Holland Publishing, 1976, pp. 257-287.

Forster, K. I., & Bednall, E. S. Terminating and exhaustive search in lexical access. *Memory & Cognition,* 1976, *4,* 53-61.

Forster, K. I., & Chambers, S. M. Lexical access and naming time. *Journal of Verbal Learning and Verbal Behavior,* 1973, *12,* 627-635.

Forster, K. I., & Olbrei, I. Semantic heuristics and syntactic analysis. *Cognition,* 1973, *2,* 319-347. Used by permission.

Foss, D. J. Decision processes during sentence comprehension: Effects of lexical item difficulty and position upon decision times. *Journal of Verbal Learning and Verbal Behavior,* 1969, *8,* 457-462.

Foss, D. J. Some effects of ambiguity upon sentence comprehension. *Journal of Verbal Learning and Verbal Behavior,* 1970, *9,* 699-706.

Foss, D. J., & Fay, D. Linguistic theory and performance models. In D. Cohen & J. R. Wirth (Eds.), *Testing linguistic hypotheses.* Washington, D.C.: Hemisphere Publishing, 1975, pp. 65-91.

Foss, D. J. & Jenkins, C. J. Some effects of context on the comprehension of ambiguous sentences. *Journal of Verbal Learning and Verbal Behavior,* 1973, *12,* 577-589. © 1973 by Academic Press, Inc. Used by permission.

Foulke, E. The perception of time compressed speech. In D. L. Horton & J. J. Jenkins (Eds.), *Perception of language.* Columbus, Ohio: Charles E. Merrill, 1971, pp. 79-108.

Fouts, R. S. Acquisition and testing of gestural signs in four young chimpanzees. *Science,* 1973, *180,* 978-980.

Francis, W. N. Linguistics and reading: A commentary on Chapters 1 to 3. In H. Levin & J. P. Williams (Eds.), *Basic studies on reading.* New York: Basic Books, 1970, pp. 43-56.

Franks, J. J., & Bransford, J. P. Abstraction of visual patterns. *Journal of Experimental Psychology,* 1971, *90,* 65-74.

Franks, J. J., & Bransford, J. D. The acquisition of abstract ideas. *Journal of Verbal Learning and Verbal Behavior,* 1972, *11,* 311-315.

Fraser, C., Bellugi, U., & Brown, R. Control of grammar in imitation, comprehension, and production. *Journal of Verbal Learning and Verbal Behavior,* 1963, *2,* 121-135.

Frederiksen, C. H. Representing logical and semantic structure of knowledge acquired from discourse. *Cognitive Psychology,* 1975, *7,* 371-458.

Fromkin, V. The non-anomalous nature of anomalous utterances. *Language,* 1971, *47,* 27-52.

Fromkin, V. A. *Speech errors as linguistic evidence.* The Hague: Mouton, 1973.

Fry, D. B. Duration and intensity as physical correlates of linguistic stress. *Journal of the Acoustical Society of America,* 1955, *27,* 765-768.

Fujisaki, H., & Kawashima, T. The influence of various factors on the identification and discrimination of synthetic speech sounds. Paper presented at the 6th International Congress on Acoustics, Tokyo, Japan, August, 1968.

Fujisaki, H., & Kawashima, T. On the modes and mechanisms of speech perception. Annual Report No. 1, Engineering Research Institute, University of Tokyo, 1969.

Gardner, R. A., & Gardner, B. T. Teaching sign language to a chimpanzee. *Science,* 1969, *165,* 664-672.

Gardner, R. A., & Gardner, B. T. Early signs of language in child and chimpanzee. *Science*, 1975, *187*, 752-753.

Garnica, O. K. The development of phonemic speech perception. In T. E. Moore (Ed.), *Cognitive development and the acquisition of language*. New York: Academic Press, 1973, pp. 215-222.

Garrett, M. F. Does ambiguity complicate the perception of sentences? In G. B. Flores d'Arcais and W. J. M. Levelt (Eds.), *Advances in psycholinguistics*. New York: American Elsevier, 1970, pp. 48-60.

Garrett, M. F. The analysis of sentence production. In G. H. Bower (Ed.), *The psychology of learning and motivation, Vol. 9*. New York: Academic Press, 1975, pp. 133-177.

Garrett, M., Bever, T. G., & Fodor, J. A. The active use of grammar in speech perception. *Perception & Psychophysics*, 1966, *1*, 30-32.

Gazzaniga, M. S. *The bisected brain*. New York: Appleton-Century-Crofts, 1970.

Gelman, R., & Shatz, M. Appropriate speech adjustments: The operation of conversational constraints on talk to two-year-olds. In M. Lewis & L. A. Rosenblum (Eds.), *Interaction, conversation, and the development of language*. New York: Wiley, 1977, pp. 27-62.

Geschwind, N. Language and the brain. *Scientific American*, 1972, 226, *4*, 76-83.

Gibson, E. J., & Levin, H. *The psychology of reading*. Cambridge, Mass.: M.I.T. Press, 1975.

Gillooly, W. B. The influence of writing-system characteristics on learning to read. *Reading Research Quarterly*, 1975, *8*, 167-199.

Glanville, B. B., Best, C. T., & Levenson, R. A cardiac measure of cerebral asymmetries in infant auditory perception. *Developmental Psychology*, 1977, *13*, 54-59.

Gleason, J. B. Code switching in children's language. In T. E. Moore (Ed.), *Cognitive development and the acquisition of language*. New York: Academic Press, 1973, pp. 159-168.

Gleitman, L. R., & Gleitman, H. *Phrase and paraphrase: Some innovative uses of language*. New York: Norton, 1970.

Gleitman, L. R., Gleitman, H., & Shipley, E. F. The emergence of the child as grammarian. *Cognition*, 1973, *1*, 137-164.

Gleitman, L. R., & Rozin, P. Teaching reading by use of a syllabary. *Reading Research Quarterly*, 1973, *8*, 447-483.

Glucksberg, S., Krauss, R., & Higgins, E. T. The development of referential communication skills. In F. D. Horowitz (Ed.), *Review of child development research, Vol. 4*. Chicago: University of Chicago Press, 1975, pp. 305-345.

Glucksberg, S., Krauss, R. M., & Weisberg, R. Referential communication in nursery school children: Method and some preliminary findings. *Journal of Experimental Child Psychology*, 1966, *3*, 333-342.

Goldin-Meadow, S., Seligman, M. P., & Gelman, R. Language in the two-year old. *Cognition,* 1976, *4,* 189-202.

Goldman-Eisler, F. Speech production and the predictability of words in context. *Quarterly Journal of Experimental Psychology,* 1958, *10,* 96-106.

Goldman-Eisler, F. Hesitation and information in speech. In C. Cherry (Ed.), *Information theory.* London: Butterworths, 1961.

Goldman-Eisler, F. Speech and thought. *Discovery,* April, 1962.

Goody, J., & Watt, I. The consequences of literacy. *Comparative studies in society and history,* 1963, *5,* 304-345.

Gough, P. B. The verification of sentences: The effects of delay of evidence and sentence length. *Journal of Verbal Learning and Verbal Behavior,* 1966, *5,* 492-496.

Gough, P. B. One second of reading. In J. F. Kavanagh & I.G. Mattingly (Eds.), *Language by ear and by eye: The relationship between speech and reading.* Cambridge, Mass.: M.I.T. Press, 1972, pp. 331-358.

Gough, P. B. The structure of language. In D. D. Duane and M. B. Rawson (Eds.), *Reading, perception and language.* Baltimore, Maryland: York Press, 1975, pp. 15-37.

Gough, P. B., & Cosky, M. J. One second of reading again. In N. J. Castellan, Jr., D. B. Pisoni, & G. R. Potts (Eds.), *Cognitive theory, Vol. 2.* Hillsdale, N.J.: Lawrence Erlbaum Associates, 1977, pp. 271-288.

Greenberg, S. R. An experimental study of certain intonation contrasts in American English. *UCLA Working Papers in Phonetics,* 1969, *13.*

Greenfield, P. M., & Smith, J. H. *The structure of communication in early language development.* New York: Academic Press, 1976.

Grice, H. P. Logic and conversation. In P. Cole & J. L. Morgan (Eds.), *Syntax and semantics, Vol. 3: Speech acts.* New York: Seminar Press, 1975, pp. 41-58.

Haggard, M. P., & Parkinson, A. M. Stimulus and task factors as determinants of ear advantages. *Quarterly Journal of Experimental Psychology,* 1971, *23,* 168-170.

Hakes, D. T. Does verb structure affect sentence comprehension? *Perception & Psychophysics,* 1971, *10,* 229-232.

Hakes, D. T. Effects of reducing complement constructions on sentence comprehension. *Journal of Verbal Learning and Verbal Behavior,* 1972, *11,* 278-286.

Hakes, D. T., Evans, J. S., & Tunmer, W. The emergence of linguistic intuitions in children. Final Progress Report submitted to The Grant Foundation, Inc., October, 1976.

Hakes, D. T., & Foss, D. J. Decision processes during sentence comprehension: Effects of surface structure reconsidered. *Perception & Psychophysics,* 1970, *8,* 413-416.

Hardyck, C. D., & Petrinovich, L. F. Subvocal speech and comprehension level as a function of the difficulty level of reading material. *Journal of Verbal Learning and Verbal Behavior,* 1970, *9,* 647-652.

Harnad, S. R., Doty, R. W., Goldstein, L., Jaynes, J., & Krauthamer, G. (Eds.), *Lateralization in the nervous system.* New York: Academic Press, 1976.

Harris, K. S. Cues for the discrimination of American English fricatives in spoken syllables. *Language and Speech,* 1958, *1,* 1-7.

Harris, R. J. Memory and comprehension of implications and inferences of complex sentences. *Journal of Verbal Learning and Verbal Behavior,* 1974, *13,* 626-637.

Hausser, R. A theory of systematic deviants. Unpublished paper, The University of Texas at Austin, 1971.

Hayes, C. *The ape in our house.* New York: Harper, 1951.

Heider, E. R. Universals in color naming and memory. *Journal of Experimental Psychology,* 1972, *93,* 10-20.

Heider, E. R., & Olivier, D. C. The structure of the color space in naming and memory for two languages. *Cognitive Psychology,* 1972, *3,* 337-354.

Henle, M. On the relation between logic and thinking. *Psychological Review,* 1962, *69,* 366-378.

Herriot, P. The comprehension of active and passive sentences as a function of pragmatic expectations. *Journal of Verbal Learning and Verbal Behavior,* 1969, *8,* 166-169.

Hockett, C. Logical considerations in the study of animal communication. In W. E. Lanyon & W. N. Tavolga (Eds.), *Animal sounds and communication.* Washington, D.C.: American Institute of Biological Sciences, 1960, pp. 392-430.

Hockett, C. The problem of universals in language. In J. H. Greenberg (Ed.), *Universals of language, Second Edition.* Cambridge, Mass.: M.I.T. Press, 1966, pp. 1-29.

Hollan, J. D. Features and semantic memory: Set-theoretic or network model? *Psychological Review,* 1975, *82,* 154-155.

Holland, V. M., & Palermo, D. S. On learning "less": Language and cognitive development. *Child Development,* 1975, *46,* 437-443.

Holmes, V. M., & Forster, K. I. Detection of extraneous signals during sentence processing. *Perception & Psychophysics,* 1970, *7,* 297-301.

Holmes, V. M., & Forster, K. I. Perceptual complexity and understanding sentence structure. *Journal of Verbal Learning and Verbal Behavior,* 1972, *11,* 148-156.

Hook, S. (Ed.), *Language and philosophy.* New York: New York University Press, 1969.

Huey, E. B. *The psychology and pedagogy of reading.* Cambridge, Mass.: M.I.T. Press, 1968.

Huggins, A. W. The perception of timing in natural speech I. Compensation within the syllable. *Language and Speech,* 1968, *11,* 1-11.

Humphrey, G. *Thinking: An introduction to its experimental psychology.* New York: Wiley, 1963.

Huttenlocher, J. The origins of language comprehension. In R. L. Solso (Ed.), *Theories in cognitive psychology: The Loyola Symposium.* Potomac, Md.: Lawrence Erlbaum Associates, 1974, pp. 331-368.

Huttenlocher, J., & Higgins, E. T. Adjectives, comparatives, and syllogisms. *Psychological Review,* 1971, *78,* 487-504.

Hyman, H. *Phonology: Theory and analysis.* New York: Holt, Rinehart and Winston, 1975.

Irwin, O. C. Phonetical description of speech development in childhood. In L. Kaiser (Ed.), *Manual of phonetics.* Amsterdam: North-Holland, 1957.

Jakobson, R. *Child language, aphasia, and phonological universals. Janua Linguarum, Series Minor, 72.* The Hague: Mouton, 1968.

Jakobson, R., Fant, G., & Halle, M. *Preliminaries to speech analysis.* Cambridge, Mass.: M.I.T. Press, 1963.

James, W. *The principles of psychology, Vol. 1.* New York: Holt, 1890.

Jenkins, J. J., Jiménez-Pabón, E., Shaw, R. E., & Sefer, J. W. *Schuell's aphasia in adults. 2nd Edition.* Hagerstown, Md.: Harper & Row, 1975.

Kalish, D. Semantics. In P. Edwards (Ed.), *The encyclopedia of philosophy, Vol. 7.* New York: Macmillan, 1967, pp. 348-358.

Kaplan, E., & Kaplan, G. The prelinguistic child. In J. Eliot (Ed.), *Human development and cognitive processes.* New York: Holt, Rinehart and Winston, 1971.

Kaplan, R. Augmented transition networks as psychological models of sentence comprehension. *Artificial Intelligence,* 1972, *3,* 77-100.

Kaplan, R. On process models for sentence analysis. In D. Norman & D. Rumelhart (Eds.), *Explorations in cognition.* San Francisco: W. H. Freeman, 1975.

Katz, J. *Semantic theory.* New York: Harper & Row, 1972.

Katz, J., & Foder, J. A. The structure of a semantic theory. *Language,* 1963, *39,* 170-210.

Kemp, J. C., & Dale, P. S. Spontaneous imitation and free speech: A grammatical comparison. Paper presented at the meetings of the Society for Research on Child Development, Philadelphia, March, 1973.

Kessel, F. S. The role of syntax in children's comprehension from ages six to twelve. *Monographs of the Society for Research in Child Development,* 1970, *35,* No. 6 (Serial No. 139).

Kimura, D. Cerebral dominance and the perception of verbal stimuli. *Canadian Journal of Psychology,* 1961, *15,* 166-171.

Kimura, D. Speech lateralization in young children as determined by an auditory test *Journal of Comparative and Physiological Psychology,* 1963, *56,* 899-902.

Kinsbourne, M. The ontogeny of cerebral dominance. In D. Aaronson & R. W. Rieber (Eds.), *Developmental psycholinguistics and communication dis-*

orders. New York: New York Academy of Sciences, 1975, pp. 244-250.

Kintsch, W. Notes on the structure of semantic memory. In E. Tulving and W. Donaldson (Eds.), *Organization of memory*. New York: Academic Press, 1972, pp. 249-308.

Kintsch, W. *The representation of meaning in memory*. Hillsdale, N.J.: Lawrence Erlbaum Associates, 1974.

Kintsch, W. Memory for prose. In C. N. Cofer (Ed.), *The structure of human memory*. San Francisco: W. H. Freeman, 1976, pp. 90-113.

Kintsch, W., & Keenan, J. M. Reading rate as a function of the number of propositions in the base structure of sentences. *Cognitive Psychology*, 1973, *5*, 257-274.

Klatt, D. H., & Cooper, W. E. Perception of segment duration in sentence contexts. In A. Cohen & S. G. Nooteboom (Eds.), *Structure and process in speech perception*. New York: Springer-Verlag, 1975, pp. 69-86.

Kleiman, G. M. Speech recoding in reading. *Journal of Verbal Learning and Verbal Behavior*, 1975, *14*, 323-339. © 1975 by Academic Press, Inc. Used by permission.

Knafle, J. D. Auditory perception of rhyming in kindergarten children. *Journal of Speech and Hearing Research*, 1973, *16*, 482-487.

Knafle, J. D. Children's discrimination of rhyme. *Journal of Speech and Hearing Research*, 1974, *17*, 367-372.

Kolers, P. A. Reading and talking bilingually. *American Journal of Psychology*, 1966, *79*, 357-376.

Kolers, P. A. The recognition of geometrically transformed text. *Perception & Psychophysics*, 1968, *3*, 57-64.

Kolers, P. A. Three stages of reading. In H. Levin & J. P. Williams (Eds.), *Basic studies on reading*. New York: Basic Books, 1970, pp. 90-118.

Kosslyn, S. M., & Pomerantz, J. R. Imagery, propositions, and the form of internal representations. *Cognitive Psychology*, 1977, *9*, 52-76.

Kramer, P. E., Koff, E., & Luria, Z. The development of competence in an exceptional language structure in older children and young adults. *Child Development*, 1972, *43*, 121-130.

Krauss, R. M., & Glucksberg, S. Social and nonsocial speech. *Scientific American*, 1977, *236*, #2, 100-105.

Kucera, H., & Francis, W. N. *Computational analysis of present-day English*. Providence, R.I.: Brown University Press, 1967.

Kuczaj, S. A., & Maratsos, M. P. What children can say before they will. *Merrill-Palmer Quarterly*, 1975, *21*, 89-111.

Kuhl, P. K., & Miller, J. D. Speech perception by the chinchilla: Voiced-voiceless distinction in alveolar plosive consonants. *Science*, 1975, *190*, 69-72.

Kuhl, P. K., & Miller, J. D. Speech perception by the chinchilla: Phonetic boundaries for synthetic VOT stimuli. Paper presented at the 89th Meeting of the Acoustical Society of America, Austin, Texas, April, 1975.

LaBerge, D. Attention and the measurement of perceptual learning. *Memory & Cognition*, 1973, *1*, 268-276.

LaBerge, D., & Samuels, S. J. Toward a theory of automatic information processing in reading. *Cognitive Psychology*, 1974, *6*, 293-323.

Labov, W. The logic of nonstandard English. In F. Williams (Ed.), *Language and poverty: Perspectives on a theme*. Chicago: Markham Publishing Co., 1970, pp. 153-189.

Labov, W. "Academic Ignorance and Black Intelligence." *The Atlantic Monthly*, June, 1972, pp. 59-67.

Ladefoged, P. *Preliminaries to linguistic phonetics*. Chicago: University of Chicago Press, 1971.

Ladefoged, P. *A course in phonetics*. New York: Harcourt Brace Jovanovich, 1975.

Lakoff, G. Linguistics and natural logic. In D. Davidson & G. Harmon (Eds.), *Semantics of natural language*. Dordrecht, Holland: D. Reidel, 1972, pp. 545-665.

Landauer, T. K. Rate of implicit speech. *Perceptual and Motor Skills*, 1962, *15*, 646.

Lantz, D., & Stefflre, V. Language and cognition revisited. *Journal of Abnormal and Social Psychology*, 1964, *69*, 472-481.

Lashley, K. S., The problem of serial order in behavior. In L. A. Jeffress (Ed.), *Cerebral mechanisms in behavior*. New York: Wiley, 1951, pp. 112-136.

Lasky, R. E., Syrdal-Lasky, A., & Klein, R. E. VOT discrimination by four to six and a half month old infants from Spanish environments. *Journal of Experimental Child Psychology*, 1975, *20*, 215-225.

Lecours, A. R. Myelogenetic correlates of the development of speech and language. In E. H. Lenneberg & E. Lenneberg (Eds.), *Foundations of language development, Vol. 1*. New York: Academic Press, 1975, pp. 121-135.

Leech, G. *Semantics*. Baltimore: Penguin Books, 1974.

Lehiste, I. Phonetic disambiguation of syntactic ambiguity. *Glossa*, 1973, *7*, 107-122.

Lehmann, W. P. *Historical linguistics: An introduction*. New York: Holt, Rinehart, and Winston, 1962.

Lenneberg, E. H. Cognition in ethnolinguistics. *Language*, 1953, *29*, 463-471.

Lenneberg, E. H. Understanding language without ability to speak: A case study. *Journal of Abnormal and Social Psychology*, 1962, *65*, 419-425.

Lenneberg, E. H. *Biological foundations of language*. New York: Wiley, 1967.

Lenneberg, E. H. In search of a dynamic theory of aphasia. In E. H. Lenneberg & E. Lenneberg (Eds.), *Foundations of language development, Vol. 2*. New York: Academic Press, 1975, pp. 1-20.

Lenneberg, E. H., & Lenneberg, E. (Eds.), *Foundations of language development*. (2 volumes) New York: Academic Press, 1975.

Lenneberg, E. H., & Roberts, J. M. The language of experience: A study in methodology. *International Journal of American Linguistics*, 1956 (Memoir No. 13).

Lesgold, A. M. Pronominalization: A device for unifying sentences in memory. *Journal of Verbal Learning and Verbal Behavior*, 1972, *11*, 316-323.

Lettvin, J. Y., Maturana, H. R., McCulloch, W. S., & Pitts, W. H. What the frog's eye tells the frog's brain. *Proceedings of the IRE,* 1959, *47,* 1940-1951.

Levelt, W. J. A scaling approach to the study of syntactic relations. In G. B. Flores d'Arcais and W. J. Levelt (Eds.), *Advances in psycholinguistics.* Amsterdam: North-Holland, 1970, pp. 109-121.

Levin, H., Silverman, I., & Ford, B. Hesitations in children's speech during explanation and description. *Journal of Verbal Learning and Verbal Behavior,* 1967, *6,* 560-564.

Levy, J., Nebes, R. D., & Sperry, R. W. Expressive language in the surgically separated minor hemisphere. *Cortex,* 1971, *7,* 49-58.

Lewis, C. H., & Anderson, J. R. Interference with real world knowledge. *Cognitive Psychology,* 1976, *8,* 311-335.

Lewis, D. General semantics. In D. Davidson & G. Harmon (Eds.), *Semantics of natural language.* Dordrecht, Holland: D. Reidel, 1972, pp. 169-218.

Lewis, M. M. *Infant speech.* London: Routledge, 1951.

Lewis, M., & Rosenblum, L. A. (Eds.), *Interaction, conversation, and the development of language.* New York: Wiley, 1977.

Liberman, A. M. The grammars of language and speech. *Cognitive Psychology,* 1970, *1,* 301-323.

Liberman, A. M., Cooper, F. S. Shankweiler, D. P., & Studdert-Kennedy, M. Perception of the speech code. *Psychological Review,* 1967, *74,* 431-461.

Liberman, A. M., Harris, K. S., Hoffman, H. S., & Griffith, B. C. The discrimination of speech sounds within and across phoneme boundaries, *Journal of Experimental Psychology,* 1957, *54,* 358-368.

Liberman, I. Y., Shankweiler, D., Fischer, F. W., & Carter, B. Explicit syllable and phoneme segmentation in the young child. *Journal of Experimental Child Psychology,* 1974, *18,* 201-212.

Liberman, I. Y., Shankweiler, D., Liberman, A. M., Fowler, C., & Fischer, F. W. Phonetic segmentation and recoding in the beginning reader. In A. S. Reber and D. L. Scarborough (Eds.), *Toward a psychology of reading: The proceedings of the CUNY Conference.* Hillsdale, N.J.: Lawrence Erlbaum Associates, 1977, pp. 207-225. © 1977 by Lawrence Erlbaum Associates. Used by permission of the authors and publisher.

Lieberman, P. Some effects of semantic and grammatical context on the production and perception of speech. *Language and Speech,* 1963, *6,* 172-187.

Lieberman, P. *Intonation, perception and language.* Cambridge: M.I.T. Press, 1967.

Lieberman, P. Primate vocalizations and human linguistic ability. *Journal of the Acoustical Society of America,* 1968, *44,* 1574-1584.

Lieberman, P., & Crelin, E. S. On the speech of Neanderthal man. *Linguistic Inquiry,* 1971, *2,* 203-222.

Lieberman, P., Harris, K. S., Wolff, P., & Russell, L. H. Newborn infant cry and nonhuman primate vocalizations. *Journal of Speech and Hearing Research,* 1971, *14,* 718-727.

Lieberman, P. H., Klatt, D. H., & Wilson, W. H. Vocal tract limitations on the vowel repertoires of Rhesus monkey and other honhuman primates. *Science,* 1969, *164,* 1185-1187.

Limber, J. The genesis of complex sentences. In T. E. Moore (Ed.), *Cognitive development and the acquisition of language.* New York: Academic Press, 1973, pp. 169-185.

Limber, J. Unravelling competence, performance and pragmatics in the speech of young children. *Journal of Child Language,* 1976, *3,* 309-318.

Lindblom, B. E. Spectrographic study of vowel reduction. *Journal of the Acoustical Society of America,* 1963, *35,* 1773-1781.

Lindblom, B. E., & Sundberg, J. Neurophysiological representation of speech sounds. Paper presented at the XVth World Congress of Logopedics and Phoniatrics, Buenos Aires, Argentina, August, 1971.

Lindsay, P. H., & Norman, D. A. *Human information processing,* 2nd Edition. New York: Academic Press, 1977.

Lisker, L., & Abramson, A. S. A cross-language study of voicing in initial stops: Acoustical measurements. *Word,* 1964, *20,* 384-422.

Lounsbury, F. G. Transitional probability, linguistic structure and systems of habit-family hierarchies. In C. E. Osgood & T. A. Sebeok (Eds), *Psycholinguistics: A survey of theory and research problems.* Bloomington, Indiana: Indiana University Press, 1965, pp. 93-101.

Lyons, J. *Noam Chomsky.* New York: The Viking Press, 1970.

MacKay, D. G. To end ambiguous sentences. *Perception & Psychophysics,* 1966, *1,* 426-436.

MacKay, D. G. Input testing in the detection of misspellings. *American Journal of Psychology,* 1972, *85,* 121-127.

Maclay, H., & Osgood, C. E. Hesitation phenomena in spontaneous English speech. *Word,* 1959, *15,* 19-44.

Macnamara, J. Cognitive basis of language learning in infants. *Psychological Review,* 1972, *79,* 1-13.

MacNeilage, P. F. Motor control of serial ordering of speech. *Psychological Review,* 1970, *77,* 182-196.

MacNeilage, P. F. Speech physiology. In J Gilbert (Ed.), *Speech and cortical functioning.* New York: Academic Press, 1972, pp. 1-72.

MacNeilage, P. F., Krones, R., & Hanson, R. Closed-loop control of the initiation of jaw movement for speech. Paper presented at the meetings of the Acoustical Society of America, San Diego, November, 1969.

MacNeilage, P., & Ladefoged, P. The production of speech and language. In E. C. Carterette & M. P. Friedman (Eds.), *Handbook of perception, Volume VII.* New York: Academic Press, 1976, pp. 75-120.

MacNeilage, P. F., & MacNeilage, L. A. Central processes controlling speech production during sleep and waking. In F. J. McGuigan & R. A. Schoonover (Eds.), *The psychophysiology of thinking.* New York: Academic Press, 1973, pp. 417-448.

MacNeilage, P. F., Rootes, T. P., & Chase, R. A. Speech production and perception in a patient with severe impairment of somesthetic perception and motor control. *Journal of Speech and Hearing Research,* 1967, *10,* 449-467.

Mandler, J. M., & Johnson, N. S. Remembrance of things parsed: Story structure and recall. *Cognitive Psychology,* 1977, *9,* 111-151.

Mandler, J. M., & Mandler, G. *Thinking: From association to gestalt.* New York: Wiley, 1964.

Maratsos, M. P. Children who get worse at understanding the passive: A replication of Bever. *Journal of Psycholinguistic Research,* 1974, *3,* 65-74.

Marshack, A. Upper Paleolithic notation and symbol. *Science,* 1972, *178,* 817-828.

Martin, E. Toward an analysis of subjective phrase structure. *Psychological Bulletin,* 1970, *74,* 153-166.

Martin, J. E., Kolodziej, B., & Genay, J. Segmentation of sentences into phonological phrases as a function of constituent length. *Journal of Verbal Learning and Verbal Behavior,* 1971, *10,* 226-233.

Martin, J. G. Hesitations in the speaker's production and listener's reproduction of utterances. *Journal of Verbal Learning and Verbal Behavior,* 1967, *6,* 903-909.

Martin, J. G. Some acoustic and grammatical features of spontaneous speech. In D. L. Horton & J. J. Jenkins (Eds.), *The perception of language.* Columbus, Ohio: Chas. Merrill, 1971, pp. 47-68.

Martin, J. G. Rhythmic (hierarchical) versus serial structure in speech and other behavior. *Psychological Review,* 1972, *79,* 487-509.

McGhee, P. E. Cognitive mastery and children's humor. *Psychological Bulletin,* 1974, *81,* 721-730.

McNeill, D. Developmental psycholinguistics. In F. Smith & G. A. Miller (Eds.), *The genesis of language: A psycholinguistic approach.* Cambridge, Mass.: M.I.T. Press, 1966, pp. 18-84. © 1966 by the M.I.T. Press, Used by permission.

McNeill, D. *The acquisition of language: The study of developmental psycholinguistics.* New York: Harper & Row, 1970.

Mehler, J. Studies in language and thought development. In R. Huxley & E. Ingram (Eds.), *Language acquisition: Models and methods.* New York: Academic Press, 1971, pp. 201-225.

Mencken, H. L. *The American Language.* (4th Edition). New York: Alfred A. Knopf, 1963.

Menyuk, P. *Sentences children use.* Cambridge, Mass.: M.I.T. Press, 1969.

Metzler, J., & Shepard, R. N. Transformational studies of the internal representation of three-dimensional objects. In R. L. Solso (Ed.), *Theories in cognitive psychology: The Loyola symposium.* Potomac, Md.: Lawrence Erlbaum Associates, 1974, pp. 147-201.

Meyer, D. E., & Ruddy, M. G. Lexical-memory retrieval based on graphemic and phonemic representations of printed words. Paper presented at the meetings of the Psychonomic Society, November, 1973.

Meyer, D. E., & Schvaneveldt, R. W. Facilitation in recognizing pairs of words: Evidence of a dependence between retrieval operations. *Journal of Experimental Psychology*, 1971, *90*, 227-234.

Meyer, D. E., Schvaneveldt, R. W., & Ruddy, M. G. Functions of graphemic and phonemic codes in visual word recognition. *Memory & Cognition*, 1974, *2*, 309-321.

Mikès, M. Acquisition des catégoires grammaticales dans le langage de l'enfant. *Enfance*, 1967, *20*, 289-298.

Miller, J. D., Wier, C. C., Pastore, R. E., Kelly, W. J., & Dooling, R. J. Discrimination and labeling of noise-buzz sequences with varying noise-lead times: An example of categorical perception. *Journal of the Acoustical Society of America*, 1976, *60*, 410-417.

Miller, G. A. *Language and communication*. New York: McGraw-Hill, 1951.

Miller, G. A. The mathematicians who counted. Review of J. R. Newman (Ed.), *The world of mathematics*. 4 Volumes. New York: Simon & Schuster, 1956. *Contemporary Psychology*, 1957, *2*, 38-39.

Miller, G. A. Some preliminaries to psycholinguistics. *American Psychologist*, 1965, *20*, 15-20.

Miller, G. A., & Johnson-Laird, P. N. *Language and perception*. Cambridge, Mass.: Harvard University Press, 1976.

Miller, G. A., & McNeill, D. Psycholinguistics. In G. Lindzey & E. Aronson (Eds.), *The handbook of social psychology*, 2nd Edition, Vol. III. Reading, Mass.: Addison-Wesley, Co., 1969, pp. 669-794.

Minsky, M. A framework for representing knowledge. In P. Winston (Ed.), *The psychology of computer vision*. New York: McGraw-Hill, 1975, pp. 211-277.

Miyawaki, K., Strange, W., Verbrugge, R., Liberman, A. M., Jenkins, J. J., & Fujimura, O. An effect of linguistic experience: The discrimination of [r] and [l] by native speakers of Japanese and English. *Perception & Psychophysics*, 1975, *18*, 331-340.

Moerk, E. Changes in verbal child-mother interactions with increasing language skills of the child. *Journal of Psycholinguistic Research*, 1974, *3*, 101-116.

Moore, T. E. (Ed.), *Cognitive development and the acquisition of language*. New York: Academic Press, 1973.

Morse, P. A. Infant speech perception: a preliminary model and review of the literature. In R. L. Schiefelbusch & L. Lloyd (Eds.), *Language perspectives— acquisition, retardation, and intervention*. Baltimore: University Park Press, 1974, pp. 19-54.

Morse, P. A. Speech perception in the human infant and Rhesus monkey. In S. Harnad, H. D. Steklis, & J. Lancaster (Eds.), *Origins and evolution of language and speech*. New York: New York Academy of Sciences, 1977.

Morse, P. A., & Snowdon, C. T. An investigation of categorical speech discrimination by Rhesus monkeys. *Perception & Psychophysics*, 1975, *17*, 9-16.

Morton, J. Interaction of information in word recognition. *Psychological Review*,

1969, *76*, 165-178.

Murai, J. The sounds of infants, their phonemization and symbolization. *Studia Phonologica*, 1963, *3*, 18-34.

Nakazima, S. A comparative study of the speech developments of Japanese and American English in childhood (2)–The acquisition of speech. *Studia Phonologica*, 1966, *4*, 38-55.

Neisser, U. *Cognitive Psychology*. New York: Appleton-Century-Crofts, 1967.

Nelson, K. Structure and strategy in learning to talk. *Monographs of the Society for Research in Child Development*, 1973, *38*, Nos. 1-2 (Serial No. 149). (a)

Nelson, K. Some evidence for the cognitive primacy of categorization and its functional basis. *Merrill-Palmer Quarterly of Behavior and Development*, 1973, *19*, 21-39. (b)

Nelson, K. Concept, word, and sentence: Interrelationships in acquisition and development. *Psychological Review*, 1974, *81*, 267-285.

Nelson, K. The nominal shift in semantic-syntactic development. *Cognitive Psychology*, 1975, *7*, 461-479.

Nelson, K. E., Carskaddon, G., & Bonvillian, J. D. Syntax acquisition: Impact of experimental variation in adult verbal interaction with the child. *Child Development*, 1973, *44*, 497-504.

Newport, E. L. Motherese: The speech of mothers to young children. In N. J. Castellan, D. B. Pisoni & G. R. Potts (Eds.), *Cognitive theory, Vol II*. Hillsdale, N.J.: Lawerance Earlbaum Associates, 1977.

Norman, D. A. *Memory and attention: An introduction to human information processing, 2nd Edition*. New York: Wiley, 1976.

Norman, D. A., & Rumelhart, D. E. *Explorations in cognition*. San Francisco: Freeman, 1975.

Offir, C. E. Recognition memory for presuppositions of relative clause sentences. *Journal of Verbal Learning and Verbal Behavior*, 1973, *12*, 636-643.

Ohala, J. J. Aspects of the control and production of speech. *UCLA Working Papers in Phonetics*, 1970, *15*.

Oller, D. K. The effect of position in utterance on speech segment duration in English. *Journal of the Acoustical Society of America*, 1973, *54*, 1235-1247.

Osgood, C. E. Where do sentences come from? In D. Steinberg & L. A. Jakobovits (Eds.), *Semantics: An interdisciplinary reader in philosophy, linguistics, and psychology*. London: Cambridge University Press, 1971, pp. 497-529.

Paivio, A. *Imagery and verbal processes*. New York: Holt, 1971.

Palermo, D. S. More about less: A study of language comprehension. *Journal of Verbal Learning and Verbal Behavior*, 1973, *12*, 211-221.

Papandropoulou, I., & Sinclair, H. What is a word? Experimental study of children's ideas on grammar. *Human Development*, 1974, *17*, 241-258.

Pastore, R. E., Friedman, C., Baffuto, K. J., & Fink, E. A. Categorical perception of both simple auditory and visual stimuli. Paper presented at the meetings of the Acoustical Society of America, Washington, D.C., April, 1976.

Penfield, W., & Roberts, L. *Speech and brain-mechanisms.* Princeton, N.J.: Princeton University Press, 1959.

Piaget, J. *The language and thought of the child.* New York: Harcourt, Brace, 1926.

Pisoni, D. B. Auditory and phonetic memory codes in the discrimination of consonants and vowels. *Perception & Psychophysics,* 1973, *13,* 253-260.

Pisoni, D. B. Speech perception. In W. K. Estes (Ed.), *Handbook of learning and cognitive processes, Vol. 5.* Hillsdale, N.J.: Lawrence Erlbaum Associates, 1977.

Pitman, Sir J., & St. John, J. *Alphabets and reading.* New York: Pitman, 1969.

Port, D. K., & Preston, M. S. Early apical stop production: A voice onset time analysis. *Haskins Laboratories Status Reports on Speech Research,* SR-29/30, 1972, 125-149.

Premack, A. J., & Premack, D. Teaching language to an ape. *Scientific American,* 1972, *227,* #4, 92-99.

Premack, D. Language in chimpanzee? *Science,* 1971, *172,* 808-822.

Premack, D. Language and intelligence in ape and man. *American Scientist,* 1976, *64,* 674-683.

Putnam, H. *Mind, language, and reality. Philosophical papers, Vol. 2.* Cambridge: Cambridge University Press, 1975.

Pylyshyn, Z. W. What the mind's eye tells the mind's brain: A critique of mental imagery. *Psychological Bulletin,* 1973, *80,* 1-24.

Pylyshyn, Z. W. The role of competence theories in cognitive psychology. *Journal of Psycholinguistic Research,* 1973, *2,* 21-50.

Reber, A. S., & Scarborough, D. L. *Toward a psychology of reading: The proceedings of the CUNY Conference.* Hillsdale, N.J.: Lawrence Erlbaum Associates, 1977.

Rips, L. J., Shoben, E. J., & Smith, E. E. Semantic distance and the verification of semantic relations. *Journal of Verbal Learning and Verbal Behavior,* 1973, *12,* 1-20.

Rochester, S. R., & Gill, J. Production of complex sentences in monologues and dialogues. *Journal of Verbal Learning and Verbal Behavior,* 1973, *12,* 203-210.

Rogers, S. *Children and language: Readings in early language and socialization.* Oxford: Oxford University Press, 1975.

Rohrman, N. L., & Gough, P. B. Forewarning, meaning and semantic decision latency. *Psychonomic Science,* 1967, *9,* 217-218.

Rosch, E. Natural categories. *Cognitive Psychology,* 1973, *4,* 328-350.

Rosch, E. On the internal structure of perceptual and semantic categories. In T. M. Moore (Ed.), *Cognitive development and the acquisition of language.* New York: Academic Press, 1973, pp. 111-144.

Rosch, E. Cognitive representations of semantic categories. *Journal of Experimental Psychology: General,* 1975, *104,* 192-233.

Rosenbaum, P. S. *The grammar of English Predicate Complement construction.* Cambridge, Mass: M.I.T. Press, 1967.

Rozin, P., Bressman, B., & Taft, M. Do children understand the basic relationship between speech and writing? The mow-motorcycle test. *Journal of Reading Behavior,* 1974, *6,* 327-334.

Rubenstein, H., Lewis, S. S., & Rubenstein, M. A. Evidence for phonemic recoding in visual word recognition. *Journal of Verbal Learning and Verbal Behavior,* 1971, *10,* 645-657.

Rumbaugh, D. M. (Ed.), *Language learning by a chimpanzee: The Lana project.* New York: Academic Press, 1976.

Rumelhart, D. E. Notes on a schema for stories. In D. G. Bobrow & A. Collins (Eds.), *Representation and understanding: Studies in cognitive science.* New York: Academic Press, 1975, pp. 211-236.

Sabol, M. A., & DeRosa, D. V. Semantic encoding of isolated words. *Journal of Experimental Psychology: Human Learning and Memory,* 1976, *2,* 58-68.

Sachs, J. S. Recognition memory for syntactic and semantic aspects of connected discourse. *Perception & Psychophysics,* 1967, *2,* 437-442.

Sachs, J., Brown, R., & Salerno, R. A. Adults' speech to children. Paper presented at the International Symposium on First Language Acquisition, Florence, Italy, September, 1972.

Sachs, J., & Devin, J. Young children's use of age-appropriate speech styles in social interaction and role-playing. *Journal of Child Language,* 1976, *3,* 81-98.

Sack, H. G., & Beilin, H. Meaning equivalence of active-passive and subject-object first cleft sentences. Paper presented at the Developmental Psycholinguistics Conference, State University of New York at Buffalo, New York, 1971.

Savin, H. B. What the child knows about speech when he starts to learn to read. In J. F. Kavanagh & I. G. Mattingly (Eds.), *Language by ear and by eye: The relationships between speech and reading.* Cambridge, Mass.: M.I.T. Press, 1972, pp. 319-326.

Scarborough, D. L., Cortese, C., & Scarborough, H. S. Frequency and repetition effects in lexical memory. *Journal of Experimental Psychology: Human Perception and Performance,* 1977, *3,* 1-17.

Schaffer, H. R. *Studies in mother-infant interaction.* New York: Academic Press, 1977.

Schane, S. A. *Generative phonology.* Englewood Cliffs, N.J.: Prentice-Hall, 1973.

Schlesinger, I. M. Production of utterances and langauge acquisition. In D. I. Slobin (Ed.), *The ontogenesis of language: A theoretical symposium.* New York: Academic Press, 1971, pp. 63-102.

Schuell, H. M., & Jenkins, J. J. The nature of language deficit in aphasia. *Psychological Review,* 1959, *66,* 45-67.

Sebeok, T. A. Review of Lindauer, 'Communication among social bees;' Kellogg, 'Porpoises and sonar;' and Lilly, 'Man and dolphin.' *Language,* 1963, *39,* 448-466.

Selnes, O. A. The corpus callosum: Some anatomical and functional considerations with special reference to language. *Brain and Language,* 1974, *1,* 111-139.

Shankweiler, D., Strange, W., & Verbrugge, R. Speech and the problem of perceptual constancy. In R. Shaw & J. Bransford (Eds.), *Perceiving, acting, and knowing.* Hillsdale, N.J.: Lawrence Erlbaum Associates, 1977, pp. 315-346.

Shatz, M., & Gelman, R. The development of communication skills: modifications in the speech of young children as a function of listener. *Monographs of the Society for Research in Child Development,* 1973, *38* (5, Serial No. 152).

Shepard, R. N., & Chipman, S. Second-order isomorphism of internal representations: Shapes of states. *Cognitive Psychology,* 1970, *1,* 1-17.

Sherman, J. A. Imitation and language development. In H. W. Reese and L. P. Lipsitt (Eds.), *Advances in child development and behavior, Vol. 6.* New York: Academic Press, 1971, pp. 239-272.

Shipley, E. F., Smith, C. S., & Gleitman, L. R. A study in the acquisition of language: Free responses to commands. *Language,* 1969, *45,* 322-342.

Shultz, T. R., & Pilon, R. Development of the ability to detect linguistic ambiguity. *Child Development,* 1973, *44,* 728-733.

Shvachkin, N. Kh. The development of phonemic speech perception in early childhood. In C. A. Ferguson & D. I. Slobin (Eds.), *Studies of child language development.* New York: Holt, Rinehart & Winston, 1973, pp. 91-127.

Sinclair, H. Sensorimotor action patterns as a condition for the acquisition of syntax. In R. Huxley & E. Ingram (Eds.), *Language acquisition: Models and methods.* New York: Academic Press, 1971, pp. 121-130.

Sinclair, H., & Bronckart, J. P. S.V.O. A linguistic universal? A study in developmental psycholinguistics. *Journal of Experimental Child Psychology,* 1972, *14,* 329-348.

Singer, H. & Ruddell, R. B. (Eds.) *Theoretical models and processes of reading, Second edition.* Newark, Delaware: International Reading Association, 1976.

Sinnott, J. M., Beecher, M. D., Moody, D. B., & Stebbins, W. D. Speech sound discrimination by monkeys and humans. *Journal of the Acoustical Society of America,* 1976, *60,* 687-695.

Skinner, B. F. *Verbal behavior.* New York: Appleton-Century-Crofts, 1957.

Slobin, D. I. Grammatical transformations and sentence comprehension in childhood and adulthood. *Journal of Verbal Learning and Verbal Behavior,* 1966, *5,* 219-227.

Slobin, D. I. Developmental psycholinguistics. In W. O. Dingwall (Ed.), *A survey of linguistic science,* 2nd Edition. Stamford, Conn.: Greylock Publishers, Inc., 1977. © by William Orr Dingwall, Used by permission. (a)

Slobin, D. I. *Psycholinguistics.* Glenview, Ill.: Scott, Foresman, 1971. (b)

Slobin, D. I. Cognitive prerequisites for the development of grammar. In C. A.

Ferguson & D. I. Slobin (Eds.), *Studies of child language development.* New York: Holt, Rinehart & Winston, 1973, pp. 175-208.

Smith, E. E., Shoben, E. J., & Rips, L. J. Structure and process in semantic memory: A featural model for semantic decisions. *Psychological Review,* 1974, *81,* 214-241.

Smith, F. *Understanding reading: A psycholinguistic analysis of reading and learning to read.* New York: Holt, Rinehart & Winston, 1971.

Snow, C. E. Mothers' speech to children learning language. *Child Development,* 1972, *43,* 549-566.

Snow, C. E., & Ferguson, C. A. (Eds.), *Talking to children: Language input and acquisition.* Cambridge: Cambridge University Press, 1977.

Sperling, G. The information available in brief visual presentations. *Psychological Monographs,* 1976, *74,* No. 11 (Whole No. 498).

Sperry, R. W. Hemisphere deconnection and unity in conscious awareness. *American Psychologist,* 1968, *23,* 723-733.

Steinberg, D. D. & Jakobovits, L. A. (Eds.), *Semantics: An interdisciplinary reader in philosophy, linguistics and psychology.* Cambridge: Cambridge University Press, 1971.

Stevens, K. N. The potential role of property detectors in the perception of consonants. Paper presented at the Symposium on Auditory Analysis and Perception of Speech, Leningrad, 1973.

Stevens, K. N., & House, A. S. Perturbation of vowel articulation by consonental context: An acoustical study. *Journal of Speech and Hearing Research,* 1963, *6,* 111-128.

Stevens, K. N., & House, A. S. Speech perception. In J. Tobias (Ed.), *Foundations of modern auditory theory, Vol. 2.* New York: Academic Press, 1972, pp. 3-62.

Stewart, W. A. Urban Negro speech: Sociolinguistic factors affecting English teaching. In R. W. Shuy (Ed.), *Social dialects and language learning.* Champaign, Ill.: The National Council of Teachers of English, 1965.

Stewart, W. A. Toward a history of American Negro dialect. In F. Williams (Ed.), *Language and poverty: Perspectives on a theme.* Chicago: Markham Publishing Co., 1970, pp. 351-379.

Stich, S. P. Competence and indeterminacy. In D. Cohen & J. R. Wirth (Eds.), *Testing linguistic hypotheses.* Washington, D.C.: Hemisphere Publishing Corp., 1975, pp. 93-109.

Strange, W. The effects of training on the perception of synthetic speech sounds: Voice onset time. Unpublished Ph.D. dissertation, University of Minnesota, 1972.

Strange, W., & Halwes, T. Confidence ratings in speech perception research: Evaluation of an efficient technique for discrimination testing. *Perception & Psychophysics,* 1971, *9,* 182-186.

Strange, W., & Jenkins, J. J. The role of linguistic experience in the perception of speech. In H. L. Pick, Jr., & R. D. Walk (Eds.), *Perception and experience.* New York: Plenum, in press.

Streeter, L. A. Language perception of two-month-old infants shows effects of both innate mechanisms and experience. Paper presented at the Acoustical Society of America meetings, Austin, April, 1975.

Studdert-Kennedy, M. Speech perception. In N. J. Lass (Ed.), *Contemporary issues in experimental phonetics.* Springfield, Ill.: C. C. Thomas, 1976, pp. 243-293.

Suppes, P. The semantics of children's language. *American Psychologist,* 1974, *29,* 103-114.

Swinney, D. A., & Hakes, D. T. Effects of prior context upon lexical access during sentence comprehension. *Journal of Verbal Learning and Verbal Behavior,* 1976, *15,* 681-689.

Taft, M., & Forster, K. I. Lexical storage and retrieval of prefixed words. *Journal of Verbal Learning and Verbal Behavior,* 1975, *14,* 638-647.

Tannenbaum, P. H., & Williams, F. Generation of active and passive sentences as a function of subject or object focus. *Journal of Verbal Learning and Verbal Behavior,* 1968, *7,* 246-250.

Tannenhaus, M. K., Carroll, J. M., & Bever, T. G. Sentence-picture verification models as theories of sentence comprehension: A critique of Carpenter and Just. *Psychological Review,* 1976, *83,* 310-317.

Taylor, I. Content and structure in sentence production. *Journal of Verbal Learning and Verbal Behavior,* 1969, *8,* 170-175. © 1969 by Academic Press, Inc. Used by permission.

Taylor, I., & Taylor, M. M. Another look at phonetic symbolism. *Psychological Bulletin,* 1965, *64,* 413-427.

Thomson, J., & Chapman, R. S. Who is 'daddy' (revisited)? The status of two year-olds' over-extensions in production and comprehension. *Papers and Reports on Child Language Development* (Stanford University), 1975, *10,* 59-68.

Thorndyke, P. The role of inferences in discourse comprehension. *Journal of Verbal Learning and Verbal Behavior,* 1976, *15,* 437-446.

Tinker, M. A. *Bases for effective reading.* Minneapolis: University of Minnesota Press, 1965.

Tulving, E., & Gold, C. Stimulus information and contextual information as determinants of tachistoscopic recognition of words. *Journal of Experimental Psychology,* 1963, *66,* 319-327.

Turvey, M. T. On peripheral and central processes in vision: Inferences from an information-processing analysis of masking with patterned stimuli. *Psychological Review,* 1973, *80,* 1-52.

Valian, V., & Wales, R. What's what: Talkers help listeners hear and understand by clarifying sentential relations. *Cognition,* 1976, *4,* 155-176.

Venezky, R. L. Prerequisites for learning to read. In J. R. Levin and V. L. Allen

(Eds.), *Cognitive learning in children.* New York: Academic Press, 1976, pp. 163-185.

Venezky, R. L. Research on reading processes: A historical perspective. *American Psychologist,* 1977, *32,* 339-345.

Wada, J., & Rasmussen, T. Intracarotid injection of sodium amytal for the lateralization of cerebral speech dominance. Experimental and clinical observations. *Journal of Neurosurgery,* 1960, *17,* 266-282.

Wales, R., & Campbell, R. On the development of comparison and the comparison of development. In G. B. Flores d'Arcais & W. J. M. Levelt (Eds.), *Advances in psycholinguistics.* Amsterdam: North-Holland Publishing, 1970, pp. 373-396.

Walker, E. C., Gough, P. B., & Wall, R. E. Grammatical relations and the search of sentences in immediate memory. Midwestern Psychological Association, 1968.

Wanner, E. *On remembering, forgetting, and understanding sentences.* The Hague: Mouton, 1974.

Warren, R. M. Perceptual restoration of missing speech sounds. *Science,* 1970, *167,* 392-393.

Warren, R. M., & Ackroff, J. M. Dichotic verbal transformations: Evidence of separate neural processors for identical stimuli. Paper presented at the Acoustical Society of America meetings, St. Louis, November 8, 1974.

Warren, R. M., & Obusek, C. J. Speech perception and phonemic restorations. *Perception & Psychophysics,* 1971, *9,* 358-363.

Warren, R. M., & Sherman, G. L. Phonemic restorations based on subsequent context. *Perception & Psychophysics,* 1974, *16,* 150-156.

Watson, J. B. *Behaviorism, Revised Edition.* New York: Norton, 1930.

Watt, W. C. Competing economy criteria. In *Problèmes actuels en psycholinguistique/Current problems in psycholinguistics.* Paris: Editions du C.N.R.S., 1974, pp. 361-389.

Webster, R. L., & Lubker, B. B. Interrelationships among fluency variables in stuttered speech. *Journal of Speech and Hearing Research,* 1968, *11,* 754-766.

Webster, R. L. Schumacher, S. J., & Lubker, B. B. Changes in stuttering frequency as a function of various intervals of delayed auditory feedback. *Journal of Abnormal Psychology,* 1970, *75,* 45-49.

Weiner, S. L. On the development of *more* and *less. Journal of Experimental Child Psychology,* 1974, *17,* 271-287.

Weinschenk, C. *Die erbliche Lese-Rechtschreibeschwäche und ihre sozialpsychiatrischen Auswirkungen.* Bern: H. Huber, 1965.

Wells, R. Predicting slips of the tongue. In V. Fromkin (Ed.), *Speech errors as linguistic evidence.* The Hague: Mouton, 1973.

Wernicke, C. *Der aphasische Symptomencomplex.* Breslau: Max Cohn & Weigert, 1884.

Wetstone, H. S., & Friedlander, B. Z. The effect of word order on young children's responses to simple questions and commands. *Child Development,* 1973, *44,* 734-740.

Whorf, B. *Language, thought, and reality.* Cambridge, Mass.: M.I.T. Press, 1956.

Wilcox, S., & Palermo, D. S. 'in', 'on', and 'under' revisited. *Cognition,* 1974/75, *3,* 245-254.

Wilkes, A. L., & Kennedy, R. A. Relationship between pausing and retrieval latency in sentences of varying grammatical form. *Journal of Experimental Psychology,* 1969, *79,* 241-245.

Winograd, T. Understanding natural language. *Cognitive Psychology,* 1972, *3,* 1-191.

Winograd, T. Frame representations and the declarative-procedural controversy. In D. G. Bobrow & A. M. Collins (Eds.), *Representation and understanding: Studies in cognitive science.* New York: Academic Press, 1975, pp. 185-210.

Witelson, S. F., & Pallie, W. Left hemisphere specialization for language in the newborn. *Brain,* 1973, *96,* 641-646.

Wittgenstein, L. *Philosophical investigations.* New York: Macmillan, 1935.

Wolff, P. H. The natural history of crying and other vocalizations in early infancy. In B. M. Foss (Ed.), *Determinants of infant behavior, Vol. IV.* London: Methuen, 1966, pp. 81-109.

Woods, W. A. Meaning and machines. In A. Zampolli (Ed.), *Computational and mathematical linguistics.* Florence, Italy: Leo S. Olschki, 1977, pp. 769-792.

Woods, W. A., Kaplan, R., & Nash-Webber, B. *The lunar sciences natural language information system: Final report.* Report No. 2378. Cambridge, Mass.: Bolt, Beranek, and Newman, 1972.

Ziff, P. Understanding. In J. L. Cowan (Ed.), *Studies in thought and language.* Tucson, Arizona: University of Arizona Press, 1970, pp. 65-77.

Author Index

426

Subject Index